W9-BVZ-795

The RIVER STOPS HERE

Saving Round Valley
A Pivotal Chapter
in California's
Water Wars

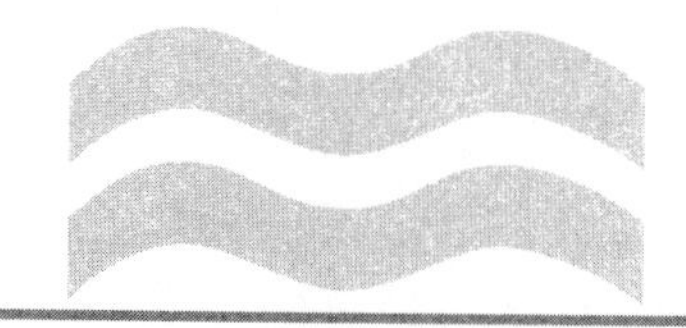

TED SIMON

Afterword by Robert Gottlieb
and Ruth Langridge

UNIVERSITY OF CALIFORNIA PRESS
Berkeley · Los Angeles · London

University of California Press
Berkeley and Los Angeles, California

University of California Press, Ltd.
London, England

First Paperback Printing 2001

Grateful acknowledgment is made to *The Sacramento Bee* for permission to reprint an excerpt of an editorial from April 25, 1968. Copyright © 1968 by The Sacramento Bee. Reprinted by permission.

Library of Congress Cataloging-in-Publication Data

Simon, Ted, 1931–
The river stops here : saving Round Valley, a pivotal chapter in California's water wars / Ted Simon ; afterword by Robert Gottlieb and Ruth Langridge.
p. cm.
Originally published: New York : Random House, c1994.
Includes bibliographical references and index.
ISBN 0-520-23056-6 (alk. paper)
1. Flood control—California—Eel River. 2. Water resources development—California—Eel River. 3. Round Valley (Calif.) I. Title.
TC424.C2.S56 2001 333.91′13′09794—dc21 00-047520

Book design by Carole Lowenstein

Printed in the United States of America

08 07 06 05 04 03 02 01
9 8 7 6 5 4 3 2 1

The paper used in this publication meets the minimum requirements of ANSI/NISO Z39.48-1992 (R 1997) (*Permanence of Paper*). ♾

For William

Many waters cannot quench love
Neither can the floods drown it

—Song of Solomon 8:7

Contents

Corps of Engineers' Plan for Round Valley

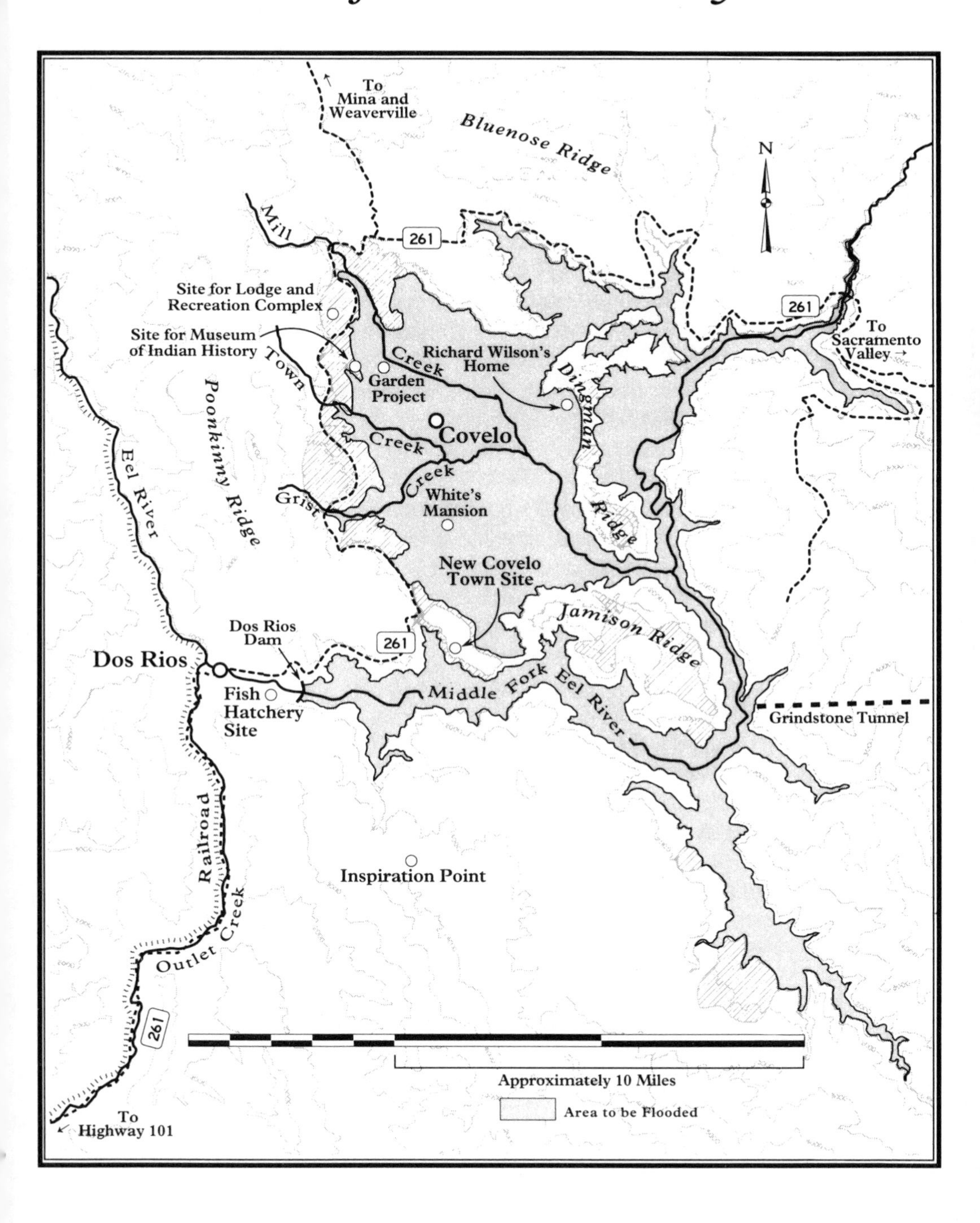

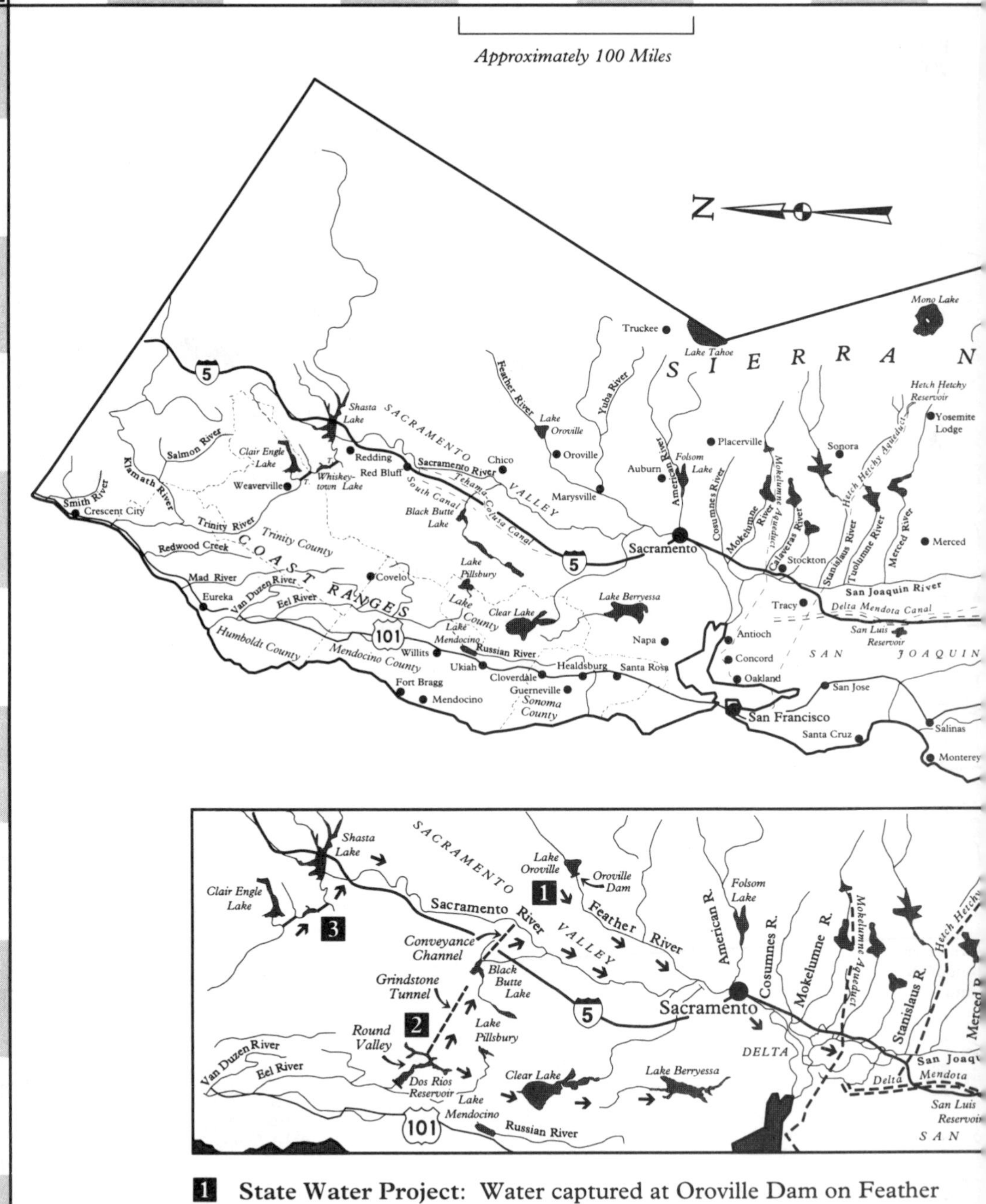

1 **State Water Project**: Water captured at Oroville Dam on Feather River is released via the Sacramento River to the Delta and pumped via aqueduct to irrigate the west side of the San Joaquin Valley and to supply Southern California. Surplus water is banked in the San Luis Reservoir.

2 **Dos Rios Project**: North Coast water for the State Water Project was to be captured in Round Valley and sent south, either through Grindstone Tunnel to the Sacramento Valley or through Clear Lake and Lake Berryessa.

Water Systems in California

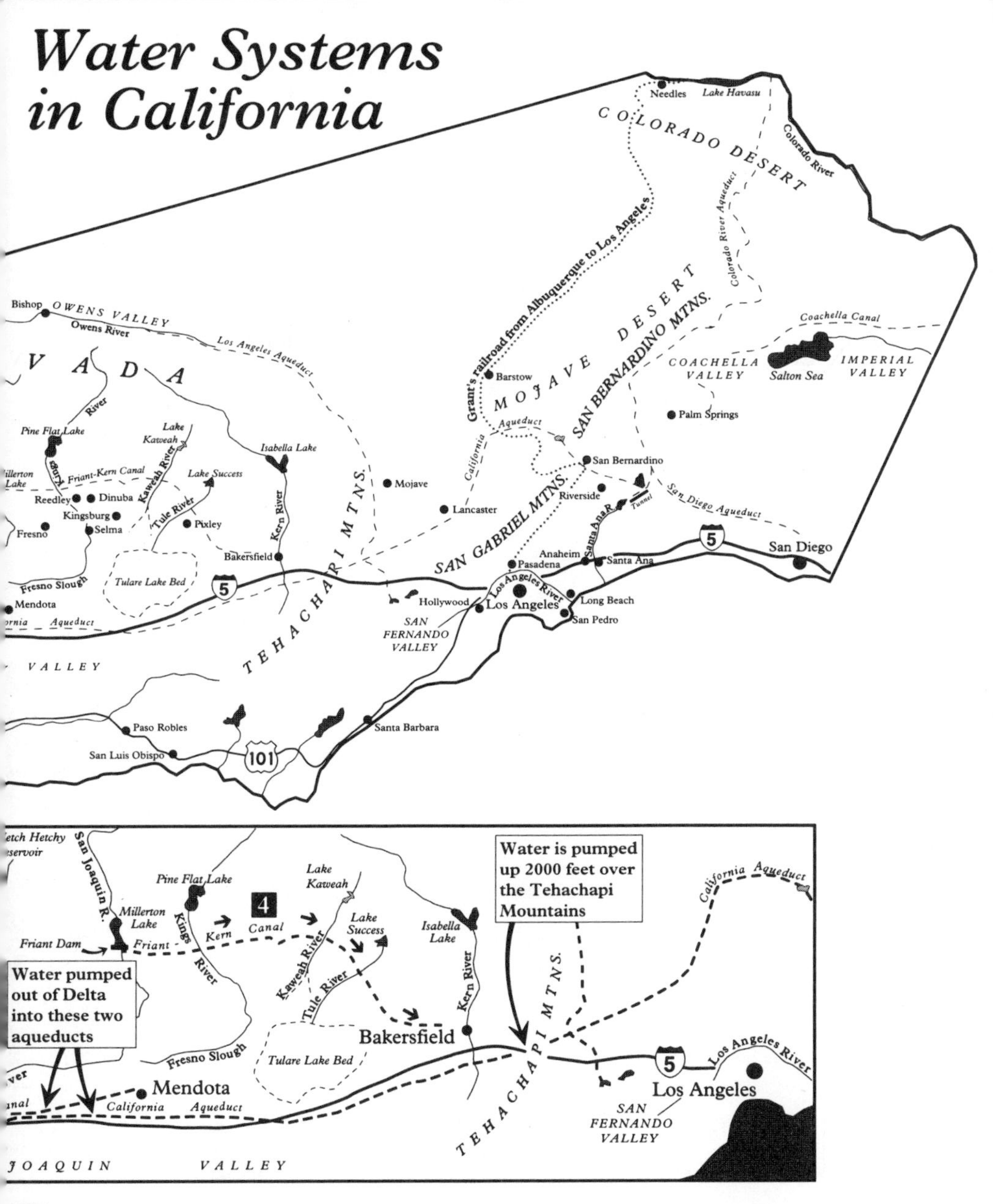

3 **Central Valley Project:** Water captured at Shasta and Clair Engle lakes is released into the Sacramento River to irrigate the Sacramento Valley and to replenish the Delta.

4 **Central Valley Project:** Water captured from the San Joaquin River irrigates the east side of the San Joaquin Valley via the Friant-Kern Canal. Water in the Delta is pumped via aqueduct into the San Joaquin River at Mendota to replace water taken out by the Friant Dam.

THE RIVER STOPS HERE

1

In the Wake of the Flood

THE GREAT FLOOD OF '64 hit Northern California hard, and came as a cruel surprise. The farmers, ranchers, and townspeople who lived and worked alongside the creeks and rivers had barely recovered from the deluge of 1955, which at the time was the worst on record. Statistically, such a catastrophe was expected only once in a hundred years. The 1964 flood was not just shockingly ahead of schedule, it was devastating.

All the wild rivers of Northern California were swollen to bursting, but the most violent and unrestrained of them was the Eel. It tore a hundred million tons of rock and silt out of the coastal mountains and scoured the riverbanks all the way to the Pacific. It took away bridges, railroad tracks, houses, animals, and nineteen people. It rose to previously unrecorded heights, and marked the fury of its passing by leaving uprooted trees perched in unlikely places as evidence to confound future skeptics.

The worst damage to life and property occurred in the lower reaches of the river, in Humboldt County. Before arriving at its delta, the river ran through a broad gorge, where small lumber towns were situated on a narrow riparian strip. The river raked through them, and the immense stockpiles of logs, known as "decks," were swept away causing terrible damage and loss. A haunting photograph of the town of Pepperwood shows it entirely destroyed by randomly flung timber dropped as though in a giant game of pick-up sticks.

In the delta area the existing levees were quite incapable of restraining the flood. People had built, as they do everywhere from Bangladesh to San Francisco, without troubling themselves too much about disasters that might never happen. Emerging from the gorge with its cargo of lethal battering rams, the river overflowed the entire area, drowning dairy herds and flooding the towns of Fortuna and Ferndale.

Far back inland, where the river gathered its strength, there was flooding too, but it caused less comment. The population was sparser, and the dollar value of the damage was less. The Eel inhabits rough, mountainous country inhospitable to man, and there was little room for development on the steep slopes alongside the riverbed—with one remarkable exception. Amid the jumble of peaks and canyons surrounding the Middle Fork of the Eel, there appeared, quite dramatically, a broad valley with a perfectly flat floor, some thirty square miles in extent, known as Round Valley.

The size and unexpectedness of this valley gave it a Shangri-la quality that has always fascinated newcomers gazing down from the surrounding ridges. It seemed to demand an explanation, and some outlandish theories developed to account for it, from Indian mythology to New Age mysticism. In fact the valley was formed during the intense squeezing, folding, and fracturing of the earth's crust, which created the Coast Range, a broad belt of mountainous territory that separates the Pacific Ocean from the Sacramento Valley.

Rivers and creeks twist and turn in this crumpled terrain, seeking some way out to lower ground, and those that do not drop down into the Sacramento River eventually have to find their way to the Pacific by the most tortuous of routes. All of those in the vicinity of Round Valley empty into the Eel River, which itself extends numerous forks into the mountains. A huge tract of this convoluted rock, 3,600 square miles of it all together, constitutes the watershed of the Eel. Round Valley is nearly at the center of it, and perhaps the most surprising geologic fact about the valley is that the river never ran through it but found a lower path around it.

When the cost of the 1964 flood was counted, the damage done at the delta and the lower reaches of the river amounted to about $42 million, and the media flashed pictures of the devastation across the country. By contrast, although Round Valley was flooded, the losses were estimated at less than a million dollars. Some small bridges went; the rest of the damage was agricultural.

No reporters thought it worth their while to tackle the long and arduous drive to Round Valley, with earth slides to bar the way and rock falls to crack an oil pan. The valley remained largely unknown and ignored, as it had been for decades. Not even the keenest observer could have anticipated that this quiet backwater of rural society would before long become the focus of a statewide feud involving the most powerful political forces in California.

There was one small town in the valley, named Covelo by its first postmaster to recall his native Switzerland. It housed a few hundred people and lay low among shade trees toward the northwest corner of the valley. The rest of the population of some two thousand all told was scattered around the valley and the nearby hills. On first entering the valley from the south, the town was scarcely visible. Great redwood barns, spreading their wings over a hundred feet or more, were the first structures that told of man's presence. Fields of hay or pasture stretched back to the foothills, sometimes bearing sheep or cattle, sometimes brilliant with wildflowers, depending on the season. The road ran straight and flat across the valley floor, between fences that were still built in the old style with split rails and crosses.

The southwest quarter of the valley was drier than the rest, and was the part that had been most favored by the early settlers. They had spread themselves over thousand-acre parcels in the nineteenth century and the holdings remained large, so that there were few houses to be seen there. About two miles into the valley, past a hundred acres or so of pear trees, stood a building with a second-story balcony supported on columns, reminiscent of the South.

Across the road from it was an avenue of surprising pretension, lined with tall redwood trees planted seventy-five years earlier. The avenue led to a grand white-stucco mansion, the only building of its kind in the valley, with broad bay windows and balconies, decked out with decorative ironwork and elaborate Victorian ornamentation. It harked back to the reign of one of the most successful and despotic kings of the Wild West, George White. At the time of the flood, both houses were occupied by the Rohrbough family, which had inherited White's estate after his death.

Another mile or so farther along, over two narrow wooden bridges, the road entered town and became Commercial Street, but unlike most towns Covelo had none of the familiar hamburger and ice cream franchises, no sprawl of busy lighted signs, nothing to even pretend at urban excitement. For most people arriving in the valley, this was the final destination. There was no passing trade of tourists or truck drivers to cater to. Only local people took the Mina road to the north, and very few crossed the Coast Range to Interstate 5 by the Mendocino Pass road, which was mostly dirt. When night fell, Covelo went to sleep.

Covelo was built, like all frontier towns, to straddle a "main drag" made broad enough to drive cattle or hogs, to park the half-ton Ford and Chevy pickups of the sixties, and to hitch horses, for many people still rode in on horseback. However, there was another visible element of the population that generally rode neither horses nor pickups, but walked. As well as being virtually the end of the road, Covelo had one other significant distinction. A mile north of town was the boundary of the Round Valley Indian Reservation, one of the most important reservations in California.

Another street, named Howard, crossed Commercial Street from east to west at the other end of town and ended up after half a mile at the school. In the area quartered off by these two streets most of the better houses had been built. They were, for the most part, tidy wood-framed structures with painted siding and porches and neatly fenced front yards. The roofs curved far out against sun and rain, and dripped wisteria. Imposing black walnut trees shaded the roads.

The valley was big enough to contain its own climate, and more than most rural communities, Covelo was dominated by its weather, which ran to extremes. Wet winters and dry winters usually came in cycles. In dry winters, at night, the air was crisp and clear and the thermometer might plunge to fifteen degrees or less. In the morning the valley's bowl filled with a heavy freezing mist, until the sun became high enough to burn it off. That winter sun, shining from a brilliant blue sky, could take the temperature up to seventy or even eighty degrees, before fading behind the trees, and whatever grew in the valley had to survive these dramatic swings.

Different crops flourished there at different times. Wheat was once profitable, and an imposing nineteenth-century flour mill stood abandoned in the town. Hops, too, were a moneymaker for a while, and a big ranch in the southern part of the valley, renamed the Diamond

H, was still known to some as the Hop Ranch. There used to be much diversity of livestock raised on the ranches, including turkeys, hogs, sheep, and dairy herds, but by the sixties the land was devoted almost entirely to raising beef cattle, and was put either in permanent pasture or used to grow other kinds of feed such as corn or alfalfa.

Round Valley was a natural home for the valley oak, a grand, patriarchal tree often 150 feet high, whose massive and contorted boughs shade an area almost as broad as the tree is tall. The oaks were a glorious feature of the valley and, in the northern areas where they were still numerous, gave the pastures the appearance of parkland. They drew prodigious amounts of water from the underground streambeds and their transpiration in the searing heat of summer helped to cool the surrounding air. On chill winter mornings, draped in their veils of Spanish moss, they loomed through the heavy mists with the grandeur of galleons under sail. Their brittle wood was of small value for construction, but they produced immense harvests of acorns, which settlers used to feed their hogs and which the native population once cooked into an edible mush. An alternative name for the tree was "mush oak."

In the wet winter cycles the valley was full of rain. The trees, houses, animals, and people lost their outlines and seemed to dissolve in the downpour. From ridge to opposing ridge, without ceasing sometimes for weeks on end, rain obsessed the valley. It fell at a steady, relentless pace, advancing slowly from the southwest, from the Pacific Ocean, soaking the hillsides to the limit of their capacity and laying heavy blankets of snow on the high surrounding peaks, which couldn't be seen, however, until the rain was interrupted.

The rain usually would start in September with a few tentative storms, catching people with their roofs unfinished or a cut of alfalfa ungathered. People would meet each other in the street and wonder aloud: "Is this it?" Would this be the beginning of the one that never stopped? You could never tell. It might come in October. It might not come until February.

When it came, the valley turned gray, and the fainthearted fled or were weighed down in misery. Often, in those times, the valley might be cut off for days by rock falls on the Covelo road. Power and phone lines would come down. Grist Creek and Town Creek, which crossed the road just before town, became unruly and rose up to threaten their bridges. Mill Creek and Short Creek, bigger streams, which ran a couple of miles east of town, ripped and roared across their floodplains, tossing great banks of gravel hither and thither as they tried to heave out of their beds. Branches and trees came down from the mountains, and cross fences that hadn't been removed in time were quickly reduced to tangled skeins of barbed wire.

East Lane, where it crossed Mill Creek, would be under a foot or two of water for a while, and sheets of water lay over the fields on either side of the rising torrent. Then, as it subsided, in all but the worst years, the flooded areas would slowly drain, and the fish would come surging up the creeks searching for a place to spawn. The salmon were three feet long or more, each female bursting with crimson eggs. Visibly battered by rocks, their skins patchy and bruised, their flesh bled white by exhaustion, they followed their memories from the Pacific Ocean to the valley and the climax of their last desperate voyage up 120 miles of turbulent water.

A few days later, if the rain had not returned to bring the creeks into flood again, their carcasses lay on the banks and gravel spits, waiting for the vultures to feed on them. But in some years, the rain would not stop, and it would blow in warmer than usual from some tropical storm and melt the snowpack on the mountains, and the water would flow over the sodden sides of the northern ridges and simply swamp the valley. That's how it was in 1955, and again in 1964.

Then water flowed over the land slowly, maybe two feet deep, removing loose earth and seed, and floating the dead salmon and everything else that was loose away.

Among those who suffered losses in 1964 was a young rancher named Richard Wilson. He had established himself in the valley only a few years before, when he bought some two thousand acres of land there and on adjacent Dingman Ridge. He calculated that by adding this property to the three thousand acres of rangeland he had inherited from his father, he would have the basis for a thriving cattle operation.

Building up his ranch and raising his family on this land that he had known and loved most of his life seemed to Wilson enough of a challenge to satisfy any man's ambition. If he had been forewarned of the extraordinary role he was destined to play in California's affairs, he might have taken extreme measures to avoid it, but blissfully unaware of his fate, he pursued the life he had chosen from among so many opportunities, convinced that it would be the most rewarding for himself and his children.

Yet it was clear then, as later, that he was no ordinary rancher. In 1964 Richard Alexander Wilson was only thirty-one years old, a tall, athletic man with an imposing manner and an erect bearing that made the most of his six feet, two inches. He had dark hair brushed back flat from a high forehead, a strong aquiline nose, a determined chin, and deep, penetrating eyes, all set in a square, handsome frame. The combination of boyish enthusiasm and natural authority made a pleasing impression on some. Undoubtedly he offended others, who resented his wealth. They took his gravity for self-importance and thought him arrogant. He probably added fuel to their discontent, for he was not politic with his attentions, gave no half measures, and disguised his personal judgments poorly.

He and his wife, Susan, also tall and strikingly attractive, with a mass of wavy black hair and an open, affectionate manner, both loved the mountains. They came from Southern California, and had given up a prosperous way of life to live high above the valley. They had a modest house without electricity that Wilson's father had built twenty years earlier on Buck Mountain, and for several years they moved back and forth between the mountain and the valley. The eighteen miles of rough logging road to their home could take up to an hour to negotiate, and eventually, with three small children to care for, it took its toll.

Reluctantly they conceded that it made more sense to live on the valley floor, close to town, schools, and the ranch office. In 1963 they moved to a house tucked into the northeast corner of the valley, where most of Richard's ranch activities now took place, but they still yearned for their mountain home. Whenever possible, at Thanksgiving or at Christmas, they took the children up the hill to Buck Mountain, and in 1964 when the storm came in from the Pacific, just before Christmas, Richard was there with his family.

A short distance below the house the road crossed a wooden bridge over Hull's Creek. Rainfall during those few days varied between five and six inches a day. The creek literally jumped out of its bed, took the bridge away, and obliterated the road. For several days they were cut off entirely by an impassable torrent. With woodstoves, gas light, and provisions, they were well equipped to wait out the storm, but Richard waited anxiously day after day, wondering who might be down there to rescue his cows and feed them, and Susan prayed that none of the children would suddenly develop appendicitis or break an arm.

On the fourth day Richard was able to bridge the swollen creek and get to his ranch. Most of his fields were still under water. The pasture would not be seriously affected, but other fields that had been tilled in preparation for spring sowings would need a lot of work. His buildings were largely intact. On the whole, he felt that he had got off lightly, especially compared with those on the delta who had lost everything, even their lives.

Like most people, Richard had seen, down in the valley, the television reports of rescue operations. News of the disasters on the coast flashed across the nation. The network TV crews flew in and politicians jostled for opportunities to contribute their sound bites. He heard Governor Pat Brown declare a state of emergency, and during the weeks and months that followed he listened to various officials and pundits promising action and offering solutions to curb future floods. All of them suggested building dams and levees somewhere or other.

In California, where water is such a precious commodity, water projects had been growing in size and complexity since the turn of the century, and many thousands of engineers, bureaucrats, and developers had come to depend on them for their livelihood and prospects. At the same time as they were creating one system, they were naturally searching out the next. It was an oft-spoken dictum that there was nothing like a flood or a drought to have water projects approved. Well-paid lobbyists were always eager to get them past the legislature in Sacramento, and they greeted major flood disasters with the same scarcely concealed enthusiasm felt by reporters, for whom the best news is usually bad.

The flood in 1955 had hastened the approval of a master plan to capture and control more of California's rivers and send them south. This project, known as the State Water Project, was already under way on the Feather River, narrowly voted into being in 1960, and underfunded at $1.75 billion. Few voters realized that this was merely a first stage, which could not on its own fulfill the promises that had been made to justify its existence. Before very long, yet more water would have to be found to funnel into that plumbing system, and the planners had their maps and models all ready.

Tantalizing amounts of water spilled off the coastal ranges into the Pacific Ocean, and for many this was a state of affairs verging on criminal neglect. The terrain was notoriously difficult, making water projects expensive and hard to justify, but the wild rivers of the north coast and, in particular, the Eel, presented an irresistible challenge. Among engineers and politicians it was understood that the Eel would be the source of their next big increment of water, and they had been planning for it for many years.

However, their ambitions went far beyond that. In the offices of the big construction companies and consulting firms were maps showing how all the rivers would be tamed. Where an atlas would show the Eel, the Klamath, and the Trinity as a tracery of thin black lines meandering from the mountains to the ocean, the engineers' maps showed them gorged and swollen like varicose veins by a multitude of dams and reservoirs, backed up to each other like steps in a staircase. The whole scheme, statewide, was to cost something in the order of $12 billion.

The engineers and planners who had drawn up this extraordinary scenario were convinced that, ultimately, the state would have to buy it. Population increases would demand it. For California to go on growing, more water had to go south, and as long as there was water "wasting," as they said, to the ocean, it was unthinkable that the state would hesitate to turn it around and send it where it was needed.

These long-range ambitions of the water lobby were concealed, if only by omission, from the public. The voters, it was thought in 1960, had enough to think about with just one monster plumbing project costing less than $2 billion. The next step would have to wait until the time was politically ripe. That time seemed to have arrived in the winter of 1964.

During the '64 flood more water poured out of the Eel River in eight days than it took to irrigate the entire cotton crop of California for a year.[1] For engineers eager to build bigger and better dams, for city managers of the rapidly growing suburbs of Los Angeles, for corporations with a few thousand acres of arid land somewhere south of Bakersfield, for politicians anxious to increase the state's gross product and rake in more tax dollars, for developers with dreams of lakeside condominiums on the shores of new reservoirs, the lights turned green. They lost no time in condemning this profligate outpouring as an intolerable threat to life and limb, and in the political climate of those days there were very few who disagreed. Liberated by this new sense of urgency, the engineers emerged from the closet as knights errant, flying the banner of flood control, and once again the area was beset by dam fever.

Throughout the century, long before the State Water Project, there had been plans to build dams up and down the Eel River, though few people in Round Valley got to hear of them. Every few years, some agency or other drew a map showing these hypothetical dams, with names like Sequoia, Bell Springs, English Ridge, Willis Ridge, Spencer, Jarbow, Dos Rios, and Etsel. They were motivated by two quite distinct aims. In one form the engineers came in the guise of kindly godfathers, bearing water to nourish the valley. Their dams were generally smaller, local affairs, diverting water from the Eel into a ditch that might irrigate the foothills of the valley. The dam at Etsel Crossing would have been one of those, and had been talked about for decades.

In their other incarnation, the engineers were very different. Then they came as the mighty manipulators of nature improving on God's work, the men who drilled through mountains, who raised immense inverted pyramids of rock and concrete and sent great rivers uphill. In pursuit of their Herculean purposes, they could hardly be expected to concern themselves much with a scattering of farmers and natives eking out a living in a remote valley. To such men the proximity of a valley to a river suggested only the question: Should we fill it with water?

2

"We Like to Leave a Clean Floor."

SCHEMES TO DAM the Eel River led inevitably to the idea of using Round Valley as a reservoir, and this had been discussed among engineers in the past. Rumors had circulated in the valley, especially back in the fifties when state engineers came to investigate, but nothing had come of it and the notion had seemed too fantastic to be taken very seriously.

When it appeared once, in print, briefly mentioned as a possibility, in a state report published in 1964, the supervisors who ran Mendocino County immediately resolved to oppose the idea. Although they were normally glad of any development that might bring money to their impoverished constituency, how could they possibly favor such an extravagant project? Round Valley was the largest single expanse of agricultural land in the county. To drown it and lose it as a tax base was absurd.

Richard Wilson, too, was convinced it was nonsense. Like the plastic pipe that had been proposed to carry Columbia River water under the Pacific to Los Angeles, like the plan to ship the Snake River around the Rockies, it was just another of those crazy water schemes that would never fly, invented by self-serving bureaucracies "down below" to keep themselves in business. All the same, a seed of doubt was planted in his mind, and he kept his ears open.

He pushed on with his plans to make his valley land more productive and to increase the size of his herd. Beef prices were dropping, and the bloom had gone off agriculture lately, but he felt confident that with enthusiasm and efficient management he could make his ranch pay. It was true that some of the old-time ranchers were hurting, but then they had been sliding along in their easy way for decades, resisting new ideas. The situation, he thought, called for a much more intensive use of resources. Energy and fertilizer were abundant and cheap, and consuming them in quantity seemed almost a patriotic duty. A great lake of groundwater lay under the valley, and he installed bigger pumps to bring it up to his fields. He invested in the most modern sowing and harvesting equipment and stuffed ever more nitrogen, phosphorus, and potash into the soil to bump up his corn crop.

His older son, Alex, went to kindergarten at the public school in town. Susan busied herself with re-creating in the valley the garden she had left behind on Buck Mountain. There were new demands on her time, which she resented but accepted stoically. Being now only five minutes from town, she found herself drawn willy-nilly into the affairs of the community and especially the church, for the Wilsons were both devout Catholics.

There were no more floods, but everybody in the valley knew that something was going on. The land Richard had bought was partly valley land, but it also extended over Dingman Ridge and down to the Eel. He could not help but be aware of the surveyors and engineers working up and down the streambeds, drilling and taking measurements. At one time the Corps of Engineers wrote asking his permission to drill a hole on his land while "making a study for location of a dam on Short Creek," but that surely could only be a dam to protect the valley, not flood it.

Members of the unofficial town council met most mornings for coffee in the comfortably dilapidated Covelo Hotel. The two-story stucco building, conveniently close to the Buckhorn Saloon, had a few rooms upstairs and two large rooms below, which served as restaurant and cafe. Around the walls of the rooms hung a multitude of redwood shingles, each with the brand of a Round Valley rancher burned into it. On the right of the entrance a long wooden counter followed the wall and led to the kitchen, the province of large, slow-moving women who loaded generous amounts of hash browns, eggs, sausages, and pancakes onto heavy porcelain platters.

It was at one of the first tables beyond the entrance that Covelo's opinion leaders gathered over their coffee mugs to figure out the latest rumors. The baseball cap had not yet come to change the nature of the indoor landscape, and men sitting at table usually took their hats off, all the better to scratch their bare heads.

During the second year after the flood they had plenty to talk about. The rumor that the state's engineers wanted to flood the valley was common currency again, but nobody would confirm or deny it. Engineers were turning up everywhere, and most particularly now in the Eel canyon downstream from Round Valley and a few miles north of the town of Dos Rios.

To most old-timers the idea still seemed ridiculous. Little J. D. Rohrbough, who was born with the century, could look far back down the decades, and he just "knew" there would never be enough water to fill that huge valley. He was convinced, and persuaded many others, that the scheme would come to nothing. Rolland Hurt, who was only a bit younger, liked the idea at first. He figured that if they did buy him out, why, it would be to his advantage because he had land in the hills that would maybe become prized lakeside property. Some shopkeepers and tradesmen, like Walter Winters, Mervyn Gravier, Cliff Foster, and Jan Stewart, had more faith in engineers than in old J. D.'s memories. Compensation was a hot topic for a while. What would the government pay? When would they pay it? For some, who had never before considered any other life, their humdrum daily routine suddenly took on a dreary, oppressive air. It would be like winning the lottery; a second honeymoon; a new start in life.

Then, as time wore on, the steam seemed to go out of the rumor. Richard convinced himself the threat had blown over. In 1966 the state published another report, describing progress and future plans for its north coast projects. There was no mention of flooding the valley. It was the same mixture as before, a number of smaller dams with some of the water going to irrigate the foothills, and the rest going south. There was also some talk of variations on the plan, with dams that might flood just a part of the eastern side of the valley where Mill Creek ran. Since that was where Richard had most of his land, he was concerned and made a note to find out more. Then the engineers stopped their prospecting and went away, and with them it seemed went the excitement. The coffee club stopped talking about water and went back to valley business and to the more entertaining game of sizing up newcomers.

Richard's efforts and investments were beginning to pay off. His operation promised to turn a healthy profit. His second son, Chris, was in school now, too, and his daughter, Marjo, was close behind. The state elections of 1966 claimed some of his attention. He was a Republican, like his father and most of his family in Southern California, and the party had an intriguing candidate for governor, a minor film star with a major political talent named Ronald Reagan. In 1964 Richard had worked in the campaign to elect a Republican congressman, Don Clausen, for his district, and in 1966 he was asked to help again.

He took an opportunity, early in 1967, to ask Clausen to find out what he could about prospects in the valley. Clausen wrote to Floyd Dominy, who headed the Bureau of Reclamation in Washington, and Dominy sent the letter on to the Corps of Engineers. The stuffy reply Clausen received from the army was only ironic in retrospect. "You may be assured," wrote Lt. Col. Lewis A. Pick, Jr., in June of 1967, "that full consideration will be given to any drainage problems that may be related to any project such as the Dos Rios Dam, which is under study."

It was midsummer, Reagan was governor, it was "Morning in California," the hay crop was in, and the corn was shooting up. The Field Day Parade and Rodeo had come and gone. There was still grass in the hills, and the main job was keeping track of the cattle and mending fences. Beef prices were reasonable. It looked to Richard to be a pretty good year.

The bad news was that his political connections were trotting out the same old rumor, but spiced with a good deal of extra urgency.

"What're you going to do about that dam they're working on over there?" they'd say. "Won't it flood you out?" And he'd say, "Well, they're going to dam the river, maybe, but not the valley." Then they'd say, "Well, the way I hear it, that's one hell of a big dam," and he'd explain, "Look, the river runs around the valley on the other side of the ridge, like this, see. And they're working on a dam down here at Dos Rios, and then, up here, they've got the Spencer Dam and this other one on Short Creek, and they're supposed to keep the water out of the valley, and give us water for irrigation, though it looks like they may give me a bit too damned much. That's if they do anything at all, which I very much doubt." And they'd say, "Well, don't count on it. I'd look into it if I were you."

In truth, Richard was a lot less sanguine than he pretended to be. He tried talking with Rollie Hurt and the other important old-timers, but they were evasive. They told him, laughingly, that property interests in the south were already speculating on the prospects of lakefront real estate. For him this was no laughing matter. Richard's own experience told him to take such warnings seriously. He knew what developers had done to Southern California, and he felt that if they once got into gear, the valley would be lost, but like anyone living a busy, productive life he wanted to ignore those little twinges that told him all was not well with the body politic. If a man tried to anticipate every pessimistic forecast and rumor, there'd be no time to get on with life. Anyway, he believed the state project was already in dire financial straits. How could they afford to come up here and spend another billion dollars in *his* backyard? He very soon found out.

Most daily newspapers were not delivered to the valley in the sixties, and came by mail subscription, but the *Ukiah Daily Journal* generally arrived on the rack at Gravier's store by late morning and was a popular choice. In those days, before TV had absorbed most of the advertising revenue, it was still struggling to provide a complete news service. It carried dispatches from Vietnam, Europe, and across the nation, and these clipped, professional accounts sat oddly alongside the quaint habits of parochial reporting in which notable people "succumbed" rather than died, and the affairs of various Masonic orders were reported at length.

In the world at large the news was generally less than good that summer. The ugly reality of the Vietnam War was becoming apparent. The San Francisco Giants were caught in a downward spiral and seemed headed for the Second Division. Adding insult to injury, the wind at Candlestick Park smothered Willie Mays in dust. On the other hand, a standing rib roast was eighty-nine cents a pound, gas and cigarettes were almost free, and Mendocino County's timber barons were chopping down trees at a record rate, undeterred by those radically inclined persons who thought they had some responsibility to the public.

The paper's "Covelo Comments" were supplied by Tessa Jesenko, who lived in the small hamlet of Dos Rios, fifteen miles downstream from Round Valley. She reported many joyful and sad occasions that summer. She announced the completion of the Dos Rios Bridge in May and the formation of the Covelo Chamber of Commerce (James

Fisher, president) in June. She noted that Susan Wilson had become a new member of the Luella Biggar Health Foundation, and that old Elmer Bauer, Sr., had succumbed on May 18.

On July 14, 1967, however, Round Valley was touched obliquely by the big picture. A three-column headline on page one announced: CLEAR LAKE LOSES BID FOR EEL RIVER WATER

Two groups of citizens with a thirst for water development had treated each other to lunch at Sausalito, a pleasant bayside resort north of San Francisco. They belonged respectively to the Eel River Association, drawn from the counties of the Eel River basin, and the California Water Resources Association, a pressure group self-styled as "Californians for Water Action." Over their mineral water they listened to the latest conclusions of the state's second-ranking water engineer, John R. Teerink.

The burden of the story was that the water they planned to divert from the Eel River would be much more efficiently conducted by a tunnel through the mountains east of Round Valley than by a southerly route through Lake County. This was a blow to the citizens of Lake County, who had been counting on that water to come to their lake and clear out the weeds that were beginning to seriously affect their tourist industry.

In the course of accounting for this unpopular stand, Teerink explained that they needed to get the water up high enough so that it would run down their tunnel by gravity, which meant building a really high dam. And so it emerged, almost by accident, that the state had decided the best thing to do, after all, was to fill Round Valley with water.

Anyone reading through the first two thirds of the story would have had no idea that Round Valley was threatened—an accurate measure of the *Journal*'s indifference. As for Tessa Jesenko, she let it perturb her not one jot. It was a full month before she even referred to the matter again, and by then the news had come to Covelo in a much more definite manner. It arrived in the valley in the shape of a young, diffident, but eager engineer who came to address the Round Valley Water District.

The water district had been invented in the fifties, at the suggestion of a far-seeing state senator, whose place in Covelo history was assured by the naming of Biggar Lane (although he became mysteriously Bigger when his lane crossed over highway 162).

The senator foresaw that outside water interests might want to meddle with Round Valley, and he advised the citizens to organize in some fashion to meet the threat. Appointment to the district's board was honorary and not onerous. The members consisted for the most part of good old names. Rollie Hurt was president, and then there was Walt Winters, Joe Millet, Joe Clark, and, of course, old J. D. Rohrbough himself. Alta Moore, the wife of Leo, the Pacific Gas and Electric man, was secretary and took the minutes.

With few funds at their disposal there was little for them to do but talk about trying to keep the creek beds clear. In 1967, however, their destiny was at last fulfilled. The State Department of Water Resources in Red Bluff wrote to say they wanted to share, with the district and the people, the results of all that hammering, drilling, marking, and measuring along the Eel River. Thinking they had better allow for a crowd, the district members convened a meeting for July 26 at the Masonic Hall, where most of them went regularly anyway as Freemasons. With its bare, cement-block walls, it was not a pretty building—nothing decorative had been built in the valley for years—but it was big enough to house a meeting of a hundred or two. News of the meeting got around, and the hall was pretty full that night. Richard Wilson was there, too, at the back, and saw a lean young man being introduced as George Baumli, the project engineer.

Although Richard had never met him, Baumli was not new to the valley. He had had a major part in the investigations over the previous eight years, had eaten at the hotel, and knew some of the people present. He spoke earnestly and knowledgeably, a little nervously perhaps, in short bursts, with a quick laugh that vanished without a trace from his mobile face. When he arrived in Round Valley for the meeting, he was already convinced that the project would go through and that the valley would become a reservoir. Of course he didn't say so. It was not his place to make such statements, but he thought the facts would speak for themselves, and he laid them out as dispassionately as he could.

He knew, that evening in Covelo, that some of the people assembled before him would not like what he had to say, but it was one of those awkward things you just have to get through. He explained that plans to build the dam and still save the valley had not worked out. The Franciscan Dam site, the one the corps was drilling for on Richard's land, the one that would have protected the valley, was found to be very poor, with a fault running right through it, and, putting his expertise between them and him on that hot July night, he went on to say something like:

"The Franciscan formation is susceptible to erosion and unraveling of the mountainsides, and this is demonstrated by the railroad that runs down the Eel River Canyon—and the difficulties the railroad has had for years to control the landslides—which are pushing the railroad into the river. They have had experts in from around the world trying to develop some measure to restrain this erosion."

The Etsel site, which the Corps of Engineers had researched, was equally questionable, with its own landslide creating additional problems. The Dos Rios damsite was all right, but to be worth doing, it would have to be 700 feet high, and that would put the valley under 200 or 300 feet of water. George Baumli took the same tack as his boss, Teerink, and tried to engage his audience in the fascinating controversy over where the water would go once it left the valley. He spoke about it at some length. Would it go south through Lake County or east through the mountains? To the valley residents this was, understandably, a less than gripping topic. They were caught up in the dread and excitement of this thing, wanting it dramatized in some way that was relevant to them. How could it happen to them? How *would* it happen? They stumbled in pursuit of questions that might enlighten them, but caught only prosaic, flabby answers.

Who would build the dam? Not decided yet, said Baumli. Perhaps the state, perhaps the Army Corps of Engineers, perhaps both together. When would they start? Well, first it had to be approved, and authorized, and . . . well . . . sometime soon. How would they be compensated? Baumli turned them over to his colleague, Bob Reeves, the right of way and condemnations expert, who gave them eloquent evasions.

Finally, Richard asked what Baumli would have to do, physically, in the valley to prepare for the reservoir.

Baumli explained that when everybody was safely out of the way, they would bring in the dozers and the earthmovers and flatten everything. And the trees? asked Richard. Same thing, said Baumli. Knock them down, pile them up in heaps, and burn them.

"We like to leave a clean floor," he said.

Finally there was a vision, something apocalyptic for them to savor, a scene of organized destruction by steely men in soulless machines, scraping their lives and memories into immense burnpiles. People brought to mind the homes they would return to that evening, pictured them as splinters and rubble in a scene of eerie devastation, and shuddered.

No doubt there were some in that hall that night who thought about their leaky shacks or their dismal, cramped mobile homes and murmured, "Good riddance to bad rubbish." Certainly there was poverty in the valley. Those who came later to look for it, needing some dispensation for the deed they had in mind, found it easily enough. There were others who simply lacked the quality of imagination or sentiment that would allow them to grieve over the loss of something old, who would always be ready to take the money and run. And there were some who had come to the valley hoping to enjoy a rural idyll and were bitterly disappointed.

Among these last was the wife of Jan Stewart, the hardware merchant. They had moved there from Montana, and it was she who had insisted on buying the fine house in the northeast corner of the valley, failing to realize until it was too late that the lumber mill, whining and clanking next door through twenty-four-hour shifts, would intrude on them night and day. Alta Moore remembers the Stewarts' endless complaints, and was not surprised when Jan Stewart later became the Corps of Engineers' most fervent ally in support of the project.

The lurid glimpse of hell that George Baumli unwittingly afforded his listeners that night gave Richard a stimulus that he had lacked. Envisioning the valley ravaged by bulldozers, an infernal scene adrift with fire, smoke, and ash, it was not even so much the loss of the houses and barns but the fate of the trees that haunted him. He had always revered those trees, the grandest examples in the state and, hence, the world, since they were a species limited to California. He simply could not bear the thought of those trees going down. It went beyond self-interest, beyond property and ambition, to more elemental and selfless emotions. It went as far as sacrilege. He would not let it happen. He would stand, with the trees, and fight this thing to the bitter end if need be.

That realization stayed bright within him for twenty-five years. Recalling it he said, with a grin: "Baumli pushed all my buttons. Buttons I didn't even know I had."

3

"Oh Shame, Shame! Where Is Thy Blush . . . ?"

FROM THE OUTSIDE WORLD Round Valley is most easily approached from highway 101. About 140 miles north of San Francisco, beyond Willits, a turnoff leads to a road that winds alongside Outlet Creek, a tributary of the Eel. At one point it crosses Bloody Run creek, a memento of one of the more egregious early massacres of Indians. After ten miles the road meets and crosses the main stem of the Eel River and follows it to its confluence with the so-called Middle Fork, where Dos Rios clings to high, eroded banks. Again the road crosses the river and follows the Middle Fork, climbing high above the river gorge. Three miles upstream the gorge narrows at Windy Point, and here the road is a thousand or so vertiginous feet above the riverbed. It was here, in this narrow V, that the engineers were proposing to raise their dam. From this point the road snakes back and forth, up and down, another eight miles to the rim of Round Valley. Here a graveled area has been cleared as an observation site, known as Inspiration Point. A bronze plaque put up by the California Parks Commission and the Covelo Women's Improvement Club commemorates the moment when a white man, Frank Asbill, "discovered" the valley in 1854, and it honors the pioneers who followed him.

Asbill was camped nearby on the Eel with a small party of horsemen, exploring the region for a supply route north to the gold diggings in Trinity County. He rode up above the river one day and found himself looking down on a cattleman's paradise—a broad and level stretch of woodlands, meadows, and marshes inhabited by wildlife and by Indians who knew it as "the valley of tall grasses." According to an early history, "he returned to camp and reported that he had seen a valley that was perfectly round. . . . The party saddled their horses and rode over into the valley and had a fight with the Indians, killing about forty of them in their camp."[1] After carving their initials on a madrone tree, they continued north, but Round Valley, as Asbill named it, left a deep impression on them, as it did on all who saw it, and they were determined to return.

There is, in any valley, the suggestion of a vast garden, and the more exactly it reproduces those soothing characteristics the greater the tug at man's better instincts. To see from a high, rocky place a sheltered expanse of fertile grassland spread out below brings an involuntary sense of relief, of refuge, of peace and future prosperity. Some famous valleys, like Africa's Great Rift, or Yosemite with its intimidating craggy walls, are too awe-inspiring to promise much comfort. Round Valley is in a cozier class, and of its kind it is superb. It is bounded on all four sides by ridges high enough to contain the spirit of the place without imprisoning it. In its proportions it is very close to those that universally have been found most attractive in large rooms or public squares—that is to say, it is longer than it is wide but not by very much, like the Piazza San Marco or a Regency ballroom, and though it may seem odd to employ such examples of high sophistication, amid those hundreds of square miles of wild, disordered mountain territory, the valley appears more as an artifice than a phenomenon of nature.

From Inspiration Point in the south to the foothills below Bluenose Ridge in the north is a distance of seven or eight miles, about the limit for clear vision with the naked eye, so that the entire huge bowl can be comprehended in one glance, and this undoubtedly adds to its attraction. Its appearance in the sixties was very different from Asbill's first view of the place. Fencelines now branded the valley floor with the same rectangular grid of sections and quarter sections that generally disfigures the face of the country. Where trees once proliferated, large areas had been cleared, but even so, many trees remained, particularly at the edges and in the more distant northern parts.

In the foreground of the view as Richard saw it on his many trips in and out, below him and to the right, were the big red barn, the outbuildings, and the hay fields of the Diamond H ranch, the largest single spread in the valley. The road ran straight across the valley floor from south to north, through the all but invisible town of Covelo, alongside the Indian reservation lands in the northwest section of the valley, and, finally dwindling from sight, it snaked up into the northern foothills. There it was little more than a good logging road to service the mountain ranches that were still numerous and active in the sixties.

On the ridges that confined the valley—Poonkinney to the west, Dingman to the east, Jamison to the south, Bluenose to the north—high conifers like Douglas fir naturally predominated, interspersed with madrone and manzanita. From the far northwest corner of the valley, meandering diagonally across to the southeast, a string of alders, pepperwoods, and locusts marked the course of Mill Creek, a tributary of the Eel. In summer it was a dry bed of granite pebbles, in winter a spawning bed for salmon and steelhead and sometimes a track for a family of bears wandering down from the hills for dinner. In older times, it is said, the flow of Mill Creek into the Eel had been impeded by bars of rock and gravel, so that for much of the year the southeast corner of the valley had been a marshy sanctuary for migrating birds, but settlers had blasted that obstacle away to drain the land.

The valley was originally populated by a tribe of Indians known today as the Yuki. Like most of these names, Yuki meant nothing to the tribe itself. White men would ask one tribe the name of another tribe, and be given a word in a foreign language usually meaning "man." In this case, Yuki had the approximate meaning of "enemy" in the language of the Wailakies, with the result that the principal group of Indians in Round Valley today know themselves as "the enemy."

These were the people Frank Asbill, with his brother Pierce and a certain Samuel Kelsey, encountered and massacred in the valley. Nobody will ever know quite what happened. Although Asbill is credited with discovering the valley, it is almost certain that slave raiders had been there before to steal women and children. This atrocious but lucrative trade had been practiced for some years and it is estimated that between 1852 and 1867 two or three thousand children were stolen in the northern counties and sold into slavery at about $40 a head. That the Asbills were taken to be slavers and felt themselves threatened is possible but unlikely. Given those suspicions, the Yuki were much more inclined to hide.

Even though the Asbills were not a particularly vicious pair—in fact their later exploits, though sometimes criminal, were touched with whimsy and an almost quixotic generosity—they must have shared the prevailing attitude toward Indians. A good account of it appears in a history of Round Valley by Carranco and Beard titled *Genocide and Vendetta.*[2]

> The Americans, coming fresh from two centuries of bitter border warfare and intolerant aggression, brought with them a deep hatred of the red race and made no discrimination between tribes and individuals. . . . All Indians were regarded as predatory animals, to be treated as such. It is therefore not surprising that physical violence was the rule rather than the exception. The native's life was worthless, for no American could be brought to trial for killing an Indian. What little property the Indian possessed could be taken or destroyed at the slightest provocation. He had no civil or legal rights whatsoever. Finally since the quickest and easiest way to get rid of his troublesome presence was to kill him off, this procedure was adopted as standard for some years.

Of course, this was not official policy. Several treaties had been made promising to reserve land for the Indians but the U.S. Senate had rejected them as being too generous. Instead, in 1853, an army lieutenant, Edward Beale, devised a plan for communal farms, where Indians would be instructed and disciplined by resident agents and protected by army posts. Congress authorized five of these military reservations and Round Valley became one of them. Col. Thomas J. Henley, an ex-postmaster of San Francisco, was appointed superintendent, and at first he appears to have worked honestly and conscientiously, but before long he fell out with the army and was widely attacked by newspapers. With his hopes of political success dashed, he seems to have decided to feather his own nest. Although the entire valley was supposed to be reserved for Indians, he encouraged his own friends and relations to settle there on the pretext that they would protect the reservation. The promise was dreadfully betrayed. During the years that followed, far from protecting the Indians, the settlers tore the reservation and its members to shreds for their own profit and amusement, and committed most crimes known to man.

The Indians had no recourse to justice anywhere in California. Serranus Clinton Hastings, the first chief justice of the California Supreme Court and a personal friend of the governor, had himself conspired to persecute the Indians in Round Valley. He owned a horse ranch nearby, and he sanctioned the formation of a volunteer company to "chastise" the Indians. Local men were mustered as the Eel River Rangers and led by an obsessive Indian killer named Jarboe.

J. Ross Browne, the secret treasury agent who investigated Henley's misappropriations, also wrote about Captain Jarboe and his rangers:

> What neglect, starvation and disease have not done, has been achieved by the cooperation of the white settlers in the great work of extermination. . . . Peaceable Indians, including women and children, were cruelly slaughtered by the whites. . . . Oh shame, shame! Where is thy blush that white men should do this with impunity in a civilized country, under the very eyes of an enlightened government!

For their five months of service, during which they killed several hundred Indians, the rangers were paid $9,347.39 by a grateful state, which congratulated them on their campaign and "the manner in which it was conducted." Before the arrival of the Asbills there are thought to have been about eleven thousand Indians living in and near the valley. Ten years later, the number was reduced to a thousand, for the most part destitute and undernourished, who worked for six ears of corn a day or begged outside the saloons.

Henley and his sons had hoped to establish a cattle empire in and around the valley, but they had miscalculated badly. There was another man, George White, whose ruthless ambition and cunning far exceeded theirs. White had entered the valley for the first time only a few days after the Asbills. He, too, grasped its potential immediately, resolved to return, and did so in time to grab a thousand acres between the properties of the Henley family. White's progress was mysterious and spectacular. Without visible means, and despite laws regulating the acquisition of land at the time, the census of 1860 showed him as owning five thousand acres. Soon he became unstoppable.

A huge area of rangeland known as the Yolla Bolly country (now a wilderness area) came almost entirely under his control, and his "buckeroos," who were more than likely to be outlaws, policed it for him. Carranco and Beard have a convincing description of these men:

> His buckeroos wore blue jumpers and Levi Straus overalls, which would usually develop into the outline of the saddle they rode, giving them the appearance of having very bowed legs. They wore small-rowelled, silver-mounted spurs well down on their run-over boot heels. Their hats were pushed down on their heads because they rode among trees and brush after the wild cows. These long-haired men with red or blue bandanas around their necks rarely carried six-shooters. Their gun was the .44-40 model 1873 Winchester, which shot sixteen times and was carried in a sling made from the top of a discarded boot and looped over the loggerhead.
>
> The wild buckeroos, yelling and screaming, would come riding into the small town of Covelo from the hills to blow off steam, heading for Alec Perry's saloon, which was owned by George White, and there they would sing their favorite songs as they stood at the bar and drank seven different kinds of liquor that came from the same barrel.[3]

White's swift expansion was probably due, in large part, to an extraordinary man who came to work for him around 1857. John Wathen, known as "Wylackie John," was described as a soft-spoken, quiet-mannered man, neatly dressed, suave, and courteous, with a polite word for anyone he met in town. In reality he was a gifted schemer, a robber, a poisoner, an arsonist, a perjurer, and a murderer, and he knew how to control White's desperate men. All these talents he put at White's disposal. He arranged to have bothersome homesteaders shot, or killed by other means (strychnine, used to kill bears, was a popular method). He stole herds of sheep and cattle from rival ranchers, organized perjured testimony, and murdered his own unfortunate creditors.

He did well for himself as White's henchman. He was partner in one of White's many ranches and embroiled himself in White's unsuccessful attempt to create a new county, with Covelo as the seat and White as "king." He was finally shot dead in a barroom in Covelo by the outraged brother of White's estranged third wife, whom Wathen was trying to discredit with false witnesses. Wathen's executioner was brought to trial and acquitted, to the great joy of many, including the judge who got drunk at the subsequent celebrations and was almost arrested for disorderly conduct.

The divorce suit, which led to Wathen's death, dragged on for ten years or more, and the papers gave great notoriety to White's bizarre marital affairs, his obsession with spiritualism, and his unscrupulous plots. Wylackie John Wathen was irreplaceable, and although others continued to do White's dirty work, they were less skilled at covering themselves. Eventually a sensational and interminable murder trial also focused statewide attention on White's tyranny, and yet he continued to frustrate the law at every turn. He remained undisputed king of his territory and was able to operate his repressive reign pretty much unhindered.

Needless to say, life under such a dictatorship was uneasy and corrupt. Many men under White's protection lied, robbed, and murdered on their own account. Any form of social evolution was impossible. From the beginning the atmosphere favored ruthless solutions to all problems. Although White became extremely rich, he was not the only one to do well. The Henleys and others also prospered by a system of exploitation that was brilliant in its simplicity. They exploited the Indians directly and herded their sheep and cattle on Indian land at no cost to themselves in rent or taxes. At the same time they were able to profit handsomely from all the government's funding of the reservation. As an early example, during Henley's four years as superintendent, the government expended more than a million dollars on the reservation, a good part of which was converted to the private uses of Henley and his cronies.

In the winter of 1874, a congressman visiting Round Valley reported that the reservation system amounted to slavery. Most of the remaining Indians, he said, had little clothing, lived in bark, slab, or grass huts, were poorly fed, and forced to work for very little return. He added that more than two thirds were suffering from advanced syphilis. At the time, the reservation was being run by a Methodist minister, John Burchard, who whipped his charges to instill them with Christian grace.

White's death in 1902 left the valley rife with resentments and vengeful accounts to be settled. Men who had been afraid to speak of what they knew now came forward with evidence of crimes, and expensive trials continued through the decades. One of White's nephews, John Rohrbough, had done well in business, with several thousand acres of his own. It was he who established the flour mill in town. He took over White's lands and estate, which White had deliberately plunged into debt in order to defraud his ex-wife, and worked hard to rehabilitate them and to improve Round Valley's reputation. He also acquired White's splendid mansion, built in 1878, complete with ballroom, gas-burning chandeliers, and piped water, and eventually passed it on to his son John II, who in turn left it to his son John III.

The remaining Indians, a few hundred in all, continued as second-class citizens, segregated and employed in menial positions. Despite the whippings of the Reverend Mr. Burchard, the Methodist church remained the principal religious influence in the Indian community, but while it may have offered some consolation, it did little to satisfy their worldly needs. Poor economic circumstances and a fractured culture kept them socially and psychologically depressed, a situation that has continued up to this day.

The legacy of White's lawless rule effectively distorted the social development of Covelo. It was never incorporated as a self-governing community, and has always been administered and policed from the safe distance of the county seat at Ukiah. In practice, a handful of old families, the Winters, the Hurts, the Vanns, and the Rohrboughs, kept a firm grip on the valley and made most of the important decisions, and the community was stilted to the point of suffocation. The years of the Second World War brought prosperity, but in the light of those stirring global events Covelo came to seem more of a backwater than ever. War industry as well as war service had drawn many younger people away, and they were loath to return. To the older generation it must have seemed, after the fifties, that their good times were fading away, and perhaps it was that which colored their attitude when plans for the high dam were finally confirmed. For some of them it must have come as a providential way of quitting while they were ahead.

The incumbent families had always been quietly cynical about Richard's determination to build up a ranching operation. They saw him as a young rich kid who would get burned, and they probably had half an eye on profiting by the harsh lessons they felt sure he would have to learn. But now, with the dam coming, none of that mattered. Many supposed the government would compensate them well, and soon. There were even some who wondered whether, given Richard's connections "down below," he might have known about it ahead of them and bought his valley land as a speculation.

Naturally none of them relished the idea of seeing everything they had grown up with vanish beneath the waves. The very idea that the largest area of fertile farmland in Mendocino County could be simply disposed of in that way was beyond anybody's comprehension. Yet it was the age of the disposable. Society lived by rules that contradicted all the experience of earlier generations, and everybody seemed to be doing very well by them. Farming itself seemed to have lost its significance, as wonderful new ways of cultivating and synthesizing foodstuffs emerged from the laboratories. There was no way old-timers could predict how things would go, and if the government was determined to put them all into easy retirement, there was no point in fighting it.

All the same, it made you wonder. It was a crazy world, all right.

4

"As Far as I'm Concerned, They Can Have It."

WITH BAUMLI'S ACCOUNT of the shape of things to come still in his mind, Richard traveled around the valley and saw it with fresh eyes, like a dearly loved relation doomed to an early death. Everywhere he recalled past experiences—as a boy visiting with his father, or as a young man out of the army and ready to make it his life. He tried to imagine it all gone, washed away or rotting beneath a huge lake. The thought was obscene, impossible to accept.

On his visits to town, at the Shell station, the hotel, and Gravier's market, all owned by old-timers, he talked with ranchers, store owners, and others, expecting them to express the same outrage and defiance that he felt. He was surprised by the general sense of acquiescence, even defeatism, among the ranchers. Some, to be sure, still believed the dam was a fantasy, and saw no need to take action, believing it would die its own death. Others thought it would be futile to oppose the government. Some of them were already spending the money they were convinced they would get in compensation. Most of the store owners were openly enthusiastic. Covelo had not been as good to them as they hoped, and the dam offered them an easy prospect, they thought, of getting their money out.

Richard knew he would have to find some support among the older settlers, and thought he might have some luck with Elmer Bauer, Jr.

The Bauer family is widespread in Round Valley, with both white and Indian branches. The white branch was chiefly represented in the sixties by the two brothers, Elmer and Zola. Zola was a short, peppery, hard-driving cattleman, and some of his entrepreneurial spirit seems to have entered into his cows known as "Zybies" (after Zola's middle name) because they were famous for breaking through fences and grazing on other people's property. News of these bovine initiatives was always received by Zola with wide-eyed astonishment and a "Well, I'll be darned. How did they ever git in there?"

Elmer and he had been in partnership once, but their differences became too great, so they split the property and went their separate ways. Elmer took the mountain ranch and Zola stayed in the valley until his death.

Speaking in the fall of '86, Elmer Bauer was reaching back over a long and busy life. His fair hair had turned to feathery white. His full, pale-complexioned face, candid blue eyes, and contented expression conveyed a childlike innocence and more than a hint of childlike stubbornness behind it.

"When they first started talking about a dam on the Eel River, my folks had a homestead out on what they call the Middle Fork Eel, out past the old ranger station. I don't know if I was born yet. That was back there around about nineteen seven . . . eight . . . nine . . . or ten—back into there.

"Mother told me these people came and talked about it—lookin' around Etsel Crossing. The Bureau of Reclamation came in. The whole hillside was going to be irrigated.

"I think back and I think it was ten or fifteen years, then you find it was thirty or forty, or more. Time flies you know. They say once you're over the top of the hill and goin' down, you gain speed." He grinned amiably. "Flyin' right along now. . . ."

The hillside where his parents had homesteaded, the one that was to have been irrigated with money from Washington, was the east side of Dingman Ridge, the long hill that separates the Eel from Round Valley. Elmer Bauer had lived all his long life within sight of that ridge.

"My dad had one ranch, and sold it to buy another across the river from there. Then he added two more. He drove cattle over the summit here, over to Willows—got two and a half cents a pound. A cow got fifteen dollars. They drove hogs to Ukiah, too.

"In later years he retired and my brother and I ran it for a while.

Then we split up our partnership and I bought the mountain ranch, see, and I run that for years.

"When I was building this house they were getting awfully serious about this dam. And I got in the same predicament a lot of farmers were in—when prices began to fall, I'd bought a whole lot of extra stuff. I'd bought equipment and property, and I'd got myself bogged down. When you're in debt and everything, and nothin's goin' too good, the dam was one way of gettin' out of it.

"Richard Wilson came to me one day and said: 'You know, if we're going to do anything about this we'd better get busy—if we're going to stop it.' And I says, 'As far as I'm concerned they can have it.' "

Elmer Bauer's valediction summed up the feelings of most of the valley's residents pretty well, and Richard was seriously frustrated. The most he could achieve was Elmer's promise that if Richard organized some kind of meeting, Elmer would come to it.

Through the church and Susan's social contacts, there were other families who offered support. A colony of Seventh-Day Adventists had bought land in the Indian reservation area, in the northwest corner of the valley, and they were vehemently opposed to being displaced. However, Richard knew he had to have more solid support from the grass roots of the valley.

He had no more luck with the Indians than he did with the old white families. Most of them, he discovered, were not even aware of the danger. Characteristically they had paid no attention to the water district meeting where Baumli spelled out the threat. Shy of exposing themselves in a white-dominated arena, they simply ignored it. Only a few discovered the truth, but among them was a very determined and forthright woman named Ida Soares. Richard sent a message to Ida Soares imploring her to find a way to let him talk to the Indian community. She remembers calling him that night.

"I said, 'Mr. Wilson, there's somethin' going on in this valley I think maybe you can tell me about.' From then on we started. I said, 'What you have to do is call a meeting. I'll see if we can get some notices up.' So we put the notices up. You know, EVERYBODY WELCOME—CONCERNING THE DAM.

"Richard came out and spoke to us on it. Of course we had people in the audience who were for the dam. 'What we have to have here,' he said, 'is a representative right now, so we can get that person into Sacramento to testify. Who will go?'

"People said, 'Ida can go.' I listened. Didn't say nothin'. Then I said, 'Mrs. Tuttle, you are of the tribe. Why can't you go down? You representing all of us.' 'Oh, I couldn't,' she said. 'What would I say? How would I handle it?' So they all said, 'Let's send Ida down there.' "

Tessa Jesenko picked up this meeting in her column. On August 16, she noted that the Round Valley Indian Council had met a few days earlier at the reservation auditorium, Warren Lincoln presiding. A letter was read "concerning the possibility of Round Valley being inundated," and Richard Wilson, owner of "vast properties" in Covelo and Round Valley, "spoke on the dam proposal." Aside from the dig at Wilson's wealth, she remained carefully neutral.

It was an inconclusive meeting, from Richard's point of view, and made few converts, if any. He tried to make a convincing case against the dam, but still had little information to go on. All he could do was to say, in as many ways as possible, that it was a lousy idea, and should be looked at more carefully. Elmer Bauer was there, but remained unpersuaded. However, it served one important purpose: It let the whole valley know who was at the heart of the opposition. At least people would know where to go.

Meanwhile the dam builders were gathering momentum at an extraordinary rate. The years of costly investigations up and down the Eel, which Richard had disparaged as just a bunch of bureaucrats keeping themselves busy at the taxpayer's expense, now bore gigantic fruit.

No sooner had Baumli departed the valley than a decision was made in Sacramento that the army should build the dam. This was ominous news, from Richard's point of view. It meant that the Middle Eel was no longer a state project, but a federal one, and the army, as everyone knew, was never short of money.

Then he began to hear of meetings up and down the coast between state officials, army engineers, county supervisors, and individuals sometimes described as "interested parties" or "water leaders." Everybody was in on the act, there was no discernible opposition, and Richard wondered how he could begin to crack the seamless unanimity that the water lobby had managed to achieve.

The way the threat had materialized struck him as very strange. There was something skewed and abnormal about it. This did not feel like a scene from modern America, but more like an episode from Colonial history. All these various forces, bearing down suddenly on one remote valley and its inhabitants, appeared to have been orchestrated by some distant power. But by whom?

It was not unusual for people in the northwest to think of themselves as being exploited by southern interests. They knew that their standard of living fell far below what was customary in Southern California, but it allowed them to breathe clean air, drink good water, live in spectacular scenery, and remain connected with the spirit that animated their natural surroundings, that brought the deer bounding across their roads at night, the huge fish torpedoing up the rivers, the bears and mountain lions prowling the hills, and the owls shrieking through the night skies.

For the most part, their living also depended on these primal things—the timber, the salmon, the rangeland. They knew, consciously or intuitively, that the wealth of their land was being drained, that the true value of the raw materials that passed through their hands was being reaped elsewhere, but it was a trade-off, and in hard times a little of that same wealth, which kept California growing, trickled back in the form of welfare, and food stamps, and Aid to Dependent Families with Children.

Richard had no need of welfare. By the standards of Mendocino County, he was a wealthy man, but he and Susan were satisfied to live modestly. There was a tacit understanding that if you wanted to live in this beautiful place, you had to live a simple life. Nobody seriously begrudged the southerners their shopping malls and power breakfasts, their lives in the fast lane. But the deal, as Richard understood it, included a "hands-off" clause. Let them rip us off, so long as they leave us alone.

Even Pat Brown, the governor who fathered the very State Water Project that was now reaching out to swallow Round Valley, expressed the same feeling. He came originally from the north, and confessed in an oral history in later years, that he thought sending the water south might keep the crowds away.

"I didn't think I'd ever come down to Southern California," he reflected, "and I said to myself, 'I don't want all these people to go to Northern California.'"[1]

It had to be faced. If Richard, and any other allies he might bring to the cause, were to fight this war, they might as well think of themselves as the victims of a land grab by a colonial power, with Los Angeles at the heart of the empire. The southerners wanted the water to grow more people. They were as remote from Mendocino County as the London mob was from Hindustan, and just as little concerned with what their armies did in their name. And, for that matter, the average Round Valley inhabitant knew as little about the forces unleashed against him as a dhobi wallah in Lucknow Bazaar knew about Queen Victoria and Buckingham Palace.

It was always difficult—alone in the mountains among the trees, or down on the scoured rocks and pebbles of the creek beds, or as one of a handful of people you knew moving slowly through the blistering summer heat of noon on Covelo's main street—to visualize Los Angeles. It was hard to bring to mind the sheer size, energy, and hunger of the place, even when you knew it as well as Richard did, which was intimately. But he visited the south often enough, had business down there, and didn't need to stretch his imagination. He knew exactly where the focus of all this aggressive energy was to be found, and it lay behind the filigreed facade of a long, low concrete building at 1111 Sunset Boulevard in Los Angeles, where an ostentatious display of fountains advertised the home of the Metropolitan Water District of Southern California.

The M.W.D.—the "Met," as it was usually known—distributed water to some eleven million people in the southern counties, as well as serving that area's huge industrial and agricultural base. It was then, and is today, a colossal organization.

Water utilities are hardly a glamorous sector of business. Oceans, waterfalls, and raging torrents naturally excite awe and respect. Lakes and ponds and sweet-flowing brooks soothe the mind and bring joy to the spirit. Water in pipes is simply boring, and ultimate success in the water business is to keep it that way. The only strong emotions associated with piped water are those of rage, despair, and terror when pipes burst, the supply dries up, or the water turns lethal. For this reason most water utilities try to go about their business in blissful anonymity.

The Met, often to its chagrin, is an exception, not because of its failures, but because historically it succeeded too well. In its original incarnation, as the Los Angeles Department of Water & Power, it became notorious for its brilliant and ruthless scheme to bring water to the city from Owens Valley in the Sierras, through a 240-mile-long pipe. That pipe was big enough and long enough to excite admiration; the farmers of Owens Valley were angry enough to try to blow it up, and L.A.'s water departments have had a high profile ever since.

The architect of that first aqueduct, William Mulholland, had a remarkable career trying to keep up with the thirst of his booming city in the sands. Determined to leave a legacy of complete security against drought, he patched together an organization of associated agencies strong enough to compete with states, to deal with the federal government, to capture the Colorado River and bring that water hundreds of miles across the desert. It was this mighty conglomerate of water agencies from Santa Monica to San Diego, known as the Metropolitan Water District, that was determined to feed the Eel River into its conduits.

Joe Jensen, the chairman of the Met, was the current guardian of Mulholland's legacy. He was an aggressive and intolerant man who intimidated all around him. Never shy about his ambitions, he had said in public, several times, that he wanted the Eel, and that when he was good and ready he'd come and get it. The media fashioned a MacArthur-like figure out of him. In the fifties he came on well-publicized visits to reconnoiter his future colonies, and issued "I will return" pronouncements.

He commissioned the Bechtel Corporation's engineers to make elaborate investigations, and in 1959 they delivered detailed schemes for a multiple series of dams on the Eel.[2] Three of them involved flooding Round Valley. Any one of them would have captured enough water to cover a million acres ten feet deep, and there were plans to send two of these million-acre-feet of water on a six-hundred-mile journey south, for the exclusive use of the Met. The fact that the Met was even able to contemplate financing such a scheme was a measure of its awe-inspiring strength.

Jensen's ambitions were not kindly received, however. Although Jensen always believed that Southern California should go it alone, state politicians were equally determined to supply the Met through their own delivery system, and here they had agribusiness on their side. The Met was only part of the water lobby. Agribusiness corporations in the Central Valley were equally powerful. While the interests of agribusiness and the Met often joined, they were also in conflict. There were huge tracts on the west side of the San Joaquin that were unirrigated and would become very much more valuable with a water supply. The land-holding corporations, through their irrigation districts, wanted water, too, and they knew they would get more and on much better terms through the state.

They had no difficulty arousing opposition to Jensen's plan in the northern counties. Neither faction could succeed without the other. Jensen battled mightily with his board over the matter. Eventually his directors overruled him, probably for the first and only time. The Met signed up with the State Water Project and immediately became the state's biggest customer, contracted to take almost half the water in the system, with an immense financial stake in the venture.

Now that the two factions were joined, their combined power was preeminent in the state. Only later, when the space program got under way, was there any other industrial complex to compare with the water lobby for sheer financial and political clout. It was still the Eel River they wanted, the Eel they had been promised, and Jensen was still willing to do whatever it took to bring the Eel south, but his forays into the north had taught him to be wary. He had been met with criticism and suspicion, and the Met was accused of going back to the bad old days, riding roughshod over rural communities. Jensen was persuaded to wield his power in subtler ways, and pursue his aims with blandishments rather than bullying.

A perfect instrument for this policy was already in place. It was called the Eel River Association. Richard already knew that a number of the meetings taking place around him were organized by this association, and he had made it his business to find out more about it. The ERA was, in fact, a movable feast of people with an interest in water development—mostly engineers and county supervisors—who met regularly every other month in various well-appointed hotels up and down the north coast. Jerry Gilbert, who was manager of a Marin County water agency from the late fifties, was in at the beginning and remembers how it evolved.

"It was at the urging of a congressman by the name of Miller—who died in a plane crash in '63 or so—that the north coast counties banded together. They were concerned about flood protection in the lower Eel—because of the bad floods in the fifties—and improved recreational facilities, and a water supply to local communities. Those interests drove these people to meet and talk.

"Marin, Sonoma, Mendocino, Humboldt, and, I think, Lake counties were in this informal association, and I was the Marin County representative."

Humboldt County contained the river's estuary and lower reaches, where commercial developments took the brunt of the flood damage. Mendocino County, which included Round Valley, was where most of the Eel's water fell from the skies. It was the poorest of the counties and wanted any kind of development to improve its economy. Lake County lived largely off income from the tourist trade around Clear Lake, and saw advantages in bringing the Eel water south through their lake to improve its quality. Sonoma was the fastest growing county, with huge, thirsty vineyards. Its burgeoning county seat, Santa Rosa, was mopping up the overflow from the Bay Area and Silicon Valley, and stretching the resources of its own Russian River. Marin County, the aristocrat among them, had the most affluent population, much of which commuted to the Bay Area. It had rolling hills, dairy farms, a leisure-oriented coastline, and very sparse water resources of its own.

Two things characterized these counties. The first thing was that in one sense they formed a microcosm of California as a whole. The wealthier they were, the drier they were. Or to put it another way, very few people, given the choice, wanted to live where the rain falls. The other thing was that, compared with Southern California, and with the exception of Marin, they were *all* wet and poor.

Their representatives knew what every water engineer had known for a hundred years—that the north coast had enough water to support tens of millions more people, that those millions would all go south, and that, sooner or later, the south would come for that water.

Put tactfully, according to Gilbert: "It rapidly became a general feeling that the needs of Metropolitan could be used to achieve the needs of the local folks. It was more of a partnership thing—not in the overt sense—but the Met had the money, and the folks had the political control over the resource and had some objectives to achieve, and so perhaps there would be a linkage between these two things—and it came about in the Dos Rios project."

Put bluntly, as Richard saw it, they were selling all hope of a thriving regional economy for beads and baubles. He harbored a lively suspicion of southern moneyed interests, so it came as no surprise to him that a faithful attendant at all the ERA meetings was Jensen's top man in Sacramento, his legislative representative, or lobbyist, the shrewd, affable man-for-all-seasons, Big Bill Fairbank. The Met's own aircraft flew up and down the coast regularly and Fairbank lost no opportunity to emphasize, in every way possible, the economic advantages that could be enjoyed by association with the wealth and glitter of the southland.

The '64 flood gave these engineers and officials a new sense of opportunity. Their voluntary association was formalized and dedicated to developing the Eel to the mutual advantage of its members, who then had the good fortune to hire a very smart man named Jerald Butchert as their executive secretary. In 1964 Butchert was the young chief engineer for the Fresno Water District, but already he had a remarkable talent for negotiation.

Butchert accelerated the pace of activity dramatically. The supervisors representing the counties were all business-oriented and saw it as their duty to seize any opportunity to bring immediate economic advantage. Entranced by the prospects for a recreation industry around the lake and security for business at the mouth of the Eel, they largely ignored the dangers to one of the bread-and-butter industries of the north coast—the salmon fisheries—and quickly became intoxicated with the project.

It was too big, too grand to be carped at. Lingering doubts were swept away by the engineers. They had spent years and millions of dollars arriving at their conclusions. And hadn't they all seen the maps of those thrombotic rivers, those other dams and reservoirs that would turn their counties into a sponge for all the rain that fell over the north coast. There was an exhilarating feeling of progress about it all, and obviously the Middle Fork of the Eel was a crucial component in the state plan.

According to Gilbert, the fate of Round Valley was never much of an issue.

"At some point they decided the best project would be to flood the valley, and that was a given. I remember very well, because I drove up there and camped with my family on the Eel, and personally I was exploring where the high water mark would be, and all that stuff. In '65 or '66. I don't think it was later than that. It was common knowledge."

Common, that is, to all but common folk.

Having to flood the valley was an unfortunate complication for most of the Mendocino supervisors. They were already on record as opposing it, but they were certain it was a futile stand. The engineers had convinced them that the only way to get any degree of flood control for Humboldt was by flooding Round Valley. Only one supervisor, Joe Scaramella from Point Arena, wanted nothing to do with it, and they left him out of their discussions. As members of the Eel River

Association, they were committed to finding a remedy to the flood danger. Privately they offered their support to the engineers, in exchange for whatever concessions they could win for their county. In public they continued to say they were against it. Ruefully they anticipated having some explaining to do, but with the dazzling prospect of a million happy tourists coming to play and spend around the army's enormous blue lake, they didn't doubt the voters would see reason. Anyway, like most of the people in Round Valley, they thought the government was too big to stop.

5

"Go for the Best Deal You Can Get."

AFTER THE MEETING at the Indian reservation it was difficult for Richard to resist a sense of futility and impotence. How could he and the few others even willing to raise their voices, stop the government from carrying out a major public work that it considered essential for the good of the entire state. For a brief while, he saw his prospects for success as laughable.

The state alone had spent $7 million amassing the data to design this project. An army of engineers, with all its immense prestige, was ready to stake its reputation on the dam. The state had legislation in place to fund it, but now the army was offering to pick up the tab. The water it was intended to deliver had already been sold to farmers and city managers from San Francisco to San Diego. One neighboring county was convinced it would save lives and property. Another believed it would save the tourist industry. And what did he have to oppose all these interests? The unsupported, personal conviction that it was wrong and wouldn't work. In contrast, Don Quixote's chances of defeating a windmill were excellent.

With pads and pencils, Richard locked himself away in his ranch office and drew up a laundry list of aims and priorities. If he was going to try, there was no time to waste. He knew he had to slow the onward rush of the dam builders. By now, he had a pretty good idea of their game plan. They would steamroller this thing through a staged public hearing. After a few perfunctory moves, it would go to the governor. Reagan would have every reason to sign off on it, and it would be into Congress for authorization as part of an omnibus bill within the year.

Once the corps was authorized to build, Round Valley was as good as dead. Even if the dam were never built, the authorization would effectively kill all chance of development in the valley for decades to come. He had to stop the steamroller. He saw how effective the dam builders were in deploying what he thought of as front organizations. The ERA was one. Another powerful entity of this sort was the California Water Resources Association. And there were others. All of them were supposedly voluntary organizations created spontaneously by the public to support water development projects. He soon learned that the corps and the Met were expert at "facilitating" the creation of these groups.

They had imposing letterheads, and were led by men distinguished in their fields. They sent out authoritative newsletters, lobbied in Sacramento, and cultivated an official manner that often misled the public. Clearly, Richard thought, if his opposition was to have a chance it would have to clothe itself in the same way. His firstborn entity of this kind he decided to call the Round Valley Protective Association, and he scribbled out what he thought its functions would be: to hammer away at legislators and the press, to hold meetings, look for support, and raise money to pay the expenses of sending delegations to testify at hearings. But the first priority, he knew, was to *buy time!* He was ready to use any means available to stall the dam and gain time for effective opposition.

There were many different lines of attack, and he would have to develop them all. He could criticize the dam itself. The rock formations of the Round Valley area were notoriously unstable. He knew that. Landslides and erosion were a major problem, and earthquake tremors were not unknown.

He could also argue that it was wasteful and destructive to flood so much good land, the biggest single area of farmable land in Mendocino County.

He could claim that it was an environmental abomination that would wreak havoc on the fish in the rivers and the wildlife that depended on the valley for winter sustenance.

And then there were the Indians. Surely they could make a strong case against being kicked off the only piece of land they could still claim as theirs.

He would try to show that the dam was just another, unnecessary boondoggle being imposed on the taxpayer. What was the point, he asked himself, of forever trying to provide more water for more people in the south, when the only outcome would be to attract still more people who would want more water? Wasn't it better to stop now, before everything wild and natural had been tamed or destroyed in this manic effort to keep up?

He could attack the corps directly. He already knew that the Army Corps of Engineers was only entitled to build dams for flood control. How much flood control could they get from a dam so far away from where the control was needed?

Who would he try to influence first? The closest, and softest target would seem to be the county supervisors. If he could turn the supervisors around, it would certainly muddy the waters for the ERA, and it would help him bring pressure to bear on the state government and the legislators. Those legislators, Senator Collier, Assemblyman Belotti, and Congressman Clausen, were all sold on the dam. It would be tough to overcome their natural inclination to support the greatest number of voters, and they got most of their support from the coastal interests who wanted flood control.

Richard foresaw that his opposition could easily be decried as emotional or elitist or impractical. At bottom he knew his reason for fighting would always be the sincere and simple conviction that it was just wrong, fundamentally wrong, to flood this valley. For those who did not share that belief he would have to fashion other reasons. To do that effectively he needed information, facts about everything and everybody to do with this project. Fortunately he was better placed than most. He had family and resources in the south and good connections up and down the state, and he planned to approach them all.

As to the dam itself, the corps would have to publish a report, sooner or later, describing just how they planned to build it, and what precautions they had taken. And then, as he understood it, they would have to hold a public hearing. He would organize his efforts to bring the best possible case to that hearing. Meanwhile he would concentrate on setting up his association, on searching out allies wherever he could find them, and on bringing the Mendocino supervisors around.

The supervisors seemed to him to be playing a double game. He thought they would be susceptible to pressure, and he needed someone to keep track of their weekly business. His intuition led him to cast Dural McCombs in that role.

McCombs worked in Ukiah for the Pacific Gas and Electric Company, and lived there with his wife, Nita, in the house that she had inherited, but he had been born and raised in Covelo. He was a descendant of the ninth white man to settle in Round Valley, and he still owned a ranch on the Eel River, at Etsel Crossing, where dams had been planned throughout the century. He was one of those who had read to the end of the story in the *Ukiah Journal,* and was deeply upset at the thought of Round Valley being flooded.

"I went up to the valley and talked to a lot of different people, and they didn't seem to think they could do anything. It was a strange feeling. Really strange. You'd go up and talk to the old-timers and say, 'Don't you want to fight this?' and they'd say, 'There's nothing we can do.' The government was doing it, and they were afraid of the government. But they all told me to get hold of Richard Wilson.

"Every time I'd go up I'd try to see him, and couldn't, so I finally wrote him a letter saying I'd like to help. Two or three days later I got a letter saying, 'Dear Mr. McCombs, thank you. I shall have further comment to make at a later date.' That was all. Then I got up there for that Indian meeting, and saw him, and he was calling me 'Jim.' I knew then that he'd checked up on me, because that's my nickname. He likes to check on people before he gets involved."

McCombs does not, at first, strike one as a particularly resolute or fearless man. He has a shy manner, slightly nervous, and his true height is diminished by a stooped posture. As a young man working on an overhead power line he fell from a ladder, injured his back, and was desk-bound thereafter. Belying these appearances, he became a fierce guerrilla fighter against the dam. And Nita, an even more frail-seeming individual, turned out to be as tough as her husband.

Richard wasted no time in putting the McCombs to work. The five Mendocino supervisors met weekly to manage the county's affairs, as well as conducting committee meetings at which they were inclined to slip controversial matters through unnoticed. Between them, Jim and Nita volunteered the drudgery of covering the "supes" and generally bringing anything significant to Richard's attention. Watching their activities was crucial, trapped as they were in ambiguity. The mere fact that one of them, Harvey Sawyers, went regularly to the meetings of the Eel River Association and had not declared his opposition was suspicious enough. Richard felt they could be maneuvered into taking a much stronger stand against the corps. In an effort to pin them down, one of his first pieces of business was to persuade the supervisors to come to Covelo and account for themselves before the multitude. Eventually he was able to fix up a meeting at the Masonic Hall for September 6, with August Avila, John Mayfield, and Harvey Sawyers, and felt he was making good progress. He was shocked to discover that the corps was moving even faster and had pulled a coup right under his nose. On August 25, 1967, the Eel River Association met again at one of the most desirable hotels on the northern highway, the Benbow Inn. This time it was to hear the army's newly appointed district engineer, Col. Frank Boerger, give an account of the project. The next day, Boerger slipped into Round Valley with a group of aides and managed to address some Indians and a small clique of businessmen who represented the Round Valley Chamber of Commerce. Jim Fisher presented the colonel with a written letter of approval from the chamber of commerce. Warren Lincoln, president of the Tribal Council, assured him that the Indians were in favor of the dam. Colonel Boerger left very well satisfied, convinced that opposition to the dam would be minimal, and reported these results to his superior. Soon afterward Gen. John A. B. Dillard wrote an encouraging letter to the director of the state's Department of Water Resources, saying:

> On 25 August 1967 at the invitation of the Eel River Association, members of the boards of supervisors of Humboldt, Mendocino, and Lake counties met at the Benbow Inn near Garberville to discuss this project, among other things. During the meeting, a preliminary outline of the plan to inundate Round Valley was presented by the district engineer. A significant result of these discussions was a definitive statement of unqualified support for the project on the part of the Humboldt County Board of Supervisors and from three of the Mendocino County supervisors. Since these counties are directly affected by the project, we consider these statements of support as most important steps forward.
>
> On the day following the above meeting, Colonel Boerger met with representatives of the Covelo Indian community in the town of Covelo. During the course of that meeting, spokesmen for the

> Indian community voiced strong support for the project as outlined, recognizing the necessity for inundating Round Valley, including a portion of the Indian reservation. During the same meeting, Mr. Jim Fisher, president of the Covelo Chamber of Commerce, voiced the chamber's strong support of the proposed reservoir after the pertinent facts had been presented. A letter evidencing this support is enclosed.
>
> In addition, the Executive Committee of the Eel River Association has taken a strong stand in favor of the project as it is currently proposed.
>
> We do know that one resident of Round Valley, a Mr. Richard Wilson, is actively engaged in enlisting opposition to the project and has conducted at least one meeting toward this end. . . .
>
> Obviously, we are going to run into some opposition to any project involving relocation of population centers, even small ones, and inundation of improved properties. However, in view of the nature and degree of the support already on record, I believe there is a reasonable basis for optimism that we may face less opposition than is "normal" to projects of this type.

Richard knew nothing of this letter, or he would have been outraged to hear that three supervisors who were supposed to be adamantly against the dam, were conspiring to support it. He only heard at third hand about the meeting in Stewart's hardware store, but that was a heavy blow. The dam boosters seemed to be all over him. He could only hope that getting the supervisors up to the valley might spark off some resistance.

Only two of the supervisors Richard had invited came to the meeting at the Masonic Hall on September 6. John Mayfield pleaded sick. Augie Avila and Harvey Sawyers both claimed to be against the dam, but they told the confused crowd that it was useless to oppose it.

"If I was living up here I would keep my place nice and paint up the barn," said Avila, "and I'd be against it, but there's nothing you can really do to stop it. All you can do is go for the best deal you can."

Nita McCombs spoke up with some intensity.

"Why don't we see how the people here really feel about it?" she asked.

"There aren't enough people here to give a fair opinion," said Sawyers. The room was packed with two or three hundred people, and Richard was getting angry.

"Well, why don't we see how the people who *are* here feel about it?" he said. "And if this isn't enough, we'll get everybody in the valley here."

"Those opposed to the flooding of Round Valley, raise their hands," said Avila. Many hands were raised, but Richard noticed a significant few that weren't.

"And those in favor."

The Hurts, Gravier, Winters, and most of the other old families were for it, still believing they would do better on the shores of a lake than on the valley floor. He was sad to see Elmer Bauer's hand go up, too. It was a strange reflection on them, he thought, that barely a hundred years after their ancestors had ridden into this valley, with guns and cattle, fighting and killing to make it their own, they were ready to let it all go under.

Richard worked painstakingly through his files and address books, reaching for contacts among friends, family, and organizations who might be sympathetic. He was somewhat astonished at the number of people he knew up and down the state who could be enlisted in his campaign. He started making calls, and for days his phone was busy and his desk awash with slips of paper as one contact led to another. Among the first people he resolved to meet was Norman B. Livermore, known to all as "Ike."

The Livermores were a prominent Republican family. Ike's brother, Putnam, was state party chairman, and Ike himself was in charge of the party's finances in the First District, which included Covelo. Naturally enough Richard had met Ike during the campaign to elect Don Clausen to Congress in 1964, and again during the elections in 1966. Although separated by twenty years, they had another, more personal connection in that they were both graduates of Thacher, a prestigious West Coast school, and had each helped afterward with fund-raising.

Ronald Reagan had put Ike Livermore in charge of the state's Resources Agency, which made him the man who, in principle at least, had authority over the State Water Project. Richard had to remind himself, though, that in practical politics the water project would carry a great deal more weight than Livermore. He knew Ike to be a pragmatic man, loyal to the governor and his party. Ike prided himself on his ability as a mediator, the "man in the middle" as he liked to say, who relied heavily on his common sense and an instinctive feel for balancing what was right against what was expedient. Furthermore, water matters were not in his area of expertise. To imagine that Livermore would cancel the Dos Rios project at the stroke of a pen was sheer fantasy. But just to get his ear for a moment was worth any effort.

Only the year before, Ike had persuaded a number of wealthy alumni to help Thacher acquire the lease to a summer fishing camp high in the Sierras beneath Mount Langley. All past pupils had been invited to sample its pleasures, and Richard discovered that Ike would be visiting the camp for a day or two in early September. He was determined to be there to make his pitch.

The day after the Covelo meeting Richard and Susan packed their kids into the Volvo and set off for the Golden Trout camp. It was a long journey. They took two days over it and they discussed this new turn their life had taken as they went. There was never any doubt that they would do their best to stop the dam. It was clear to them both that they faced tremendous odds, but in their different ways they each felt that it was insane to flood such a valley. On the afternoon of the second day they arrived at Lone Pine, in the Owens Valley and from there made their way by trail, partly on foot, to the Golden Trout camp.

Richard could hardly have hoped for a more appropriate spot in which to plead his case; a few rustic cabins alongside a shimmering trout stream in an unspoiled valley at ten thousand feet, and two men talking and fishing, far from the pressures and political clamor of the overheated flatlands below.

Ike had come with his wife, Dina, and the two families ate and played together. For as much of that time as Ike would give him, Richard talked about the dam but it was immediately apparent that Ike was not prepared. Ike was a lumber man. He knew all there was to know about timber, but confessed that he was almost totally ignorant of water matters. In fact he had not really anticipated having to deal with them. The Department of Water Resources was certainly among his responsibilities, but Reagan had personally chosen its director, William Gianelli, and they communicated with each other directly, rather than through Ike. There was no doubt that Gianelli was an extremely competent and decisive engineer and it was supposed that in practice Ike would be quite busy enough dealing with his own area of expertise.

Even so, with frequent cries of "Amazing!" Ike listened. Richard ploughed into his brief. He fastened on the cost of the project, on the cost overruns that such projects were notorious for, on the unstable geology of the area and the earthquake activity that the engineers seemed to have dismissed as insignificant, on the loss of good farmland, and the historic importance of the Round Valley site. He cast doubts on the economic viability of the project. The corps, he said, was only interested in getting its name on one more huge dam, and their claims for flood control were merely a pretext. He suggested that the state was simply looking for new ways to keep its bureaucrats employed. He remarked, perhaps a shade disingenuously, on the extraordinary way that this project had been sprung on the people. And of course he said, with an eye on the scenery around them, that it would be a crime to drown such a natural jewel as Round Valley.

Ike enjoyed the company of the younger man. Twenty-four years later he still recalled the visit with pleasure. "It was the first time I ever heard of Dos Rios Dam," he said. "We just sat around the campfire. He gave me a lot of stuff. It was just utter Greek to me, but he was so persuasive and such a nice guy that I said, 'Dick, I'll look into it. Keep me informed.' "

Richard came back over the pass in the early morning encouraged by at least having the ear of a man in such a strategic position. Livermore would not fight the battle for him, but he would listen. If Richard could make a good case it would be heard, but so far he was desperately short of hard facts to work with.

The nights had recently turned cool, and a thick white fog had settled in the valley. It lay below him now, completely obscuring the valley floor and reaching out into the draws where the creeks flowed in and where Mill Creek flowed out to the Eel. The fog exactly modeled the lake that the corps intended to create. It had an undeniable beauty of its own, and Richard almost experienced a sense of relief, imagining the slate wiped clean.

He looked down on this "ghost of Covelo to come" and wondered just who and what he was trying to save. A sly and obdurate bunch of ranchers, "rolling right along" in their easy, shortsighted way. A few hundred Native Americans—most of them "good Indians" available to do the menial jobs, living in a ghetto. The whole place redolent of bad blood and villainy. Maybe it *should* all be washed away.

It would not be hard to find those who agreed. The idea had great appeal to a frontier mentality, always ready to solve its problems by leaving them behind and moving on. In that view of progress, the land was just Play-Doh for the expression of man's ego.

A hundred years of tumultuous history had been made in this valley—a hundred years of struggle for survival and domination, of bitter conflict between two races and cultures. Then the engineers and planners come along. "Too bad," they say. "It didn't work out. Look at those depressed Indians living on welfare among their heaps of junked cars. Look at those dejected ranchers and shopkeepers, cut off from the mainstream of our dynamic society. Let's do them a favor; wash it all out and start again."

Easily said. Too easily done. What does history mean to them? What do they know about the slow piecing together of lives and relationships, the tentative triumphs of human feeling over prejudice, the gradual intermingling of color and culture by marriage and friendship that may eventually bring this society through to a better solution? How many hundreds of years did it take those oaks to establish their roots and grow to maturity? Why should a human community grow any faster?

This fine valley, which had attracted men of greedy and violent natures in the past would draw civilized and constructive people in the future. All the great human cultures, he reflected, were raised over bloodshed and tyranny. The past could not be obliterated. It had to be understood, absorbed, and transcended. Confronting the dam, Richard had come to realize that this was true of his own history, too.

Well, if the past could not be expunged, it could be made to work for him. There were elements in his family history that had brought him to this point. As he contemplated the actions he would have to take and the resources he would have to draw upon, the significance of that history gradually became more apparent. The tide of epic events that had brought his family across the continent—events in which they had played a significant role—had left him after all with an inheritance he could use. There was money, quite a lot of it, but that came mainly through his father's second marriage, and from his wife's family. In any case, though money was certainly useful, a personal fortune could never begin to match the resources of the establishment he was preparing to challenge. No, the truly valuable inheritance was the network he had been born into, the political atmosphere he had breathed in since childhood, his familiarity with the movers and shakers of Southern California.

Like his father, he had rather despised the sleazy compromises and accommodations of that world. The unlikely life he was leading as a back-country rancher was a protest and an attempt to free himself from the corruptness of it. Now that same world of relentless progress, which he more often described as blind greed, was reaching out to engulf him. There was no escaping it, it seemed, and as he realized how well his past had equipped him to fight this fight and turn this tide, he saw it more clearly as his destiny.

As for Susan, he knew that her love for the world they had chosen was if anything even fiercer and more uncompromising than Richard's. There was never any doubt that she would support his fight, to the finish. Already there were indications of the trouble that lay ahead. Some people in the valley were angry with the Wilsons' interference. In a valley accustomed to rivalries and feuds, they were quick to take sides, and the poison would soon spread into the clubs, the women's groups, and the schools. Alex, Chris, and Marjo would suffer, too, and all the more so for not knowing why. It was a hard prospect, but Susan did not falter. It was the despoliation that got to her. She was outraged that a government could contemplate such an act of vandalism.

"It's wrong, Rich," she said. "They can't be allowed to come in here and impose this thing on us. Ripping up these wonderful trees, destroying such a beautiful valley. You will have to fight it. No one else could do it so well. Thank goodness we have the strength and the means to try," and she undoubtedly felt that it was the strength of their mutual faith that would help them through.

Dams have been opposed before, but it is unlikely that a private citizen ever set himself up to defeat such powerful vested interests as these and, at the same time, to reverse the central policy of a great state. A megalomaniac or a fanatic could imagine that he might manage such an upheaval unaided, but Wilson was neither of those. However, he did carry within him the kind of quiet arrogance that in an older culture would be associated with the aristocracy. Although his purpose was to frustrate the establishment, he was nevertheless *of* the establishment. He had seen it manipulate affairs on a grand scale, and he knew—or thought he knew—how to tap the sources of power.

What made Wilson such a formidable opponent was that he combined within himself elements from both of the great rival attitudes that have shaped American behavior throughout its history, and he had sympathy for both. In the family strands that wove him, the twin motives of conservation and exploitation were powerfully present.

There were some characteristics that he appeared to inherit from both sides. A particular fearlessness and a devotion to work were qualities that Wilson had in abundance. Otherwise it was not a harmonious combination. To indulge the one side of his nature, he had to forswear the other, and generally they warred within him, making him a complex and often inscrutable figure.

The strongest influence on his early life was that of his father, Dr. John Cree Wilson. The middle name records an ancient family connection with the Cree Indians, part of the Algonquin family of Indian nations who inhabited the northeastern forests of America. From his father Richard Wilson inherited a respect for nature, a love of solitude, a compassion for people and creatures, an uncompromising integrity, and three thousand acres in the mountains above Round Valley.

On his mother's side he was connected to a rather different man, her uncle, Angus, who went, if not from rags, then certainly from britches to riches, and took his brothers with him. His life began, curiously enough, in that same Algonquin territory, just north of the St. Lawrence River. Later it exemplified, with almost painful accuracy, America's raucous lurch into the industrial age. The rise from narrow, rural austerity, the brutally hard labor, the rootless wanderings across the continent, the dogged persistence supported by a gradually forming grasp of the managerial magic that made profits, the progress from laborer to boss to grand entrepreneur to city father, public recognition, florid Victorian tributes, and the final days of opulence tinged with an inescapable suspicion of melancholy—all this brought Wilson a background of wealth and standing among the "old" families of Southern California. Through them he understood how things are done.

The events that shaped and prepared him were the same as those that had brought the people of California to this point of absurdity—to the point of enthusiastically and blindly trashing the very assets that had drawn most of them there in the first place. Round Valley, in this argument, was but a symbol. Everywhere in California the environment was under attack: The rivers, the beaches, the forests, the soil, and the very air were all being degraded in the effort to sustain the growth of its cities and the prosperity of its industries.

The stories of these two men, Angus Grant and John Cree Wilson, and of the times they lived in, explain not only how the water lobby became such an apparently invincible force but also how Richard Wilson acquired the strength and the skill to oppose it.

6

Timber, Gold, and the Railroad

ANGUS GRANT was raised on a hundred-acre farm near Williamstown, in the Canadian province of Ontario, close to the St. Lawrence river and the U.S. border. His father, Archibald, Richard Wilson's great-grandfather, was given the land in its virgin state as a "concession" from the British government. Taming it consumed his life, and he certainly could not have imagined that it would launch his sons into a quite different career.

In that climate a farmer needed sturdy buildings to protect animals, feed, supplies, and equipment, as well as his own family. Archibald's buildings were founded on rock quarried from his own land, and framed with timber cleared from his own fields. He devoted the days of his young manhood to transforming his land into a farm, and on many of those days he, too, must have been as wet and cold as the weather. By the time he was fifty-six years old rheumatism had crippled him so badly that physical labor was no longer possible, and he could only walk with the aid of two canes.

Of his nine children the first five were daughters, and he was fifty-three before his first son, Angus, was old enough, at fourteen, to be "put in the farm." By then the truly backbreaking work had been accomplished. For Angus, growing up to see his father laboring alone and in increasing discomfort, the emotional pressure must have been great. Too great perhaps. Only two years after he was judged old enough to do the work, he passed the burden on to his younger brother Daniel, and left the farm to cross the border and seek his fortune elsewhere. He never farmed again.

Angus Grant grew up during America's first Space Age, the space then being lateral rather than vertical, and its appeal to the adventurous and discontented spirit can only be imagined: it would be as if it were possible for an ingenious person today to ride a backyard rocket in search of treasure on the moon. When Angus left home, the opening up of the West by the gold rush was still recent news, creating a distant focus of tremendous attraction to ambitious men. Once the pull had overcome his family ties and expectations, it drew him, inevitably, west. The year was 1859, and America was on the brink of the cataclysmic violence of the Civil War.

The lure of the West and the growth of the railroads must have been common topics of conversation. Even though the easy gold was gone, gold was not the only treasure. What was in the wind, the sense of the time, was that a person might turn almost anything to account. What had seemed previously to be merely the furniture and fixtures of nature—the trees and rivers and mountains—could now be seen as lumber, irrigation, and ore. There was so much more to be gained from exploiting these resources rather than clinging to the old, agrarian ways, and yet it took an almost reckless discontent to reject the traditions and values of generations of farmers—and to reject the very land itself, from which all prosperity flowed.

Age sixteen and straight off the farm, Angus could not have known much about the world, yet news of great doings "out there" must have filtered through. Many men had begun as laborers and made fortunes in lumber. Perhaps Angus had heard these stories. In any case that's where he decided to try his luck.

Of all the resources that the North American continent yielded to its new conquerors, there is no doubt that timber was the greatest in quantity, the most valuable, and the most heavily exploited. Trees paved the way for the conquest of North America, figuratively and, in terms of the railroads, literally. All along the Atlantic seaboard, but particularly in the North, huge forests of hard and soft woods were laid low. They were cut for fuel, for construction, and for export, and they laid the basis for great industrial enterprises. By the 1850s the forests in and around the state of Maine were in decline, and the mill owners moved west across the Appalachian Mountains where new, vast expanses of virgin white pine awaited them in Michigan, on the shores of the Great Lakes.

The pace of exploitation accelerated, and thousands of square miles of forest were cleared and converted to agriculture in three decades. Under the Homestead Act a settler could acquire 160 acres for $1.25 an acre. Lumber companies, big and small, could afford to pay the $1.25 just for the timber, leaving the land free to the homesteader.

As young Angus made his way to the forests to try his luck, one can only imagine the wonders and temptations he encountered on the way, but there is nothing of that, nor of the rambunctious life of the loggers in the few stories he told his son. Nothing of the dangers and excitement of felling those great trees and of the "river hogs" who floated them downstream, of the curious Michigan Logging Wheel, with its ten-foot-high steel wheels, used for transporting logs, of the camp fiddlers, the jigs, and the tales of Paul Bunyan and his blue ox Babe that delighted the "shanty boys," as lumberjacks were first called.

Maybe he took no part in that legendary life, but more probably he was not much of a reveler and even less of a sentimentalist. As his son wrote later, "My father was not one to talk of his experiences." All we know is that he stayed there six years, acquired the skills of a carpenter, and then moved on westward. In 1865 he was in the Badlands of the Dakotas where, again according to his son, "there was mining business." This by no means implies a change of trade, since the saw was as important to mining as the pick. All the mine shafts and galleries had to be framed and supported with lumber, and some very fancy carpentry was involved in holding open some of them, particularly where vertical seams were involved. So perhaps it is not surprising to find him, a little later, in 1868, even farther west at Lake Tahoe, "with a contract to log for the Comstock."

The Comstock lode gave birth to a number of mines whose names are synonymous with legendary wealth. Yellow Jacket, Ophir, Best and Belcher, Gould, and Curry, were just a few. Virginia City, which housed the miners and catered to them, the Virginia and Truckee Railroad, which carried the ore to the mills on the Carson River, the immense and wide-ranging timber industry that Grant was a small part of, "were all the direct and unavoidable result of the prospecting, in 1859 . . . of four boozy and disreputable scoundrels who found the world-shaking Comstock Lode."[1]

The luscious prose of Lucius Beebe describes it well: "They came by the roaring thousands, on mule back and afoot, a few in Concord coaches over the old grade by Hangtown and Strawberry and Carson City: the wicked and the willful, the soiled and solvent, the gyps and the gunmen, the splendid strumpets and blowzy madames, the gamblers, the newspaper reporters, kings and clowns. Wells Fargo came, the Bank of California came and, eventually the railroad came. . . .

"In the tumultuous decade that followed . . . Virginia had exploded into a city of 20,000 wildly irresponsible inhabitants, and the fame of its wicked ways, its continued uproar and production of stupefying wealth were celebrated throughout the civilized world.

"San Francisco was being built and financed by the Comstock. Its vast industrial enterprises, its seemingly impregnable Bank of California, its fantastic Palace Hotel, its cable cars, sea port and the Nob Hill mansions of its ever-crescent colony of millionaires were all being financed by the profits from . . . [the] . . . fabled mines of Virginia, Gold Hill and Silver City."[2]

Water and timber had always been vital elements in the pursuit of gold and silver. The first miners on the western slopes of the Sierras worked directly in the streambeds, panning for gold, but when those beds were exhausted, miners moved from "wet diggings" to "dry diggings" far from the rivers, and water was diverted in great quantities to pan the dirt. At this point the flumes came into their own—water chutes built of wood and carried over rough terrain on timber trestles. They could deliver considerable quantities of water over increasing distances, and at high pressure. It was not long before miners realized they could use the water itself to do the digging for them. It was called hydraulic mining, and by now, of course, the grizzled prospector of a few years back had given way to big companies able to finance this sort of technology.

One company alone built more than seven hundred miles of flumes and tunnels to carry water to the gold-bearing mountainsides. It was fired at the earth through huge brass nozzles—at a roughly estimated rate of seventy-two million gallons a day. Every loose particle was swept away to expose the naked skeleton of the mountain. A small area of rock has been maintained in this condition as a museum exhibit at Columbia, near Sonora, and for some it holds the same obscene fascination as the buffalo carcasses that were skinned and abandoned by the thousands to glisten and rot on the plains.

While the Comstock was under way, the need for timber was always paramount. Mark Twain's western counterpart, Dan De Quille,[3] left a dramatic account of this nineteenth-century ecological disaster. Saying that Comstock "may truthfully be said to be the tomb of the forests of the Sierras," he adds that, "it is going to make sad work, ere long, of the picturesque hills surrounding Lake Tahoe, the most beautiful of all the lakes in the Sierra Nevada Mountains. Where tall pines now shade all the shores and wave on all the mountain slope, naught will shortly be seen save decaying stumps and naked granite rocks. But timber and lumber are imperatively demanded, and the forests not only of these hills but of a thousand others doubtless will be sacrificed. . . . Already one bad effect of this denudation is seen in the summer failure of the water in the Carson River. The first spell of hot weather in the spring now sweeps nearly all the snow from the mountains and sends it down into the valleys in one grand flood, whereas while the mountains were thickly clad with pines the melting of the snow was gradual and there was a good volume of water in the river throughout the summer and fall months."

Tahoe, on the roof of the Sierras, was close to the Donner Trail and the route of the newly constructed Central Pacific Railroad. In his journeys from the Dakotas, Angus must have followed for some of the way at least the tracks of the two great rival railroad companies, the Union Pacific and the Central Pacific, as they raced toward each other to complete the first transcontinental rail link. Payments and huge land grants depended on the amount of track they laid, and each was determined to engorge as much of America as possible. With the Civil War over, it was a contest that could be observed without anguish, one of the great dramas of the time. Out of Omaha and driving west on eastern capital, came Durant's Union Pacific Railroad. From the West Coast, the "Big Four," Crocker, Hopkins, Huntington, and Stanford, were dragging their Central Pacific line over the mountains on a shoestring.

The telegraph, which had only recently put the Pony Express out of business, was in operation. When Angus Grant was there, reports of the action were coming back up the line almost daily, and he followed them with avid interest. The railroads depended heavily on supplies of timber and the skills of carpenters to lay track and to bridge innumerable ravines and water courses. Before long, Angus knew where his best prospects lay. He was already acquainted with two of the three richest sources of wealth of the age, timber and minerals. It was the third—the railroad—that finally took him to his destination.

For the next ten years, according to a few surviving accounts, he moved from one contract to another, back and forth across the Rockies. The first contract after he left Tahoe was to build railroad bridges in the vicinity of Kansas City. By now he must have mastered the difficult art of bidding, and bringing his men and materials together at the right time, in unpredictable circumstances and for the least cost. The men were a rough bunch. Managing them needed nerve, cunning, and a strong presence, and he evidently had all three, for he did well.

With the Civil War over and railroad building booming, the rush to the West was accelerating. This new population was, broadly speaking, of two kinds. There were the new immigrants flooding into America, those whom Europe had treated badly. They might cling to the languages and traditions of their villages, but as for the broader culture of Europe, they wanted none of it. European society was rigid and unresponsive. Things might be tough in America, as bad in their way as anything to be endured in Europe, but at least they didn't have to suffer the intolerable weight of a rigid class system.

Thirty years earlier, de Tocqueville observed that American manufacturers were the harshest he had ever encountered, but their saving grace, in his eyes, was that they had no tendency to become an aristocracy. They were interested only in making money, and they could treat their workers badly because there was always a frontier open and waiting for those who would not endure it. The West was a safety valve for industrial discontent, constantly touted in print and in rhetoric, and millions headed west with the hope of one day owning their own farms.

Their vision was a touching blend of nostalgia and wishful thinking, which has come to be known as the myth of the garden. From the earliest days Europeans held two antithetical views of America. Some saw it as a savage and repellent wasteland, others as a paradise. Naturally the version that triumphed was the dream of America as a latter-day Garden of Eden, where the human race would be cleansed and restored to grace, and this beautiful promise, trumpeted forth in the speeches of the nineteenth century, led many to imagine that the orchards of Kent or the gardens of Pomerania could be reproduced just as well in the new territories of the west as in the Ohio Valley.

"While there are uncounted millions of acres of fertile and unoccupied land, where farmers can rear their families in peace, plenty, and privacy, under the guardian genius of our laws, we hope that farms will continue to spread to the bases of the Rocky Mountains," said the *Western Monthly Review* in July of 1827.

And appealing to their sense of destiny Cyrus L. Dunham explained the purpose of family farming as he spoke for the Homestead bill in Indiana in 1862:

"I believe, Mr. Chairman, that we are placed here for a wise and glorious purpose—to restore poor downtrodden humanity to its long lost dignity; to overthrow despots, and shed abroad the genial influence of freedom. . . ."

But for many of those whose families had already established themselves in the East, these sentiments had a hollow ring after the Civil War. That war, as brutal as any ever fought, led to a moral collapse and cynicism felt specially by men of Angus Grant's generation, men with whom Angus had to work and compete. The pursuit of material wealth had become for them the most sensible, even the only worthwhile occupation. Many of them were unscrupulous, even savage in their determination to win against what they considered a hostile world.

Some historians have suggested that the ravages of the Civil War robbed American society of a vital link in its development. Angus Grant's "gilded generation" struck gold and oil, built railroads, skyscrapers and fortunes, or died in the attempt. Following them there should have arisen another generation capable of transforming this raw wealth and energy into substantial civic achievements. Instead, the doctrine of individual aggrandizement roared on into the twentieth century.

There is little doubt that what enabled America to keep its capitalism raw was the immense balance of natural resources that remained to be exploited. It was those resources, much more than any intrinsic American virtue, that kept Americans "free."

As Henry Nash Smith wrote in *Virgin Lands*: "The character of the American Empire was defined [in the 1880s] not by streams of influence out of the past, not by cultural tradition, nor by its place in a world community, but by a relation between man and nature—or rather, even more narrowly, between American man and the American West. . . . This relation was thought of as unvaryingly fortunate. The myths of the garden and of the empire had both affirmed a doctrine of progress, of gigantic economic development. . . ."[4]

The myth of the garden was given a boost by the Homestead Act. An area of 160 acres—a quarter of a square mile—was fixed on as a reasonable size to support a family, and homesteaders could acquire it simply by living and working on it for five years. There was a general belief that millions of happy homesteaders took advantage of it. The truth is different.

The available land was all in the West, that is to say in areas where some form of irrigation would be necessary. The act was passed into law in 1862. By 1890 (the year when the West was generally considered to have been settled) the U.S. population had increased by thirty million. The number of homesteads "perfected" was a mere 372,659. During the following ten years, drought and financial crisis drove many of even this small number off their lands and forced them, instead, to work for big proprietors or to rent farms where the cost of irrigation work had already been covered and where markets were available. Yet most Americans who were not directly confronted by these facts continued to believe that the West was being settled with small, family-owned farms.

In an attempt to improve matters, Congress passed the Desert Land Act in 1877. The idea this time was that if you could put down twenty-five cents an acre and a promise to irrigate, you could have a square mile of public land. Three years later, with proof that you had brought water to the land plus another dollar per acre, the land was yours.

The Desert Land Act, like the Homestead Act, did little to improve the chances of the family farm. There are stories of men emptying a bucket of water on their land in front of a witness who would then swear he had seen the land irrigated. Cattlemen assembled great spreads by assigning their ranch hands as "dummies" to each collect his square mile. One notorious profiteer was James Ben Ali Haggin, who later played a significant role in California water development. Haggin owed the exotic part of his name to the fact that his father had married a Turkish woman. He was a colorful tycoon but not, by all accounts, comfortable to be around. Gertrude Atherton, who saw him frequently in the salons of San Francisco, said "he always entered a room as if he hated someone."[5] By manipulations and forgeries, he and his associates Lloyd Tevis and W. Carr, created what may have been "the greatest farm in the world"[6] in Kern County at the southern end of the San Joaquin Valley. Haggin did, in fact, irrigate his land and make it productive, proving, as he himself proclaimed at the time, that the job could only be done properly over a large area with considerable capital.

Other operators on a giant scale, such as Lloyd Tevis and Henry Miller, were quick to teach the same lesson, followed by Jim Boswell, Russell Giffen, and Fred Salyer. The gamble to win in the West was a desperate one, and not many succeeded, but those who did discovered that once they had accumulated some money, the prospects for making more were unlimited. California, the last frontier, attracted bold refugees from the East by celebrating individuality and self-reliance but, paradoxically, it has been dominated from the start by large corporations.

This situation caused Henry George, an eloquent defender of the poor and disinherited in California, to protest in 1871 that "concentration is the law of the time." Far from land holdings being broken up, old land ownerships were being combined, new land was being monopolized. Cities were swallowing up little towns. "A thousand little dealers become the clerks and shopmen of the proprietor of the marble-fronted palace. . . ."

In a harsh judgment of the prospects for small farmers, he went on to say: "Of the political tendency of our land policy it is hardly necessary to speak. To say that the land of a country shall be owned by a small class, is to say that a class shall rule it; to say—which is the same thing—that the people of a country shall consist of the very rich and the very poor, is to say that Republicanism is impossible."[7]

Congress was forced to make yet another attempt to remedy the situation in 1902, when President Theodore Roosevelt signed the National Reclamation Act. Under it, the government was to use money raised by the sale of western lands to build irrigation projects on public land. This federally subsidized water would be delivered to worthy homesteaders with farms not exceeding 160 acres per family. Over a ten-year period they were supposed to reimburse the federal reclamation fund for the cost of the irrigation works. Donald Worster describes how once again the purpose of the act was frustrated.

> The original intent . . . had been that the federal government would mainly concentrate its reclamation efforts on the public domain. After a site had been selected, homesteaders would file on their free claims and reside on them for the standard five years required to get title, while enjoying the water gurgling in ditches through their fields. It did not work that way at all. The appearance of Service engineers and a construction crew in an area touched off . . . a frenzied rush of speculators. They grabbed up the free homesteads, intending not to settle there but to sell them a few years later, whenever the water arrived, at a stiff price to latecomers. . . . Even more unexpected was how much reclamation was done on the private, not the public domain. By 1910 there were thirty projects in the works, and some of them had not a single acre of public land. Altogether, they included 1,199,926 acres of public land and 1,402,702 acres of private property. By and large federalization worked to enrich speculators and enhance the holdings of established owners, not to furnish new homes for homeless folks from overcrowded cities.[8]

The service that did this work later became known as the Bureau of Reclamation. Throughout its existence it has had the impossible job of reconciling the agrarian dream with the realities of western agriculture and a hydraulic society. With a brief to carry out irrigation works that were both useful and profitable, it was dogged by its failure to impose acreage limitations, and by a tendency to do favors to the rich. Whatever sermons were being preached in Washington and in the state capitals, it seemed that when man confronted the West there was only one way to go, and that was the way of the wild—survival of the fittest and largest. It was a rule that certainly governed the progress of Angus Grant. After he finished up in Kansas there was another railroad contract in California, and some more mining business. Then in 1878 he went to work for the Atchison, Topeka and Santa Fe, and stayed with it, working his way south. In 1880, via Las Vegas and Santa Fe, he entered Albuquerque in triumph. He was thirty-seven and was already considered a success.

He liked Albuquerque, a railway town at the beginnings of its growth, and built a house there in the so-called New Town across the tracks. He had already begun to reconnect himself to his family in Canada with occasional visits, and met there a young teacher, Joanna McMillan. In September of 1880, in Chicago, when she was twenty years old, they were married. They returned to Albuquerque and had a son, Daniel Garfield Grant, named in memory of the president who was assassinated on the day Daniel was born.

The following year Angus and his wife traveled to Las Vegas, then a quiet green oasis in the desert, for a holiday. While out driving in a carriage they were drenched by a sudden thunderstorm. She caught cold, which set off a galloping case of tuberculosis. A year later she died. Her second child, a daughter of six months, died a few weeks after her. Angus Grant took his son to Glengarry to be looked after by his parents and a cousin, and went back to the life he had known before his brief and tragic attempt at domesticity.

A frenzy of business seemed to overtake him. He continued to build bridges, but he seems also to have made it his ambition to create Albuquerque almost single-handedly. In only a few years he built the town's biggest office building and an opera house. To these, sometimes in association with others, he later added a reservoir to supply the city with three million gallons of water a day, an electric light company, a gas company, an ice company, a new street railway, and a wool scouring mill. He was a director of the First National Bank, and he also bought a newspaper, the Albuquerque *Democrat,* but not, it seems, to express his opinions, for he leased it out to others. In any case, he was a confirmed Republican.

After three years, he brought his younger brother Lewis out to help him. They formed a company, Grant Brothers, and got the contract to build the Santa Fe line to Needles, in California, and eventually all the way to the coast at Los Angeles. In all they built about a thousand miles of railroad track, and left a small town, Grants, New Mexico, named after them. In 1886, Grant Brothers took offices in Los Angeles. A third brother, John, had joined the firm, which now undertook contracts to lay track in Indian territory, and after that in Mexico.

An early history of New Mexico comments: "Among the enterprising men of Bernalillo County, and Albuquerque in particular, none occupies a more prominent position than A. A. Grant. Born in Canada in the year 1843, we find him to-day, a man forty-seven years of age, in the prime of life and, endowed with native ability coupled with the successful results of his labor, he stands a fitting example of honest endeavor, energy, and ambition.

"Here [in Albuquerque] he has a spacious and elegantly appointed suite of rooms, fitted for his use, and here he dispenses genial hospitality to his many staunch friends among the businessmen of the city."

Later, when an encomium to Angus Grant appeared in another history, Grant Brothers Construction Company was described as "one of the most important contracting concerns in the United States." That may have been a slight exaggeration. The biographers of those days flattered their subjects handsomely and bedecked them with fine verbal flourishes. Nevertheless, Grant Brothers was certainly a very successful firm, and Angus Grant a wealthy man. Whether he was in any sense content is hard to say.

There is a photograph showing him enthroned in an ornately carved Spanish chair; a burly figure buttoned up in a dark, heavy suit with starched collar and cravat. The head is square and strong-jawed, the features well balanced, and he gazes at the camera through deep-set eyes like a man accustomed to being obeyed. The walrus mustache does its fierce duty to his expression, but in the shadows there could be, if one cares to think so, just a suggestion of mockery.

Despite his interests in New Mexico, and the fact that the company was now in Los Angeles, Angus Grant chose to live in San Francisco. It is not clear why. Perhaps his tastes in company and entertainment had developed to a point that could only be satisfied in that relatively sophisticated city. He stayed at the Arlington, "a respectable rooming house on Kearny Street," as his son described it. Then, together with his brother Lewis and a General Williamson, he bought the Moraga ranch, many hundreds of acres in extent, five miles out of Oakland. He spent very little time there, and engaged a cousin to manage it. When his parents died and it became time for Angus to bring his son, Daniel, back with him to California, he put the boy on the Moraga ranch with his cousin. In 1901 Angus Grant died while traveling, probably of heart failure. He was fifty-eight. In all his adult life he had spent only two years at what could be called home. The rest of the time he had lived on work sites, in hotels, or on trains, laying the basis for a fortune that he seems not to have known what to do with.

He was only thirty-nine when his wife died, and although he must have been a very eligible match he did not remarry. One must assume that the untrameled bachelor existence was one he chose, but his son, telling the story to his own daughter, carefully avoided any details and made no reference to his father's state of mind. It is only when he talked, enthusiastically, about his Uncle Lewis's outgoing nature and love of life that the implication of joylessness creeps in. There is something enigmatic about Angus's choices, and it may be that his heart failed him in more ways than one.

After his father's death, Daniel Grant went to live with Lewis Grant and his wife, Hattie, in Los Angeles. "They had two little girls, Anna and Gertrude, who became the nearest things to sisters I ever had." It was Anna who was to be Richard's mother.

At age twenty-seven, Daniel became a director of Grant Brothers. According to an obituary in the *Los Angeles Times,* he later became a stockbroker and the first president of the Los Angeles Curb Exchange. He moved in the circle of those old families, whose names—Sartori, Chandler, Otis, O'Melveny, Graves, Kerckhoff, Van Nuys, et al.—continued to reverberate in Los Angeles society. He did business with them, went to the same clubs, and his children went to school with their children. In short, he played his part in establishing and maintaining one of the more exclusive power structures in America. He put on a good deal of weight, was loved and supported by his wife and family, and, no doubt, did well by them. Through his cousin Anna the benefits of those connections passed on in due course to her son, Richard Wilson.

7

"They Have Stolen the Unearned Increment."

THE GOLD RUSH was over long before the Grants and the Wilsons arrived in Southern California, but the fever never subsided, and both families were drawn and influenced by it in different ways. But for the gold, California could never have been boosted to stardom at such a tender age. Before that lick of yellow winked at James Marshall through the ruffled waters of Sutter's millrace in 1848, California was going through the same modest beginnings as other new states. Only a decade earlier, she had still belonged to Mexico, and had been loosely occupied by missionaries, then by great landowners, relatively few in number, who exploited native labor and set a pattern that has endured to this day.[1]

Adventurers occasionally wandered across the Sierras from the United States, and some became excited at the prospect of owning such wide expanses of land, most of them under only nominal control. The prize consisted of cattle country and irrigable river valleys, and to grasp the prize meant annexing the territory.

The scale of operations was minuscule compared with what was at stake. California's fate was determined in 1845 by mere handfuls of men in petty disputes. John Charles Fremont was an adventuresome (some would say meddlesome) captain in the U.S. Army Corps of Engineers, with a senator for a father-in-law. With his band of sixty-two men he was a major force in the area, and provoked a stand-off with Mexican Commandante José Castro whose "army" was little larger. Archibald Gillespie, another officer given to romantic missions, later ruled Los Angeles with fifty men. José Antonio Carillo successfully revolted against him with sixty rancheros and a toy cannon.

U.S. General Stephen Kearny, having "conquered" New Mexico, rode west to do the same in California with three hundred dragoons. At one time Kearny, Fremont, and the naval commodore, Robert Stockton, all claimed to be governors of California. All were replaced by Col. Richard B. Mason. Kearny relieved his annoyance by arresting Fremont for insubordination and taking him back over the Sierras in handcuffs, though he returned soon enough as a civilian.

And so it went on. The confrontations that loosened Mexico's grip and led, eventually, to American statehood, caused no more deaths and injuries than an average gang fight in Los Angeles today, and the victims were often innocent bystanders. The principal players—others were J. D. Sloat and Thomas Larkin—are now immortalized in the names of cities and San Francisco streets. Much of their skirmishing had a comic opera quality, and success appears to have ambushed them, but they had the good fortune, like many others who followed, to be there when it mattered, and their names glow with the same aura that has gilded all things Californian.

Those were the small beginnings of California and, but for the gold, the state would surely have matured much more gradually over time. What Fremont had in mind in 1845 when he coined the name Golden Gate for the entrance to San Francisco Bay is hard to say. He certainly had no inkling then of the hordes that would rush through it after the gold strikes of '48 and '49. In five frantic years San Francisco, from being a fort with a few hundred dependents became a ramshackle metropolis of 50,000 souls living in a frenzy of hope and despair. Editorialists in the East branded it "the Sodom of the West."

Most probably, but for the gold there would be no San Francisco—at least, not as we know it. With all the sunlit shoreline of that immense bay to choose from, why build where summer is often just a weather report heard through the fog? But the sea-born imperatives of the gold rush put it where it is, and the gold came back to it, corrupted it, embellished it, and, as in so many other mushrooming capitals of commerce, finished by cultivating it.

Los Angeles meanwhile remained a small, provincial town living off cattle and wheat. Then, several decades after the gold rush, keen entrepreneurial eyes saw it as a worthy rival to San Francisco. It had a seductive climate and a natural port. The newly built railroads took the people to Los Angeles, by the hundreds of thousands. A good deal of the money went there, too, but in spite of Hollywood (or because of it) the sophistication stayed in San Francisco for a long, long time. Much of California's social history is tied up in the rivalry between north and south; in the frantic efforts of Southern California's nouveaux riches to catch up with San Francisco's cultural dominance. California today may mean beaches and the Santa Monica Freeway, but in the prewar days of Cole Porter and his East Coast socialite fans, California was still San Francisco, and the lady was a tramp for insisting that "it's cold and it's damp."

The fascination that both these great cities have exerted on the rest of America, and indeed on the whole Western world, has obscured the most extraordinary thing about them: In all reason, they should not be there at all. Mesmerized first by gold, and then by the romance of modern transport, observers found it easy to gloss over the simple truth—cities must have water. Of all the ways in which California is exceptional, none is stranger (or more ominous) than its defiance of the basic rules of growth and development set by human civilization up to that time.

Throughout history communities have developed alongside streams, bounded by the natural limits of their watersheds. In this way they could reap all the natural diversity of their ecosystems, from the lush riparian bottomland up to the thin summer grazing of surrounding peaks. Cities grew by rivers. Big cities grew by big rivers. Commerce followed the paths of rivers, and was founded originally in the agricultural wealth created in the river valleys.

In San Francisco and Los Angeles, sudden wealth and the astonishing growth it generated came from quite other sources. For a long time it obscured the underlying absurdity of their situations—one on a dryish and very shaky rock, the other in a desert. So well did these cities project images to match the fantasies of the millions longing to go west, that it was worth incurring any expense to maintain them, and water was undoubtedly the greatest expense.

Both cities fought to prevent water from being the controlling factor in their growth, and until recently, at considerable cost to their environments, they succeeded. San Francisco, with her Bay Area satellites, remains the queen of the north. Los Angeles, whose puny streams have long been bundled away in concrete ditches, has waxed from southern star to galaxy. Both, like bloated and bedridden patients living on intravenous drip, would be helpless without armies of attendants to feed them their essential nourishment through slender tubes from improbable distances.

Land was already available in vast tracts, granted either by older Mexican decrees, or by the federal government to finance the railroads. As thousands rushed west with all the money they could scrape together, they created, suddenly, a big market for food and clothing at inflated prices, providing a further impetus for large-scale agriculture and land monopolization.

Through the years, as unbridled growth posed mounting problems, ever more elaborate solutions were financed out of that growth, but always borrowing on the future. The survival of this pyramid scheme became so essential to the economy of the state (and ultimately the nation) that it was shored up by all available means. Inevitably the same system extended beyond the cities into the southern and central valleys. Millions upon millions of people, involved in complex infrastructures of industry and agriculture, have established themselves where they have no natural hope of survival. Their very existence depends on the wisdom and cunning of hydraulic engineers and the prosperity that funds their enterprises.

Everyone knows that growth must have its limits. Among planners there was occasionally abstract talk of some such an ultimate moment, but it could not, *must* not, be imminent, for it would spell the end of a golden age, and California was to be exempt from the mortal condition. Yet all the time the pressure was building. In the sixties there were already some who felt the state would have to change course, or it would simply crash under the weight of exaggerated expectations.

Such prospects were unthinkable, however, when the Grants first came to Los Angeles. They played their part in the story, but the man whose name is inseparable from it, who one might almost say wrote the script for California's growth, arrived just a couple of years later.

Harry Chandler, who created Hollywood before movies were even thought of, first came to Los Angeles in 1888. He had dropped out of Dartmouth College, and came west to recover his health. For reasons known only to himself, at school he had taken a dare and dived into a vat of starch, with catastrophic consequences to his lungs. Everybody with an adventurous spirit was talking about striking it rich in California, but Chandler also hoped the climate and dry air would heal him. He found a job picking fruit outside Los Angeles in the San Fernando Valley. Then he thought he might do better selling it off a donkey cart. One of the vast ranches of the Van Nuys wheat empire was close by, and he took his cart to the ranch houses where a group of hands gathered.

According to the story he often liked to tell later in life, an autocratic horseman drove up and chased him off the property. He had hardly escaped to the highway before he saw his persecutor, whom he took to be a foreman, galloping up to him. The horseman apologized, and explained that he had assumed Chandler to be a bootlegger. He introduced himself as Isaac Van Nuys, and asked the young man to come back and sell his fruit anytime he chose.[2]

Van Nuys was by far the greatest of the landholders in the valley, with about sixty thousand acres. He was the flinty son of a Dutch family long established in New York State, and by a curious coincidence had also come west seeking relief from asthma, which plagued him all his life. The two men apparently became friends, much to Chandler's later benefit.

Harry Chandler appears in his photographs as the mildest of men, looking out through his round-rimmed glasses with a cheerful, naive innocence. This was entirely belied by his performance, for he quickly discovered in himself a ruthless business talent. Giving up on fruit, he went to the city and got hold of a newspaper delivery round. Soon he had a stranglehold on the distribution system, and used it to ingratiate himself with the *Los Angeles Times.* Before long he married the publisher's daughter and became the newspaper's business manager.

The publisher was Harrison Gray Otis, a retired general notorious for his colorful slanders and fulminations who used the paper shamelessly to promote his own profit.* Otis was in on all kinds of develop-

*On one famous occasion Otis was paid back in kind. "He sits there," said Hiram Johnson, campaigning for the governorship in 1910, "in senile dementia with gangrened heart and rotting brain, grimacing at every reform, chattering impotently at all things that are decent, frothing, fuming violently, gibbering, going down to his grave in snarling infamy . . . disgraceful, depraved, corrupt, crooked and putrescent." See *Thinking Big,* by Gottlieb and Wolt (Bibliography).

ment schemes and had many interests and business friends to boost. Chandler slipped effortlessly into the same role, and showed such brilliance at the game that he ultimately netted a fortune of several hundred millions—worth enough at that time to make most present day billionaires eat their hearts out.

Around the turn of the century Los Angeles seemed to change from a sleepy cattle town into a metropolis almost before its astonished inhabitants' eyes. A land boom in the eighties brought people flooding in (the Wilson family among them) and doubled the population, which by 1900 was over 100,000. It was clear to some that Los Angeles would continue to grow fast, and Van Nuys sold off twelve thousand acres at the end of his property closest to the city, to a syndicate of developers. Other parcels of land to the northwest of the city were being developed at the same time, financed by another syndicate that Harry Chandler assembled, laying the basis of his enormous fortune. This entire area became known as Hollywood. Meanwhile the town of San Fernando had already been developed at the northwest end of the valley. Between the two remained about a hundred square miles, all of which might potentially be developed as satellite communities or small farms to feed the growing market. The principal difficulty lay in water supplies.

Los Angeles was originally established by the Spanish on the banks of the Los Angeles River, a stream that drew on rainfall in the San Gabriel and Santa Susanna Mountains north of the San Fernando Valley. Beneath the valley, the water gathered naturally in a vast underground basin, which kept the river flowing through dry periods. This was the only source of water for the valley, but Spanish law had granted all the water in the river to the city, and in 1899, under American law, Los Angeles had established, in court, that this right included all the groundwater of the San Fernando Valley.

Wheat required no irrigation. Housing and other kinds of agriculture most certainly did. How, then, would it be possible to develop this land without water? It was a challenge that preoccupied the minds of Chandler, Otis, and others whose names are now plastered over the maps of modern day Los Angeles. The techniques for developing new communities, with salesmen's hype and electric trolley lines, were already thoroughly understood and practiced by a group of "financiers," but there was no source of water in the vicinity, apart from what *already* belonged to Los Angeles. The developers were opening up tracts around the city and running electric rails out to them, and it was not in their interests to rob Los Angeles of her water supply. Their plans depended on the city's growth, yet with only the Los Angeles River and its groundwater to draw upon, prospects would ultimately be limited. The population was now approaching 200,000. For men like Chandler, who had their acquisitive eyes on the next 100,000, water was of paramount importance.

It was also of great interest to a handsome, charming, and well-connected former mayor of the city, who thought he had the answer. Fred Eaton is generally credited with planting the idea of the Los Angeles aqueduct in the mind of William Mulholland, the city's legendary water engineer, but it could not have been Eaton's idea originally. In fact two surveys had been done privately in 1885 and 1891 to prove that it would be possible to take water from the Owens River 250 miles away, and transfer it by gravity to Los Angeles. Of course there were severe problems to be overcome, but they were problems of design, materials, expense, and politics.

Eventually, as most people know, the aqueduct was built. The story of its conception and construction needs a book of its own, and several have been written. The most recent, most detailed and most revealing is by William Kahrl, and deserves to be read by anyone with a taste for intrigue and a good story.[3]

Two areas of mystery and controversy have kept the story alive up to the present. One has to do with the relative rights and priorities of an agricultural valley and a burgeoning metropolis. The other, which inspired Polanski's film, *Chinatown,* has to do with the shenanigans surrounding the San Fernando Valley.

Before being elected mayor, Fred Eaton had been the superintendent of the private company that supplied Los Angeles with water. Through the eighties and nineties he had occupied himself with looking for additional sources. He settled, in the end, on the Owens Valley as the only possibility. Given what had already been accomplished by canal builders in Europe and the East Coast, let alone the flume builders of Comstock and elsewhere, the notion of bringing water over a great distance was not outlandish.

Eaton saw his aqueduct from Owens Valley as the key to the future of the city, and also as a source of personal wealth. His plan was to acquire in his own name the land through which the Owens River ran, and to profit from his ownership of the water. He discussed his ambitions with Mulholland as early as 1892, when the Los Angeles water supply was still in private hands, but Mulholland scoffed at the idea as being, literally, farfetched.

Eaton was widely liked as an all-around nice guy. During his years as city engineer and then mayor of Los Angeles, he knew everyone, had access to anyone. Surely Eaton would have mentioned his plan, in confidence of course, to whomever might be helpful. One such person was certainly Joseph B. Lippincott, the Bureau of Reclamation's resident engineer, the man who is usually cast as the villain of the piece where Owens Valley is concerned, and with good reason.

All three, Mulholland, Lippincott, and Eaton became close. All three could have discussed the idea with others. Eaton would have been looking for some way to finance it. Mulholland, at first, might just have wanted to comment on its absurdity. Lippincott's corrupt ethics allowed him to act as a double agent. His government job required him to investigate the possibilities of an irrigation project in the Owens Valley, just the kind of project that was meant to help small farmers. But in fact he thwarted his employers and prevented federal interference with the aqueduct. Obviously he knew where his bread was buttered, and he had several good reasons to tip off a few big players.

The Owens Valley aqueduct was attractive to all those entrepreneurs who had an interest in the development of Los Angeles. What made it particularly interesting for some, however, was what was obvious from a glance at a map. For the water to get to Los Angeles from the Sierras it would have to cross the San Fernando Valley, making a hundred square miles of barren ground suddenly most desirable. Furthermore, as anyone with an eye for profit quickly realized, most of the water that came down that aqueduct would have nowhere to go for a long time. This was the crucial perception. Whatever water came that way was destined for future growth. Los Angeles would have to grow to many times its size before any of it would be needed. All that water, in the meanwhile, would be available to develop communities and farms in the valley, and increase the value of the land tenfold or more. This was a very big game and the stakes were high.

There were some preconditions for the gamble to come off. For one thing, it could not, as Eaton may have once hoped, be a private venture. The Bureau of Reclamation's investigations had already begun in the Owens Valley. That was what Lippincott had been sent there to do. Taking the water to Los Angeles was in direct contradiction to his mission, for it would leave the valley high and dry. Ultimately there would have to be a showdown between Los Angeles and Washington. How could the federal government be seen to abandon the farmers of Owens Valley in favor of some private utility? Only the city, representing "the people," could muster enough moral and political power to counter the federal plan.

The aqueduct would have to be a municipal project for the greater good of the greater number, but the city's water supply was still in private hands. In 1902, just after Eaton's term as mayor, Los Angeles was able to buy the utility, and with the purchase came its superintendent, William Mulholland. In 1904, Mulholland announced his plan to build the aqueduct to a select few city officials. The project still had to be kept under wraps, for now the challenge lay in acquiring, piece by piece, the water rights in Owens Valley, without allowing the innocent proprietors to know that they could hold the city to ransom.

Acting as an agent for the city, as well as on his own behalf, Fred Eaton secretly acquired options on a number of strategically situated properties in the valley, and he did it, apparently, with the connivance of Lippincott. Eaton did very well out of these transactions, and Lippincott's consultancy business prospered mightily. But their earnings were nothing compared to the fortunes made by those who were lucky enough to own San Fernando Valley.

There was, of course, one more obstacle to overcome before the aqueduct could be built: to persuade the people of Los Angeles to pay for it. Mulholland set the bill at $24.5 million, and a bond issue was authorized for the amount, to be voted on in 1907. In the press an outrageous campaign of lies, insults, and innuendo was waged for and against the project. The two central issues were, first, whether the water was actually needed, and second, whether a syndicate of developers in the San Fernando Valley had profited by inside knowledge of the city's plans. Since the syndicate in question included both Otis and Chandler of the *L.A. Times,* and E. T. Earl of the *Express,* the mud flew thick and rank.

The rival Hearst newspaper, the *Examiner,* reveled in charges of graft and corruption, which centered in particular around an option that was picked up in the San Fernando Valley before news of the aqueduct was made public. The buyers of this option were a group of the foremost real estate developers of the day, who knew, among them, all there was to know. There was Henry Huntington, nephew and heir of Collis Huntington, prime mover of the Central Pacific Railroad. He had learned about railroads at his uncle's knee, and his bright red trolley cars were already a famous sight in the Los Angeles region. There was Moses Sherman, who laid street railways and had sold Huntington his first trolley system. There was L. C. Brand, who had once sold Huntington an electric utility company and was vice-president of the Title Insurance and Trust Company. There was Otto Brant, president of that same bank. There was E. H. Harriman, president of the Southern Pacific Railroad, which owned immense tracts of land through which the aqueduct would have to pass. There was William Kerckhoff, another utilities tycoon, and Joseph Sartori, another great banker; and there were Harrison Gray Otis and Harry Chandler.

Nobody has yet been able to prove that they knew the water was coming through the San Fernando Valley, but there is one significant piece of evidence. In 1910 Harry Chandler paid Van Nuys just over fifty-three dollars an acre for his San Fernando valley land. By this time the value of the land was well known, the water was guaranteed and on its way, and heavy profits had already been taken. Yet that earlier option picked up in 1903, in supposed innocence of any knowledge of the bonanza to come, valued the land at more than thirty dollars an acre, a ridiculously high price for semi-desert. Somebody definitely knew something.

The darkest suspicion naturally centered around the fear that these men had somehow promoted the aqueduct purely to serve themselves at the city's expense, and some progress was made with this theory. Certainly, once Mulholland had made up his mind to go for the aqueduct, he stretched the truth to promote it.

At one of several inquiries into the matter afterward, it was shown that Mulholland had understated the amount of water already available from the Los Angeles River. He had claimed it would only support 200,000 people, but he later admitted that 500,000 was closer to the mark. The drought during the first years of the century, much trumpeted by the *L.A. Times,* also turned out to be fictitious, according to rainfall figures since available. In this respect Mulholland's behavior was typical of the way water project engineers have behaved since.

They know how reluctant the people are to fund projects so far ahead of the time when they will benefit from them.

These suspicions generated a lot of fire and smoke, which have always obscured the main issue. Why, in the final analysis, should any group have been allowed to profit so hugely from a municipal project? At one of the several investigations, Mulholland himself testified that the land in the San Fernando Valley should have been available to the public at one hundred dollars an acre, but had been "seized by a few capitalists who have forced prices up to one thousand dollars an acre," and who "have stolen the unearned increment for the next twenty years"—an unearned increment that obviously should have gone to the people of the city who paid for the project.

According to those figures, Harry Chandler's syndicate could have paid the entire cost of the aqueduct and still made a handsome profit. What's more, between them the speculators (if that's what they were, given the minimal risk) owned the utilities, the construction companies, and the transport systems to service their captive communities.

Clearly the San Fernando Valley was a money-making machine on a par with the Comstock. Given that all this profit taking was being done in full view of the public, why did the city not find a way to skim off enough cream to cover at least some of its costs?

A simple answer is that the political atmosphere favored speculation and admired those with the wit and good fortune to strike it rich. There by the grace of God go I. What does it matter if one man becomes a millionaire so long as we all might benefit? And it is also doubtful whether those who voted in the bond issue understood how the cost—approximately one hundred dollars per capita—would be visited upon them as individuals.

There was a scandal, and it did lead to an inquiry, but nothing really came of it in the end. Whatever political will there may have been to recover that "unearned increment" Mulholland had spoken of was swamped by the city's phenomenal growth rate. Everyone was in a hurry. There was no time to linger over old losses. Every day was a new game, and anyone could play. The whole argument was dissolved in a pragmatic solution. The San Fernando Valley was annexed by the city, and received all the water it needed at the common price.

Both Mulholland and Eaton, quite legitimately, bought land in the San Fernando Valley along with thousands of others, and most did very well with it. The Los Angeles aqueduct proved to be the model for success in California. All the great water projects that followed were inspired by it, and all the great entrepreneurs who profited by them were emboldened by the dizzying success of Chandler's syndicate.

Chandler and his associates did not rest. South of the Mexican border they bought 840,000 acres (1,300 square miles), and sucked water out of the Colorado that had been intended for the Imperial Valley. North of Los Angeles they acquired the 300,000-acre Tejon ranch, which now draws water from the State Water Project. Both were simply variations on the same San Fernando gambit, which has continued to deliver unearned increments with satisfying regularity.

The system, discovered somewhat accidentally, depended on grasping one simple principle underlying major water projects. The user's manual reads something like this:

- Water demand grows gradually, but water supply has to be provided for in one fell swoop (because you can't gradually increase the size of an aqueduct). So when the new project comes on line, there will be a huge, but gradually diminishing surplus. If you can station yourself strategically to make use of that surplus you are liable to get it very cheap, and you can make a lot of money.
- If you can persuade the people, in whatever form they come, municipal, state, or federal, that the need for water is urgent, so much the better. A good way to do this is to stress the importance of growth because, magically, the more you talk about growth the more it happens. Growth will pay for everything, and solve all old problems. New problems will be solved by more growth.
- Once you start using the water, you have a pretty good case for keeping it even though it was only meant to be temporary. There will be jobs lost, you say, terrible hardship, loss of productivity. The answer is not to take your water away, but to get more. That will encourage more growth.

These principles have been applied, with resounding success, up and down the state of California since Los Angeles led the way. A great proportion of the water captured by the federal- and state-built systems has found its way onto very large corporate holdings at derisory prices. Variations of the gambit have been successful in many areas besides water. Great accumulations of capital have resulted from those unearned increments, supposedly compensated for out of growth. There is a fallacy embedded in this rationale, however, for the loss of the unearned increments represents a steady hemorrhage of the people's resources, an immense deficit that becomes apparent when growth finally slows to a standstill—and all those unearned increments have been spirited away to even sunnier climes.

As for the Owens Valley, whose water nourished this fevered growth, Bill Kahrl writes:

"What is important about the valley's development is that its people have had very little to do with shaping it. Many of the most vital decisions affecting the future of their lives on the land are made in Los Angeles, where their interests are not represented. The residents of the Owens Valley have thus been effectively disenfranchised. And in a system of representative government that is wrong."[4]

Not dissimilar to the fate that was being prepared for the people of Round Valley.

8

Strange Fruit

ARDUOUS AS Angus Grant's career may have been, it was also as simple and straightforward as the track he laid. He had only to seize his opportunities, give them his best shot, and pray for success. His personal ambitions and the aims of society were in excellent harmony. Whatever moral dilemmas threatened him along the way could be disarmed by the claim, generally shared, that he was bringing civilization to a savage land.

Angus and his cohorts achieved their aim. They opened up the West. It was for succeeding generations to plant the seed and enjoy the fruits, but things took an unexpected turn. During the first half of this century the true nature of a society dependent on massive irrigation projects was made manifest. Alongside sudden wealth and rapid growth, poverty, misery, and repression darkened the land, and those who lived through that time preferred, on the whole, to watch the pictures that Hollywood made rather than dwell too much on what was going on around them.

To the extent that they were forced to respond to reality and reconcile it with their beliefs, they found different ways of performing this difficult feat. Grant's son, Daniel, who was to become Richard's uncle, seems to have taken the more comfortable route. He used the advantages of inheritance to sustain the fortunes of his family, but did little else. "He was a California Club sort of person," Richard says. "A businessman, but no Chandler. He was respected, and he fit in."

Richard Wilson's father was cut from a very different cloth, and the way in which he dealt with the problems of his time was the paramount influence on Richard's later development. Through the Grant family Richard derived many of the material advantages and connections that became indispensable to his campaign, but it was his father who furnished his conscience, and the spiritual strength to follow its dictates.

John Cree Wilson was born to a farming family from Pennsylvania in 1888, the year Chandler came to Los Angeles. He grew up with his sister on a dairy farm in Santa Ana, which was then an agricultural community south of the small town of Los Angeles. In essence, his childhood was a fulfillment and vindication of the Jeffersonian dream of America. Having left behind the harsh winters of populous Pennsylvania, no doubt by dint of much hardship, the family settled on the farthest shores of the continent in what may be the world's sweetest climate, masters of their own land by the banks of the Santa Ana River. There, through a pious upbringing, hard work, and responsibility, John acquired the strength and independence of character that he displayed throughout his life.

Unlike Angus Grant, John Wilson had had no desire to escape from the farm. His respect and affection for rural life—it amounted almost to a passion—remained constant in him until his death. In the eyes of his parents and teachers, though, his evident intelligence and ability marked him out for a different career. He was accepted into the medical school of the University of Southern California, and when that institution later went bankrupt, he was able to transfer to the Berkeley school, where he graduated. He satisfied his longing for the outdoors by working his way through school at one of the roughest occupations available—running a mule wagon on the Hetch Hetchy Reservoir project. Driving the mules in those hard conditions was only part of the difficulties. Hauling his men out of whorehouses to get them back on the job was often an even greater challenge. This delight in tough physical work was all the more remarkable in the light of his academic brilliance. When he finished his training on the East Coast, in his board examinations at Massachusetts General Hospital he got, according to his son, "the highest scores of any man in the state, ever."

Back in California, before the First World War, he lived and practiced in an apartment on Sunset Boulevard. Then, as now, hospital positions were jealously protected and, often as not, awarded on the basis of influence. John Wilson had to watch the better connected but less qualified slide into plum jobs, while he struggled to make his way. However, he overcame this disadvantage by developing a specialty in helping children with clubfoot, a congenital deformity that still went largely untreated and was, of course, a damaging physical and aesthetic handicap.

He achieved most of his cures through the use of shoes and therapy. The scalpel was only a last resort, and he became known for the extraordinary care he took of his patients. He was one of the first to employ a physical therapist in his office on a full-time basis. These innovations were still experimental in the twenties, and his pioneering work earned him gratitude and respect from all levels of society.

Very early in his career he met Anna Grant, and they were married in 1916. The war interrupted their marriage for a year, when he went east again, this time as an army captain in a base hospital, and when he returned they moved out of the apartment into a large house belonging to Anna's widowed mother. The Grants and their relatives had various properties in the areas developing around Los Angeles, and soon the Wilsons were able to move again, this time to a house of their own on South Virgil, which is today a street off Wilshire Boulevard, but then was separated from Los Angeles by several miles of open country.

In those years between the wars, the upper echelons of the medical profession flourished as never before. Many of the fundamental discoveries of the previous century were brought to fruition in the medical technology of that time, and the deadly scourges of the human race no longer seemed invincible. A cornucopia of drugs, vaccines, vitamins, anesthetics, soporifics, lotions, and potions spilled out on a grateful world, and the heroes of this liberation were the pinstriped specialists, the fashionable consultants, surgeons, and physicians pictured in the papers attending at the bedsides of the famous. In an important city, in such an atmosphere, any skilled doctor who was in some way part of this new age of medicine could expect to do well. John Wilson, though he never wore pinstripes, was by all accounts an exceptionally clever and dedicated doctor as well as being a handsome, authoritative figure. With all these qualities he succeeded in spectacular style. By the time his third and youngest son, Richard Alexander, came into the world, Wilson was already an established orthopedic surgeon with a brilliant reputation. When the new Children's Hospital was opened in Los Angeles, he became its first resident surgeon.

He was a tall man with a reserved and formal manner, but behind the public face of the masterful and accomplished physician there was another side to Wilson. Though generous when he thought it warranted, he guarded his self-respect and did not forget old scores. His son recalls—with great glee—an anecdote from one of the doctors at the hospital who happened to push an elevator button at an inopportune moment. The door slid open to reveal John Wilson thrusting a panic-stricken medical functionary up against the wall with both feet off the ground.

"He was calling him a son of a bitch and threatening all kinds of mayhem because this guy had given him the business over some appointment—you might never know that physical side of him, but it was there. Oh, yes, it was there."

Both Wilsons, father and youngest son, sport hawklike noses they liked to attribute to their Cree bloodline, and perhaps it showed in John Wilson's natural preference for the country and outdoor pursuits. He was always much happier in the country. As he became more prosperous, he built an isolated beach house at Newport Beach (where today you can jump from rooftop to rooftop) so that he could hunt duck on Balboa Island (where ducks are now more commonly found frozen in the supermarket). He loved gardening and became quite expert at raising roses and tulips, which he took to flower shows.

Although his hospital work was both profitable and demanding, he deliberately offered his help to friends in the country so that he could combine his rounds with hunting expeditions, taking first his nephews and later his sons along with him. As the pressure and congestion around his workplace increased, he gradually extended his wanderings over the Tehachapi Mountains and up the San Joaquin Valley.

He did not share the general delight in the unending growth of the greater Los Angeles area, but it was a phenomenon that continued to astound the world. In 1890 the city contained some fifty thousand people being taxed on property assessed at about $50 million. By 1928 Los Angeles had a population of almost one and a quarter million and property valued at more than $2 billion. The excitement of the postwar boom in the twenties reached fever pitch in Los Angeles. Even the most cautious minds saw visions of limitless improvement.

All the big cities were developing that particularly yeasty metropolitan culture with its tang of modern times that intoxicated a generation newly arrived from the land. They were only too willing to shed the cumbersome habits of rural life and plunge into the fast-paced sophistication of the streets, and this, too, offended Wilson's sense of values, which were still strongly rooted in rural tradition. America had discovered the secret, it seemed, for making money multiply itself magically, effortlessly, and everyone was getting rich. The secret was in moving money around and, not for the last time, the true sources of wealth were forgotten in the fascination of the deal.

By now Los Angeles was directly connected with the rest of the continent by four different railroad companies, and with the seagoing trade routes of the world through her port of San Pedro. While the agricultural produce of the Sacramento Valley and northern San Joaquin Valley naturally went out through San Francisco and Sacramento, the central and southern parts of the valley fell within the hinterland of Los Angeles, as did the hugely prolific Imperial Valley that had been coaxed from the desert between the coast and the Colorado River.

Four fifths of this land was irrigated—all by private projects. Farmers had squeezed every drop they could command with their own resources from the rivers of the valley. The new All-American Canal was bringing even more Colorado water to Imperial Valley. King cotton came to California in the twenties, and did three times as well there as in the rest of the nation. And all around Los Angeles, from Santa Barbara to San Diego, from the coast to Pasadena, irrigated orange groves and grapevines covered every usable acre. The output was vast and expertly organized. The wealth nourished Los Angeles, constantly raising the stakes on real estate and later protecting her from the most brutal effects of the depression.

In 1921, J. K. Baillie of the Los Angeles *Evening Express* interviewed Joseph Sartori, founder of Security Pacific, who was then the city's most powerful and respected banker, and came away with a joyfulness akin to requited love. He wrote:

> A city is just as big as its banks, no larger. This is the day of big business. Big business makes a big city, and big business must have

> big banks with big resources. "We are building not alone for today but for the future," said Mr. J. F. Sartori this morning. And as I listened to this kindly man with the brilliant mind and the vision of an empire builder it was not difficult to see why he controlled millions and could put through a single deal involving close to $150,000,000. His force is irresistible and his logic as true as steel. "You will see a continual stream of people from the East and the Middle West pour into Los Angeles and surrounding country," said Mr. Sartori. "The possibilities of this section are almost limitless. No other place will be as densely populated as the section in and around Los Angeles. This is the garden spot of the world, and to it will come people from the four corners of the earth." And I walked up the street happy that I lived in Los Angeles, and convinced that if I were spared I would live to see the city built from the mountains to the sea.[1]

He could have written the same piece again in every decade up to the time forty years later when all the oranges were finally gone, and the city did stretch from the San Gabriels to the beach.

In 1933, the year of Richard Wilson's birth, the city and its surrounding communities continued to fulfill Sartori's heady predictions, despite the depression that was devastating the rest of America, but it was not a good year for mankind as a whole. In Germany, Adolf Hitler finally achieved full power, and most of the industrial world was mired in a financial swamp. Millions upon millions of working people were sucked into hardship and even destitution—fertile ground, it was feared, for the dreaded "red" agents who seemed to be lurking under every capitalist bed.

And indeed there was trouble on the farm. Migrant workers, laboring in the most apalling conditions, were threatening to organize. The activists who spurred the field workers to strike and revolt were a motley crew, but they all shared one belief. They were convinced that the growers could, if they wished, put matters right; that it was just greed, indifference, and not a little malice that kept the employers from paying a living wage and replacing the squalid, unsanitary encampments with decent quarters.

As for the growers, they took it upon themselves to put down migrant protest by force, and were left free to do so as long as the general public didn't interfere. Since they controlled or, at least, had the sympathy of most of the newspapers, they were largely successful in deflecting public attention. As a result, the real issues were never exposed. Neither they nor their critics ever came to grips with the underlying cause of the problem—the fundamental principle that governs large-scale agriculture by irrigation.

The unhappy truth is that all of them, owners and laborers alike, were in the grip of a system that left little to spare for social justice. Everyone involved could witness the marvels that irrigation provided; the densely packed, luxuriant orchards; the immense fields with that weird, industrial flatness, where emerald crops grew like grass; the inconceivable quantities of stuff that rolled out of this dreamlike landscape and into Southern Pacific's waiting boxcars.

What they were actually seeing was in direct line of succession to the slave economies of China, of the Nile Delta, of the Sumerian period. But what they wanted to see—this being America—was farming, American-style, and they said, "This is perverse, a travesty, a corruption of all we stand for. How can one man own so many acres, reap such immense harvests, and treat his workers like animals? Why aren't there many small farms, supporting many worthy families, enjoying and thriving on the liquid wealth that tumbles from the mountains into these thirsty fields?"

And the answer would not have pleased or persuaded them. In all that long valley, from Shasta to the Tehachapi, only a relatively small amount of land could be readily watered from the rivers. That land was soon gone. The rest was arid, and the job of bringing water to dry land was a major undertaking. This was *not* farming—this was a production plant every bit as capital-intensive as any Ford assembly plant. And the owners, of course, were not dirt farmers. They were railroads, utilities, banks, and oil companies, and interspersed among them, the last of the great land barons who had acquired, by one means or another, the huge Mexican land grants of the original "*hacendados muy grandes.*"*

The railroad companies had planned their routes carefully. As a cheap means of public financing they were rewarded with huge tracts of free land on either side of their lines. Those checkerboard patterns of land became the bases of huge farm holdings. At one time, Southern Pacific alone owned a tenth of California—over eleven million

*In 1915, of the eleven million acres under cultivation in California, four million of the best belonged to 310 proprietors. In Kern County four companies owned a million acres. In Merced County one company owned a quarter of a million. See *Factories in the Fields,* by Carey McWilliams (Bibliography).

acres. They sold, leased, or managed their lands with one object in view: to ensure the greatest volume of freight at the highest possible price. In collaboration with giant utilities such as Pacific Gas and Electric, dams were built that supplied power as well as water. To amortize the great expense of these projects, only certain crops would do, grown intensively over large acreages, tended and harvested by mobile armies of cheap labor, processed, packed, and marketed like soap or shoes or any other industrial product. Cotton, rice, alfalfa, grapes, fruit, nuts, sugar beets, and green vegetables were the major items.

Why then could not smaller farmers come together to finance a dam and a canal? There were such projects, although almost always led by an entrepreneurial developer or moneyed interest. Present day Fresno owes its existence to a certain William Chapman and his associates who, in 1875, subdivided 277,600 acres into 20-acre family farms irrigated by canal from the Kings River. Planted with saplings and vines, they were all sold off in three years to would-be farmers from the East (many of them Armenians) at a thousand dollars apiece, and the new settlers achieved a considerable level of success. Other such schemes followed, taking advantage of readily accessible irrigation water, to create the valley towns of Selma, Dinuba, Kingsburg, and Reedley.[2] Later projects, however, were poorly planned and rather cynically promoted. Some were out-and-out swindles; most were failures. The evidence indicated that irrigation farming demanded a degree of enterprise and managerial skill that conventional farmers lacked.

Overshadowing all was the simple fact that the enormous estates did exist, that they were run in cooperation with equally enormous packing houses such as Libby, Heinz, Santa Cruz Packing, Kings County Packing, Bercut-Richards, and Burton Gray, and were in collusion with the railroads so that prices for most staple commodities were shaved down to the point where small farmers could not compete. Only the plantations of the South, presenting the same challenges and opportunities, had required manpower on the same scale. This time it was not to be slavery, precisely, but something even more convenient. For the slave owner had the problem of caring for his human property year-round whereas his California counterpart had only to provide for his rented slaves as long as they were needed.

For decades the farmers had drawn their labor force from all around the globe. Wherever they could find men so miserable that they would jump at any chance to work, they shipped them in. From China, from India, from Japan, from the Philippines, from Mexico, they came in waves and, when their attendant problems outweighed their usefulness, they were expelled. Until the onset of the depression, this system passed generally unremarked by the public. Only when the numbers of any particular race became so great that they began, inevitably, to drift away from the bare-bones existence in the fields and impinge on the lives of citizens were they noticed. Then, usually in one of those times of economic hardship that hit periodically, they were perceived as a threat, prejudice grew rapidly, and the "coolies" or the "ragheads" or the "braceros" were labeled a scourge and sent packing. However, there was little or no concern over the conditions under which they labored, and sometimes died, in fields, down mines, and on railroads.

When the Great Depression of the thirties hit, the picture changed dramatically. Suddenly it was white folks, the so-called Okies, evicted from their homes and farms in the South and Midwest, who became the great drifting migrant labor force, and they could no longer be ignored or deported. Even worse from the point of view of the big farmers, the social climate had changed. Now everybody in America was being hurt, and the plight of others had become news. While employers shuddered at the specter of communism that was haunting their parish, many idealists and reformers saw in the depression evidence of the theory that capitalism was doomed. If they needed further confirmation, they had only to see the terrible price that working people were paying everywhere for the frenzied greed of the twenties, and among those victims of capitalism rampant, the most miserable were the abused innocents who later became the heroes of Steinbeck's novel *The Grapes of Wrath.*

The scandal didn't burst upon the public until 1939, when Steinbeck's book was first published, but his Joad family, and the seventy thousand or more real transients that they represented, began their dreadful ordeals during the early years of the thirties. For the first time in California's history, most of the sweat work in the fields was being done by Americans, and by *white* Americans at that. This was a truly unexpected occurrence, with grave consequences. Unlike the coolies and ragheads, they had come to California expecting to share in a paradise, only to find themselves condemned to live in hovels and ditches on starvation wages. Clearly it would not be difficult for militant organizers to arouse a fierce sense of grievance among them.

To forestall expected trouble, in 1933 the employers, prompted by big interests, combined into a statewide organization. The Associated Farmers of California—the AFC—was formed, county by county, through the Farm Bureau and the chambers of commerce, to confront what they saw as a serious challenge to their survival. The members were farmers and businessmen of all kinds, but the leading lights were also those who wielded the most power, and the money came from the railroads, the utilities, the banks, and others with more than a general interest in the survival of agriculture in California. Just to quote one example, during the depression approximately 50 percent of farmland in central and northern California came under the control of Bank of America alone.[3] These interests, with their fears of a red insurrection already inflamed, had good reason to expect a violent eruption of discontent, and they were determined to suppress it by force.

Several military men, such as Col. Henry Sanborn and Col. Walter Garrison, held positions with the AFC, as did the tear gas salesman, Ignatius McCarthy. These specialists developed connections with the sheriffs and the state bureaucracy. They could muster two thousand deputies anywhere in their area in a few hours and, together with the state's Bureau of Criminal Identification, they maintained a file on about a thousand "dangerous radicals." In Imperial Valley alone, some four thousand gun permits were issued in 1935. "Professional agitators" were rounded up merely on suspicion and held at Salinas and Brentwood in detention centers that were actually referred to as concentration camps. Vigilante groups were encouraged to burn crosses and issue threats, and their activities were reported approvingly in newspapers like the *Los Angeles Times.*

Growers controlled the state and federal employment agencies, which in turn forced the relief agencies to cut off workers' relief and deliver them to the labor camps. The growers pretended a greater labor demand than actually existed, and setting desperate workers against each other, they got their men to work for half their already miserable pay. Strikes were broken in the Santa Clara Valley in 1931, and in Vacaville in 1932; 1933 was an extraordinary year of violence, at Vacaville again, and then at Pixley, a cotton-growing area between Fresno and Bakersfield. At Pixley a posse of armed growers fired on strikers and their families, killing and wounding men, women, and children while the highway patrol looked on passively, hidden from view.

These events were presented to the population at large in a very partial light. The *Los Angeles Times* had always been rabidly opposed to any kind of worker organization. In earlier, rougher days, its vituperative founder, General Otis, had had a cannon mounted on his limousine for fear of angry union organizers. Now the paper frothed at the mouth about foreign agitators, congratulated sheriffs for averting strikes, and complimented the California Cavaliers, who burned crosses and announced that "anyone who peeps about higher wages will wish he hadn't." The readers, by and large, swallowed what they were told.

When the strikes and rebellions reached their peak, times were bad and everyone knew there were fundamental problems to be resolved, but 1933 was the very year when, far from modifying the agricultural system, California decided to extend it to its limits. It was the year when the Central Valley Project was authorized by the legislature. This remarkable plan had been brewing for sixty years. Even in 1873, it was apparent that God had gotten it all wrong. Rivers were running out to sea, when they should obviously be running someplace useful. Canals would carry them across the foothills and bring millions of acres under irrigation, and big dams on the Sacramento and the San Joaquin Rivers would generate free power.

The idea was too grand for its time, and was shelved for lack of finance and support, but in 1920 Col. Robert B. Marshall revived the splendid visions of the nineteenth century. He published his own version of the water plan, and by now there were plenty of farmers to get excited about the thought of all that icy northern water rushing through their hot, arid lands. They were dealing with the same problem that has bedeviled pioneers everywhere, the very problem that the Federal Reclamation Act was intended to solve.

Addressing the state legislature in 1925, Paul Bailey from the Division of Engineering and Irrigation described the dilemma faced by communities wanting to open up new land to irrigation. How do you get enough farmers together at one time to pay for irrigation projects on the scale that conditions in California demanded? Quoting a report from 1923, he said there were already a million or more acres in California, fertile enough and with water at hand, unable to produce adequately to pay for their costs. Those costs, of course, included the cost of bringing water to the land.

"Much of this," he wrote, "is in large holdings and in new districts that have recently been brought under irrigation." And the problem was that "at present these lands are lacking in numbers of tillers of the soil to respond to the propitious agricultural environment of the state."

He goes on to explain why so little of this irrigated land was under cultivation. It's because the projects are necessarily of such a size "that in a year or two, [they] bring under irrigation in one community, an area of land greater than can be absorbed by normal growth within as many decades."

He points out that communities find themselves between the devil and the deep blue sea. Dry farming communities cannot compete, and can be seen to stagnate, shrivel, and die. Only irrigation communities can prosper in the long run. But the engineering costs of new irrigation projects can be covered only if they supply large areas. Then, the problem is to find enough farmers to take up the option quickly enough to pay for it. Only a state-financed scheme could absorb the costs until enough farmers could be brought onto the land.

But the plan ran into powerful opposition from private utilities. An important part of the package involved generating and distributing public power. The Pacific Gas and Electric conglomerate, among others, wouldn't have it, and the growers weren't yet powerful enough to overcome them. They had one other recourse. They could pump.

It had been known for a long time that water lay below the valley in vast, primeval lakes, but at first the inefficient pumps of the time made it either impossible or too expensive to go below certain depths. Some growers were fortunate. They had artesian wells on their property. They had only to drill to the water and it spouted to the surface under geologic pressure, but for the great majority well water was no solution. Then technology got them off the hook with the invention of the electric pump. Soon there were wells thousands of feet deep, and the surface of the underground lake began to decline.

By 1930 it was clear that the groundwater reserves were becoming dangerously depleted. Evidently it was again time to move on to the next stage, and again approximately the same plan was issued, this time as the State Water Plan. It met with even more enthusiasm, but unfortunately when it came time to raise the money, the state had to concede that in the midst of the depression it could not. Agriculture could not expand without more water, and severe restrictions would limit the use of such water as already existed. This was anathema. The state needed more than production. It needed growth. California had already mortgaged its future and was living beyond its means, in a way that had become the principal feature of the American economy.

During the depression there was only one source of available finance in America—the federal government. In 1935, the Bureau of Reclamation under Roosevelt took over construction of the Central Valley Project. This would have been fine, but for one unfortunate snag: The rules governing federal water projects were all too well known. They followed the same old idealistic principles that were intended to foster the expansion of agrarian America. Federal water was supposed to be water for the people, not for the plutocrats. Nobody could have water for more than 160 acres, and if the bureau took over the Central Valley Project it should have meant breaking up the great estates.

In their camps and clubs and dining rooms, the proprietors considered their chances of taking the federal water and getting away with it, and it must have seemed to them that they held a strong hand. For the valleys of California to become what the laws and rhetoric of America had clearly intended—an extension of the Mississippi and Ohio valleys, with federally funded canals substituting for rainfall—would require a most un-American level of government interference with the existing, privately funded operations; a policy far too "socialistic" for even the New Deal to contemplate.

The big growers owned politicians, newspapers, radio stations. Their lawyers could keep justice spinning its wheels almost indefinitely. But beyond all this they could rely on a certain ruthless logic. They made the money that kept California growing. Their farming methods could keep this bounty flowing into the state's coffers, in a way that a proliferation of small farms never could. They wanted the water, there seemed no other way to get it, and political reality dictated that they would eventually have their way. They saw to it that what happened took exactly the opposite direction to what the federal law intended, and public money was used to expand their current practices to the limit of the state's capacity. They supported the federal takeover and made their own plans.

For a man like John Wilson, all these events presented an insoluble dilemma. He believed, as did most successful Americans, in unfettered private enterprise as the best of all possible systems in an imperfect world, and rather than look to bureaucratic regulation or some foreign ideology, he depended on the wholesome instincts of individuals to redress social inequities. With his strongly conservative background, he could hardly sympathize with militant unions and labor activists, and yet the factory agriculture that had brought these crises about was distasteful to him also. Unable to resolve the dilemma, he used his leisure time and resources to distance himself from it.

Anna Grant died prematurely in 1937, when Richard was only three, and Wilson remarried soon after to Marjorie Connell, of an even more wealthy and influential family. She was more socially and politically active than Anna too, and the Wilson family's range of connections widened further still. It was Marjorie's uncle, Michael, who made the Connell family fortune from lumber in Montana, and when he came to Los Angeles he used much of it to support the arts (her aunt founded the Los Angeles symphony orchestra) as well as education and health care in the city. The Connells, together with the wealthy and influential families they knew through their social, political, and philanthropic activities, were inclined to a gregarious and elaborate form of rustic fun. The men of the previous generation had established a tradition of camps in the Sierras and the redwoods. They took with them their servants and their silverware, set up tents and marquees, and played at being outdoorsmen. In these bucolic beauty spots, free from observation, the men could reinforce their opinions and indulge in those pleasures then considered to be exclusively masculine, and which usually involved heavy drinking as a competitive sport.

The best known of these retreats was Bohemian Grove, near Guernville, where various camps were established by the financial heavyweights of the age, and where they liked to entertain the politicians they had sponsored to represent their interests. Mike Connell had a special affinity with the Lost Angels camp. Though considered by the others to be a rather raffish and ill-disciplined bunch, they were still important enough, through the prejudice of one of their members, to have accidentally swung the presidential election in favor of Woodrow Wilson.[4]

The Connells had particularly close connections with the Valentines, who had a camp above Mammoth Lake where the O'Melvenys, Joseph Sartori, and others gathered—all people who became important in Richard's later life. Inevitably they became acquainted with all the families bearing the old Los Angeles names, the same people who starred in Daniel Grant's world. These were the elite of a small town grown suddenly very big. There was a tremendous amount of money to be made in this time of urban effervescence, and for several decades, through undisclosed dealings and private understandings, they succeeded in retaining control of the power structure among themselves.

Although he was not a "clubable" man, Wilson did nevertheless, through his wife's family, meet with the cream of California society. He sat on the board of a bank and knew the very people who stood behind the vast agricultural enterprises, and the financial institutions that owned or serviced them. He met them on his occasional visits to their camps. He may have met them at the opera, or in his consulting rooms, or even on the operating table, where he met all manner of people. (Once, when working as a police surgeon, he took the leg off a policeman who had previously handed him a speeding ticket. "You've got me where you want me now, Doc," said the cop.)

What they would no doubt have told him about the deplorable state of affairs in the valleys, was that the economic realities left no leeway to increase wages or do anything else that might raise the cost of their products. For once, this hoary old line from the tearful plutocrat had a measure of truth to it, but there was no satisfaction in that. Clearly there was something fundamentally wrong with attitudes on all sides of the question.

Wilson's reputation attracted many of California's most powerful citizens to his office door, but neither the businessmen nor the politicians he knew seem to have impressed him as having a worthwhile handle on the problems of the day. During his lifetime he saw their efforts debase and overwhelm ideals that he cherished. In particular he saw Santa Ana, his symbol for rural virtue, degenerate into a grimy industrial suburb, and he had a marked tendency to regard city life in general as corrupt.

Those who knew him say that he lived for his work. He was, without doubt, considered the best surgeon in that time and place. He was a compassionate man and gave help often and freely to needy people who came his way. For the rest he took what time he could to escape the urban throng and roam the valleys in search of quail and congenial friends in the country who shared his values.

He came to know a modest farming family, the Twisselmans, on the west side of the San Joaquin Valley near Paso Robles, having had to operate on one of them. He went there to hunt when he could, and, among all the rich and celebrated people he had to deal with in his life, it was Carl Twisselman whom he acknowledged as his best friend. Carl's wife, Dorothy, has survived him, and she remembers Wilson's visits among the highlights of her life. Later he brought young Richard with him.

"He adored that boy," she said, "though I don't suppose he knows it."

The Twisselmans did not irrigate, and Dorothy has become convinced that the hydraulic culture of the Central Valley is a cruel and unnecessary perversion of nature. Through all those years of political strife, she never heard Wilson endorse agribusiness. To him farming was a wonderful way of life, and a blessing on those who could sustain it. To make agriculture into an industry of exploitation, with all the attendant evils that had surfaced with it, was to make a travesty of something he revered, and he wanted nothing to do with it. Richard, who worshiped his father, absorbed that message at an early age, and it was reinforced every time they went out together.

As early as 1929, in his search for greater distance and detachment, John Wilson was drawn all the way into the mountains of Northern California, more than six hundred miles from his home and work. There, at the edge of the Yolla Bolly wilderness, he was offered a seven hundred-acre parcel that would satisfy even the sharpest desire for isolation. The only access was on horseback, after a grueling drive on dirt roads that took him through a dusty little cattle town named Covelo. It was a glorious tract of meadows and fir forests at four thousand feet, sloping down to the Eel River, where salmon spawn in winter and summer steelhead wind lazily in deep stone pools. High above the river was the crowning jewel of the place, a lovely lake named Henthorne, from which the parcel also took its name. He bought it and later added to it and, by this unlikely act he ensured that his family was, henceforth, stretched out in both space and time across the length and history of California. Although he had no inkling, in his lifetime, of the consequences, his remarks to his son show that he was doing what he could to redress a balance.

Once Henthorne became his, he went there religiously every year for almost forty years to breathe the clear mountain air. His son remembers him saying, with unforgettable conviction: "It straightens a man out."

9

Another Country

ON A WARM SUMMER EVENING IN 1941, Dr. John Wilson and his young son, Richard, left their big house in Pasadena to catch the overnight train for San Francisco. Since he had acquired Henthorne, John Wilson made it a habit to spend a month there every summer and, for him, the arrangements had become routine. For seven-year-old Richard, every detail of the journey was wildly exciting. Never before had he been to the famous ranch, where there were bears and rattlesnakes and mountain lions. It was his first long train ride as well, a thrilling event in any child's life, and it was also the first time that he had ever gone away alone with his father, all the more important to a boy who had lost his mother at the age of three. It was the beginning of a supreme adventure.

Dr. Wilson had booked a "roomette" on the Southern Pacific *Lark,* and father and son boarded the train at Glendale station after dark, heightening the sense of mystery. Richard, who claimed the top bunk, reveled in the delicious experience that was still in keeping with the generally comfortable circumstances of his life. Then there was breakfast on the train as it chugged up the Salinas Valley and through the beautiful orchard country of Santa Clara. Meanwhile a chauffeur had already driven the Buick to San Francisco, and when they arrived the car was delivered to them at the station.

Dr. Wilson dismissed the chauffeur, took charge of the big, black automobile, and they set off together across the Golden Gate Bridge and north on the two-lane highway 101.

It was an unexpectedly terrible journey. Richard remembers the fierce heat beating down on the black Buick for hours on end. The road, which is now a freeway, then passed through every dusty town along the way. There was San Rafael, Novato, and Petaluma. Even now he remembers the snarled-up traffic around the courthouse of Santa Rosa. Then came Healdsburg, Cloverdale, and Ukiah, and somewhere after that he recalls being violently and disgracefully sick into his father's lap, so that they had to stop for the night at the old hotel in Willits.

Next morning, soon after leaving Willits, they turned off the highway onto a dirt road that followed a river. They crossed a railroad, and a trestle bridge, and continued on a journey that seemed endless as the swirling dust enveloped and choked them. Along the other side of the narrow river gorge, the railroad ran on its easy, even tracks while their own road clung to the contours of the mountainside, curving up and down in search of a firm footing, with Richard getting sicker than ever.

"There was no air-conditioning in those days. It was just awful. And my father's theory was—well, you just keep driving till you get over it."

The scenery showed little change as they went. The first river they accompanied was called Outlet Creek, and it seemed to be running in the wrong direction, away from the coast. After about fifteen minutes, it was joined by a larger river flowing, with equal perversity, from the southwest. This was the Middle Fork of the Eel, and John Wilson tried unsuccessfully to explain to his son that it was really only the south fork of the Middle Fork, since there was also a North Fork and a South Fork, each of which had its own forks. The geography alone was enough to make you dizzy.

After another quarter hour of grit and nausea, at a junction named Dos Rios, they crossed a bigger bridge made of green-painted steel girders. The road then followed the new river against its flow, rising high above it in ever tighter turns, and swooping down again twice until, at last, they came to the rim of Round Valley and stopped there to look out over the flat floor of the valley, as everybody does, and as Richard has done so often since. Then the road snaked down the side of that last ridge and made, straight as an arrow, for the little town of Covelo, where they got relief, of a sort.

Many people unfamiliar with California imagine that the climate should be cooler as one goes north. In the winter this is true, but in summer in those interior valleys where the sun beats down out of a cloudless sky for months on end, the gathering heat is intense. It frequently reaches 110 degrees* or more and stays there for many days. It is a dry heat, of course, and the inhabitants grow accustomed to it, but to newcomers arriving in the middle of the day it comes as a staggering blow. Richard felt it strike as he stumbled from the car to examine, for the first time, the dusty little township that would mean so much to him later.

It was like arriving in a foreign country. A broad dirt road ran through the middle of town, flanked by boardwalks. There were horses tethered to hitching posts, and wood frame structures flaunting those false fronts so familiar from western movie sets. The main stops were on the corners of the first intersection. There was the Shell station, which belonged to the Vann family, Gravier's store—Mervyn Gravier was the owner then—with a reasonably good supply of clothes, food, and tack, an International parts store, and close to the fourth corner was the Covelo Hotel.

That first day they didn't linger long in Covelo. They drove on, north again, and up into the mountains another half hour on an even tougher road until they arrived at Hull's Valley, where they stayed with some friends called McDuffy. With the spectacular resilience of youth, Richard was scarcely out of the car before his queasiness gave way to exhilaration. He had never seen so much unadulterated country before. It astonished him and filled him with a tingling anticipation of undefined thrills. It made an immediate and lasting impact, amplified by each succeeding visit. The sense of space and opportunity was a tangible thing to a boy whose only experience so far was of the controlled, adult bustle of Los Angeles, and the polite society of Pasadena.

On the morning of the third day, when Pasadena already seemed a world away, they packed out from a spot called Beefhead with horses and mules on the three-hour trail to Henthorne. The motley crew of men who succeeded each other in Dr. Wilson's employ ran his cattle on the range, but they were based on a site just above Hull's

*43 degrees Centigrade

Valley at Buck Mountain. At Henthorne itself there were only the most rudimentary facilities, for everything that could not be made on the spot had to be packed up there by mule. The cookstove and chimney, pots, kettles and tableware, bedding and provisions, lamps, fuel, and hardware all went that way. And Richard vividly remembers that when his stepmother once broke her leg at Henthorne, his father improvised a cast with a section of stovepipe, and she had to be packed down to Buck Mountain in the same way, on the back of a mule.

So Richard began his apprenticeship in mountain living, which continued through the summers almost every year from then on. Instead of his well-appointed bathroom in Pasadena, he shared a barrel to wash in. Instead of his soft bed, he had a hard bunk. He spent his days with rough, outdoor men who spoke little but had a seemingly inexhaustible fund of knowledge about animals, grasses, trees, and water. As he grew older he was allowed to accompany them to town.

In those days, before the war took hold of the economy and changed it, there was more life in the hills. Many small ranchers lived out there with their orchards, their hogs and sheep and turkeys, and a few cattle for themselves. They came down to Covelo for supplies and entertainment. A remarkable number of them played musical instruments—a fiddle, a banjo, or a guitar maybe—and brought them down to town on Saturday nights. In later years, Richard would accompany one or other of the men who worked for his father, and listen spellbound to the music and the yarns they would spin.

"There were three saloons," he recalls, "though I was never allowed in them. There were times when it was really wild. And a little later, when the loggers came in, we had girls from town in buses coming in at the weekends—real boomtown kind of stuff. But the town looked better than it does now. It was cleaner.

"There was a traditional power structure of a few old families. Then there were the Indian families—the 'good' Indian families who didn't bother anybody. The town operated on the caste system. The Indians did the work; they'd behave themselves and stay on the reservation because they couldn't go in the bars. They didn't have the right to drink.* Then there was the old family regime. The Rohrboughs—pronounced 'Rawbies'—and the Hurts, and they ran things."

*They got the right in 1953.

During the day Richard helped the hired hands with whatever there was to do, and came to respect their abilities and enjoy their eccentricities.

"There were the Kasers, Otto and his dad, Rudy. They were Swiss German. Otto was from Covelo, and my father hired him in 1929 to go 'swamp out' Henthorne and begin to put it together. Then we used to have an old fellow named Tony Bernath—a Lithuanian, with a big mustache and a hot temper, a muscular kind of guy. He split post and built fence—he'd stay in the mountains for extended periods of time, and then he'd come to town and he'd get so drunk. I remember him clearly—very heavy accent; he was just one of the characters, we lost a whole lot of them.

"These people were skilled. Tony could take an ax, or a broadax or a saw, and make anything you needed. Just start with a tree, and hack it down into just about anything—fences, a table. He was a bachelor—stubborn and bull-headed. He was there in the thirties and forties. We had one guy called Les—came from the Bakersfield area—who decided he'd found eternal youth and he dyed his hair green and purple, and all kinds of stuff. And there was Jack who was just about an outlaw—always in trouble, drinking and stealing things. Seems like there was an endless number of these people passing through the landscape.

"It's changed, though there were still a few of them left a little while back. I remember when Cleo O'Ferrall was caught taking the tin off a barn roof out at Estle Beard's place. You wouldn't believe it. He was the deputy, too. He had a lisp that made him sound kind of cute. Well, I suppose he thought they didn't need a roof on their barn. He went out there one night, by moonlight, and started taking it off. A woman came out with a flashlight and shouted, 'You come down off there, Cleo' as if she'd known who it was all along. He lisped out: 'Goth'awmighty, if fate wouldn't have it, the on'y time I ever try anythin' an' I get caught.' "

Richard learned to build fences, to ride boundaries, and to guess where the cows would be. Gradually imprinted in his mind was a three-dimensional map of the surrounding area, with all its bewildering peaks, ridges, draws, and creeks, and with that knowledge came a visceral understanding of watersheds, and the vital importance of the snowpack. In a good, wet winter the snow packs down on the mountaintops above four thousand feet, and holds there through to the summer. As it melts it keeps the grass growing, and a knowledge of the watersheds tells you where it's growing. And that's where you go to find your cows.

Richard's first trip to Henthorne was a revelation that eventually shaped his life, and it was a special year in another respect. That was when his father decided to build a house for them all at Buck Mountain, a house that Richard would one day call home.

The contrast between the two lifestyles of Richard Wilson's childhood could hardly have been greater, and the only common link between them was his father. Marjorie Connell was very dear to him, and he thought of her as his true mother. She gave him all her affection, but she belonged very much to that other comfortable world of Southern California. His two brothers, John and Lewis, were both much older, and did not take kindly to their father's remarriage. Lewis, in particular, was of an age to resent his stepmother a good deal. Both boys had been to Henthorne, of course, but by 1941 John was already a grown man, and Lewis was seriously alienated. Richard grew up virtually as an only child, and his brothers played no big part in his "Wild West" experience.

In Pasadena his life followed the smooth routine of the well-to-do. He went to the right prep school, the Polytechnic. He took dancing classes with the young elite, learned to ride at Flintridge, and competed at shows. There were tennis tournaments, and a certain Mr. Garrish who ran a boys' club would take them to the snow for tobogganing.

When his grades weren't up to scratch his parents got him a tutor.

"I wouldn't say I was a good student, I was good enough to get my work done, but not good enough to suit my father—he was really on my back about that because of my education. I think that's when he decided to send me to the Thacher school because he just didn't think I was working hard enough. And those were wonderful years when I look back on them, because I formed many of the friendships I have today."

Both the Polytechnic in Pasadena, and Thacher in Ojai, near Santa Barbara, are private schools. The latter is quite possibly the best on the West Coast. Thacher draws its pupils predominantly from the wealthier class, but it was founded by a man whose passion was to rescue boys from the indolence, complacency, and unconscious sense of futility that a wealthy background often promotes. He did it by involving them, compulsorily, in a strenuous outdoor program of camping, climbing, and survival. Although the school is generous in its scholarship programs, the majority of its pupils do, naturally, come from wealthy, and sometimes influential, families.

The school trademark is a relaxed, confident manner, which makes for easy and unaffected social contact at all levels, and is often characterized as democratic. Nevertheless, the strongest bonds are usually those between members of a similar class. Richard Wilson was a popular, attractive figure, and his education provided him with wide-ranging connections throughout the establishment.

From Thacher Richard went to Dartmouth College, again very much an establishment choice, particularly for a generally competent freshman, good at sports but with no special passion or vocation. And in that respect, he continued to disappoint his father.

Dr. Wilson's ambitions for his sons caused a good deal of friction in the family. He was determined that they should all take up medicine. With his commanding influence in the field, and knowing from bitter experience how helpful his position could be to them, he did all he could to persuade them. His eldest son, John, took to medicine from the start, and eventually became a worthy successor to his father, and the two of them ganged up on the others. Lewis was of a different stamp, and suffered greatly from his father's domineering will. Marjorie Connell saw what damage had been done to Lewis and helped to protect Richard from her husband's zeal.

"My father used to take me on rounds every weekend when I was home. I mean, on Sunday we'd go see patients, take casts off, go through their charts, because he wanted to get me interested in medicine, but there was something about it that just never really came to life in me.

"When I was in college, there was always this thing from my brother and father—'Well, what are you going to do?' and 'How about the medicine premed?'—and, well, the coup de grâce came in '52. I was home at Christmas and they were doing an operation together on the weekend—on Sunday—and they wanted me to come down and just watch. It was in the amphitheater—actually they were going to take a calcium deposit off some woman's shoulder.

"I have an allergy to ether: If it's hot and there's ether, it makes me sick and I just conk out. I really didn't want to go, and I made quite a fuss, and my mother heard the phone call about it, too. But I gave in and we went down to the operating room. They gave me a smock and said, 'Put it on and go on up to the gallery and if you feel bad just walk out the door.'

"So I sat up there, and they were starting their procedures, and working dutifully on this woman, and I started feeling bad and I walked out and hell, I never knew what happened—I went flat down on my face, landed right here where the scar is, broke my jaw in three places, got my teeth all rattled. They took me into the operating room and got a surgeon. I had my jaw wired shut for about six weeks, and drank milk shakes. By the time my mother got through with them they were so torn up we never heard any more about medicine.

"I took history at Dartmouth, played soccer, was in one of the senior societies, was president of my fraternity, was busy, had a good time. I was in the ROTC—the air force—in the flying program until my eyes were no longer acceptable. I applied to Cornell to go on a postgraduate to take some agriculture, and I liked that pretty well. Then I came back to Berkeley and took some courses, and then I was drafted."

Still confused and uncertain about what he would do with his life, he was sent off to Fort Ord on the Monterey peninsula for basic training, passed the officer candidate test, chose the Army Intelligence Corps, was accepted, and fell ill with mumps. He recovered from this undignified illness and eventually climbed back into the training cycle to become a plainclothes intelligence agent checking up on security clearances.

Naturally, as Richard grew older his awareness of his family's position in the world broadened. He realized more clearly the extent of his father's reputation and skill. At the same time he was exposed by both parents to a stream of family acquaintances, who, it transpired, were sometimes people of considerable importance. Often they came to discuss the political prospects of one or other of their protégés, with a view to raising money for campaign contributions, or simply to look after the expenses of a representative they felt would help them out in Congress or the State Assembly.

"My father was not very political, but he knew all these people. Some of his pals—like Alfred Gormley, who ran the Carnation Milk Company—used to come round to get money for the Republicans and they'd talk politics. I think that was when Nixon was running for governor. My father despised Nixon. He said he wouldn't hire Nixon to shovel shit out of his barn in Covelo. And my mother couldn't stand him—oh boy! Well, it's interesting you see, because Susan's uncle, Ed Valentine, was one of the original people who started Nixon on his career in California. There was a whole group of Southern California people that were Nixon's original backers. They brought him along from nowhere to somewhere, and they were not my father's type.

"But it all started down there in Whittier and Pasadena—in the circle of people that I knew. No question about it, it was very manageable. There was always somebody in Los Angeles you could see who would tell you everything—tell you who was running it, if he wasn't running it himself."

Richard grew up, then, with a sense that things *could* be managed and not, as is the case for most of us, by some remote power elite but by people he knew who passed through his home, called him by name, and even occasionally asked him how he was doing at school or on the tennis court. Because he had unqualified admiration for his parents, he naturally tended to assume that things were in safe hands and that everything was arranged for the best.

Indeed, the Southern California of Richard's childhood was a comfortably ordered and pleasing environment, although it was soon to change out of all recognition.

"It's almost hard to explain now what it was like. Because there was a sense of place. Los Angeles was Los Angeles—it wasn't Westwood, it wasn't Inglewood, it wasn't Watts, it was downtown. If you went to Pasadena, there it was. A place. Or Arcadia. Or Cucamunga. You actually drove *to* these places.

"If you went to Balboa you drove through literally thousands of acres of orange groves before you ever got to the beach, and the only thing on the way was Knott's berry farm. Mrs. Knott made blackberry pies. That's all there was. Just one building, and we always stopped and bought pies. They were so good. On the way to the beach—one building!

"If you went to Santa Barbara, you went on the Friday and came back on the Sunday. I mean, it was a trip. The people in Santa Barbara didn't have anything to do with the people in Los Angeles. And Ventura was hardly even a stop on the road. It was so beautiful and productive—the citrus orchards—I can't recall anywhere in the world that looked like that.

"There used to be a farmer's market on the west side, where Westwood is now, where all the money is today. From Newport Beach down, the whole coastline was Japanese truck farmers—many of those thrown into concentration camps during the war—and they brought all that produce up to the farmer's market in Los Angeles. My mother [Marjorie Connell] would go there once a week. She'd call Roy, one of the market managers, and he'd get some things ready for her. I just had the best time. It was just like an Arab bazaar. All fresh (no refrigeration) vegetables, meat, fish, everything you want to eat. Peanut butter.

"I have a very distinct feeling about certain areas then having their own presence, their own kinds of architecture.

"In Pasadena or any of those communities, everybody had something a bit different. They really showed individual effort. There was no building inspector then, all this stuff we go through now. They'd built the house themselves—it represented their contribution. Whereas today folks have nothing to do with planning the thing, absolutely no contribution as to how the neighborhood looks—all they've done is bought in."

The rapidity of the metamorphosis, together with the realization that it was not to his father's liking, might have given him the first hint that there were forces actively undermining the values he had grown up with.

"I went to school with John Griffith, and his father built Lakewood, on the way to the beach. That was really one of the first big housing developments—one of those things where they're all the same as far as you can see. That was what changed the whole scheme of things. To me that's one of the real crimes of what happened at the end of World War II, when all that technology came back from the war. We just went crazy. To me it's as though you destroyed the individual—consumerized him—so he was no more competent to think for himself.

"We lost it with the freeway system. We just shoved it all together and made it one great mass. We lost the whole show."

These were the perceptions of a man in his fifties, looking back over three decades; judgments that necessarily became clearer and more fully realized as his career progressed. At the time they were confused and contradictory. The freeway system itself, that triumph of the Eisenhower presidency, with all its fresh, uncluttered concrete, was thrilling in its way. It was the rebirth of the "open road," promising the kind of freedom that had always glamorized the automobile. Few among the postwar generation could resist it.

The consequences followed rapidly but were assimilated without thought. As one after another of the towns Richard Wilson had known became mere pockets in the immense concrete waffle of greater Los Angeles, there were always other, more distant destinations to be arrived at even faster. The sense of increasing sameness was numbed by the ability to get somewhere quickly. Monotony should have made many journeys taken for pleasure redundant. Instead, the activity itself, using the car to go somewhere, anywhere, became the main purpose, and characterized the attitude of the time to life itself. In a broader sense, roads were just the current metaphor for a process that had begun with railroads, and that Richard would encounter again with waterworks.

Ten years later, *The New York Times* reflected on that era in an editorial:

> Once upon a time, a road was a friend to man. It enabled the farmer to get his produce more easily to city markets, and it enabled the city man to escape the crowded streets for the quiet, green countryside. Most adults can remember when "a drive in the country" was a pleasant way to spend a Sunday.
>
> At some time in the past thirty years, automobiles and trucks and the roads on which they move ceased to be man's servants and became his masters. The point in time is imperceptible, but probably it can be dated from 1956 when Congress authorized and President Eisenhower approved—with relatively little controversy—the 41,000-mile Interstate Highway System.
>
> It is not commonly realized that this is the most enormous public works project in the history of the world. In cost it is likely to exceed $60 billion by the time it is completed in 1972. In size and complexity, it dwarfs all of mankind's previous engineering works such as the pyramids, the Great Wall of China, the Panama Canal, or Grand Coulee Dam.
>
> The vast program has developed a life of its own, an inherent bureaucratic momentum that seems unstoppable. Every major city from Boston to Los Angeles is festooned, draped—or is it strangled?—with ribbons of concrete. The countryside is levelled and rolled and graded. The road builders march—imperially, relent-

> lessly, inexorably—across stream, meadow and woodland, through parks and nature preserves, through private homes, businesses, and historic sites. As neighbourhoods are sliced in two and cemeteries relocated, neither the quick nor the dead are safe. . . .
>
> The truth is that most Federal and state highway officials are alike in their basic indifference to community values, natural resources or esthetics. Their principal interest is moving people and vehicles in the shortest, cheapest way between two points. They regard concern for a historic neighbourhood, an ecologically important watershed, an unspoiled valley, a grove of handsome trees or a rare stretch of wilderness as sentimental or irrelevant. . . .[1]

Wilson was unusual in being troubled by what he saw happening around him. Undoubtedly he owed this gnawing discomfort to his childhood experience of the ranch above Covelo. He recalled his father telling him, as they stood together at Henthorne one day, looking over the lake at the boundless forest: "This place will be all right until they bring in the hot dog stands."

At school, at college, in the army, he thought of Henthorne often as a refuge, a place where he felt at ease. As the hot dog stands multiplied between Pasadena and the ocean the unspoiled beauty of the northern mountains appealed to him more and more. Yet Henthorne was identified as a place to get away to, a respite from the real work of the world. It took a major event to shake that view.

During Richard's years in the army, his father had been struggling with advancing heart disease. Despite valiant efforts, and a whole year on an exclusive diet of rice, his heart finally failed him. In 1957, toward the end of Richard's army career, came the shocking news that his father had died.

Much of Los Angeles mourned his passing, too. A lengthy obituary in the *Los Angeles Times* acknowledged his celebrity and began: "Tall, handsome Dr. John Wilson is dead. . . ."

"That's when I really began to think about whether I wanted to go back to Covelo."

It could not be denied that his social contacts and the opportunities for a career and easy money were down there in Southern California. Richard's branch of the Grant family, descended from Lewis Grant, stood on the foothills of wealth and influence. Farther up the sunlit slopes were his cousins, Angus Grant's grandsons, Richard and Daniel, and his stepmother's family, the Connells, with the income from Mike Connell's fortune to sustain them.

At the top of the heap, in those days, was whoever might be representing the Chandler family, and in Richard's time, Harry having died, it was Harry's son Norman, and his grandson Otis, who shook the biggest sticks. Another man who stood on top of the pile for a good many years was Asa Call, the president of the Pacific Mutual Insurance Company, who seemed to know better than anyone who was doing what and where. Also counted among this elite were two lawyers from the O'Melveny family. There was Stuart, who inherited the Title Insurance & Trust Company, which had an unrivalled hold on the real estate transactions of Southern California. His business was housed in a mighty, block-sized warren of white stone on Spring Street. Another O'Melveny had the law firm of O'Melveny & Myers, a giant of the legal profession.

His neighbor, Bill Valentine, was credited with a good deal of influence in Los Angeles, as was Bill's brother Ed. The Valentines owned and managed two money-spinning assets inherited from their father. There was Robinson's Department Store on Broadway, and Fullerton Oil, a major oil field in the Fullerton area of L.A. Robinson's was Ed Valentine's business, and a considerable force in the life of the city. Bill was the oil man, and apparently a very effective one.

John Cree Wilson himself had wielded remarkable influence. He had sat on various boards, including that of the city's biggest bank, Sartori's Security–First National, and he had had most of the city's leading lights under his care, as well as such Hollywood titans as Louis B. Mayer and Daryl Zanuck. Much of his influence descended directly to his son John, who inherited his skill, and his position in the establishment. Through him the family became interwoven by marriage with the O'Melvenys and another old California family, the Laphams. Daniel Grant was a powerful supervisor of Santa Barbara, and Richard Grant became the head of the biggest cement company in the state, the very stuff in which California's growth was set.

These few men, with one or two transient qualifiers, constituted the unofficial government of Los Angeles. Their social headquarters was the California Club, a great pile of yellow ochre brick on Flower Street, built in 1929 at a cost that almost ruined the club. The public rooms are of such imposing proportions that they would grace many of the chancelleries of Europe, and their twenty-foot-high walls are opulently paneled in oak bought from the British Admiralty. From these majestic quarters, they distributed their favors and reprimands to the business community. Richard, through Ed Valentine, had direct access to this coterie, and would have had no difficulty in finding a more than comfortable niche in their establishment.

In fact, Richard's interest in the Valentines was neither commercial nor political, but purely romantic. By 1957, Bill Valentine and his wife had died. Their two daughters were in the care of Ed Valentine's family, and Richard had been in the habit of escorting one of them whenever he returned home. Then she disconcerted him by getting married to someone else. The other daughter was Susan, and he found it easy to switch.

"When I got out of the army, she and I went out quite a bit and enjoyed it. She was at Stanford, and she came up to the ranch and she liked it. She was really enamored of the whole thing—she loved Buck Mountain."

He was already taking the move to Covelo very seriously.

"As far as L.A., well, if I'd wanted to go into real estate or some other business I was all connected up. . . . I mean that was a slam dunk. It frankly just didn't appeal to me. My stepmother was not well. She and I were close; she was in Pasadena, and it was really hard for me to leave her. But I felt there's a future here. I really had the feeling that this is a young country, things are going to change. There's values here—things I could relate to on a personal basis."

How far Susan's enthusiasm affected his decision nobody can know. She was an undeniable beauty, vivacious, intelligent, artistic, almost as tall as Wilson, who stands well over six feet. It seemed extraordinary that a girl of her background, wealth, and talent should want to bury herself in the back country, but she was also a very private person with a great craving for the simplicity and serenity of the mountains. They got married in 1960, when she was twenty-two and he was twenty-seven, and they moved to the house on Buck Mountain.

10

"Well, I'm Braggin' a Bit Here . . ."

IT WAS MID-SEPTEMBER when the Wilsons returned to Round Valley from the meeting with Ike Livermore. Richard was greatly encouraged by the older man's sympathy, but it just made him all the more aware of how much help he would need, and how little time there was to arouse opposition to the dam.

Then, to drive that message home, a bizarre event occurred to emphasize just how badly he needed to win more support in the valley. The Eel River Association had chosen to hold its October meeting in Round Valley, of all places, and the purpose was to thrash out, finally, its position on the routing of the water from the dam. Colonel Boerger, the state engineers, various local officials and the state senator, Randolph Collier, had all been asked to speak.

The Lake County supervisors were determined that the water should flow through their county, and furious that the matter was even being discussed. Their most precious asset was Clear Lake, and its name was becoming a joke. It was a big natural lake, the biggest in California, but it was unusually shallow. Hot summers combined with pollution from a bustling holiday population were turning it green with algae, and they thought the Eel River water would clean it out. They seized on the opportunity to demonstrate their discontent.

On the day of the meeting Covelo was invaded by a caravan of two hundred cars and buses. The protesters brought gallon jugs filled with the viridescent muck from the lake to wave under the noses of the officials. The fateful day of the meeting was Friday the thirteenth. From Richard's point of view it was neither a lucky date nor a diplomatic choice of venue. He hoped in vain for some rising indignation from Covelo residents at the sight of these incensed citizens bustling into the valley like a flock of vultures clamoring for Round Valley's blood. It was very disconcerting to see all this energy focused on the wrong objective. When it was all over, he knew he had a lot of work to do quickly to build support for his campaign, and he went back to Elmer. Of all the old guard in the valley, Elmer was the one with whom he had the closest sympathy and mutual respect. If he couldn't win Elmer over, he felt, his chances with the others must be very poor.

When Richard tried to understand the apparent unconcern of the older families in Covelo, he was forced to realize how different his interest was from theirs. As long as those families had lived in the valley, they had depended upon it for their livelihood. It had not always been easy. In the course of a century, many crops and many kinds of livestock had been tried, had succeeded for a while, and then become unprofitable. In some cases disease was the enemy. Wheat, for example, had fallen to black smut fungus. In others, the climate proved too harsh and unpredictable.

Sometimes it was a change in prevailing fashions that left them stranded. The taste for pork, turkey, lamb, and beef fluctuated. The demand for hops failed. Sometimes government busybodies were the enemy, imposing regulations like those that closed down Covelo's dairies and slaughterhouses. Most often economic competition was too stiff, and here Round Valley was always at a disadvantage because of its distance from markets.

Bred into the ranchers of Covelo by many disappointments was a skepticism that did not allow them to wax too lyrical about their valley. They knew what it could do to them. The easygoing lifestyle certainly appealed to them, but there was a risk in becoming sentimentally attached to a piece of land, when financial wisdom might demand that you sell it and move into something else.

Richard and Susan viewed Covelo from a very different perspective. They were financially independent and had come to Round Valley to escape from the artificiality of their privileged existences in the south. Susan came to the mountains as a young bride, to be free at last of the social demands that she found so stifling, and the bitter experiences that followed the death of her parents. For Richard, the hills and the valley were still suffused with the joy he felt as a young boy finally allowed to accompany his father from rich, suburban Pasadena to this wild, unthinkable, extraordinary frontier. So it was a while before they measured the width of the abyss that separated them from their neighbors.

Richard found Elmer up on the hill where he was building his house.

"Well, Elmer," he said, "do you still think your troubles are going to float away with the dam?"

Elmer responded with his toothy, childlike grin and said he'd been doing some thinking. He had made it plain to Richard that he was driven by financial need, but eventually he had been forced to realize that concern for money was exactly why he should oppose the dam with all his might. On reflection, Elmer saw that his problems were not going to be solved by the government at all. On the contrary, they might get worse.

Like many others, he says, he had not thought it through. Elmer recalled his conversion clearly.

"Suppose they had got it passed down there, authorized. It would bring everything to a standstill. You might sit here for twenty years."

In July the engineers had told them that the government wouldn't start buying their property until 1973. For six years at least, land prices would be frozen. But what if things changed? In six years a lot could happen. By 1973 perhaps the dam wouldn't seem so attractive anymore. Costs could escalate. New data could emerge. Politics could change. The water could seem too expensive. That authorization would be a death sentence on the valley. Once imposed, it would take the devil to lift it. Round Valley would be a twilight zone, in limbo.

"Those people would all be settin' here yet," said Elmer in 1987, "and they couldn't sell. I don't think they realized it. I didn't. When you start thinking about it, it gives you a shock."

Once converted, Elmer viewed the activities of his erstwhile comrades in a much different light.

"You know, we had a chamber of commerce here. Well the chamber is supposed to promote your area. I belong to it. So do a bunch of us, but we never went. We got careless, see, and this group got in there—these people who'd bought stuff, like Judge Weber and Glen Davis. And they had this meeting of the chamber of commerce, kind of secret, and they voted to send a letter to the governor that the Round Valley Chamber of Commerce was for the dam. And they sent it."

Sliding past the fact that when the letter was sent Elmer was still a dam supporter, he recalled his outrage.

"Well, I got hold of that, and I called another meeting and we made new bylaws on the thing, that if anything like that comes up, then we had to have a public meeting and notify the whole valley. And then we took a poll, and we sent another letter to the governor to say it wasn't so, and they'd put one over on us. Well, I'm braggin' a bit here . . ." and he smiled complacently.

"The corps just put it out that there was no opposition. And they had opposition. They lied. They absolutely lied. That makes you kinda mad. I hate a liar. I think he'll steal. That is absolutely how I think about it."

Richard carefully disguised his tremendous sense of relief, and received Elmer's change of heart as though it were only natural. At least he now had someone in the valley to plan with, and they both agreed that their next target should be the Indians. While Elmer was able eventually to turn the chamber of commerce around, the Indian Tribal Council presented a much more formidable challenge. Richard knew it was vital to convince the Indians if he was going to demonstrate serious opposition in the valley. Not for the first time, the Indians took an approach that was both perplexing and frustrating to the whites.

The two halves of this community, white and Indian, were separated by thick scar tissue, beneath which much feeling, good and bad, was suppressed. Individuals might be able to establish trusting relationships in special circumstances on particular occasions, but there was an almost insuperable barrier of suspicion between the two groups.

"It was more like a society from the Deep South," Richard says, recalling how it was in those days.

To add to the difficulty, Indians were much less inclined to express a personal opinion on matters affecting the tribes, and to a white man this reluctance often gave the impression of apathy, confusion, or fecklessness.

In reality there was a good deal of discontent within the tribes at the role their chairman had played. It turned out that Warren Lincoln's decision to offer Colonel Boerger the tribal council's support was almost entirely his own idea. The council had barely discussed the matter, and was ignorant of the terms. The problem now was clearly one of "face." While presenting this bland, noncommittal air to the whites, they were looking for a way to resolve their internal dilemma. Eventually, two older women were able to seize the initiative and stage a coup d'etat. Warren Lincoln was ousted by a vote, and the vice-chairman, Norman Whipple, took his place. One of the leaders of the coup was Whipple's mother-in-law, Vivian Frasier. The other was the chairman of the Indian Methodists, Ida Soares.

One crisp and sunny winter's day in 1991, Norman and Ida met to help each other dig into their memories. Norman, now in his fifties, was a tough, stocky character with short-cropped graying hair. He was wearing a plaid shirt and a woolen jacket, and had a small, black baseball hat jammed down on his broad head. Ida was considerably older, and her tiny body had all but vanished beneath a heavy dark coat and slacks, but her head, poised above this shapeless ensemble, glowed with cherubic vitality, and her frequent laughter made Norman seem, at times, older than she was.

Talking about Warren Lincoln, Norman said: "What he did, without even the knowledge of the council, was that he met with the Corps of Engineers. Some way or other, they got to him, and before we knew it we were just about ready to accept the whole program. But that didn't go along after the council found what was going on.

"What I think really happened with Warren Lincoln—he's passed away now—was that it gave him prestige. Saying, 'I'm dealing with the Corps.' He wasn't the only council man. He had another one with him. If they could get what they wanted, you know, and be named into something . . ."

His gestures were more eloquent than his words. It was a matter of pride. Lincoln wanted to be the one who negotiated, and signed, the treaty with the "white chief."

"Then the council reversed the whole thing. They had an election, and voted him out and put me in there."

When the council "reversed itself" and appointed Norman, Richard thought he had the support of the Indians in the bag. He was on good terms with both Norman's wife, Annabelle, and her mother, and he was confident of persuading Norman to bring the Tribal Council out against the dam. But the more he argued, the more remote Norman seemed. Richard was baffled. He was morally certain that Norman was opposed to the dam. He was equally sure that a majority of the Indians were, too. Why didn't Norman exercise his leadership, and persuade them to take a stand against it?

Norman laughed. "You can persuade an Indian so easy. Say for example you're talkin' to an Indian and you say, 'Well, I'm goin' to do this tomorrow, and I'm goin' to need some help. Would you help me? I'll give you ten dollars.' He says, 'That's good.' So he leaves you and meets another guy, who says, 'Hey, I'm going to go out the valley. You want to go for a ride?' 'Sure. Let's go. To hell with the ten dollars.' It's not funny or comical," Norman added, with a short laugh. "That's just the way it is."

"It's our nature, I think," said Ida.

"It is a problem," Norman said, "getting Indians to make up their minds."

Norman's strategy was simple. They would wait and bargain with both sides until they had a decent deal on paper for what they would get if the dam did go through, and what they would get if it didn't. But best of all, he thought, was that it would give his community time to arrive at a mature decision.

"Then we could say to the Indian community, 'If you're "for," then this is what it is. And if you're "against," this is what it is. And we don't do any particular way persuading anybody. So when people come and votes are counted they can't say, 'Well, I didn't understand.' "

With impressionistic slices of meaning, Norman tried to paint a picture of how he saw his responsibilities at that time.

"What the council did—and it was really, really smart and real nice—they didn't say, 'Well, the council is goin' to do this and this.' They says, 'Let the Indian people do it.' "

"Because there was people for and against," broke in Ida. "One lady said, 'This is worse than Peyton Place, this is Hatin' Place.' "

"Even if it went through," said Norman, talking about the dam, "we were going for everything we could get. For example, when the whole plan was made, it was that the Indians would be on the north shore. Okay, but the access to the whole lake was on the south shore. So that was where everything would stop."

The corps had, in fact, fallen in crassly with the mood of the time. The town of Covelo, as they saw it, would be relocated to let the white businessmen take advantage of the tourists. The Indians would be given more land near their reservation, hill land that Ida scornfully characterized as "only fit for rattlesnakes." There, remote from the action, with their second-class status perpetuated, they would continue to be dependent on the whites for employment in white-owned enterprises.

"That was one of the things we were really fighting for. More access to the entrance of the whole thing. We'd want land there, to utilize these people as a business. Recreation."

For many months the Indians refused to declare themselves on the issue. Frustrated, Richard tried to pressure Norman to a decision, until Elmer stopped him and tried a more gentle approach.

"Elmer used to talk to me every day," said Norman, "and . . . he's so slow. Kinda cute . . . and every day he'd say, 'Norman, you got to do this. If you don't do this, we're goin' to end up here.' Really he was an inspiration to keep goin'. I've knew him ever since I was a little bitty feller. Elmer has always been a nice man. He was good.

"But it got to the point where everybody, the county supervisors, the Corps of Engineers, the rest of the valley, were all waiting for the Tribal Council to make a decision."

In those first days, when Richard was trying to stitch together some sort of garment to cover the nakedness of the opposition, the Indian community was no help to him. As Richard traveled around the valley, canvassing for support for his new association, he met with surprising reactions. He had felt sure he could count on Cliff Foster, who was one of the great characters of the valley. Ancient and weathered, he was the Mr. Fixit of Covelo. There was nothing he wouldn't tackle, but he got his biggest charge out of electrical jobs—literally. It was not uncommon for him to stick his wetted finger into a receptacle and say, "Yep, this is 110" or "That's 220, all right."

Apparently his father had met President Lincoln, and, it turned out, Cliff was a great believer in government as guardian of the people in the tradition of Roosevelt and the New Deal. When Richard suggested to Cliff Foster that the Corps of Engineers had something beyond the people's interest and welfare at heart, he became outraged.

"What are you doing, challenging the corps?" he demanded furiously. "They would never be doing this if it wasn't for the good of the people." In all the years that Richard had known him, it was the first time that he had showed any anger.

By contrast there was Bud Barnes, a hard-talking native of Round Valley, raised in the cowboy tradition. He rose through high school to the county road crew and ultimately became road boss. When Bud found out about the plan to dam the valley he was outraged and called Richard on the phone. Like many men with his background, he talked always as though his volume control were stuck on "loud," and with the defiant emphasis of a man standing his ground. On one occasion Richard overheard a checkout girl at Gravier's ask Bud how he was doing. He thrust his face forward and declared:

"I've got plenty of potatoes . . . and a sack of beans . . . *and a friend with an aeroplane who'll come and get me any time I ask him.*"

He was nothing if not peremptory, says Richard.

"He instructed me, as a fellow cow man, to come over some evening because he and Isabel wanted to have a talk. It was toward the end of the day. Bud was in his rocking chair, with his slippers on and his false teeth in a glass on a side table. They were both watching the evening news on TV. He said, 'Dick, this is a great thing you're doing, trying to stop the rascals. Isabel and I have talked it all over. We know this is going to take money to fight, and Isabel and I have decided to give you ten dollars now. AND THERE MAY BE MORE LATER!' Well, then I knew we were on our way."

Los Angeles was about five hundred road miles from Covelo, if you crossed the Coast Range on the Mendocino Pass road, and traveled down Interstate 5. Richard knew every inch of that route. He had business in Los Angeles that he had to attend to regularly, and drove up and down at least once every two months. On his way south he would pass through either San Francisco or Sacramento. By taking the alternative route back, he could keep his finger on the three political pulses of California.

As soon as he had Elmer sworn in to keep up the campaign in Round Valley, he planned to go south again, scheduled to meet with several people he hoped to enlist in his cause. As he was about to leave, all hell broke out in the feed lot on Dingman Ridge; one of the calves was in trouble, and the only available ranch hand had broken his arm chasing Zybies off the property. Richard was four hours late when he got into his Volvo and tore out of the valley, still wearing jeans, boots, and a dirty farm-supply shirt, with a hamburger beside him in his upturned hat.

11

A Rancher in a Stained Hat

RISING UP from the shoreline of San Francisco, on the south side of the bay, steeply terraced rows of mansions, mile upon mile of them, display their ever more elaborate pillars, pediments, cornices, and curlicues. On these costly ribs of rock, from Pacific Heights to Russian Hill, sits much of the gold and silver of Comstock and the virgin redwood of Mendocino—all consumed in less than a century. Once over this gilded crest and down the other slope to more mundane thoroughfares, the scale of grandeur diminishes. Down there, where the roller coaster roads flatten out, in a quiet avenue between California Street and Geary Boulevard, lives Lewis Butler, attorney-at-law, and one of those who had seen California's troubles growing a while back.

Butler is in his sixties now, a tall, impressive fellow with good features and pale, graying hair. He views the world with a bland expression that gives little hint of his passion for egality. His well-cut, light gray suits denote dignity with accessibility. His unlined face suggests an enviable ability to wrestle with the world's troubles without being consumed by them. He lives in a nicely appointed house that understates its generous proportions, valuable by virtue of its location but bought at a time when the price was reasonable.

He was born in the late twenties to a liberal but well-to-do family, was raised in California and "did his bit in the navy" just before finishing law school. The ultimately reputable firm of Pillsbury, Madison, Sutra, one of the country's great legal mills, welcomed him with open arms and offices. He could have remained there for the rest of his life.

He spent ten years with Pillsbury, Madison—ten years that he considers, in retrospect, to have been almost totally wasted. One sunny afternoon in his living room he described how this charming, apt, and elegant personage had become a crusader. It was a sense of futility—sharpened by Kennedy's election to the presidency—that drove him to Washington to try for a job in the Peace Corps. With characteristic self-deprecation, he explained: "I found out afterward that I was the only Republican to apply, so no matter how big an idiot I was, I was a useful person to have around."

It should be quietly assumed, of course, that he was the only Republican to apply for a job of some authority, because he went off not with just a headband, jeans, and sneakers, but as the new deputy director of the Peace Corps in Malaysia. Before leaving for Kuala Lumpur with his wife, Sheanna, and his two children, he secured their return by buying the house on Commonwealth Street. Four years later, "having declared my independence" and having made contact with a more unruly reality, he returned to San Francisco to set up the kind of law practice that made sense to him.

"I had a close friend from law school—Pete McCloskey—who had just successfully sued to stop an overhead power line running out to the Stanford Linear Accelerator. In 1964 there was no such thing as an environmental movement—the word wasn't even heard of—but I thought that sounded like a lot of fun and I didn't know what else to do, so we started a law firm—Butler & McCloskey—to deal with what we called 'conservation problems.'

"Pete already had a successful law firm in Palo Alto, so it was never really Butler & McCloskey, it was Pete being nice to me so that I could have another name on the door of this stupid little rented office down here in San Francisco.

"So we went around representing various people who had only one thing in common—none of them had any money or paid their lawyers. We acquired very funny clients, and that went on for two or three years. I made my living—I wrangled—working on problems with black unemployment, supported by the Ford Foundation, et al.

"In 1965, a bunch of us started the Planning and Conservation League—an environmental lobby. Bill Evers, a friend of mine from school and the navy, was one of them. His mother had started something called the Roadside Council to keep billboards off the highway. There were three extraordinary women in Marin County in the thirties who started the Marin Conservation League and had gotten Mount Tamalpais turned into a state park—all wealthy dowager ladies who wanted to beautify their turf over there. It's a strange thing, but the conservationists in those days were all Republicans, like Evers, because they'd come out of the families that had property and had gone to the mountains and wanted to save things.

"So Bill grew up in that tradition. He'd taken over as president of the Roadside Council, and they were trying to save Lake Tahoe, but they were totally out to lunch as to how to deal with the legislature. They [the lawmakers] were very nice to you, and invited you to come and testify, and then the vote was rigged, and off they'd go.

"So the conservationists came to the conclusion that if everyone else had a lobbyist, they needed one, too. They didn't know what the hell a lobbyist did, but you ought to have one.

"The Sierra Club didn't have one either, so we got a guy who had been doing some work with the Sierra Club, named Zierold, and he became a lobbyist. The Sierra Club was in on the deal and we sent this guy to Sacramento and he was to go around fighting for bills that we were interested in, which were mainly to keep freeways from wrecking farmland or to keep power lines from going all over the countryside, stuff like that.

"We were very ineffectual, but we were passionate. And it was the only statewide conservation lobby in the United States. Just showing up there was something, because then they had to deal with you.

"At that time a guy named Alfred Heller was doing good stuff for the environment with an outfit called California Tomorrow. He had a magazine called *Cry California*, and they were doing articles saying, 'Hey, the water plan is crazy' and, 'Chewing up farmland for freeways isn't doing any good.' There was a whole sentiment around then to support these things. And of course there was air pollution in L.A., and water pollution, so we came along at about the right time, and even though we didn't accomplish a lot we worked right along and I had to learn something about politics in Sacramento.

"Then Pete ran for Congress. We closed the office. I ran his campaign, and, to our great amazement, he beat Shirley Temple. That was the fall of '67."

With his reputation fortified by that success he reopened the office. The Planning and Conservation League became a force to be reckoned with, at least in Northern California.

"Just about the time Pete went to Congress I had a call from Heller. He said there was some rancher in his office and that I ought to see him, and—I remember very well, because it was about six-thirty at night—it must have been November—this guy comes to the building and knocks on my door, and I let him in, and I remember this very well, too, he's got on a dirty hat—a short-brimmed Stetson, stained, very carefully stained, and a dirty shirt and dirty pants and dirty boots, and he said his name was Richard Wilson.

"He said he had a problem. Had I heard of the Dos Rios Dam? No. Had I heard of Round Valley? No. He got out a map and showed me. I saw the town marked Covelo. I said, so what's the story? Is the dam supposed to flood out this CoVELo place (putting the accent in the middle of the word). He said the name of the town is not CoVELo—it's COvelo."

Lewis's mispronunciation of "Covelo" illuminated the problem dramatically. Beyond a thirty-mile radius of Round Valley, virtually nobody knew how to pronounce the word Covelo, because they had never heard it spoken. In a country where multiple millions are spent on advertising to win name recognition, how do you hope to save a town nobody has heard of, with a name nobody can pronounce? And do it in a few months?

Richard outlined the situation, and Lewis, who believed that lost causes should be fought on principle, recognized that this one was a dilly.

"I said to Richard, 'You don't have a legal problem. I mean you don't need a lawyer, you just have a huge political fight on your hands,' which, by the way, it never occurred to me could be won. And frankly I didn't expect to have a lot to do with him then.

"I do remember also asking Richard, 'How many people like you are there up there?' And he said, 'Oh, a few.'

"I didn't realize that this was a one-man show. All I knew about him was that he was a rancher in a stained hat.

"I said, 'Well, it sounds important. We have the Planning and Conservation League, and we ought to get together with the Sierra

Club and see if we can't help you.' Because the Corps of Engineers was supposed to build this dam, and we always had a kind of gut instinct that if the Corps of Engineers was for something, then it must be bad.

"After all, we knew what the Corps of Engineers was doing in general. It was paving over Los Angeles. I have an uncle who had been an officer and later a general in World War II in the corps, and at some point I asked him about it. I really wondered what they were about. And he said that the Corps of Engineers in the twenties and thirties had been a great organization. He had been in charge of building Treasure Island out here in the bay, and he said in those days it was really run by the military, and the things they did were the highest priority kind of things.

"But now it's this gigantic bureaucracy that lives off federal money. So he'd kind of confirmed my bias that a lot of the stuff they did was the old rivers and harbors boondoggle. Political pork barrel. But people didn't know. The corps had this heroic image. People thought it was sacrosanct—beyond criticism."

In those days the Wilsons kept an apartment in San Francisco, on Arguello near the park. Richard returned there that evening after his meeting with Lewis Butler and peeled off his work clothes, well satisfied with his progress. On this same day he had wrestled with both Zola's errant cows, and America's sacred cows. It was a healthy combination. He liked very much the mixture of physical and intellectual effort. The idea of balancing politics with practical labor was one that had always attracted him. Richard believed there was a natural, down-home wisdom only to be learned on the land, something that in his own father's words "straightened a man out." Now barely 2 percent of the population lived that way. No wonder, he thought, things had gotten out of kilter.

The meeting with Lewis Butler had gone well. Clearly, they liked each other, and it would certainly become very important to have someone watching things in Sacramento. And Heller had promised to give him what support he could with his magazine. There was much more to this California Tomorrow than he'd realized. These were serious people grappling with serious problems, and they looked like a valuable resource.

Not a bad day's work. Richard called Susan in Covelo, said goodnight to the kids, and collected messages. Most were from Los Angeles. He had meant to sleep in San Francisco and leave in the morning, but he was feeling too alive, too vibrant to stay still. If he left for L.A. now, he could nap somewhere on the way, get his other business done early, and have time to look up other people he hoped might help him. He liked the long car journeys, and used them to think things through. He threw his farm gear into a bag, pulled on casual clothes, and by nine he was threading his way through the nighttime traffic on 19th Avenue and heading south.

12

An Invitation to Battle

UNTIL THE DAM threatened to wash his world away, Richard had never had to account for Covelo to his friends in Pasadena. Except for the rare few who had traveled that far north, the world he inhabited remained a mystery, and they could not comprehend why he had chosen to live there. When they joked and joshed him about it, he was just as flippant in his replies, and talked about good water and clean air. Now, however, that he needed their help, he had to make a serious effort to confront their ignorance and indifference. He found that it really was as though he inhabited a different country, with customs and expectations as exotic as any in the Third World.

In the long hours of driving, he tried to prepare himself for their questions. What was so important about the north coast? Why should they try to preserve a part of the world they never saw, of which they knew little and cared less? The more he considered the problem the more dramatic the alienation of north from south seemed to him, and the more challenging the problem of finding common ground, particularly since what he was really asking was their help in maintaining the separateness.

The fact that Covelo was shown on almost every map of California published anywhere was not a measure of its importance, but rather of its isolation. And it does signal a rather strange state of affairs. The state of California, from the tip at Crescent City to the toe at Tijuana, is eight hundred miles long. People who don't know the state at all identify it with images of Hollywood, surfing beaches, and the uglier phenomena of Los Angeles. This crude and obsolete array of symbols denotes what people locally know as Southern California, which extends roughly from Ventura to the Mexican border.

Those who know enough to make the distinction realize that there is also a Northern California, centering around San Francisco (although Sacramento is usually included) and symbolized by the Golden Gate Bridge, trolley cars, and the bay. Few appreciate that San Francisco and Los Angeles are four hundred miles apart. Even fewer are aware that San Francisco, far from being in the northern part of the state is actually at the middle. And for the great majority, including most Californians, some three hundred miles of mountainous territory north of the Bay Area is off the map altogether.

As a result, little of what goes on up there has rated much attention from the rest of the state and even less from the world at large. California's far-northern counties make up more than a quarter of the state's total area, and yet the population, approximately a million, is scarcely enough to fill one good-sized suburb of Los Angeles. With so few people scattered so widely, any small gathering of houses is worth a mention. Mina, on a dirt road north of Covelo, was given the same status by cartographers as Ojai, near Santa Barbara. Ojai harbored seven thousand people. Mina, when last seen, boasted one building with a subpost office and a dry gas pump.

Those forty thousand square miles of rocks and rivers have been California's larder, a vast storehouse for five out of the six great natural resources of the state. Only the oil, so far, has come from the south. The furs, the gold, the fish, the timber, and the water have come preponderantly from the north.

The larder has been thoroughly plundered. The furs and gold are about done. The fish are seriously imperiled. The last of the old redwoods are under seige, and a good part of the available water has already been diverted to farms, homes, and industries farther south. California lumber has provided homes for countless millions here and abroad; northern water has raised trillions of dollars in crops in the Central Valley. In the process, fortunes have been made and empires built.

Richard knew that there was nothing surprising or revelatory about this. For two hundred years America had fueled its growth by the unrestrained exploitation of its natural resources. Since the founding of the Republic it had been an article of faith that Americans had the right, even the duty, to use this land and all it had to offer. The Indians lost it because, it was said, they had no business wasting such God-given bounty. The new Americans needed it to fulfill a manifest destiny.

Now it was finally becoming apparent that Nature, as we needed her to be, could not sustain the demands made on her. Furthermore, Nature was one, and her processes were interdependent. Not very long ago, most people thought you could take every fish out of the rivers and oceans and all else would remain the same. Some still seem determined to do so, as if fish existed only to be fried, or trees to be logged. For such people, the general rush to the south of California was a blessing, leaving them to operate largely unsupervised in this forgotten wilderness of the north. Yet it would not be too farfetched to suggest that these northern counties were to California what the Amazon rainforest was to the world. In 1968 these were still novel, even subversive, concepts for most people, and as Richard grappled with them himself, he knew there would be many in the south who would find them quite obscure and unacceptable.

In a situation so heavily weighted against them, there was one factor that Wilson and his supporters thought might give them a chance—a very slim chance. It was a subtle change in the mood of the nation, one that Lewis Butler had already identified. Some sections of the public were beginning to rebel against obvious and arbitrary damage, like pollution.

Unfortunately, voters were a long way from recognizing more general environmental issues. The very word *environment* was still as little charged with significance as the word *relationship* had been in the forties. Given time, enough time, this new awareness might come to their aid, but the generation that blossomed into flower power in the sixties, was absorbed either in an inner-directed revolution around issues of the soul or in violent opposition to the war in Vietnam.

Secure in the wealth that the despised "straights" of the fifties had amassed through the Eisenhower years, they were engaged in exposing and examining their consciences. To the extent that they related at all to the nuts and bolts of government ("the system," as they knew it), their tendency was to deny validity to all of it. In this dropout climate the establishment was, if anything, even more free to go its own way, albeit with some uneasiness about the future.

It was true that, lately, certain so-called "environmental" matters had surfaced. In the bureau's projects on the Trinity River and elsewhere, fish had suffered. Some reservoirs were silting up, others were leaching out. The corps also was confronting some neighborhood resistance to their less than beautiful concrete levees. But both agencies were adapting to the coming age of the environmental impact statement. Both were very well equipped to deal with paperwork, and they saw it by and large as another extension of the bureaucratic activity on which they and the legislators thrived. All in all Richard Wilson thought it was too early to hope for an ecological backlash. A more promising approach might be to rouse indignation at the way this plan had been foisted on valley dwellers and taxpayers alike.

The general concept of the State Water Project was published as a bulletin by the Department of Water Resources in 1957 when Harvey Banks was the director, and Pat Brown was governor. Titled "The California Water Plan," it was a magnificent example of visionary engineering. In its hundreds of glossy pages, it described just what could be done with all—absolutely all—the water in California, to further the prospects of the state and its inhabitants. It reached out into the farthest corner of the state, and not a drop that fell escaped its Olympian eye. It counted every rivulet, stream, lake, or raging torrent that coursed above or dwelled beneath the crust of California. It laid out the guiding principles by which the philosopher-engineers had arrived at their conclusions, and then described in detail how they would use all the remaining available water resources of the state to fulfill what they took to be society's expectations.

The project that emerged from the plan was known as the State Water Project. It was the backbone of the present system—the California aqueduct and the various organs attached to it, which funnels some two million acre feet of water annually from north to south. The great arguments of the time focused on the usefulness and the cost of this first stage. After all the governor was asking for a hefty bond issue of $1.75 billion. The debate also dealt with some major political conflicts in the Sacramento Delta area, with its dense population and rich industrial and agricultural interests.

All these immediate and controversial matters kept the media busy, and it is hardly surprising that plans to get more water from the Eel

River at a later date received little attention. Yet it was all there in the plan. The state engineers were nothing if not thorough. They devoted 120 pages to a list of local water projects throughout the state. Round Valley was included among the regional projects, and earned one long paragraph describing how the valley's "ultimate requirements" of water would be met by irrigation canals, as part of the general plan.

There was certainly no hint that these "ultimate requirements" would turn into a "final solution" by drowning. There were maps showing just how Round Valley was to be irrigated, and they are a joy to behold. There are many of them, and they fold out to several times the width of the book. The colors are pleasant pastel washes laid over light brown contours and boundary lines. Aquamarine defines areas where lakes and reservoirs are already established. Vivid brick red splashes aptly show the boldest proposals of the planners. Purple patches indicate projects of local importance, while the agricultural land supposed to benefit from the irrigation projects are shaded in beige.

On sheet 5 of plate 5, Round Valley is by far the largest beige area west of the Sacramento Valley. Close by, to the north of it, the small Franciscan Reservoir is outlined in purple, but it is overlaid by the larger brick red area of Etsel Reservoir. Clearly Round Valley, as the largest piece of farmable land in the Coast Range, was an important service area. No layperson observing this map would dream that it could one day be colored blue and submerged.

In 1957, when the plan was published; in the succeeding years when the legislature battled over water rights and age-old disputes between north and south; in 1959 when Governor Brown was authorized to go to the public for the money; and in 1960 when the bond issue was passed, newspapers carried an abundance of stories about the water plans. Not once in that time was there any mention of the possibility that such a large and productive—let alone beautiful—valley could be flooded. In particular, the *San Francisco Chronicle,* a major newspaper that included Round Valley in its bailiwick and had a traditional interest in water issues, carried no hint of it.

In 1963, when Governor Brown announced that it was time to go on to the next even more costly phase of the plan—a $12 billion project (at today's prices) to capture the north coast rivers—maps appeared in the press, but the main configuration of dams and reservoirs was the same, and Round Valley was still clearly protected as an area to be serviced.

In 1964, the news focused even more closely on the Middle Fork of the Eel, as the *Chronicle* reported that "an Upper Eel River project costing more than $200 million has been added to the State Water Project" and that it is "the first to be added to the multibillion dollar state plan to develop water in the north and transport it to arid Southern California." Although the reporter wrote about the threat to salmon runs on the Eel, and was evidently open to discussing potential hazards and disadvantages, there was still no hint of a threat to Round Valley.

Then in one bulletin, number 136 published that same year, the idea actually surfaced in print. It was the last of four variations on a theme. Anyone reading the four proposals could have guessed that this was the one the engineers preferred. The first three were either smaller or too costly, but in the fourth: "Water would be conserved in a large Dos Rios Reservoir, which would inundate Round Valley. . . . This plan would combine the very good Dos Rios damsite with the large storage potential of Round Valley, and would enable full development of the Middle Fork Eel River." As in all such engineering proposals, the political implications were simply ignored.

Until the state and the Corps of Engineers unveiled their plan as a virtual done deal in 1967, a serious proposal to use Round Valley as a reservoir was never entertained in public. All the published maps and reports continued to foster the illusion that the state intended to protect the valley and irrigate it for the benefit of its agriculture. Yet all this time, unbeknownst to innocent readers of the daily papers, there is no doubt that there were engineers in the Department of Water Resources who believed that Round Valley would and should be drowned.

From Richard Wilson's point of view, this was nothing less than a conspiracy by state officials to foist their pet project on an unsuspecting people, and to ride roughshod over the valley and its inhabitants. To a man like Richard, already accustomed to being heard and taken seriously, such treatment was an affront. It struck him as an outrageous act of bureaucratic arrogance, and it made his wholehearted opposition to the project a certainty.

It was not long before Richard identified, to his own satisfaction, just who had engineered this coup. His finger pointed to the vigorous and ambitious director of water resources, William Gianelli, a wartime officer in the Corps of Engineers personally appointed by the new governor, Ronald Reagan. For all the talk of desperate water needs, Richard saw very quickly that the Dos Rios Dam would also satisfy a different kind of need. It would allow the Department of

Water Resources to keep its 4,300 employees on the payroll.* Already Gianelli had set up offices at Red Bluff, in the north of the state, staffed them with engineers, and spent several million dollars on planning and surveys. While the Corps of Engineers might be at the head of the project and responsible to the federal government for its execution, the work would be carried out by the same huge establishment of engineers, contractors, and suppliers that had been put together by the state to build the first stage of the water plan. When that first great job was done, where would this carefully assembled workforce go? There had to be another project.

The way in which it had been managed, and the motivation behind this boondoggle, appeared all too clear to him. It seemed obvious that the information had been held back until the corps was ready. Opposing the state government, when plans were still fluid, would have been difficult enough, but not out of the question. Opposing the Corps of Engineers was almost unthinkable. And when the corps came bearing a gift from Washington of a quarter billion dollars, what politician would be foolhardy enough to refuse?

Richard might have found it very satisfying to go after Gianelli right away, but he knew that would be foolish and fruitless. The benefits of water were not questioned. Ever since it was used to blast the gold out of the Sierras, its power to create wealth had brightened every ambitious eye. From the twenties on, two propositions became the unquestioned pillars of the state. First, California was synonymous and identical with growth. The two concepts were mystically and inseparably united. In this sense the Golden State became the apotheosis of the American vision as it was promoted in the nineteenth century; the hyperbolic curve that began its slow crawl along the ground when the wagons moved west and took its final, triumphant fling into the infinite in California.

The second proposition followed inevitably from the first. There could be no growth without water; therefore, whatever water was needed must automatically be placed at the service of the state. It is written into the state's constitution. Obstacles were purely technical. Under the pressure of growth, they would inevitably be overcome. By the same token all water that did not contribute to California's growth was labeled as "wasted."

*4,300 in July '68, down to 4,000 in July '69: Doody memo to staff

Knowing these things, Richard understood that he would have to show first that the dam was a bum deal. He would have to tangle with the engineers. It was the harder road to take. It would involve building a case on technical and financial grounds in an area where the corps was always considered most competent, but it had to be attempted.

The public hearing Richard had anticipated was less than a month away. The notice had arrived in Covelo on the day of his hurried departure. It would be his first opportunity to confront Col. Frank Boerger, the soldier whom he was determined to defeat in battle. Even though the battle would be fought with arguments, statistics, reputations, connections, and press releases instead of with muskets and cannon, the outcome would be no less serious. Richard's little band of rebels, his "Covelo militia," was defending the valley against an occupying army, yet it was one of the oddities of this "phony war" situation that his enemy had scarcely even heard of him, and certainly would not be taking him very seriously. Like the leader of any well-trained regiment marching against civilians, the colonel was surely feeling confident of the outcome.

It was vital to stop that army in its tracks, and he had a few months, no more. He would be fighting for time, gasping for it. He was determined to build a sober, respectable case against the dam—no wild, rhetorical attacks, no flights of fancy. He'd kill them with facts and figures, if possible their own. But there is no doubt that it helped him mightily to identify the enemy in person. His anger at Gianelli's maneuvers, at the corps's arrogance, and at the Met's complacent power plays was a slow-burning core that fueled his campaign to the end, and justified all the dirty tricks he might be lucky enough to play himself. As it turned out, there were a few.

Richard's stay in Los Angeles and Pasadena was short but fruitful. He met and spoke with a number of people, including his brothers and other members of the Grant and Connell families, who promised to help if they could. There were some state senators and assemblymen he needed introductions to. He tried to gauge the state of knowledge in the Los Angeles business community in regard to Dos Rios, but scarcely anyone had heard of it. In one respect though he struck lucky. One of the Connells tipped him off about a brilliant press agent who might help him with his campaign. The name was Curtis Roberts. He operated out of San Francisco, and Richard arranged to meet him on his way north.

13

Curt Lights Up

CURT ROBERTS was an inspired promoter of political people and causes. He had successfully sold many politicians to the electorate, including two mayors of San Francisco, Jack Shelley and Joe Alioto. He had worked for a rising political star, Alan Cranston, as well as for Rockefeller in his challenge to Barry Goldwater, and he was in great demand by action committees trying to get this or that proposition past the voters.

In the sixties, before polling and automation changed everything, brilliant ideas counted for more, and Curt was a prolific source of them. He is remembered by many for driving a Southern Pacific train up San Francisco's busy Market Street to publicize the United Way, but he devised many other equally effective, if less bizarre campaigns. A colleague of his, Wes Willoughby, found him awesomely innovative, and cites his billboards for Shelley's mayoral bid as an example. They were years ahead of their time, he remembers.

"Everybody then thought you had to have reams of words—Vote for Jack Francis Shelley, Democratic Candidate for Mayor of the City of San Francisco, the man you can trust, and so on. Curt just had a picture and three words: VISION SHELLEY MAYOR.

"When Jack saw it he was horrified. 'You can't do that!' he said. But Curt persuaded him, and he won. These days it's normal. Then his posters were the talk of the town. He was one of those people—well, you could almost see the bulbs light up."

For all Curt's brilliance as a promoter of other people's careers, probably the most successful job he did was on himself, and he was very proud of it. Starting in radio in the thirties, in the company of friends like Ralph Edwards and Art Linkletter, he joined in the general infatuation with the demon rum, and soon discovered himself to be an alcoholic. He quit with the help of AA, and nothing he did later could surpass that triumph. He became a mainstay of the AA movement in Northern California, and many celebrated men in sport, business, and the media acknowledged a great, if unpublicized debt for the strength he lent them when they needed it—most usually, of course, at night.

This early struggle provided a moral background to his career, as well as a network of influential admirers. He was executive director for many years for the United Crusade, which became United Way, and he rarely, if ever, took on clients he couldn't sympathize with.

Once met, he was unforgettable. He was a very small man, hardly five foot four, thin, and physically frail. He was most often fastidiously dressed in a three-piece suit, with button-down collar, regimental tie and horn-rimmed glasses. His silver-white hair was carefully controlled, his shoes immaculately polished, and he used all this formality and precision to set off a wild and irreverent sense of humor that delighted everyone. He was a liberal Republican, of the kind known in those days as "Tom Kuchel Republicans"—very much after the style of Ike Livermore, whom he knew, and of Lewis Butler whom he soon met.

He lived in some style on Russian Hill, in the bottom half of a house in Lombard Street, and it was there that he and Richard first met. The rapport was instantaneous. Curt had an automatic distaste for government by bureaucracy, and for great, soulless projects that sacrificed real lives for the undetermined good of the amorphous many. Richard began to explain his purpose, but Curt cut him off.

"I'm ahead of you," he said, and picked up a piece of greenish newsprint from a table. "I guess they didn't tell you I'm a fly fisherman. Here, let me read to you. This is Bud Boyd writing in the chronicle *Sporting Green,* three years ago. I quote: 'This column has put the magnifying glass to the Guv's big water plan'—that's yours—'and realistically noted that the fish life losses will be the greatest in California's history.'

"And again here he says: 'We can already see the handwriting on the wall when looking at the dams proposed for the Eel River system.'

"There's nothing here about your valley, but do you know how many sport fishing licenses are sold in California every year? I'll tell you. Two million. Of course, those guys have either forgotten about this, or never read it, but if you want to pay me to bring it to their attention—what a job. I'll take it. And I'll do the hard stuff for free."

He grinned, stubbed out his cigarette, and lit another. It was his only obvious—all too obvious—weakness. "I can lick the booze," he told Wes once, "but not the other." He smoked unfiltered Camels, constantly. He was in his fifties when Richard came to know him, and already emphysema had shortened his breath, but his mind was still as bright as a glowing filament, and the lightbulbs were starting to pop.

Richard got Curt and Lewis Butler to meet with him the next day at Lewis's office on Bush Street in downtown San Francisco, and Richard told them stories from the Wild West of Mendocino County. His spare, phlegmatic style suited the characters and situations he described. He recounted some of Round Valley's violent history, and talked about his childhood experiences there. Bright images of forests and meadows, mountains, and deep canyons began to supplant the Hollywood stereotypes of John Wayne country in his listeners' minds. He tried to give them a feel for what it was like to live with the natural boundaries of watersheds and high passes, and the strong sense of belonging that people in and around the valley would naturally develop.

Already Richard was beginning to toy with thoughts that stretched far into the future. He had ideas for a different political structure that would define administrative limits in a much more rational way: an Eel River County, for example, that would encompass the entire watershed of the Eel, and have control over its own resources. In just a few short months of frenzied activity, he had uncovered in himself a powerful streak of idealism. The desire to save the valley became inextricably linked with thoughts of why and what for, and he found, to his own surprise, that he had been subconsciously accumulating information and ideas on the subject ever since he first came to identify with Henthorne. It was a startling time. So many things he had not examined before: His feelings about Los Angeles, his choice of history as a college major, and the very decision to live the life he did were all suddenly illuminated and given a new dimension.

He spoke of none of this, but something of these passionate stirrings communicated itself through his manner and laconic speech, and gave his listeners a strong sense of his conviction and determination. Curt, who had a sharp ear for a likely candidate, already saw Richard as ideal campaign material, and became as eager as Lewis was to see this valley and its occupants.

"Why they don't just kick the engineers out, I don't know," he said.

Richard smiled. "Well it is strange the way they roll over on their backs when the corps comes along. There are plenty of people up there who don't want this dam. But they think if the government wants it, they can't stop it."

"What kind of people?" asked Lewis.

"Well, ranchers, Indians, a lot of people in town."

"Who else has come out against it, apart from you?" said Curt. "Is there a city council, a mayor?"

"That's a big part of the problem," Richard explained. "Covelo is unincorporated. It's not a city. Officially everything comes from Ukiah—deputies, road maintenance, inspection, the whole bureaucracy. But Ukiah's a long way away. Unofficially the town is still run from the Masonic Hall by those same old families, and they don't like interference. They'd rather go under than lose control. I guess I qualify as interference. But Elmer's working on that, and I think he'll be able to pull them around."

"So there's you and Elmer fighting this thing?" Curt sounded amazed. "What about the county officials? I suppose they think it's great."

"What they think is hard to say," said Richard sourly, "but thank heavens they are officially on record as opposing the flooding of Round Valley. They took that position in 1964, and we're doing everything we can to keep them to it. We have Jim and Nita McCombs—you'll meet them—breathing down their necks all the time. There's only one supervisor on the board I'm really confident of, and that's Joe Scaramella. He won't change his mind, but he won't fight, either. Its not his district, and the others don't talk to him about it.

"Harvey Sawyers is the supervisor for Round Valley, and he's from Willits. He says he's opposed to the dam, but Jim McCombs says he's practically sleeping with the corps. He's the county representative on the Eel River Association, which is just a straight-out water lobbying front for the Met, and I'm pretty sure he tells them a different story."

"What reason do they give for opposing it?" asked Lewis.

"First, they lose the tax base. The county makes fifty thousand dollars a year in taxes. Second, there's the extra strain on the county resources—schools, health, roads, and so on—from all the construction workers that would come in. For them it's primarily a question of money. If the Feds could come up with a big enough bribe, the supes would cave in. And of course the corps is always telling them how the lake will bring untold wealth from tourists. Joe's the only one who says he cares about saving the land, even though it's the biggest spread of good farming land in the whole county."

"Well, what happens next?" asked Curt. "You said there was going to be some kind of meeting."

"Yes. On the fifteenth of December—that's three weeks from now—the corps will hold a public hearing at the Willits High School."

"Are you ready for it?" asked Curt.

"Well, we're pushing ahead. I'm in the process of registering the Round Valley Protective Association as a non-profit, so that we can recruit supporters and raise money. Then we'll call a meeting in Covelo to get things started. I'm working on a speech for the hearing. The main problem is that we don't know much more about the dam than it says here in this notice.

"It's going to be a rockfill dam, 730 feet high—it gets higher every time they mention it. In 1964 it was 600 feet, in July it was 700 feet, now it's almost the highest dam in America, and one of the first things I want to know is where all that rock is coming from. They call it 'borrow,' and you can imagine the amount of it, and what it costs to move it. That's got to be the largest single item of cost, and an extra mile would add millions. They always underestimate costs, and that's one of the ways to attack them.

"They say it will hold more than 7.5 million acre-feet of water. That's like Shasta and Oroville put together. Definitely the biggest man-made lake in California. Only Clear Lake is bigger. That's if it ever fills up. I don't think it will. There's not enough water. It's too high up the river, and it'll be full of mud.

"Then they want to drill a hole seventeen feet wide and twenty-one miles long through the Coast Range to take the water to Grindstone Creek and then into the Sacramento River. The state has to find $153 million for that."

"Why?" asked Curt. "If the corps pays for the dam, why not the tunnel, too?"

With a touch of weariness, Richard went over ground that was already too familiar.

"The only reason the corps gets to build this dam, is because it can claim a flood control function. It's not supposed to build dams for water storage. That's the bureau's business. In reality, as everyone knows, this dam is being built to send the Eel River south to Los Angeles. But the corps claims the dam will, and I quote, 'effect substantial reduction in peak flows along the main Eel River.' Somehow they calculate that this is worth $57 million in flood damage. The state has to pay back the rest over a hundred years. The interest rate is only 3.25 percent, but it's bound to go up.

"Since the state can't even find the money to finish what it has already begun, this is supposed to be a terrific deal. We get the dam now, and future generations can eat it.

"But the tunnel has nothing to do with flood control, so the state has to buy that now. For $153 million. This whole project is a white elephant, and I am sure we can prove it, but we have to get hold of the facts and so far all we've got are these three paragraphs. Somewhere there is a full engineering report on this project, and as soon as I can get hold of it, I'll find someone qualified to take it apart. Meanwhile, all I can see to do is make enough noise so that it doesn't slip through unnoticed. Obviously we need to pack the meeting in Willits with as many people as we can."

Lewis came back from the other side of the room with three cups of coffee. Curt, who was taking notes with large flourishes of a pen, said, "Okay. You get a lot of local people to come along on the fifteenth and say 'We don't like your dam.' Does the corps have to listen?"

"Listen, yes. Change anything, no. They have to incorporate the objections into their final report and send it off to Washington. But of course the state has to approve it, too, and that's another story. Lew and I have been talking about that."

Curt pulled a crested Zippo lighter from his vest pocket and lit another Camel. Lewis poured more coffee and said, "As far as I can tell, and amazing as it seems, there is no legislation needed for this project. I've got something here I'll read to you. 'Under the terms of this act'—that's the State Water Project—'the legislature is denied its traditional powers to approve or disapprove construction of additional units of the project as they are undertaken.'

"And then, 'Unless this proposal is reversed by the Supreme Court itself, we can be sure that every effort will be made by Southern California representatives to further weaken historic northern rights to northern waters.' That was written by Senator Charles Brown, who incidentally represented Owens Valley in his arguments against approving the State Water Project in 1960. His warnings have come home to roost.

"But in the case of Dos Rios, the state has to give approval to Washington before it can be authorized by Congress, and that means the governor has to recommend it. The way Reagan works, it seems he relies on his cabinet. If they say go, he'll sign it. But there's nothing to stop the water committees of the Senate and the Assembly from holding hearings if they want to. And their advice would have to carry some weight.

"Normally, if we could get to them, the water committees would be our main hope, but it doesn't look good. The Assembly committee has fifteen members. Ten of them are from Los Angeles or from agribusiness districts. The chairman is Carly Porter, who sponsored the bill that put the whole State Water Project in business, so his record is at stake here, too.

"The Senate committee doesn't look much better. There are fewer of them—only nine members—but seven of those are from Los Angeles and points south. I asked John Zierold, our lobbyist, about this and the truth is nobody expects anyone to raise an eyebrow over it. They think it's one of the best-studied, most trouble-free schemes in the history of water."

Richard looked across at Curt. "You've got to realize," he said in measured tones, "that there is absolutely no opposition to this project. It's all wrapped up, and there's a piece of pie for everyone. Once they get their foot in the door at Dos Rios they'll get the whole north coast. There will be dams for all."

This was not news to Lewis, but Curt had a strange light in his eye.

"And when will this pie be served?" he asked.

"Pretty damn soon," said Richard. "From this hearing they can go straight to the committees, and on to the governor. I'm sure Reagan is sold. Our only hope there is Ike Livermore, the Resources secretary. He's the one figure who hasn't already been brainwashed by the water lobby, and I think he'll listen to us. He's asked me to keep him informed, but we'd better have a tremendous case, because he'd be putting his neck on the block to oppose it. Once it gets past Reagan, it need never see the light of day again before Congress swallows it up in an omnibus bill."

They talked a while longer. Curt and Lewis both agreed that a preliminary meeting in Covelo was very important, to drum up support before facing off with the corps at Willits. If they could make a really strong showing at Willits, Curt would try to make the ripples spread. Lewis would help him with the conservation groups, and Curt would work at getting the anglers and hunters involved. The *San Francisco Chronicle,* he thought, would be a natural ally. He knew people there.

"This may be the least controversial water project since rain," Curt said, "but I have a feeling we'll change that. Oh, and there's something else I'd like to change. That Round Valley Protective thing you're registering, Rich. Can we still work on that? Doesn't ring right for me."

Richard looked at Lewis, who shrugged.

"Sure. What do you think then?"

"Conservation's better than protection. How about Round Valley Conservation something or other?"

"League?"

"Good. And then I think we should consider running up another one, for the Eel River, don't you? A lot of people will want to save the Eel who have never heard of Round Valley. Think about it. Okay? Now, I've got to meet a bishop. I'll see you in a week."

That period was the first of a succession of miraculous times for Richard. Everything he did, everyone he met, seemed to have some relevance to his cause. He took it to be a guarantee of the rightness of the path he had chosen. Individuals of all kinds responded to his energy, and he became aware for the first time just how many there were struggling in so many different areas to shed light on the problems of their times. The people associated with California Tomorrow—Alf Heller, Sam Wood, who effectively ran the operation, and Bill Bronson, who edited *Cry California,* among others—were a fount of insights about the innumerable ways in which society, with its ingrained habits and expectations, was degrading its own environment.

Richard was specially impressed by people that Lewis knew, like Joe Paul, Dick May, and David Lennihan, with their angler's associations, like Trout Unlimited, who fought to protect the rivers under the more readily recognizable banner of saving the fish runs.

Opportunities resulted as a matter of course from these meetings. An obvious one was to marshal the anglers in defense of the Eel. They knew, as they appealed to the simple desires of their membership to be allowed to wade into a stream and hook a steelhead trout, that they were really fighting on behalf of an incredibly complex ecosystem involving countless life-forms, beautifully and incomprehensibly linked with the surrounding life of forests, marshes, meadows, and ponds—a complexity of immense value that could not possibly be replaced by a concrete hatchery, no matter how many millions were spent on it.

A week after their conversation, at the beginning of December, Lewis and his wife, Sheanna, went up with Curt Roberts to Round Valley for Richard's community meeting.

"We drove up in Curt Roberts's Mustang," Lewis recalled. "Sheanna was crammed into the backseat and I was up front with Curt. He had a CB radio—a ham radio really—he loved to talk to people around the United States on this radio.

"He really liked Richard. I think he thought Richard was going to be candidate for governor. Certainly state senator. He'd talk about it. 'Here's this rancher, and he looks like Gary Cooper, and his wife looks like everybody's wife ought to look, living up there in the woods, with beautiful little kids.'

"Richard was thirty-four then, and Susan was twenty-eight—a strikingly beautiful young woman. Curt was intrigued by the whole thing, and he was getting paid, too.

"We drove up in the morning. I'd never been to Round Valley before. It was very bleak and wintry. We stopped at a sort of observation place at the top. It was all very exciting."

They drove over to the far corner of the valley where the Wilsons now lived, and Lewis was surprised by the modesty of the place. He had become accustomed to thinking of Wilson as a man of means, and was expecting something more palatial than the four small rooms of their house. Susan took them to an annex of two equally modest guest rooms furnished with heavy, dark oak pieces that had clearly belonged to much more spacious quarters. A grand piano almost filled the small anteroom it occupied. The feeling was of a household that had been deliberately shrunk, and both men received the impression that the Wilsons were determined to avoid any hint of ostentation. They washed up and went back to the house for coffee.

The inaugural meeting of the Round Valley Conservation League was held that morning in the Wilsons' kitchen. It was a cozy room with an eight-foot ceiling and a view of the garden that Susan had already reclaimed from surrounding pasture, and filled with flowers and shrubs. The room was not crowded, but thanks to Elmer one or two other valley stalwarts had come to bless the proceedings. Mabel Brown, who owned land down East Lane, was there, and he had persuaded one member of the Hurt family, Wayne, to join, too. The prize supporter, though, was old J. D. Rohrbough, who had begun to think that maybe the Corps of Engineers was crazy enough to go through with their ridiculous plan. Elmer was there, of course, with Jim McCombs and the cantankerous Bud Barnes.

Richard was duly installed as president, and Elmer, looking very pink and vice-presidential took his place a heartbeat away. They spent the afternoon touring the valley. Curt was a bundle of energy, throwing off ideas like sparks from a grindstone, and as Richard colored the scene for them with anecdotes about the valley characters they met, it was obvious to him that both of them were getting emotionally involved with this crusade.

By the time they came to attend the meeting Richard had convened at the Masonic Hall, Lewis was aglow with enthusiastic expectations. The reality dampened his ardor.

"There was a little stage and room for maybe a hundred people at the most. There was a mixture of ranchers there and . . . I remember looking down and seeing very broad-shouldered and big-chested Indian guys standing at the back of the hall looking at me . . . just absolutely expressionless.

"Richard told me that he wanted me to tell the people who were gathered there that the Corps of Engineers could be beaten, and the fight could be won. And my credentials were that I was a veteran of all these wars over preservation things. At that time I was the attorney for the Save the San Francisco Bay Association, and against all the odds the Bay Conservation and Development Commission had been created, and the bay was in the process of being saved. But I still didn't think *this* fight could be won."

Already it was December 5, and only ten days away from the public hearing with the corps at the Willits High School auditorium, but it had taken that long to get together the kind of show Richard wanted. It was the first demonstration of organized opposition to the dam, and he wanted it to count. Lewis was not the only one to speak. Richard led off by introducing himself as the president of the new Round Valley Conservation League, with Elmer Bauer as vice-president and Jim McCombs as secretary and treasurer. The price of membership had gone up, from two to ten dollars. It was already clear that this was going to be a costly campaign.

"Our primary purpose," he told the audience, "is to conserve Round Valley and the surrounding area as an agricultural, residential, stock, and timber region and to keep it from being converted into a man-made reservoir."

He tried hard to limit his arguments so that nobody need feel excluded. There were no references to fancy ecological and environmental issues.

"We want to make it clear that we are not opposing the export of excess water to other parts of the state, nor are we opposed to flood control. We simply believe these things can be achieved without the loss of this valley. There are other solutions."

Richard was anxious to alert people to his belief that for the engineers Dos Rios just meant getting their foot in the door. This was the key project that would unlock a host of others. Already Congress had authorized feasibility studies for the Klamath, the Lower Trinity, the Mad, and the Van Duzen rivers, all of them north coast rivers.

"They are treating us like children," he said, "who can't be trusted with too much bad news at once. This should be looked at on an overall basis. Disinterested parties should be allowed to study it."

Elmer Bauer rose to say a word or two to inspire his fellow ranchers, and then Lewis told his stirring tales about battles with the corps, and he recalls how disconcerted he was by that first exposure to the citizenry of Covelo.

"I got up and made a very brave speech, and what I remember is that there was no change of expression on anybody's face. Just not anything. There was just dead silence."

The audience was no more responsive to the others than it was to Lewis. After the meeting, Richard seemed uncharacteristically distracted. He talked for a while with a reporter from the *Press Democrat*, whom Curt had persuaded to come up from Santa Rosa. Then Lewis described his bewilderment at the stony faces in the hall.

"Oh, that's just the Covelo welcome," Richard said, with a tired smile. "They don't get that fired up by words, the way they do down below. But you made your points. Here's Bud Barnes. We'll ask him."

He turned to Bud, who was standing by, solemnly, with Isabel.

"Bud, this is Lewis Butler and Curtis Roberts. Lewis was wondering how his talk appealed to the multitude."

Bud took hold of Lewis and Curt's hands and gave them a severe shaking.

"Isabel agrees with me, Dick. Mr. Butler done good."

Richard's spirits rebounded like magic, and his big grin flashed across his face.

"There you are, Lewis," he said. "You'll never get a finer compliment than that."

14

How the Corps Lost Its Innocence

URBAN WATER ENGINEERS had had their eye on the Eel River since the turn of the century, when the city of San Francisco was looking around for water supplies. Even then it seemed perfectly possible to bring Eel River water 150 miles south. San Francisco chose to flood Hetch Hetchy in Yosemite Park, instead, but the city of Oakland, across the bay, got interested and for a while, in the twenties, had serious plans to bring Eel water down to the east bay.

The Corps of Engineers became involved in the thirties, but their interest was with the other end of the river, at the delta, where there was a flood problem. It seemed there was enough commercial activity around the Eel delta to justify a flood control project. At first they were limited to Humboldt County, but in 1940 a big flood enlarged their franchise to include the entire river basin. From that time on, corps engineers have tramped the length of the river, looking for places that could be considered as potential damsites. They installed stream gauges to measure the flow at various places along the river. They investigated the geologic structure, measured earth movements, costed out railroad relocations. They studied the possibilities of hydroelectric power generation, and they named and designed, in outline, dams to hold back the Eel along half its length. All in vain. Every project they conceived was just too expensive. Even levees couldn't be justified.

In his fight to save Round Valley from flooding, Richard Wilson invested in a portfolio of glossy color photographs designed to demonstrate to legislators the scenic splendors that would be lost forever. *Above,* an aerial view, and *below,* a creek and some of the cattle so characteristic of the valley.

PHOTO COURTESY ELMER BAUER

Above: Looking north up Covelo's Main Street around 1900. The area to the west was called "Dog Town," and to the east, "Frog Town." These buildings burned down in 1905. *Below:* Peering out of a rain-damaged print from the turn of the century, Covelo men gathered outside the people's Cash Store with their dogs and horses for what looks like the start of a bear hunt.

PHOTO COURTESY ELMER BAUER

PHOTO COURTESY ELMER BAUER

Grain was an important crop in Round Valley earlier in this century. *Above:* A harvester in action in 1913. It took a team of about thirty-two horses to pull one. *Below:* The flour mill built by John Rohrbough between 1888 and 1914. It was eventually bought as a museum piece by Richard Wilson, in an effort to upgrade the town center.

PHOTO COURTESY ELMER BAUER

PHOTO COURTESY ELMER BAUER

The Winter Stage from Covelo to Dos Rios in 1927. It was driven by the aptly named Bill Goforth.

PHOTO COURTESY ELMER BAUER

PHOTO COURTESY ELMER BAUER

George White, *left,* the legendary cattle king who operated his huge cattle empire from Round Valley for forty years. His mansion, *above,* was the finest and most sophisticated in the region. White's gifted hatchet man, "Wylackie" John Wathen, was shot dead in the saloon bar of the Gibson House, *below,* in 1888.

PHOTO COURTESY ELMER BAUER

PHOTO COURTESY WILSON AND GRAND FAMILIES

Angus Grant (*above, left*) fled the family farm in Canada as a boy and won huge success as a railroad construction magnate. He took his brother, Lewis (*above, right*), into partnership. On the left is Angus Grant's son Daniel as a boy of eleven when he was living with his father at the magnificent Palace Hotel in San Francisco. Lew Grant's daughter Anna, Richard Wilson's mother, is shown (*below, right*) kneeling, with her mother and Daniel Grant, who by this time was a well-known Los Angeles businessman. Dr. John Cree Wilson (*below, left*) was Richard Wilson's father and principal influence.

PHOTO COURTESY WILSON AND GRAND FAMILIES

Richard Wilson, his wife, Susan, and their three young children, Alex, Chris, and Marjo in 1971. The leading proponents of the dam were Joseph Jensen (*below, left*), chairman of Southern California's Metropolitan Water District, and William Gianelli (*below, right*), who was Governor Reagan's director of Water Resources.

PHOTO COURTESY OF CALIFORNIA DEPARTMENT OF WATER RESOURCES

PHOTO COURTESY OF THE METROPOLITAN WATER DISTRICT

Sixties flood scenes like these (*left*) made a powerful argument for building dams and aqueducts like the ones pictured below, and for turning Round Valley into a reservoir.

Pictured at right are the Kern-Friant Canal, and the Shasta dam, both built for the Central Valley Project. Lovely as Lake Shasta appears, the photo shows clearly the denuding effect on the shoreline when a reservoir is consistently drawn down through the summer months.

Above: Governor Reagan at the Round Valley garden project, standing alongside horticulturalist Alan Chadwick, and facing state senator Peter Behr. Richard Wilson watches, poker-faced, from the left. *Below, left,* the irrepressible Elmer Bauer manages to upstage even Ronald Reagan. *Below, right:* Ida Soares in 1974.

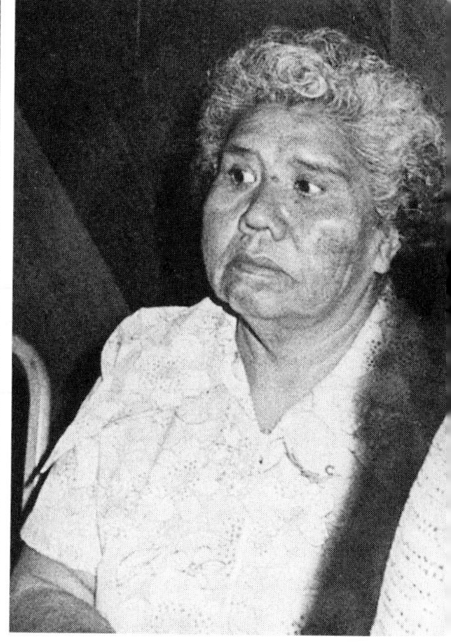

Hank Pape, who was chief of engineers when Dos Rios was being designed, recalls the flood of February 1940 as the biggest they had known. All the emphasis then was still on protecting the lower reaches of the river, where the lumber mills stood and the dairy farmers grazed their cows. The obvious thing to do was build levees. Hank says, "Our ideas were the simplest in the world, but always we came up with these horrendous costs. With butterfat and milk at the prices they were in those days, you just couldn't come up with a benefit. You could feel for the people. You knew the disasters they went through, but it was the old cost versus benefits."

The benefit/cost ratio is the iron rule that controls the corps. Before the engineers can hope for permission to spend the people's money on anything they build, they must prove to Congress that their efforts will be profitable, that there will be a net gain in value to the people. Sometimes the approach to these calculations is relatively simple, as in forecasting, for example, the value of damage a flood may do if it is not restrained. Sometimes it gets abstract, as in quantifying the future recreational value of a lake that was not there before, or the probable loss of wildlife due to the diversion of water. Simple or complex, the calculations are always arduous and prolonged, and involve mountains of data.

Despite all this effort, none of the corps's ideas for the Eel made financial sense as long as the only object was to protect the people and property on the river delta. Then came the '55 flood, again the biggest in living memory.

One has to sympathize with the corps. Hydrologists have nothing to go on but precedent. Who can possibly know how big the next flood will be? Now they had to start over, figuring what was needed to protect the Eel delta, just supposing someone felt like paying for it. They gave the '55 flood top ranking, and an official-sounding label. They classified it as a hundred-year flood—that is to say, in any year there would be a 1 percent chance of that flood happening again.

The '55 flood sent six hundred thousand cubic feet of water out to the ocean every second. After they had cleaned up the mess, the corps designed levees capable of containing that much water if it should ever come again. They couldn't make the levees any higher, because then the highway and the railroad would have to be relocated, making the expense astronomical. It was at the limit of what levees could do, but the corps was satisfied that their hundred-year flood could be controlled. Now, too, there seemed a faint chance of getting them built, because populations in the neighboring towns of Eureka and Arcata were growing. With the danger of flooding averted, it was thought, people would want to come and build on the delta plain, too. That would increase the value of the land, and bring up the benefit. The magic ratio was within reach.

Actually, things were getting a lot more exciting than that. The state was working up its own water plan, using many of the corps's earlier findings. In 1957, when the California Water Plan thumped onto the desks of engineers across the state, four dams were proposed for the Eel at an estimated cost, in today's money, of roughly $3 billion. Although these dams were being proposed for water storage, they would obviously help to control flooding, too, giving the corps a chance at the action.

That was just for openers. After the Eel came the Klamath and the Trinity rivers, with dams, power stations, and tunnels worth three times that amount. It must have seemed as though the golden age of dam building had only just dawned.

The corps was all too eager to jump in. All it had to do was cover itself with a bit of flood control, and it would be in business. But there were problems. Naturally the dam that made the most sense for flood control on the Eel was the one that would capture the most water, and that was a dam, already named Sequoia, closest to the mouth of the Eel. Unfortunately it was also the one that came last on the list for the state of California. The obvious place to start, for the state's purposes, was right at the other end of the Eel, up in the mountains, as close as possible to the Sacramento Valley, on the Middle Fork. But with so little flood control, such a project would make the corps very vulnerable to criticism.

It was a canny New Deal Democrat, William Warne, who found a solution to the dilemma. In the early sixties, when Pat Brown was still governor of California, William Warne was his director of water resources. Warne was a onetime journalist and speechwriter for Franklin D. Roosevelt. Later he had become an assistant commissioner of reclamation under Floyd Dominy, and it was there he had learned his lessons about water. The story goes that Governor Brown first offered him the job of running the Resources Agency, the same job that Ike Livermore held later. Bill Warne, it is said, refused in favor of the nominally inferior position of director of water resources. He knew where the power was.

Bill Warne had two major dams in mind. One was on the Middle Fork of the Eel at Dos Rios. The other was on the main stem of the Eel at English Ridge. All together, he was looking at a bill of more than half a billion dollars, and the obvious tactic was to get Washington to pay for it. That could be done by having either the bureau or the corps build for him. Warne figured out a way to bring both these archrivals into the state's service.

Though much has been made of the feud between the bureau and the corps in the past, they were simply reverse sides of the same coin. They employed the same people and contracted with the same companies. When Bill Warne suggested they sit down together and figure out ways to share the booty, he experienced little difficulty.

The federal agencies were like pieces on a chessboard, and they had to move according to rules devised by Congress. There was the bureau; the bishop, perhaps, with its quasi-religious mission, eager to dig and pour, but it was only supposed to make cheap water flow to small farmers and municipalities.

There was the corps, as gung-ho as ever, the knight ready to jump in anywhere, but it was only supposed to build dams for flood control. The state was queen of the board, who could go anywhere, do anything, provided she had the money. Sadly, the queen was broke.

There is not much doubt that when Bill Warne and Pat Brown sat down with their legal adviser, Ralph Brody, to consider this matter, they thought the game was absurd and determined to play by their own rules. The obvious first question was: If we do it our way, who is going to blow the whistle? And the obvious conclusion was: Nobody, as long as everyone gets something.

The bureau could be kept happy with the dam on English Ridge. Its real function was to act as a way station for the water from Dos Rios, if it should be decided to send it south to Clear Lake, but it would also capture some water of its own, which would be available to farmers in and around Willits, Ukiah, and Redwood Valley. That was enough to give the bureau legitimacy.

This would leave the corps free to build the dam at Dos Rios, if only they could prove that it really would control some flooding at the mouth of the Eel. This was always a weakness in the plan. Colonel Boerger made a brave, if cynical, effort later to deny it, but Hank Pape admitted as much. Talking about the corps's earlier investigations, he said, "There was little consideration that any of these dams, any place along the headwaters, would have any impact on flood control."

But with the state eager for the dam, and the bureau with its own piece of the action, who was going to argue?

The engineers went to work with a will. In one area of investigation alone, that of landslides, it was the most extensive engineering research effort ever made anywhere. The conclusions from the damsite investigations were clear. Only the Dos Rios damsite would hold up, and filling Round Valley would make for a splendid project. Far more water would be captured. Delivery would be far more efficient.

Bill Warne's original authorization actually specifies the building of dams to protect Round Valley. It may never be known whether Warne knew, when he signed that document, that Round Valley would have to be flooded. He himself says now he cannot remember, and this is entirely credible given that, for him, it was never an issue. He would have been for it, necessary or not, because he came of an age when lakes were thought to be more valuable than valleys. He believed then, as he still does, that damming the Eel was not just expedient for the state, but was an important contribution to the quality of life on the north coast.

Even in his eighties, and "not as chipper as I used to be," he remains sturdily unrepentant about developments on the Eel. He says, "I was convinced at that time, and still am, that regulating the Eel River was one of the prime conservation activities that we ought to take."

The question of whether it would be permissible politically to flood the valley was not raised. Nobody even thought it worth asking. Plainly, in the light of this great public work and the good it would do for millions of Californians, the valley had no importance. *Pro bono publico:* Whatever does the greatest good for the greatest number. The buck passed up the line, and Bill Warne was more than happy to carry it. However, he was a Democrat, and a very political one at that. He campaigned loudly against Reagan in 1966, and Reagan made it equally clear that he would kick Warne out first chance he got. Reagan won, and Warne passed the buck on to the new man, a distinctly nonpartisan Democrat named William Gianelli, who had even fewer qualms.

By 1967 there were 1,200 dams in the state of California, and 150 of them were of considerable size. Some were built privately by farmers or power companies; some were built by associations of irrigators—known as "water districts"—or by municipalities, but a large number of them, and certainly the flagships among them, were built by the two great federal agencies, the Bureau of Reclamation and the Corps of Engineers.

By the sixties, time had hallowed both these federal entities. Their roles were hardened in dogma and they were generally regarded as twin deities, exempt from suspicion, good, wise, and all-powerful. They showered blessings on the faithful and brooked no opposition. In 1967, when the corps issued its first ponderous proposal to flood Round Valley, nobody could remember a time when the engineers had been seriously thwarted. They seemed to have Congress in their pocket, and authorizations were virtually automatic.

It is almost impossible to overestimate the momentum behind the big water projects. Their legitimacy went far beyond their practical value as bearers of water and power to farms, homes, and factories. They were monuments to the most successfully productive nation the world has ever seen. Most illustrious were the grand dams of the thirties. For sheer potency nothing could rival the Grand Coulee, Hoover, Shasta, and Bonneville dams, with their vast sweeping surfaces of gleaming concrete, their mind-boggling statistics of cubic yards and kilowatts and megagallons, representing whole statesful of light and power. Those images flashed around the globe as symbols of what resolute men in an enlightened society could achieve, and countless boys (this writer among them) read of those marvels and said, "I want to be an engineer and change the world."

Grand Coulee was finished in 1941, just in time to swing the productive balance in the Second World War to the side of the Allies. Its hydroelectric power output produced vast quantities of aluminum, enough to build the armadas of planes that terrorized Germany's war economy. Afterward, in a society still imbued with the mindset of total war, it had seemed logical to engage in total peace. We had the know-how, the technology, and the newly demobilized manpower. The transition was simple: from tanks to Caterpillars, from fortifications to dams. Postwar America's capacity to churn out concrete and stick it in the ground was awesome. A host of massive water projects sprang to life—in Texas, in the Mississippi basin, and, above all, in California. American Man (for women still had little or no primary function in the grand scheme of things) had finally achieved full mastery of his natural resources and was bending them to his will.

Most Americans were comfortable with the thought that this degree of supremacy over Nature was no less than their due. They were children of an age when modern science routinely hatched a miracle every Friday, from penicillin to polyester; an age in which America's vast industrial resources had overwhelmed the Nazi threat to democracy, were now holding in check an equally powerful Communist adversary and yet were strong enough to shower material prosperity on its people and simultaneously rescue Europe and Japan from postwar chaos.

The bureau and the corps were both revered forces in that same legend, and morally invulnerable. Up until the war years, the bureau was by far the more glamorous of the two, having built all the famous dams. Then the corps became more ambitious, actively searching for projects to enhance its prestige and inflate its budget. A rivalry developed between the two agencies that quickly became vicious and cutthroat, and in their efforts to outdo each other, they incurred enormous waste and duplication. The bureau began losing ground, and its commissioners unleashed torrents of abuse. Floyd Dominy, the then-commissioner of the bureau, was known to hate the corps. His predecessor, Harold Ickes, described the corps publicly as lawless, irresponsible, self-serving, and "hand in glove with land monopolies." But although they regularly lambasted each other, rarely if ever did the public question the essential integrity of these two beneficent giants.

When Ickes hurled his curses at the Corps of Engineers, the shock was all the greater because he was blackening a whited sepulchre. Cliff Foster in Round Valley was not alone in his unqualified admiration of the corps. Millions felt as he did. This was the army engaged in good works, and what finer example of service and patriotism could you hope to find?

The corps, in fact, is innocent by definition. The rules governing its conduct were created to protect the corps against the besmirching effect of politics, and it seems that for a long time they were successful. For example, the corps is forbidden from initiating a project. It may not say to itself: "Gee, we've got all these engineers idle. Let's find something useful for them to do." As a servant of the people it must suffer in silence, laying off redundant workers until the people call. And when the call comes, it must come via a congressman, who in turn has to convince a public works committee in Washington, which may then authorize the corps to investigate the project.

Only at this point does the word go out, and down the chain of command to the local district engineer, usually a lieutenant colonel nearing the end of his career. With not much to be gained either way, he holds hearings in strict fairness to make sure that the public really does want this thing done, whatever it is, and that the army is not being used to favor one interest at the expense of another.

Well that's how it used to be, more or less, for most of the corps's history. In 1852, in California, the corps began work on San Diego harbor. Since then it has built breakwaters, dredged channels, and restored jetties all the way up the coastline to Crescent City. Inland it built levees, bridges, and small dams to save communities and farmland from flooding. Its work was specific, relatively small scale, and much appreciated. It may not always have been beautiful, but then until recently function bestowed its own aesthetic.

Of course, the rules could not prevent congressmen and generals from lunching together. In the forties, it seems, the lunches got longer and more creative. The corps had grown in the war, and was understandably reluctant to shrink again. Meanwhile there were a few well-heeled citizens who thought the army could help them out of a dilemma.

It began with some land in the San Joaquin Valley, some very rich land that got flooded periodically by rivers running down the slopes of the Sierras. The owners of this land wanted dams on the rivers. They wanted the water that those dams would capture, at times of the year when it would be useful to them. And although the Bureau of Reclamation was already very active in that area, they definitely did not want the bureau to build them, because these were not farmers with 160 acres each. These were a few very big farmers, with half a million acres among them. So they tempted the corps to bid for the job, in competition with the bureau, and that was how the corps lost its innocence. The army could not resist the temptation to get into some real, heavy dam building, and a deal was struck. With an agribusiness lobby to support it, the corps went to battle with the bureau and after a decade of bitter contest, it won. The fruits of that victory fell mainly into the hands of great corporations like Tenneco, Miller & Lux, Salyer, and Boswell. Those who were paying attention saw the corps's reputation sullied beyond redemption.[1]

Naturally, that did not make villains of them all. The engineers in the field remained as honest as ever and dedicated to the same original principles of disinterested service. Such qualms as they felt about their leadership could never prevail against the obvious value of the work they did. By all the standards they had grown up with and applied throughout their working lives, these were fine projects, and if politicians misused the benefits, that was not the fault of the engineers.

On the whole, civil engineers do what they do because they believe implicitly in comfort and convenience above all else: not for themselves, necessarily, but for society at large. If there's water, let's capture it. If there's wet land, let's drain it. Whatever can be used by man should be used. They are instrumentalism incarnate. The environment exists for man to exploit, and if that creates problems, we'll fix them the next time around.

They are certainly not indifferent to beauty, but much prefer the man-made variety. Nature can be awesome in its wildness, and engineers do not like to be awed. They like to do the awing. In this respect they are uncomfortably close to the corporate mentality they often serve. Where an ambitious engineer like Bill Gianelli would deliver a talk titled "Wild rivers, who needs 'em!"[2] a timber tycoon like Harry Merlo would say, "A tree that isn't logged is worth no more than its shade on a sunny day."[3]

This proximity of interests is awkward for many engineers, and a desire to protect their innocence leads them to hide from responsibility for what they do. It is not their business to "quantify aesthetics." It's not their job to judge the consequences of their labors, or to feel for the lives they disturb. God knows, it's tough enough having to figure all this stuff out and get it right.

For a dam builder, the penalty for getting it wrong can be horrendous. Making sure becomes a habit. It requires engineers to be drenched in information, for years and years, with little relief. That was certainly true of Hank Pape, who had a lot to do with designing the Dos Rios Dam. His education at U.C. Berkeley was an example of what engineers traditionally endure for the sake of their vocation.

"I did a straight four-year course in civil engineering, which meant 142 units to graduate, with only four electives, and those were six months on economics, a couple of courses on architecture, an irrigation course. Everything I had at university related to engineering—physics, chemistry, mathematics, strength of materials, structural design, irrigation, sewage, transportation, and so on. I'm just telling you this to show you that I'm, well, narrow-minded in a sense."

An unusual admission, but tunnel vision is an occupational hazard, and most engineers know it. With so much to be learned, most of it by rote, there's not much time left for the arts and humanities. Hank is cheerfully modest about such limitations. That was the price you had to pay, particularly in the grim days of the depression when he was growing up. He feels fortunate because he knew, early in life, where he was headed, and he had parents who gave him a chance.

"Way back in grammar school I developed an interest in engineering. In fact, back in sixth or seventh grade I put together a paper on the Hetch Hetchy project."

Hetch Hetchy was the name of a much admired valley in Yosemite, which the city of San Francisco flooded for its water supply. Regarded by men like the naturalist John Muir as an act of vandalism, the dam ignited the environmental movement in the twenties, but that was not what excited Hank's youthful enthusiasm.

"I can still remember this thing, which my mother very carefully typed up for me. I made up this beautiful cover with diagrams of O'Shaughnessy Dam and, in fact, I even made a little working model of a reservoir, which I thought was Hetch Hetchy. It had a little copper pipe in it, and water ran out."

Hank laughed, obviously moved by this happy memory of a tough, working-class childhood sixty years before.

"I happened to be raised in the Bayview District—you know, Candlestick—when it was families of immigrants, and second- and third-generation Americans. I was one of three who went to Lowell High School in San Francisco, which meant commuting a long way. We got permission because we intended to go to university. This was not exactly the dream of most people at that time.

"For me, engineers were great people, doing great things. Hetch Hetchy had only recently been built. I watched San Francisco growing around me, structures like the telephone building, and later the bridges. But I guess the primary motivator was—Get your degree! Get out! Get a job! Get off your parents' back! Things were tough then. This was from 1935 to 1939. Dad got paid by the hour, for the hours he worked. No work, no pay! So obviously they sacrificed for me.

"I graduated, and I put in two months as a clerk with Bethlehem Steel because there was nothing else, until in September this opening came up in the Corps of Engineers and I went to work for them as a 'subprofessional engineering aide.' About as low on the ladder as you can get. Subprofessional. That's right."

With his foot on the ladder Hank hung on, and climbed until he was chief of engineers in the San Francisco District of the U.S. Army Corps of Engineers. Then he retired to a comfortable home in Cupertino, a town in the Santa Clara valley.

Always a small man, he is now shrunken and bowed by age, and his eyes have difficulty peering through heavy lenses. Beneath a long, receding forehead, his prominent features still hint at determination and fortitude. He speaks with a mixture of conviviality and caution, evidently proud of his accomplishments yet still, even now, a little shy in the face of broader issues he never felt sure about. He knows there is much criticism of the work engineers have accomplished, work that once seemed so admirable.

"My exposure to politics, policymakers, that type of thing, was minimal," he says, with a touch of vulnerability.

"Engineers were looked up to. They built the Panama Canal, they built skyscrapers, dams, they did things that served mankind. Nobody could doubt the value of these things. But people developed other values. They began to think about animals, plants, esoteric things they didn't consider at the time. Maybe some people even began to look way, way back in history. What happened on the Nile with its intensive crop use.

"I just heard the other night of what's happened in Russia with the Aral Sea. The comrades in Moscow decided they were going to dam this thing up and make it into an agricultural wonderland. Now apparently this has destroyed life for a whole group of people. Communications have changed everything."

In the early sixties, the corps was completely reorganized. The San Francisco District lost all its military construction, and many jobs as well, but civil works were increasing, and Hank was chosen to be head of the design branch. The work atmosphere was changing, too. Men took off their dark coats and vests and worked in shirtsleeves, with air-conditioning. The old, scarred wooden furniture loaded with ledgers had given way to bright new offices, replete with shiny metal filing cabinets, the first computers, tubular steel chairs, fluorescent tubes, push-button phones, and a host of other innovations. It felt good, productive, and praiseworthy.

In those days the district was working out of a converted furniture mart in San Francisco, but as the workload increased more people were hired and they moved to 100 McAllister, on the corner of 7th

Street close to Market. The extreme orthodoxy of the corps contrasted strangely with its accommodations. A furniture mart might seem exotic enough, but 100 McAllister was a truly extraordinary building. It was built in 1929, before the "crash," by members of the San Francisco Methodist congregation. What they really wanted to build was a church, but, caught up in the spirit of the time, they thought they should make money as well, so they built a church with a hotel on top. This unpromising concept was translated into something as tasteful as it was bizarre by Lewis Hobart, the architect who designed Grace Cathedral.

The grand Gothic portico of the church rose four floors above street level, with the lobby of the hotel alongside it. However, there was a city ordinance forbidding alcohol to be consumed within two hundred feet of a church, and the hotel bar was moved up to the twenty-fourth floor, creating quite by accident, San Francisco's first "skyview" bar and restaurant. Before long, the hotel was converted to office space.

It might be reasonable to assume that the Corps of Engineers is a military organization, but that is very far from the truth. The Pacific Division is commanded by a general, but his staff is almost entirely civilian. The general oversees three districts, each commanded by a colonel. This colonel and his deputy might be the only military personnel. All the others would be civilians, and it is they who provide the continuity, because the uniformed men are moved on every three to four years.

The colonel and his corps of civilians play as much a part in the construction of their projects as a conductor does in the performance of a symphony orchestra. They have to choose the work, to know the score, to keep the players together, to maintain standards and spot mistakes, and to bring the whole thing to a timely and harmonious conclusion. Most of the grinding, meticulous labor associated with a major civil construction has always been done under contract by the big engineering companies like Kaiser, Bechtel or Stone & Webster, to name only a few in an immense industry. How otherwise could Hank Pape and his design branch, consisting of fewer than twenty people, deal with the workload equivalent of a billion dollars?

The corps, the Bureau of Reclamation, and the state's Department of Water Resources, all operate in much the same way. At their zenith, they employed many thousands of people in California, but this was nothing compared with the numbers engaged by the construction companies themselves, let alone the suppliers of cement, iron, machinery, and other matériel. And all this, or a billion dollars' worth of it, was orchestrated from the offices of Hank Pape and his colleagues.*

Among the most visible of the men who worked out of 100 McAllister was Charles Elmore. He was project coordinator on the Dos Rios Dam and spent more time than most connecting with local authorities in the counties. He accompanied Colonel Boerger on his many visits to reassure and inform the public, and at meetings with the Indians, with supervisors, with Jan Stewart's hard core of dam boosters, he was often the man who represented the bureaucracy behind the uniform.

He came to know the valley and the Eel River as well as anyone, and took his wife, Eleanor, and their young children camping there. They were all struck by the beauty of the place, and it is one of the enigmas of the story that not one of those engineers who so admired Round Valley ever considered crossing the line and saying, out loud, "This must not go!"

Elmore was a youthful-looking black man of thirty-nine, handsome, intelligent, exceedingly well groomed, and deeply committed to his job. He had overcome considerable obstacles to pursue his career, and his first encounter with the corps in the fifties was the stuff movies are made of. As a newly demobilized veteran, with an engineering degree from Kentucky, he sent job applications out in all directions and eventually got a favorable response from the Corps of Engineers in Jacksonville, Florida. They were interested, and in due course he got the job. Somehow he was hired without ever having been interviewed in person.

It was a time when black men were still distinctly unwelcome among white engineers. His arrival at the office on his first day of work provoked horror and disbelief. He told a friend later that he would never forget the look on their faces when they realized that this was the Charles Elmore they had hired. It caused turmoil throughout the building. They didn't know what to do with him, and he spent the whole of the first day sitting in the personnel office, while the curious poked their heads through the door to examine the freak. A place was

*$370 million in 1967 dollars

found for him the next day by a window in a remote corner of the planning department, where he sat idle and exposed to the rubberneckers who paraded past in the street outside to catch a glimpse of him.

Merit, and a capacity to absorb punishment brought him through this ordeal, but he was glad of the opportunity to move to the West Coast. There was no doubt about Charlie Elmore's competence, and Hank knew him as an excellent planner. He played an important part in the Dos Rios team. There was, obviously, an esprit de corps among these men. Pape, Elmore, and the others who look back on that time remember working well with each other, and believing firmly in the value of their work. It was important to them all that their boss, the district engineer, was a man they could trust and respect professionally. In earlier days, when the job was often the last before retirement, this was sometimes a problem. Later, when the corps rejected its more humble role and became a fully fledged self-serving bureaucracy, the quality of the command improved, and more qualified and ambitious men were appointed.

"Many of them," says Hank, "came from being top of the class at West Point, headed for command. They were all competent engineers, and as time went by there were some with advanced degrees in engineering or in business. They could be briefed and brought up to speed."

Col. Frank Boerger, the district engineer in charge of bringing the Dos Rios Dam through to authorization, was one of the first of the brightest. All those who remember him, whether opposed to the dam or not, recall him as an impressive individual and an eloquent advocate. The official portrait shows a square, boyish countenance with bright eyes, and a confident smile. His career details might be a model for the army's claim to make a man all he can be. Born in South Dakota, he enlisted in World War II and won a place at West Point. He graduated as a civil engineer at the University of Illinois, distinguished himself in various service schools, and held both command and staff positions in Germany, Italy, and the Far East. He came to San Francisco as a sophisticated, traveled, and highly qualified man. Perhaps the most significant part of his experience, though, was his last position, where he was acting as deputy division commander of the Missouri River Division.

It was there, in the fifties and sixties that the corps and the bureau, in unaccustomed collaboration, had spent billions of dollars to convert the "wild Missouri" into a barge canal, by building a controversial and widely criticized series of dams, locks, and levees. It was there also that the corps had submerged a valley occupied by three Indian tribes—the Mandan, the Arikara, and the Hidatsa—with its Garrison Dam. Since the Middle Eel project was originally planned as a cooperative venture with the Bureau of Reclamation, Boerger's experience of working with the bureau on the Missouri could have been a welcome and rare qualification. As for the drowning of the Fort Berthold Reservation, that was done by his predecessors with a minimum of fuss. Boerger came to Round Valley with personal knowledge of the ease with which such things may be accomplished "for the greater good of the greater number." When the army appointed him as San Francisco district engineer in 1966, it seems they could hardly have chosen a man better qualified to shepherd the Eel project through to Congress and beyond.

Boerger was a quick study, and it didn't take long to bring him up to date. There could never have been a doubt in his mind that they would go for the high dam and take the valley. The difference between that and the next best plan was a phenomenal amount of water. Without that extra capacity, the promised flood control, which was their pretext for doing the job, didn't have a chance. Anyway they needed to have the higher water level to be able to run it out east under gravity.

Nor could he have had any doubt that the dam would be built. That was a foregone conclusion. For decades the north coast had been recognized as California's last, great water bank. Even as the objections mounted, he knew they could never weigh seriously in the balance against the needs of the state. One had only to look at it from a detached point of view to realize that this must be so.

Where was the political power in the state? In the south. Where was most of the growth, the industry, and the agriculture that supported the state? In the south. Where was the money coming from to build the State Water Project? Preponderantly from the south. Who had already signed contracts and paid for the water Dos Rios would provide? The Metropolitan Water District. How many voters would have their water needs assured by this dam? About ten million. How many voters would be displaced by this dam? Fewer than a thousand. Which politicians would have egg on their faces if the State Water

Project couldn't deliver what it promised? The same politicians who would have to approve this dam.

The arithmetic was overwhelming, and not a single public figure had yet emerged to challenge it. So what could possibly come up to stop it? Was there anything intrinsically wrong with the design? Nothing. He had never seen so much work done on a single dam project, and nobody involved had anything but absolute confidence in it. They had been lucky with the Dos Rios site, certainly. It was probably the only stable and competent site along that whole reach of river. In a sense they had also been lucky that the other damsites were no good. That removed the temptation of trying to compromise by shielding the valley. No compromise solution could come near the value of having the whole storage area available.

So given that the project was a sure thing, Frank Boerger's duty was clear. It was to negotiate a smooth passage, at the least expense, with maximum local cooperation. There was a significant prize to be won. Time. If Boerger managed to steer the project through the hearing in Willits without raising any serious objections, he could hope to get it past Sacramento and off to Washington for authorization in 1968. Because of the way Congress worked, any serious delay now—even a month or two—could cost two years. And two years could grow to more. There was a war on, after all. Vietnam was costly, and already there were rumors that federal budgets might come under attack. Boerger knew what was expected of him. He had ten months to get the governor's signature.

It ought to be plain sailing. Statewide the seas were calm. In Ukiah, it was true, a small storm was brewing, but there were always bound to be objections. People hated to be turfed out of their homes. They would be furious. Some would resist and make angry speeches. Part of his duty was to explain, patiently, how they would be compensated, and to bring them to terms with the inevitable. However violent those objections might be, they were not the kind that counted. The objections had to be substantive. They had to raise the possibility that there might be some serious flaw in the design or the calculations.

Using standard procedures, he had gone through every phase of the project as carefully as he knew how. Gianelli's Department of Water Resources had a national—in fact an international—reputation for engineering competence, and his men had spent millions doing their homework. The corps, too, was world-renowned for its expertise. It didn't surprise Frank Boerger to find that everything of importance was in order.

It was extraordinary, when you looked at it, how many criteria they had to satisfy. Not only did the dam have to work and pay for itself but also they had to plan and calculate for fish, wildlife and vegetation, land use and population growth, roads and railroads, industry, agriculture and recreation, local power, and water supplies. They were involved in the economic and social well-being of several counties. Putting in a project like this was almost like redesigning a small nation.

But it all made sense, it all hung together. Some future flood damage would be averted, Mendocino would, eventually, get a wonderful lake, and a huge amount of valuable water would go south to create economic wealth. He did not have to ask himself who would get wealthy. That wasn't his job. Full of confidence in his project he steered toward the storm in Ukiah. A storm in a teacup, maybe, but it could be awkward, and it was Colonel Boerger's duty to deal with it.

15

A Flood of Praise and Ridicule

RICHARD WAS having trouble with his speech. Not so much the one he had given in Covelo, or the one he was preparing for Willits, but with the very words that came out of his mouth. Curt didn't like them. Pompous pronouncements, he called them, and cumbersome circumlocutions. Try as he would, though, Richard couldn't stop the officialese from taking over. Those time-honored segments of gobbledygook kept creeping in. That old tradition of taking refuge in the third person, in quasi-objectivity, and in sonorous sentences of multisyllabic meaninglessness was hard to shed.

He had never addressed a public audience in his life, and it had not occurred to him that he would have to make speeches. He had gone into this crusade assuming that he would do whatever there was to do, but he had certainly not given any thought to the matter. Now, suddenly, Curt was telling him it was crucial, and that he was no good at it.

"Whatever Bud Barnes may say, *You done terrible,*" Curt charged. "Nobody will be able to remember a thing you say. What are you going to tell them in Willits on Friday?"

For the first time, Richard found himself resenting this mercurial midget who was taunting him so impudently. He was not accustomed to such irreverent treatment. If he hadn't been on Curt's home ground, in his house on Lombard Street, he might have found a way to end the ordeal, but he'd made the trip specifically for this, and having ordered the medicine felt he had to swallow it. Stiffly, he drew a stapled document from his briefcase, and started reading from a draft of the speech he'd written for the hearing.

"Gentlemen, we have listened to your report on findings of cooperative studies and investigations on the Middle Fork Eel River, California. We believe the main purpose of the study is—"

"Jesus Christ," yelled Curt. "Shut up, will you! You'll put everybody to sleep. Why are you telling them what they already know? This isn't a comprehension test. Listen! What's the point of this speech? Do you think that you're going to overwhelm the corps with logic and persuade them to fold up their tent and steal away?"

"Of course not."

"Well, maybe you want to impress your supporters with your statesmanship. No? Okay. This speech you're going to make, and all the other speeches you're going to make after this one, will have one purpose, and that's to be reported. You've got to get the press.

"Maybe you've seen those newspaper movies where the brilliant reporters push back their fedoras, loosen their ties, and reduce reams of prosy porridge into crisp one-liners. I think I met one of those once, but you'd better not count on him being there Friday. Actually I think he's dead.

"You have to do the job for them. The guys there on Friday are going to be wallowing in hours of that same tedious stuff. They'll be like crows looking for anything that gleams. If you want them to tell your story, you have to polish up a few nuggets for them. See, you're going to make this speech, with variations, over and over and over again. It's called a stump speech. This is just the start. Every time it will get neater and tougher and hit harder. We'll tape Friday's performance and work with that. I'm going to coach you as if you're running for office, because one day I think you will. We'll work on the speech together. You'll make it. I'll get it in the papers.

"Now, see if you can tell me what you're going to say on Friday—and put that other awful thing away."

It was one of the hardest tasks Richard had ever put his mind to, but gradually, with Curt badgering him ceaselessly, it began to flow a little more easily.

"Who are you?"

"My name is Richard Wilson. I'm a rancher and farmer in Round Valley."

"Why are you here?"

"I'm here to represent the people of Round Valley, who don't want their beautiful valley taken away for dubious purposes which seem economically unsound and probably unnecessary."

"Try not to to use 'which.' It'll shorten your sentences."

"All right. I am here to represent the Round Valley Conservation League. We don't want our beautiful valley taken away for dubious purposes. We believe that this plan to flood our valley may be economically unsound and probably unnecessary."

"Good! What are you doing about it?"

"A nonprofit corporation has been formed—"

"No, no! Not passive. We have formed, or I have formed . . ."

"All right. We have formed the Round Valley Conservation League as a nonprofit corporation . . ."

And so it went on through the afternoon.

There was plenty more to do during those few days, drumming up support for the valley. The sport fishermen in San Francisco seemed to be the most enthusiastic, and they were already spreading the word to other groups. Then he came across a geologist, Frank Spurlock, who reminded him of the Vaiont disaster in Italy, just four years earlier in 1963, and gave him an account of it.

As he read, mentally transposing the event to countryside and people he knew, it had a chilling fascination. It was the worst dam disaster in history, with three thousand lives lost. The cause was a sudden and massive landslide—three hundred million cubic yards of rock fell into the reservoir at a speed of sixty miles an hour, displacing the water and driving it out with phenomenal force. Amazingly the dam itself was unharmed, and still a three-hundred-foot-high wave swept over the top of it and destroyed everything in its path. The tremors were recorded hundreds of miles away.

One of the major concerns in the Eel River basin had always been landslides. The railroad had struggled with them for half a century, and Richard already knew that the engineers, both state and army, had devoted tremendous resources to studying the problem. They claimed the Dos Rios site was stable. They claimed that the problem of landslides had been taken care of. To Richard it still seemed like a vulnerable area and (being honest with himself) a fruitful source of alarm. For now the challenge was to raise any objections he could think of to cause delay. He added it to his Friday speech, and invited Spurlock to come up, too, and say something about the geology of the area.

His relationship with the people at California Tomorrow had grown strong and productive, and he was filling sheets of legal paper with names of potential allies. He began to get a sense of the network of groups with environmental interests that Lewis and his friends had created over the years, and was surprised how extensive it was. The numbers of people involved were relatively small, but they were all highly motivated.

Tess Jesenko in the *Ukiah Journal* cheered him up when she finally came down off the fence.

"The newly formed Round Valley Conservation League deserves all the support it can get," she wrote. "Funds are urgently needed to preserve the Valley. Membership dues are $10."

Then he got some more encouragement from Clem Vanoni of the Geyserville Chamber of Commerce. Geyserville is a small city on the Russian River, about halfway between Covelo and San Francisco. Coyote Dam, which the corps had built near Ukiah, was supposed to protect the Russian River from flooding, but Vanoni said the flood control was a joke. He was going to the hearing himself, but he gave Richard a bunch of figures on Coyote and another dam the corps had planned. He said they showed what a financial mess you could get into when you swallowed the flood control bait.

Friday the fifteenth arrived almost before he knew it, and he found himself driving up from the Bay Area, with Curt, still trying to digest the information that was pouring in.

The auditorium of the high school in Willits is an unusually handsome one. Unlike the more usual multipurpose gymnasium that accommodates every kind of activity and doesn't properly suit any, this was built as a real theater. It is large enough to seat six hundred, with one large, sweeping balcony and a deep stage framed by plum velvet curtains. By two-thirty a large crowd was already seated, cigarette smoke wafted through the air, and small groups were conferring here and there. Richard recognized many people from Round Valley. Elmer was there, of course, and Bud, and many members of the Hurt and Rohrbough families had arrived.

Distinctly separate was a small knot of people gathered around a stocky man with glasses and an amiable grin. This was Jan Stewart, the hardware merchant from Montana, talking to other dam boosters from Covelo. A solid contingent of Indians had taken places toward the back, as was their tendency, but Ida was close to the stage with Norman and a few of their friends. Jim McCombs welcomed them and introduced Nita, and his brother Norman, who was there to represent the Covelo Grange.

Richard had notes for his speech on cards, as Curt had advised him, and he busied himself looking over them while they waited for the meeting to begin. Public meetings generally have a dilatory beginning, but not when the army is in charge. The corps doesn't enter a hall. The corps invests it, as in a military operation.

Colonel Boerger, Charlie Elmore, and the boys marched up the aisle in a phalanx and took possession of the stage. Vigorously, efficiently, exuding confidence, they set up their maps and charts. Then the colonel faced the audience and, assuming command, entered into the business of the day. The business went on for hours, covering every aspect of the project, from the original exploratory surveys the corps had made in the thirties, to the golden vistas of opportunity that would be opened up to Mendocino in the coming millennium.

As anticipated, come "happy hour" the crowd began to thin. After the corps, an engineer from the Department of Water Resources held the stage for a while, the Department of Fish and Game read a statement of concern about the inadequacy of hatcheries and water to keep the fish running, and then the counties had their say. Boerger had a list of would-be speakers, and he controlled the order of appearance. Mendocino's county engineer presented his analysis and spoke at length about the detriment to the county. Lake County reiterated its determination to get the water to go through Clear Lake, saying if they couldn't get the state to change its mind they would oppose the project altogether.

The two anthropologists Richard had enlisted made a surprisingly strong case for spending several million to salvage the record of the Yuki culture before it was too late. Don Todd of the Mendocino Farm Bureau said they were opposed because it was all for the benefit of Los Angeles. So far, nobody had said anything about saving the valley for its own sake. If the army's purpose was to convince the meeting that the question was not whether to build the dam but merely how to make the dam more palatable, they seemed to have succeeded. At last Richard was called, and, as he rose, Curt switched on the recorder.

Nervous but determined, Richard began: "Ladies and gentlemen, I am Richard Wilson, rancher and farmer from Round Valley and representing the Round Valley Conservation League, a nonprofit corporation. I am here today to enter a plea—a plea for your support and a plea for restraint upon those federal and state agencies which have moved into our area and submitted a proposal that the only way of meeting their demands is to take our beautiful valley and its surrounding mountains and turn it into a reservoir for flood control, water storage, and recreation."

He went on to talk about the uniqueness of the valley. "Perhaps it is because the state of California is so richly blessed with beauty and natural resources that we take this area for granted, but please let me say that it will not take too many more dams like this, and the children of future generations can look at the inland valleys of our state in picture books only. Nature's architect still commands more respect than man-made projects."

He invited contributions to the league. He questioned the value of the promised flood control, using Coyote Dam as an example. He asked, facetiously, whether the army's desire for "local cooperation" meant the cooperation "of those who are going to lose their homes, who are going to lose their land, who are going to have their cemeteries dug up and who are going to move their means of livelihood?"

He did his best with landslides, quoting a state bulletin on the danger of destructive waves, and he went into some detail about Sonoma County's financial history with a different corps project, pointing out that "in projects of this size and magnitude you can think once and only once. If the dam is built and we wish we hadn't done it, all we can do is pay for it." He warned that if the north coast abandoned all its traditional occupations—lumber, fisheries, and cattle—in favor of an uncertain future based in tourism, they might be spawning a second Appalachia. Flooding Round Valley ran contrary to California's own resolutions regarding the preservation of land.

"Look before you leap," he said, and sat down.

As a speech it was not very good. Too sketchy in some places, too involved in others, with arguments that sometimes were difficult to follow and sometimes seemed to miss the target. But he had learned some of Curt's lessons. It was immeasurably better than the stilted peroration he had drafted first. In one important respect, though, he did very well. He demonstrated a commanding presence, the only one to match Colonel Boerger's, and his supporters recognized him as a worthy champion. His sincerity was unmistakable, and when he finished there was enthusiastic applause.

"Mr. Jan Stewart? It's your turn to speak next," called out Boerger, and Jan Stewart stood up. There was no grin on his face now. He said he was there to speak for Covelo businessmen, and the Covelo Action Committee. The economy of the area had suffered seriously, he said, and they felt the dam was a way out, but as soon as he began to speak, angry voices called out to contradict him. Ninety-five percent of the businessmen in Covelo supported the dam, he insisted.

"Well, how many businessmen are there?" called somebody.

"Twelve or fourteen," he said, flustered.

"I hope you go under," said another scathing voice, and booing resounded through the hall. The owner of a 28,000-acre property unwisely got up to offer his support to the corps and got the same treatment, with shouts of "What about the rest of us?" and "You'll be sitting pretty."

Jim's brother got up to speak for the farmers in the Round Valley Grange, and his simple statement obviously drew a lot of sympathy. Saying that all the corps could offer people like himself was a chance to make money off tourists, he said: "We try to keep the ticks off our cattle, but we would be parasites, too, living off somebody else."

It was nearly eight o'clock as the last speakers trailed off, Frank Spurlock among them, raising the specter of earthquake damage. Boerger closed the meeting politely, as imperturbable as ever after a grueling five hours, and promised to include the points raised when he presented his final report. Jim McCombs had been standing with a group of engineers at the back of the hall while Richard made his arguments.

"One of them turned to me," he recalled, "and said, 'We often get guys like that. They come along and make a big speech, and then we never hear from them again.' "

When Jim passed the comment on to Richard and Curt after the meeting, they laughed. They felt they had reason to be pleased, particularly with the support from the valley. On top of that, they had opened up many lines of attack that Curt thought would be fruitful.

Richard was a little hesitant there.

"Our criticisms have all been made with too little information. It's a cute game. They let us blast off about earthquakes, landslides, flood control, and the rest of it, and leave us to think we've scored points. But they've got this mass of information that they can use to rebut everything we put up, and if we don't have anything new to add we may never get a chance to come back at them.

"We have to get the corps engineering report, and we have to get an independent analysis done. Just as Lake County has done over the routing question."

"We'd better decide how we're going to handle that," Curt pointed out. "It's good for us in a way, because it may cause delays, but if they get their way, they are going to push for the dam like crazy, and to hell with us. That Lake County group is a sleazy bunch, in my opinion."

"Let's not get involved with them," said Richard. "We should just concentrate on the dam. We have to come up with the right corporation to do a review. I've been looking, and so have a number of people I've talked to. Kaiser are out. They've got their snouts in the trough already. Same goes for Bechtel and the others I've come across. Also they're horrendously expensive. Maybe the Sierra Club will pay for some of this."

Richard made a note to mention it to Lewis. He could talk to Mike McCloskey, who was the Sierra Club's conservation director. Curt said he'd get the tape transcribed, and then Richard had better get together with him and plan some more activity.

"But I guess it's pretty much over for the year. Don't forget to read the papers. Pray for rave reviews."

The Santa Rosa *Press Democrat* devoted sixty column inches to the meeting in its Sunday edition. STREAMS OF PRAISE AND RIDICULE FLOOD HEARING ON DOS RIOS DAM flowed the headline. An exhaustive account included three paragraphs on Richard's "lengthy" speech, and reported that he had drawn heavy applause. But the icing came off the cake two paragraphs later, when the paper mistakenly printed his name in place of Jan Stewart's, making it seem as though he had gone from acclamation to abuse in no time flat.

Curt called from San Francisco to congratulate and commiserate.

"It happens all the time," he said. "Don't worry. People will sort it out for themselves, if they care. But did you notice that the three of your points he picked up in his report were all made at the end of your speech? That's really common, and really important. People write down the last thing they hear. Try to summarize your most important points at the end, in a snappy way. Amazing how many don't. Even professionals. Merry Christmas."

16

Wish-wash at the Courthouse and Hogwash at the Fair

COLONEL BOERGER AND RICHARD WILSON were locked in battle over the Mendocino County supervisors. Both men had allies on the board, and both were bringing all the pressure they could to bear. For Richard it was a critical conflict. He had to keep them at the very least undecided, or it would weaken his chances tremendously, maybe fatally. For Boerger there was not quite so much at stake. He was confident that the project would go through with or without their agreement, but it would greatly help the project to have the supervisors on his side.

He could have nothing but sympathy for their predicament. On the one hand, they subscribed $5,000 a year to the Eel River Association, and were in full agreement with its aims and purposes. On the other hand, they represented a poor county, in terms of tax dollars, and there was no doubt that taking Round Valley off the books would cut the county budget even further. They were bound to put the interests of their county first, and while Round Valley may have been worthless to the other seven counties, it was worth $50,000 a year in taxes to Mendocino.

Looking for some positive benefit they could hold out to their voters, he hoped to convince them that the recreational facilities at the lake would bring in much more money than they would lose.

He had met them all several times, and must have known that some would be more open to his arguments than others. The two supervisors from the coast, Joe Scaramella and Augie Avila, were not happy about the dam. Perhaps a lingering connection to their European peasant origins left them with stronger feelings about the value of land. Joe, in particular, was adamantly opposed to flooding the valley. Augie seemed a lot more flexible and would probably come to terms.

Ernie Banker, the charmer, was wavering somewhere in the middle but would probably come down with the majority. Harvey Sawyers he already knew from Eel River Association meetings, and of course there was no doubt where he stood. Sawyers and the new young guy, John Mayfield, were the hard-headed businessmen, eager to have something happen. They would go for anything that would breathe some life into their stagnant districts.

Sawyers was a handsome and pleasant man, playing a difficult role. Mayfield had a rough edge to him—maybe a touch of ruthlessness—and he no doubt realized the project was a fact of life, and could see past the tax problem to how it could generate income. He also knew his nuisance value, and Boerger foresaw some hard bargaining. Mayfield was due to take over the chairmanship of the board in the new year, and would be a force to reckon with.

For the moment, though, Joe Scaramella was chairman, and at the board meetings, which Boerger and Charlie Elmore attended, he talked harshly about the loss of land and agricultural productivity.

"This is fourteen percent of our usable farmland," he said. "Is it worth flooding twenty thousand acres up here, in order to save twenty thousand acres downriver?"

Boerger was tactful, and said nobody relished inundating the valley, but there simply wasn't any evidence that Round Valley would develop much economically. In any case, he added, though flood control was a very important element, what made the project feasible as well as essential was the great value of the water that would be sent over the hill to Sacramento.

"What I think you're saying," said Joe, "is that the state wants this water and is paying for it with flood control. But we in Mendocino County don't get any flood control. What we get is to lose our biggest area of farmland. That's why we can't support this dam."

Boerger nodded. He knew this was the critical issue and he approached it carefully. He argued that the county would not, in fact, lose money in the long run.

"Going by experience elsewhere," he said, "land values around the lake may rise rapidly. Mr. Elmore here has some early estimations of the additional tax revenue that will accrue simply from the arrival of the construction crews, and they are considerable. I have asked for this and other information to be included in an office report, and I would like to come back and discuss this with the board."

Trying to win support in the community, Boerger made himself available to address service club luncheons. He was an impressive speaker. His style was necessarily formal and restrained, as befitted a soldier, but a hint of suppressed emotion added great force. And he knew his stuff. He had the facts and figures at his fingertips. It was a delight to his audiences in these small towns to be treated to such a polished, professional performance, and they were flattered. He brought a pleasing sense of purpose, a glimpse of wider perspectives, and, best of all, a reminder that there was more to life than petty parochial concerns.

Smartly uniformed, brisk and reassuring in his explanations, he was welcomed by Lions, Kiwanis, taxpayers, women voters, and spoke to anyone who would listen. Talking to the Rotarians in Willits, he said recreation facilities on the lake would "unquestionably have a favorable and lasting effect on the economic situation in the north coastal area, and especially Mendocino County, the county of origin."

The highways, he said, were getting better all the time, and bringing more and more people up north. And he played a potent card when he said that the dirt road across the coastal range to the Sacramento River would become a fast highway, bringing thousands if not millions of happy spenders across to the coast from the Central Valley.

"At the Greer's Ferry Reservoir in Texas," he said, "land values in the area adjacent to the reservoir increased from $6.4 million in 1960 to $9.9 million in 1966." More figures followed to whet the appetites of the assembled businessmen. No doubt there were some there who began to think seriously about picking up some of the action. There were people with parcels of land in the hills who were already congratulating themselves on their lakeside properties. Some of them were growing marijuana, the county's major cash crop. Some had been tipped off ahead of time that the lake was coming. With a shoreline of more than two hundred miles, there would be plenty of room for development. Boerger had only to point out that eventually it would bring money to the county. Then he ended with the perfectly modulated salesman's pitch. "Hurry!" he said. "The longer we wait to take advantage of this fortuitous combination of circumstances . . . the greater the penalty will be."

There was a Churchillian ring to his coda.

"The time is now to seek authorization of this project. The time is now when construction can best be accomplished at least expense. The time is now when demand can best be satisfied economically. The time is now when best to use federal assistance without federal control, to help the people of this area in meeting their needs."

Because of the controversy, the supervisors were attracting a lot more attention than usual. Richard was trying to get as many of his supporters into the meetings as possible, just to create a presence. Still it was difficult to oppose Boerger. If there was one thing the corps could do with ease and aplomb, it was provide information. Boerger could tap into reams and stacks of it. Reports, analyses, comparisons, surveys, studies, statistical summaries from projects past, present, and putative tumbled out at his command, available to clarify or confuse as the case might be. While Richard could not even get his hands on the one report he needed most—the hefty Interim Project Report that he knew the corps had already put out for review to selected officials—Boerger reveled in his resources. Quoting from two thick documents, he forecast that by the year 2000 lands around the lake would increase in value by $15 to $23 million, that personal income would go up by over a million, that there would be almost 200 new jobs, and 720 more people. As to the immediate future, "due to the flooding of Round Valley in 1980, temporary declines are expected," but, he said, "these declines are abruptly reversed and are expected to be offset within two to six years." There would be "larger numbers" of summer residents and other recreationists, a "minimum disruption" of business activity in a relocated Covelo "due to the influx of construction and maintenance workers." He said his staff had calculated the county would take in about half a million dollars just from increased sales, license fees, and cigarette taxes from the construction workers and their families alone. That would be almost as much as the county feared losing.

To Richard's great relief when Jim McCombs reported to him on the meeting, Joe Scaramella did not buy Boerger's package. Joe said the board had opposed the dam in 1964, and all that he had heard since offered "few, if any, benefits to Mendocino County." Their own engineer, he said, waving a report at the colonel, had concluded that the county got no flood control benefits and nothing for their water, but instead would have to pay for roads and recreation facilities and would lose substantial agricultural productivity.

Then he introduced a resolution to make clear the county's total opposition to the entire project. The recreation scheme was all well and good, he said, but the county would have to fork out $2 million, half the cost of setting it up, as well as half the maintenance costs.

"If anyone should pay for the recreation facilities," he said, "it should be the people who are going to get the water."

No way could the county afford it, and there was already a resolution refusing to accept this burden. To a scattering of applause from the crowd, he declared, "The corps and everyone should know what the position of Mendocino County is."

Boerger may not have been too perturbed by this outburst when he left the courthouse that afternoon. He could see which way the wind was blowing. Someone else might have to come up with that $2 million. Maybe the state. Maybe the Met. In a $400 million project, $2 million was hardly a big consideration. Then the supes could say they'd done a good deal for the county and get reelected. As for Joe's resolution, he didn't think it had a hope. This was Joe Scaramella's last meeting as chairman. Next time John Mayfield would be in the chair.

The recreation facility became the major bone of contention with the supervisors, and Richard did everything he could to discredit it. He knew how important it was to the corps to keep that element of the project alive. It helped to improve the benefit/cost ratio. It added to the impression that this really was a multipurpose project, and not just a water tank for Southern California. At the same time—and this was what endeared it to Gianelli's Department of Water Resources—through some smart arithmetic, it made the water cheaper for the ultimate consumers.

But the most obvious advantage was that it did wonders for the corps's image. The corps and its believers in Congress had always known the importance of the swimming, boating, camping, and fishing they offered at their reservoirs. It was the human face of dam building; it projected the impression they were eager to make, that they weren't just stony-faced men evicting helpless citizens for the benefit of remote interests or careless urban communities. It was particularly important to them to keep the recreational element alive in this case because it helped to justify the argument that this dam was a boon to the north coast. It was the argument Bill Warne had made, that Gianelli and the cohorts of the Eel River Association had repeated, and that all the water buffs were chorusing. Recreation, they said, would revive and protect the economy of the north coast. They knew the flood control element was weak, though they never admitted as much. They needed a positively attractive ingredient.

The trouble was, the county couldn't afford to take on the burden of building and maintaining the campsites and boating ramps, and roads and sanitary facilities you need when a million people come and go. The corps was forbidden from paying for it, because it had nothing to do with flood control.

What Richard had to fear most was that someone would come up with the money, because then, it was almost certain that the county would have to support the project. As the new year began, Boerger and Gianelli both put their departments to work looking for a way to sweeten the deal.

In Mendocino the year opened with a flurry of activity. Farmers and ranchers belonging to the Grange and the Farm Bureau met to consolidate their opposition to the dam. Richard had already pointed out that without Round Valley, 85 percent of the cattle in Mendocino County would disappear, and when the idea sank in they were outraged. Even though the corps had already rejected the idea as unworkable, they pressed for a lower dam that wouldn't flood the valley, seeming unable to grasp that the corps was not interested in simply doing them favors.

Meanwhile the Lake County supervisors had created another huge distraction. They had invested $32,000 with the Kaiser engineering corporation for a report to rescue their claim on the Eel. The study was to be unveiled at the Lake County fairgrounds, more usually used for the judging of livestock. Everybody with an interest hurried over there to marvel at it, and Richard went, too, to see if he could find out what the opposition was up to.

Kaiser's exhibit turned out to have all the allure of a pedigree bull with fertility problems. Kaiser's vice-president, Frank Matthias, smiled down merrily at his hapless clients and told them the report wouldn't be ready for another thirty days, but he revived their flagging spirits by hinting that the results looked really promising and worth waiting for. However, this nonevent had great significance for Richard. He took advantage of the opportunity to ask one of the Kaiser engineers some questions about water supply and flood control, only to be rebuffed.

"These water matters are very complicated," the engineer told him. "It would not be possible for a layperson to understand them." This remark dug as deeply under Richard's skin as Baumli's offhand reference to piling up the oak trees and burning them. He repeated it often, and it spurred his determination even further. These engineers, he thought, have a real knack with language. Later, as he struggled to master all the complexities of water projects, the memory of that Kaiser engineer helped to keep him going.

Colonel Boerger was at the fairground, too, to hear Kaiser's news, but refused to comment on the lack of it. It hardly mattered to him how they took the water out of the reservoir. It would be the same dam whichever way they went. At least the Kaiser report reaffirmed that the high dam was the best and only way to go, so there was honor among engineers. He just wished there could be an end to the arguments. However, the rumor of good news to come was rushed to the Eel River Association, which met a few days later at Concord, with all five Mendocino supervisors joining in.

The association passed another resolution in favor of building the dam and flooding Round Valley by seven votes to two. Harvey Sawyers, who voted for Mendocino County, explained that he was obliged to vote no because he was hamstrung by that old 1964 resolution. However, he and the other Mendocino supervisors were still playing both ends against the middle. Richard observed, with some concern, that they had managed to get included in the resolution a plea to the state government to put up the money for the recreation facility.

Colonel Boerger was now a presence at all these events, and it was obvious to everyone that things were moving his way. He said he was pleased with the vote and that he had some new ideas for helping Mendocino County out of its dilemma, like moving and rebuilding Covelo much sooner than was planned. Next day, with his staff, he was in Covelo again. He met with Warren Lincoln, who was then still chairman of the Indian Tribal Council, to reassure him that Indian gravesites would be moved with great care and reverence. He spent a good deal of time with Jan Stewart's people explaining how the relocation and recreation schemes would work. There were engineers in the valley all the time now, and Boerger's presence there for three days emphasized the fact that they were now part of the scenery. All but the staunchest opponents to the dam assumed that they would never leave.

The Mendocino supervisors returned from their various excursions south, and reassembled in the Ukiah courthouse in a state of mounting indecision. With the exception of Scaramella, there is no doubt that they now all thought they should go with the dam, whether they liked it or not, and extract whatever crumbs of comfort they could get in exchange for their cooperation. Only Joe Scaramella would not let them simply slide into acquiescence. He insisted on reviving his motion to reaffirm opposition to the dam.

John Mayfield, who was now the chairman, appeared to do everything in his power to avoid the issue. The situation as it stood must have suited him fine. To those who were opposed to the dam, he could say, "The board of supervisors is on record against flooding Round Valley." To those who wanted the dam, he could say, "That was a different board, voting in 1964. Circumstances have changed, and we are just holding out for the best deal."

But Scaramella's resolution would close down the options. Mayfield was an ambitious young politician who already had his eyes on Sacramento and a position in the bureaucracy there. He probably didn't want to look like some provincial hick standing in the way of progress. He argued that there was no need to put the resolution to the vote. Why rub it in? It smacked of harassment, he thought, and it might complicate matters as the county tried to negotiate for more benefits, like roads, bridges, and compensation in case the dam was built anyway, meaning of course, "*when* the dam was built anyway."

Joe was adamant. He felt morally obligated to restate the county's opposition, and he got Ernie Banker to second him. However, the affair was neatly turned to Mayfield's advantage. Harvey Sawyers, the other dam booster on the board, proposed to table Scaramella's motion, and succeeded, with Mayfield's casting vote, in putting the motion into cold storage by a vote of 3–2. The effect of this was that Mayfield and Sawyers could now say, when it suited them, that the county had voted not to oppose the project, which was even better.

Nita McCombs watched this display with wrath and dismay, and wrote the board a scorching letter of criticism for their wishy-washy performance. She derided them, and Sawyers in particular, for being brainwashed by the corps. Her letter was read out at the next meeting, but had no appreciable effect other than to let them know that little sister was watching them.

It was plain now that Colonel Boerger had the momentum. Despite Kaiser's delinquency, he planned to wrap up his report and send it to his superiors as promised on the fifteenth of January. The routing question could be finally settled later. He had the great majority of the north coast counties solidly behind him. Mendocino was obviously ambivalent, and he could count on the state's approval. Richard had been right in thinking that the objections raised at the hearing would not count for much. Boerger, like his staff, was quite confident that they could all be overcome, and he saw no reason why the Dos Rios Dam should not be authorized by Congress that summer, as planned. He had only to be patient and polite, and Richard Wilson's local rebellion would fizzle out.

17

Dr. Brown Flies the Eel

RICHARD WAS very serious about getting an independent analysis of the Dos Rios Dam project. If he was going to pull it apart, it had to be credible. He also knew it would cost a fortune to go to one of the big engineering design companies for it, but he was prepared even for that. As it turned out, he was spared the expense.

"None of them would touch it," he says. "They wouldn't run the risk of offending the corps."

It occurred to Richard then that if he couldn't find an established engineering consultant to take an adversarial position on Dos Rios, maybe he could find an academic who would, and he called, among others, a zoologist he knew who was doing field research at Hopland, south of Ukiah.

Dr. William Longhurst, from U.C. Davis, was sympathetic. Longhurst was convinced that the dam would ruin the fishing in the Eel, with or without hatcheries. Davis itself, he said, would not be likely to produce the kind of help Richard needed. Almost all the research they did there was funded by agribusiness corporations, and the staff was pretty much sold on the State Water Project. He promised to look around elsewhere. In fact he did better than that. He instituted a systematic, nationwide search, and in mid-January he called Richard.

"I've found your man," he said. "He's teaching at the University of Washington in Seattle, and his name is Gardner Brown. He's a Ph.D. from Berkeley, a resource economist, and he did his doctoral thesis on the California Water Plan. He's no friend of the corps either. He's been working up a case against them on the Snoqualmie River. I think he'll do a good job."

As it happened, Richard had at last been able to get a copy of the corps report that same day, and it sat now on the desk in front of him. In its canary yellow cover (the cheerful color seemed incongruous and vaguely insulting) it had a peculiar fascination. It was a roughly bound block of copier paper, two inches thick, and it sat on his desk like a small tombstone. There were 572 pages of text, with 62 sheets of maps, graphs, and tables. The bland title read:

DRAFT
EEL RIVER BASIN
CALIFORNIA
INTERIM REPORT
ON
WATER RESOURCES DEVELOPMENTS
FOR
MIDDLE FORK EEL RIVER
NOVEMBER 1967

A stenciled number showed it to be the 136th copy distributed. The sheer weight of it, the exhausting industry required to produce it, the thoroughness and expense of it, the infinite detail, the cool assertions and the implacable conclusions it presented, all gave it the shocking reality of a terrible, irreversible accident. If he had been presented with this six months ago, he might well have thought, My God, nothing can stop this!

Now he could hardly wait to rip into it, hoping to find embedded in this block of lethally boring bureaucratese the seeds of its own destruction.

He began to glance through the report, at the authorizations by Congress, the maneuvers of various agencies as they staked out their claims, the list of previous reports, and then, in section after section, reports on topography, geology, soils, vegetation, surface and groundwater resources, fish and wildlife, mineral resources, population, land use, transport, water supplies, recreation, growth trends, climatology, stream flows, rainfall statistics, flood damages, water quality, electric power, improvements by other federal agencies, public hearings, the California Water Plan, the State Water Project, the Central Valley Project, the master conveyance system, the delta pool concept . . . and that was just the background reading.

The bulk of the report was about the project itself, how, where, and when it would be built, how much it would cost, who would pay for what, how it would work, and what would happen to the fish, the wildlife, the people. Here, on four pounds of wood pulp, was a complete plan to redesign the destinies of thousands of people, to wipe out all traces of an Indian tribe's ancestral home, to obliterate all the hopes and achievements of white settlers during their brief and sometimes gory history in the valley.

Again he was made vividly aware of the consequences, of three hundred feet of water sitting over Susan's garden, over his new ranchland, the trees, the churches, the schools, the prolific berry bushes, the old flour mill, the Indian burial grounds, the cattle baron's stately mansion, all under the biggest man-made lake in California. How could such a project have advanced so far without anyone in Round Valley having had a chance to object? What had happened to the supervisors and their stirring resolution? Had they all slept through it, like a community of Rip Van Winkles in "the valley that time forgot"?

One item caught his eye. In listing the flood damage that the dam was expected to avert in the future, the corps included an item of $28,000 a year for Round Valley. Of course Round Valley would be safe from flood damage. It would be under water. Richard later took grim satisfaction in exposing this gem of rationality.

Most of the report depended on observations and measurements it would be hard to challenge, but wherever he did have some basis for comparison, the report seemed to be at least vulnerable. The corps valued Round Valley at $12.5 million. That seemed low, and he found that the state had quoted a value of twice that amount. If he as a layman could find such discrepancies, what could an expert do with it? He dialed Gardner Brown's number in Seattle.

Richard was very fortunate once again. Longhurst had indeed found the perfect protagonist to face up to the water lobby. Gardner Brown, a young assistant professor, had come out of Berkeley with an encyclopedic knowledge of California water. He also believed that it was being largely misused, and he took nothing but pleasure in the opportunity to prove it, and to be paid in the bargain.

Richard asked him to fly down to San Francisco, met him there, and drove him back up to the Wilson residence in Round Valley, where he met Susan and the kids. They saw a tall, thin man with fair skin, angular features, and reddish blond hair receding from a high forehead. The cerebral intensity of his expression, emphasized by deep-set eyes and a rather high-pitched voice, disguised a dry sense of humor.

At first Brown was nervous in their presence. He had expected more formality and an overbearing display of wealth. He had dressed a little defiantly in casual hiking gear, and was surprised to find Richard in farm clothes that had obviously seen a lot of wear. As he put it later, "I have a problem with rich people. I regard them as guilty unless proven innocent, and so I had a certain amount of reserve when I first met them. Besides," he said, laughing, "they're Republicans."

Brown and his parents came originally from Boston. He ended up at Antioch College in Yellow Springs, Ohio, which was one of the last strongholds of resistance against McCarthy's "loyalty oath." Brown called it a "reservoir of radical kids," and he emerged with his idealism intact, but without the ideology. In fact he was totally committed to an open society.

Whatever his prejudices before he arrived in Covelo, he says Richard and Susan quickly disabused him of them. He remembers sitting in their kitchen talking through the evening, and remembers how gracious they were. As they talked that night, it was an opportunity for Richard to feel his way through some of the broader issues of his campaign. After all, he had to be able to justify, in his own mind, the stand he was taking. Was it really fair to deny so much water to the south? He had claimed, in his speeches so far, that he was not opposed to exporting water. The great water authorities, the men who were supposed to know, said the water was "desperately needed." Those words were heard again and again. Could they be true? To be sure of sharing common ground in any future discussions, he went over the project with Gardner from the bottom up.

Dos Rios was a so-called multipurpose project, meaning it set out to satisfy a number of different needs simultaneously. There were two ways to look at that. Either you could say the engineers had been commendably smart and inventive, and had found ways to get a lot of extra value without spending much more money, or you could say they were covering for what was essentially a weak project by tacking on bits and pieces of politically attractive trimming to win them support. The truth, as always, lay somewhere in between, and the problem was to identify the weaknesses.

To get Congress to buy a project, it had to be shown that it would deliver more in value than it cost, including the cost of construction. That is what was meant by a benefit/cost ratio higher than one—A simple problem to demonstrate in theory, though quite difficult in practice.

Here was a dam and a tunnel that cost $398 million to build. That was called the first cost. When finished it would provide water for export, protection from flooding, some hydroelectric power, and a recreational facility. Those were the four benefits. First you had to pick a time frame to say how long these benefits would last, and the usual time for such a project was a hundred years (a figure that covered a multitude of assumptions). Then you had to figure out what it would cost to repay that $398 million over a hundred years, just like a mortgage. Obviously the result depended on the rate of interest. Federal projects up to 1967 were charged at about 3.4 percent. The annual payments in this case came to $14,800,000.

Then you had to calculate the cost of maintaining it, and in the case of Dos Rios, the corps had arrived at a figure of $900,000. So these two figures added together were the annual costs: $15,700,000.

Because the corps's mandate was flood control, this was the benefit the report dealt with first. There were thirty-five pages of analysis devoted to figuring it out, but it broke down into two basic categories. How much future damage would be avoided? And how much extra value would the land have because it was now protected? The total annual benefit came to $1,510,000.

The biggest benefit by far was the water. How much water could be pumped out each year? According to the corps, 900,000 acre-feet. But what was it worth? This was the most important and most difficult part of the whole calculation. What the corps report said about it was: "Benefits . . . are based on the least cost of producing an equivalent annual yield from an alternative source."

But what would be an alternative source? The state insisted that there was nowhere else in California where they could hope to find this quantity of water. The only alternative source was the ocean.

In the sixties it was firmly believed that nuclear power would soon make it possible to get unlimited supplies of fresh water from the ocean at a reasonable price. In desert countries like Israel and Saudi Arabia, desalinization plants were already operating. Former President Eisenhower had published an article in *Reader's Digest* touting the prospects. A plant built in California had recently been shipped to Cuba to provide America's Guantanamo base with water, after Fidel Castro cut off the supply. And the Met was sponsoring a huge plant on Bolsa Island. These were just a few of the projects under way, and the information about this process was accumulating steadily. It seemed at the time that technological progress would bring the cost of energy down and make the desalting process more efficient. The only questions were, how much and how soon?

To put a value on Dos Rios water, the Department of Water Resources calculated what they thought water from the ocean would cost in 1980. They came up with a figure of $25 per acre-foot, which was what they said Dos Rios water would be worth to the Met. So the annual benefit from water was 900,000 times $25, or $22.5 million a year.

The next benefit was recreation. The corps usually built recreation facilities around its lakes, and in the sixties it published a booklet listing hundreds of lakes and pools throughout the United States where people could play. Lake Covelo was claimed to be a potential winner, where up to seven million vacationers might spend a day each year, but for this report it contented itself with projecting a million "visitor-days," and worked out what that might be worth as income. This section of the report was incredibly complex. The calculations to arrive at the dollar value of a recreational facility involve a host of considerations, including the impact of the dam on wildlife, fish, and vegetation. Nevertheless, the corps trudged on undaunted, and arrived at a figure of $1,210,000.

The last benefit, the hydroelectric power, was relatively simple to work out, and the smallest item in the list, although some assumptions were made that could be challenged. The amount given was $210,000.

So, the annual benefits added up to $25,430,000. Compared with annual costs of only $15,700,000 it was obviously a good deal. The benefit/cost ratio was 1.62.

Of course, Richard wanted to know where Gardner Brown thought he would start. The biggest item was water. If you could show that the water was worth less than $25, you could bring the ratio right down. For example, if the water was worth only $20 an acre-foot, the ratio came down to 1.33. At $15 an acre-foot, the project was not worth building, and Congress could never authorize it. Gardner would have to get more information from the state about their calculations, and collect data on desalinization. He could not tell what that would bring, but there was one area where Gardner was fairly confident. He felt sure the costs had been underestimated.

He told Richard that the corps had been seriously embarrassed recently by cost overruns. Their estimators were trying to get it right, but he felt sure of finding some heavy discrepancies there, and their bad record would help to give his criticisms credibility. At the same time, he knew they were trying all kinds of tricks to increase the benefits, because they really wanted these projects.

"On the Snoqualmie," he said, "I discovered that they were, in effect, cheating. They had developed procedures that systematically overestimated benefits, and underestimated construction costs."

With the pleasure of a Little Jack Horner pulling out a plum, he added: "The thing about the corps is, they're not allowed to lie. If you ask them straight questions, they have to give you straight answers. You can really get at them."

Richard wanted to be sure that Gardner would not content himself with the obvious criticisms. Those would not do here. He would have to be original and creative. Obviously knocking down the value of the water would be great, but he had in mind another major factor in the cost of the dam, and that was the rock, or "borrow," that they would have to find to build it. How could the corps know it was to be found so close by? Dragging twenty-five million cubic yards of rock an extra mile would cost a penny or two!

Richard had given much thought to Gardner Brown's visit. He knew he would be asking a lot from the economist, and he wanted to engage Brown emotionally in the battle to save the valley. He came up with an inspired idea.

A great practical advantage to Richard's patrician upbringing was that he never felt obliged to make personal enemies of the people he opposed. Disgusted though he might be with the intended outcome of their efforts, he was on cordial terms with the engineers he met working around the Eel River. In particular, he had become friendly with a helicopter pilot named Byron, whose job was to patrol the river and make observations of its behavior for the Department of Water Resources.

Byron said he would be pleased to take Richard's friend on a sightseeing trip along the Middle Fork of the Eel, and this became an experience that Gardner would never forget. He still admires Richard's vision in realizing how effective it would be for him to see, from this unusual vantage point, the terrain he would be helping to protect. The incident also had its comic aspect, which gave Richard a little quiet pleasure. Byron, employed by the state, had little idea that he was transporting a man who was dedicated to terminating the whole project, while Gardner was deeply impressed by this display of largesse, thinking Richard had commissioned the helicopter at his own expense especially for him.

The experience was inspiring to Gardner. They circled up over the valley for a while until Byron tilted the machine forward and they dashed across the high southerly ridges to Dos Rios. The hillsides were dark and moist from recent rains, clothed here and there with brush and smaller trees. Then, as they began to drop down over the green bridge, he saw winding away below him the bright gash where the river had ripped away the skin of earth and exposed the silvery gray rock beneath.

They swooped down into the canyon, very close to one tall sentinel of rock that jutted out into the river's path, and rushed upstream over the livid boulders and pebbles of the riverbed. It was too young a river for mossy banks and trees to line its course. Every winter in flood it reamed out its bed and tore away whatever life had found a precarious foothold during the summer, bringing yet more debris tumbling down from above. And so it would go on year in, year out, until some unimaginably distant time when "every valley shall be exalted, and every mountain and hill made low."

Or, of course, until the river was dammed.

Gardner knew enough about rivers to know that this annual purge was not just an act of senseless destruction. Countless life-forms had adapted to the cycle. Nobody could know the consequences of interrupting it. He was very glad to have a chance to keep at least this one natural process alive.

Before Richard took him back to the airport, he reiterated just how much they would be relying on him. Brown had to come up with something that would shake the legislature's confidence in the project and justify another hearing—something Ike Livermore could use to question his own water department. Only then could they hope to delay authorization. Only that way could they buy the time to bring the legislature and the governor to their senses.

Gardner was thrilled and a little apprehensive. Here was something rather different from what he was used to. As an academic he was accustomed to doing radical reappraisals of public policy, being complimented on them by his peers, and largely ignored by the engineers and planners whose work he was criticizing. Now, to his surprise, he was being offered a chance to stick his oar right into the mainstream of action by a man who evidently had access to the decision makers.

He entered into the spirit of the thing, and from his knowledge of the California Water Project, was able to suggest an even more potent weapon with which to beat Gianelli. In effect, he said, the Department of Water Resources might well be lying when they said there was no other source of comparable amounts of water. Richard was excited with the results of this visit. He had confidence in Gardner. And what a kick it would be to prove that Dos Rios was not only uneconomic but completely unnecessary, too? If only the issue could be kept alive long enough to get to the truth!

Richard paid Gardner's airfare and expenses out of his own pocket, and promised him three thousand dollars for his report, or more if he could get financing from some of the other groups. While the conservation league was raising a few dollars here and there, it was obvious that without Richard to bankroll the campaign, they could never have gotten the action going in time. Not for the first time, he appreciated that having a few thousand dollars in the bank could mean the difference between effective action and paralysis.

18

What Is Wilderness Worth?

FEW HAVE MUCH SYMPATHY for the problems of the wealthy, least of all with the problems of wealth itself, but they exist nonetheless. Richard was made acutely aware of them by his upbringing. In the first place his father, though married to a rich woman, worked extremely hard in a conspicuous and much-admired profession and plainly considered money one of the less important rewards of his life. Then, in his summers he was immersed in a life far removed from ease and luxury, challenged by men who rarely had more than enough to see them through the week. He thrived on their appreciation and respected their skills regardless of the wages they commanded, and the style of his education at Thacher reinforced these values.

As time went by he saw many well-endowed young lives in his own social circle dissolve in a haze of alcohol or, later, end violently in drug-related deaths. Given the advantage of his particular perspective, he could see and act on what his peers either failed to realize or were unequipped to deal with: that money often supplanted relationships, and that too much money could render a person worthless.

He talked about it later in relation to his own children.

"I thought it was much more beneficial to bring them up in the kind of environment that we have had, and let them go into the world armed with that, than to have me busting my ass making money and setting up trusts, and watching them go down the drain, as so many of my friends have done.

"They get nothing from it. Nothing. The kids are zero. I've seen it."

He was lucky to inherit his father's strength of character, for all its intransigence, and he also inherited his father's religion, which supported him spiritually, but he did not inherit the vocation, and the lack of one was seriously troubling at first. It was bred into him that he had to have some purpose on this earth to which he could harness his spirit and resources. It was that need that undoubtedly decided him to move to Round Valley, and he was more than lucky that Susan was ready to join him in his adventure.

You could not run a cattle operation in the hills without acreage in the valley to grow winter feed. Buying land in the valley was all-important.

"The ranch was known as the Perata ranch. Johnny Perata was an undertaker. He had it for years, but it fell into difficult times and went into a bankruptcy sale. I bought it in Monterey County. It didn't have water and was all run down. I drilled the first big well, and built the feedlot up on Simmerly Flat, and at one time I had three thousand head of cattle out there."

At first he was simply engrossed in the challenge of making his ranch profitable. Being relatively wealthy made him all the more determined to succeed. He knew very well that there were some in the valley who had taken advantage of his father's generosity and absences, and that was all very well for a man whose reputation was securely based in a quite different world, but it would not do for him to be seen as an easy mark. He did not want to be considered a gentleman farmer. He was determined that he would be an integral part of his ranching operation.

He had seven or eight people working for him, but there was no job he did not do himself. He fed the cows and chased them. He worked the fields and mended the fences. He worked with all the farm machinery and helped repair it as far as he was able. It was in his treatment of vehicles that he perhaps most resembled his father, for he drove them all with a fearless abandon, and people whom he visited, hearing him roar up to their doors in his pickup, wondered what he might have driven over in his abstract haste.

It was normal for him to be seen slouching home at high noon with that forward leaning stance of the tractor driver, covered in grime and oil, with his striped denim shirt flapping over hip-hung pants, his face sunk in heat and exhaustion. He could have paid a dozen men to do what he did, but he was determined to beat the money into second place, never talked about it, refused indeed to acknowledge its existence except as the coin by which the integrity of his work was measured.

People naturally were bemused by the desire of this rich man to roll in the dirt with the rest of them. He had to struggle hard to earn respect as a cattleman. His temperament was far from the placid ideal for a stockman. He thrived on action, new ideas, and modern methods, which naturally invited skepticism and even quiet mockery. What he lacked in natural empathy for cows, he made up with hard work and tough decisions, and his greatest success as a rancher was appropriately political. For the year of 1967, he was elected president of the Mendocino Cattlemen's Association.

Richard's innovations were very much along the lines of orthodox agriculture as practiced at that time in the Central Valley. They were designed to draw as much value as possible from his valley acreage, without too much concern for long term effects or broader considerations. In essence they meant pushing his corn yields for winter feed with maximum amounts of artificial fertilizer and energy-intensive irrigation. His treatment of the land only differed from that of agribusiness in the scale of the operation. In the fall of '67 he was supervising the construction of a trench silo—a huge trench with a concrete floor that would hold three thousand tons of cattle feed and ferment it. Surrounded by a big investment in costly machinery and land, he had plenty to do without having to fight the government as well.

With hindsight it is clear that his achievements as a cattleman could not have satisfied him for long, and the threat mounted against Round Valley, though most unwelcome was also, in a sense, timely. It found in him a great fund of unused energy and stretched him as ranching alone never could. Now, as his campaign to protect the valley became the principal focus of his life, Richard devoted more and more of himself to that end. His own awareness shifted and deepened, and expressed itself in different ways. His childhood familiarity with the terrain, the peaks, slopes, draws, and river canyons, was transformed into an ecological map, and the information he had subconsciously absorbed about grasses, rock formations, forests, and wildlife became a personal encyclopedia of resources.

The river, Richard's river, the "Middle Eel," as he had always known it, begins in the Yolla Bolly Mountains, on a great array of peaks and slopes, fanning out in a fifty-mile arc east of Round Valley. There among subarctic vegetation such as foxtail and lodgepole pine, the snowpack slowly seeps between particles of decrepitating rock, performing innumerable small life-giving acts as it goes. From San Hedrin Mountain, Bald Mountain, Black Butte, Anthony Peak, Buck Rock, Hammerhorn Ridge, Castle Peak, and Leech Lake Mountain—all of them over 6,000 feet—the moisture gathers and slowly descends.

Long before the water becomes even as definable as a rivulet, it has been midwife to myriad organisms and brought nourishment to uncounted shrubs and small trees. In their turn these life-forms knit the rock particles together, shed their dead matter to mingle with the rock, and hold the moisture back. All of this has a profound effect on what is crudely called a river. Delaying the percolation of the water on its downward path, it keeps the river alive through the rainless months from April to September, and even through the seven-year drought cycles that come and go.

Farther down the slopes, where it is warm and the snow turns to rain, the water follows more recognizable paths. Trickles become streams and move with enough momentum to carry soil and organic matter down the hillsides. Countering this downward pull, the warmth encourages more growth. Douglas fir, California bay, live oak, madrone, maple, and scores of other trees put out deeper and more extensive roots. This area also hosts one of the world's widest selections of berry bushes and plant growth, established here during an unusually welcoming glacial period. Thick layers of humus cover the forested ground on these steep slopes, holding back both the water and the soil and supporting a hierarchy of wildlife that is only hinted at by its more visible members, the bears, deer, mountain lions, bobcats, foxes, possums, coyotes, snakes, and lizards.

All the time there is the slow, unceasing descent of inanimate matter, drawn by the river through its tracery of veins into the canyons below, where the main arteries—Elk Creek, Black Butte River, Williams Creek, Beaver Creek, and the Middle Eel itself—run. Some of the detritus is rock, fine particles or sizable chunks, depending on the force of the stream. Some is vegetable matter, which feeds the aquatic life of the river. Along the watershed, from the mountains to the mouth, different versions of the same process occur, feeding the river with what it needs where it needs it, and protecting it.

In the upper reaches in the summer the most visible life in the river is the steelhead, and nobody who has seen these big, colorful fish curving lazily through the golden waters of sunlit rock pools will easily forget the peacefulness of the moment. They subsist on the insects fed by the measured increments of floating matter from the forests and, like the salmon, they spawn on the gravel beds washed clean of silt by winter floods.

Farther down are the ducks, water ouzels, turtles, otters, frogs, rainbow trout. Above them flutter wild turkeys, grouse, quail, and owls, and above these soar golden and bald eagles and the ever-present vultures.

It takes a good deal of familiarity and reflection to conceive of the river as being not just a visible body of water moving over a bed but a pulsating system of moisture, with most of the attributes of a living organism, covering a piece of land shaped not by political boundaries but by the law of gravity. The river is really the watershed. It is intimately commingled with the earth. Everything that lies in the watershed affects the river, all one ecological entity, through which water moves. Whatever lives naturally within the watershed can be sustained by it. Is it so absurd, then, to think that human society, too, would be healthier and function better as an integrated part of the watershed?

As Richard examined his own knowledge in this new light, he became much more consciously aware of the interdependence of all these elements. He had become, without even intending it, a conservationist. Inevitably, some of his farming practices did not fit very well with this expanded vision, and gave rise to yet more internal debate. While he continued in public to talk about saving Round Valley, in his inner thoughts it was the entire watershed that he saw as being at stake, and he asked more probing questions about the evident degradation of rural life.

It had to be admitted that there was depression in Covelo, that things did not look bright economically, but surely it did not have to be so. Wasn't this a symptom of some much more general malaise rather than an isolated blight that could be excised and forgotten? Surely it would be better to restore vigor and optimism to Round Valley rather than drown it?

It was too easy, he realized, for city people in California to dismiss agricultural land as expendable. With such a long history of making large tracts of desolate land blossom, and bringing in huge harvests of cheap produce, why should any one smallish area be preserved if it could produce more profit with a shopping mall or a reservoir on top of it.

It was also easy to see how an immense conurbation like Southern California would act as a center of gravity to suck more and more of the state's wealth into its orbits, impoverishing the surrounding countryside. As Richard developed his ideas of the watershed as an economic and cultural unit, the wastefulness and damage of current unplanned and unrestrained growth became more apparent, and he was inclined to blame it for destructive social consequences, too—the Watts riots being one example.

Looking for the causes of Round Valley's decline obliged him to take a historical view as well, and he found himself searching through his own history and his family's long reach back into the beginnings of the white man's America. Those people, like his own ancestors, the Grants, who first came to America from Europe in the eighteenth century or before, were impressed by what appeared to be an inexhaustible abundance. Everything seemed to be in excess. What first struck the early colonists was the extraordinary variety, quantity, and size of fish and seafood.

The rivers of Virginia, it seems, teemed with fish, to the extent that horses stepped on them and "colonists scooped them up in frying pans." An observer wrote in 1636: "I myself at the turning of the tyde have seen such multitudes of sea bass that it seemed to me that one might goe over their backs dri-shod."

Often the Pilgrims in Massachusetts had nothing to eat but lobster. There was talk of vast crabs, each sufficient to feed four men, and of patriarchal lobsters five and six feet long caught in New York Bay until Revolutionary days, when "since the incessant cannonading" they disappeared. The great codfish banks off New England supplied not just America but the whole of Europe. The Chesapeake Bay furnished prodigious quantities of swan and wild duck. The arrival of a flock was said to sound "like a great storm coming over the water," and the abundance of trees and plants was described in similar terms.

By comparison, the America Richard knew would have to be described as anemic, yet governments and engineers were behaving as though they were living in the America of his great-grandfather, when natural beauty was in profusion and resources were a glut on the market, when the entire West was up for grabs. Just to think of those times could make one's heart ache. To think of how it had all gone, piecemeal, bit by bit, to settle a family, make a business, lay a track, excavate a mine, run a road, fuel a factory, always for a reason that was sufficient if not good.

The great rivers, in all their fury and magnificence, dammed from end to end—the Ohio, the Mississippi, the Missouri, the Colorado, the Rio Grande, just a string of basins and levees. The fish that once thronged the rivers and the ocean banks, the great herds that drifted across the grassy plains, the deep dark forests where that Indian life, that other mysterious fraction of his patrimony, had flourished—all decimated, sacrificed to progress, security, and the dollar.

Now this northwestern corner, big in itself maybe but tiny in relation to the continent, was all there was left of the wild world. That vast expanse, from the Atlantic to the Sierras, had been rolled up like a carpet and sold. Surely it must be obvious to anyone with an ounce of imagination that what little was left was too precious to lose. These were the last wild rivers, the last forests, the last great fish runs; here was the last natural home of bears and mountain lions in the contiguous states of America. And together with those rather shopworn symbols of wildlife, lived the unknowable, unimaginable, wealth of nature; an infinite, intricate tapestry of species woven by the master; unreproducible and laid out in this last mountainous attic of the U.S.A. Anybody willing to give it any objective thought would have to realize what priceless assets the valley and the river and the surrounding forests were.

And that was precisely the problem Richard faced. Nobody could put a price on them. The corps could get away with treating Round Valley as though its only value was in the crops and cattle that ranchers were raising on its eighteen thousand acres. As a natural phenomenon it had no more dollar value for them than it would have had to Angus Grant a hundred years before. Less, indeed, because the corps could say, with every expectation of being believed, that their lake was more valuable than anything nature could provide.

Although he felt obliged to do battle with the corps on economic grounds, he could not help being aware of the artificiality and absurdity of the rules. In his heart, he knew that what offended him most about the sacrifice of the valley was the indifference to its beauty, the wanton disregard of a value that was so evident to all who saw it.

It was obvious that they also ignored what should be a major factor in the calculation, and that was the cultural significance of the watershed. It was ignored, in part, because people had not yet learned to appreciate its importance, and also because nobody had yet found a way to attach a monetary value to it. Its wealth resided not just in the wildlife, the vegetation, and the topography but in the values formed by the men and women who had learned to live well with it.

Here he was at odds with the majority of the ranchers of Round Valley. They, for the most part, were trying to have their cake and eat it. They wanted the freedom and independence of a rancher's life, but with the fruits of a technological society as well. They saw no contradiction, but Richard did. He began to realize that a farm could not provide an urban lifestyle without becoming itself a kind of factory, with ever greater dependence on high-priced inputs, debt-laden machinery, and a market that was unrelated to local conditions.

The value of a rural area, Richard thought, was better expressed in the lives of earlier generations. Not the casually brutal cowpokes who did George White's dirty work, but the men and women like Elmer Bauer's parents and the Kasers, his early mentors at Henthorne, who adapted themselves to their environment and made it flower, who planted orchards or raised livestock in modest numbers that the land could support. In this fond regard for a simpler, and in some respects more devout, existence he was linked across time not just to his father's youth in Santa Ana, but right back to the time of his great-grandfather Archibald Grant. And as he roamed back and forth in his imagination, the sense of what had been lost grew sharper, and the importance of saving what was left more urgent.

Richard saw how boxed in he was. Always he would be forced back on dollar values. How many acres? How many buildings? How many cattle? How much hay? How many fish in the river? How many deer on the hillsides? Interesting, but beside the main point. How was he going to make that point—that wildness, wilderness, has great real value? How could that value be expressed so that he would not always be comparing apples with oranges?

It was not enough to fight the corps on one issue. He would have to go the whole hog. He would have to deal with the whole, interdependent mess of resource use and exploitation and evaluation. It could never be just water or just trees or just soil or just people. Richard observed his progress with a certain wry humor. Within a few months of deciding that he was not going to let the corps drive him off his ranch, he had become one of those who were trying to save the world.

It was difficult to limit the scope of the task he had set himself. The ramifications rippled out across the state, and seemed to impinge on virtually every aspect of daily life. And since ordinary people were touched by the issue in so many ways, he had to assume that their support would have to be enlisted in as many ways. They might face the issue as domestic water users, as taxpayers, as vacationers, as fishermen, as hunters, as businessmen, as home buyers, as consumers of food, as wilderness lovers, white-water rafters, as Democrats and Republicans, and on and on.

Their attitudes would be affected by a regional bias, too. Those looking for flood control, as opposed to those who feared that their rivers would be the next to be regulated. Those who hoped for more water for their regions, as opposed to those who didn't want to pay for it. Those southerners who saw their future in more growth, as opposed to those who feared more congestion. Not to mention the people with special interests, who would be most vocal in support or opposition, ranging from Indians to cement companies.

Richard's first short-term objective was to create and announce his Eel River support group. Together with Curt he came up with the name Save the Eel River Association, which they thought would bounce nicely off the name of their principal adversary, the Eel River Association. Together they worked on the membership of the steering committee, which would appear on the left-hand side of the letterhead, and they agreed there was no point in pulling punches. Richard's connections, after all, were his principal asset.

"We might as well hit 'em with everything we've got," he said, and he reeled off a formidable list of rich and influential names who had offered to support him. There were the great patrons of California's Republican party, Allen Chickering, Robert di Giorgio, and Palmer Fuller III. He had the San Francisco police commissioner, John Mailliard III, whose brother was a congressman and whose wife, "Tex," was San Francisco's number one hostess.

He had Roger Kent, an extraordinarily distinguished Democrat, whose family had given its name to Kentfield, a small city in Marin. There was Dean Witter, the stockbroker with branches from coast to coast, who lived in San Francisco. He had a very personal reason for opposing the dam. He had a large ranch on the Eel River, just below

Dos Rios, and was a fanatical fisherman. He knew very well what the dam would do to his favorite sport. William Siri, the president of the Sierra Club, was on the letterhead. So was Richard's older brother, John Cree, Jr., as well as the dean of the USC Medical School, Roger Egeberg. Lewis and Elmer were on it. A few prominent industrialists and some dignitaries from cities up and down the state brought the total to twenty-six names.

"I don't know what good it'll do," said Richard with some satisfaction, "but at least they won't be able to ignore us. That's half the battle won."

19

The Steelhead Jumps and Gardner Delivers

WITH GARDNER BROWN primed and aimed at the target, Richard turned his energies to other things. The supervisors were still dancing their wearisome minuets and polkas in Ukiah, and with Jim McCombs's help he was doing his best to support Joe Scaramella and keep them from falling into the corps's lap. Support in the valley was growing, and together with Elmer he was doing all he could to bring the Indians out against the dam. It was time to get out in the world, so he planned the next phase of his offensive.

It was all geared to a time, about three months away, when the corps would produce its final report for Washington. By then he needed three things: some solid ammunition from Gardner, some publicity to make the world aware of what was happening, and some friends in the legislature.

Early in January he got his friends in Covelo together at Elmer's house and outlined his campaign. He explained that from now on in they would be working all out to spread the word. He wanted them to keep up the pressure in Covelo, to get people to write letters to anyone and everyone—to Clausen, Collier, Belotti, the supervisors, the governor, the president, the man on the moon. The most important thing was to let it be known that there was opposition.

"*We* all know about it. It's the first thing that comes to our minds.

But out there, they're not thinking of us. They're thinking about Vietnam or the economy or anything but us. Do you realize that since this dam was announced, not a single major newspaper has carried a story on the subject? We really only have three months now to make this a public issue.

"The Army Corps of Engineers is convinced that they can get this dam through Congress this summer. They have been told by our friend Gianelli at the Department of Water Resources that this project is already authorized by the legislature. They believe that all the corps needs is Governor Reagan's signature. It doesn't even have to touch the Assembly or the Senate.

"Right now the only counties opposing it are Mendocino and Trinity. Trinity really doesn't count. And if we're not careful, the Mendocino supervisors will slip into the corps's hands.

"When the corps sends that report away to Washington, they will have to allow a certain amount of time for new evidence to be presented. We must accomplish two things here. We must *have* some evidence, and we must extend that period of appeal as far as possible.

"We need to create such a wave of protest that the legislators will have to get involved. If we can get a hearing in front of legislative committees, we may delay the proceedings long enough to derail the corps's timetable. Then we have a chance to find even more evidence against this dam."

He explained that he planned to open an office in San Francisco and get a secretary. Most of the time he expected to be in Sacramento, San Francisco, or the southland. Curt, Lewis, and he were trying to arrange speaking engagements, build alliances, create news.

"Anything we can do to give Curt material for press releases will be valuable. I propose that Elmer and you, Bud, organize a poll of the residents here so that we can show the support of the valley. Then we should hold a meeting to announce the results and solidify our opposition."

Something had changed in Richard, and they all noticed it. In the past he had been persistent enough, questioning and prodding maybe, but listening a lot, too; initiating action but quietly, cautiously, a little diffident. Now he was leading from the front. Seized by the urgency of the matter and his own commitment, he made his proposals forcefully, as demands rather than ideas. Like his father, he did not suffer fools gladly and often had difficulty disguising his impatience. These traits became more exposed as his resolution hardened. His listeners were left in no doubt about his intentions and expectations. Few of the jokes made that evening came from him.

Correspondence flowed out of his office to points all over the state, and he endeavored always to make his letters generate other letters that would eventually come home to roost somewhere in a strategically important office. For example, to Jack Mailliard, brother of the congressman, who also happened to have a ranch in Mendocino County, he sent a letter suggesting he write to a list of people, including Reagan, Livermore, five senators, two congressmen, and three assemblymen.

He also listed a number of others he wanted Mailliard to convince to do the same thing, and more. They included some of those already on his steering committee, like Egeberg and Witter, as well as Herbert Hoover, Jr., in Los Angeles. Mailliard did as he was asked. Not a bad haul for one letter, and the first wave of mail began to arrive at the legislators' mailboxes.

Lewis was pestering the corps with questions designed to expose areas of weakness, and to make sure that his side wasn't caught unawares by some surprise move. With his partner McCloskey in Congress and other young Republican friends in the Nixon administration, he was able to fish for information about the corps's prospects in Washington. The war, which was draining the economy, was also provoking talk about cutting back on federal water projects. But that was a slim straw to grasp at, and they knew it. Congress was extremely fond of these pork barrel projects, and a threat to reduce them might prompt the corps to redouble its efforts to get what it could authorized that year.

In fact, Lewis was beginning to catch signals that the corps was accelerating its schedule. In February he wrote to a lawyer he knew who was working with Senator Kuchel at the Department of the Interior in Washington, asking every question he could think of about the corps's past, present, and future prospects on the matter of Dos Rios. That led eventually to a meeting with Colonel Boerger in San Francisco.

Lewis remembered Boerger being very cordial, but he could not help feeling that same condescension that had so riled Richard in Lakeport.

"He regarded us as these nice, misguided people. It was as though the corps had trained him to do this. We should not be treated as the enemy, because there would always be citizens who didn't understand and had some particular ax to grind. You would be nice to them because they couldn't conceivably have an effect on what you're doing."

For his part, Richard went for the legislators in person. Having played some part in getting Don Clausen elected to Congress, he badgered him for help, but all Clausen would or could do openly was to pass his letters on and forward the replies. His problem was that he represented Humboldt as well as Mendocino, and so long as Humboldt wanted flood control, he was in a no-win situation, with no personal beliefs to guide him.

State Assemblyman Frank Belotti was in the same bind, but he was closer to the action and couldn't get by just shuffling papers. He had to talk to the engineers and state officials and the supervisors of all the north coast counties, and listen to their complaints. He had little sympathy, it seemed, for Richard's stand, and before long he was drawn inevitably into the Mayfield/Sawyers camp of pragmatic opportunism.

They saw him as a way to get what they wanted, which was money from the state to pay for the recreation facilities. Belotti became the key that Boerger had been looking for, and Richard could do nothing to stop him. In April, Belotti appeared in a photograph in the *Ukiah Journal,* a short, squat man with a froglike aspect, talking to supervisors and water officials at a crab feast in Sacramento. Soon afterward he announced a measure, Assembly Bill 552, requiring the state to put money into recreation at Dos Rios. In Richard's eyes it was tantamount to supporting the dam. He knew that it had been prompted by Gianelli, and it was a major blow to him and his followers. Belotti's bill, like every other bill, would have to go through a seemingly endless series of committee hearings, in the Senate and the Assembly, and Richard felt he would have to contest it every inch of the way. It was a heap of trouble he thought he could well do without.

And then there was State Senator Randolph Collier. Of the three, Collier was potentially the most influential ally and the most dangerous enemy. He was an old-style politician with maximum seniority in the Senate, chairman of the Transportation Committee, and a member of George Miller's all-powerful Finance Committee.

There was never any doubt about what animated Randolph Collier's political philosophy. He was one of those who identified so strongly with the people he represented that he never bothered to ask them what they wanted. He already knew that what was good for Randy Collier was good for the north coast, which he had represented, without interruption, for twenty-nine years. This uncomplicated approach to the job gave him a freedom of action that was envied and loathed by many other legislators.

He established his power base early in his career, judging quite rightly that what his far-flung and sparsely populated constituency needed most of all was an adequate road system. He became known as the father of the freeways, allied himself openly and shamelessly with all the big interests involved, and made sure his constituents got plenty of fat contracts, even if it meant occasionally building a freeway that began and ended nowhere. He grew in influence as the freeway system grew. Starting as a tall, lean, dark, and hawklike man, he grew over the years into a florid, overbearing, and rather gross figure. He made the Transportation Committee his fiefdom, dispensing favors and collecting campaign contributions with such disregard for appearances that many thought him to be the archetype of the corrupt politician.

Lewis Butler certainly thought so, saying he had watched Collier move through the corridors of the capitol annex, grasping the envelopes that lobbyists thrust into his hands and stuffing them carelessly into his bulging pockets. So flagrant was this exhibition that one of the *San Francisco Chronicle*'s best men spent three months working to expose Collier's venality. He returned empty-handed, as did the FBI after him. Finally it became clear that Collier was not interested in money nearly as much as those who watched and despised him. It was the power that he enjoyed, and he used it as he saw fit, without regard to party or ideology.

Thus far Collier had been in favor of the dam, but Richard thought he had a decent chance of bringing him around. As soon as the Legislature was back in business after the holidays, he phoned Collier in Sacramento, made a date for the following Thursday, and mailed him a copy of the speech he had made in Willits.

Collier had an office in the Senate Building, but he also kept a small suite in the Senator Hotel a block away, and was often to be found there instead. Unlike most of his colleagues, he conducted his business on a small and personal scale. He had a strong-minded, older secretary named Ellen Winslow, and one assistant who Richard remembers being always heavily frosted with dandruff. Collier listened to Richard with a kind of offhand concern, promised to think about it, and asked, as had Livermore, to be kept informed.

From then on, Richard and Lewis were often seen ducking into the Senator Hotel with one thing or another, and Ms. Winslow seemed to have gotten rather attached to her tall, handsome young men. She assured them, frequently, that the senator was sympathetic.

"Now boys," she would say, according to Lewis, "the Senator's having an executive session this evening at the hotel, but I guarantee you your issue will not come up." These promises were never enough to relieve Lewis's anxiety. He watched Collier nervously, having been warned his power was such that he might easily do some secret deal in executive session, trading approval of the dam for some other favor. And in public Collier continued to make statements supporting the dam.

Richard, against all the evidence, seemed oddly sanguine about Collier. It was almost as though they had a secret understanding to which Lewis was not privy, and later Richard made the same remark about Collier that he had made about Reagan.

"You know, all things being equal, he generally tried to do the right thing."

In their efforts to make a dent in Sacramento, they were barraging lawmakers with material bound into huge red binders, and the production of these ponderous missives amounted to a cottage industry.

"McCloskey told me how to do it," said Lewis. "It was the most important thing I ever learned from him. I went to a store and bought twenty of these red binders, three inches thick, with dividers. It started off with these pictures all carefully taken to make Round Valley look like one of the great agricultural areas of the world. And with George White's mansion, as though there were dozens of them." There were copies of letters and telegrams, editorials from the *Chronicle*, a *Reader's Digest* article by Eisenhower about desalinization (including a good joke about de-Stalinization), poll results from Round Valley, and a long state report about other water sources. All in all, it made a massive tome.

"So I put all this stuff together and took it over to Curt and said, 'Will this sell?' and he said I had the right idea, so we started banging these things out over the weekend. Then we'd go into senators' offices and say, 'This is about the controversial Dos Rios Dam.' Well, nobody knew what to do with this gigantic binder. You couldn't throw it away. It had obviously taken too much work. It was too heavy. And the pictures cost Richard an arm and a leg. But it was all directed toward the hearing we were determined to get."

While they were running in and out of offices in Sacramento, the *Mercury-News,* a much-respected newspaper from San Jose, published a two-page spread attacking high dams, which was a rare position to take in those days. Lewis was reminded of Lou Cannon, his old ally in the fight to save San Francisco Bay. Lou was the young reporter who held the Sacramento desk for the *Mercury-News,* and Richard met him, read his pieces and was greatly impressed. He thought immediately of *Cry California,* and called Bill Bronson. Would he ask Cannon to write a few thousand words about the fight to save Round Valley? Bronson agreed.

Lou was not enthusiastic at first. He said he'd go up and look, but he wouldn't commit himself. He thought Richard was probably just some rich guy trying to buy influence to protect his own.

"Frankly, I was skeptical," Lou Cannon recalled later. "There was such an obvious self-interest in it. I mean, whenever things are built, like roads and shopping malls, there are always nice spots that are going to be taken—and people thinking that their own little area is so precious. But I did go up there and talked to Richard and Susan . . . and it captivated me—the beauty and the isolation.

"Of course there was self-interest, and he didn't disguise it, but he really, honestly felt it was a bum project. So I took the assignment, and my first call was to the guy who headed the Corps of Engineers then, Colonel Boerger. He was kind of arrogant, I thought. He just wanted to brush everything aside—any objections you had. In most of my dealings with the corps up to that time, they could generally make a good case for their projects. But with Dos Rios, even before I went into them very much, the figures just didn't make a lot of sense, and you knew they were going to take the most optimistic view.

"After that first visit I became very interested in the Middle Fork of the Eel—there just aren't that many wild rivers. I took a cabin up there for three days, and we went with the children. On the third day I came down with my son Jack—he was two years old—to the river. I always used to take my fishing pole with me in those days. All it had was a monofilament line, a five-pound test line, and I had this super-duper lure, and I just threw it in, and immediately I got an enormous steelhead on it. I was working at it for ages, half an hour I suppose, letting it run and bringing it back, until it jumped up the way steelhead do to throw off the hook. At that time people were saying the summer steelhead were gone because of the '64 flood. If Richard had stocked that stream with steelhead for my benefit, he couldn't have made his point better. . . ."

It was the summer steelhead that first got the argument into the major media. To fishermen, the summer run of steelhead on the Eel was a rare and priceless phenomenon, and they were ready to go to the barricades for it. Lewis, Joe Paul, David Lennihan, and Curt Roberts all met with Richard at the Bar Association Lounge one evening in February, and Richard was invited to address Trout Unlimited at the annual meeting in March. Both the *Chronicle* and the *Examiner* had popular outdoor columnists, and they were the first to pick up the story of the threat to fishing on the north coast.

At first sight there was a sense of the elite versus the people in this clash between two views of recreation. On one side were the happy campers, glad to crowd around the shore of a lake, enjoying the noisy atmosphere of power boats and barbeques, with RV generators buzzing merrily in the background. Against them was the solitary asceticism of the fly fisherman, silently communing with Nature. It was the kind of contrast that worked well for the corps, with its creed of "the greatest good for the greatest number," but the caricature did not stand up to examination.

Sport fishing on the Eel, it transpired, was worth at least $2 million a year, and there were serious concerns that a dam at Dos Rios would ruin it. As Lou Cannon observed in his piece: "A strong case can be made that the Dos Rios project would destroy some of the best recreation remaining in the state, substituting power-boat recreation for the quality experience of a wild river. . . . The corps project plans a hatchery to compensate for the loss of eight million chinook salmon eggs, but the record of previous hatcheries and previous high dams suggests that fishing will never be the same again."

This was a challenge the dam boosters had to take seriously. Jerald Butchert had the assistant regional director of the U.S. Fish and Wildlife Service, Jack Hemphill, over to talk to the Eel River Association. At a hotel in Santa Rosa, the engineers and supervisors listened, eager for guidance and solace. To Hemphill, as to most fishery experts at that time, the problem was easily stated in two propositions: First, you can't have fish without water, so you have to let enough water run out of the dam to keep the fish afloat. Second, you can't have fish without eggs, so if you block the fish off from their spawning habitats, you have to build hatcheries where the fish can be bred and released.

That was it. Enough water, big enough hatcheries, problem solved.

Well, not quite. One can almost see him frowning in perplexity at his audience as he goes on to admit that "estuarine ecology is extremely complex. The subject is one which has been largely neglected in the past. . . . Upstream Eel River developments . . . will adversely affect fish and wildlife of the estuary . . . a reduced water supply will shrink waterfowl habitat. . . . Channel work in the Lower Eel could eliminate holding pools for salmon and steelhead and thus interfere with their normal migratory patterns. . . . We are working closely with the corps . . . we do know that the potential for damage is great . . . we would expect that the great reduction in Eel River flow . . . would produce a rather dramatic change in the chemical characteristics and species composition of estuarine waters. This could have a marked effect on species such as salmon and steelhead, which will depend on the estuary during certain stages of their life cycles." In other words, he didn't truthfully know what would happen. It was a pretty good guess that any major changes to the river would damage its ecology. But then, with one bound he was free. Emerging into the sunlight of technology he shook off his pessimism.

"Our crystal ball," he said, "indicates that four or five super hatcheries for anadromous fish will be developed as mitigation factors for losses on the north coast of California." Effectively ignoring all he had said about the rest of the ecosystem, he concentrated purely and simply on reproducing salmon and trout by the ton. As a last thought he added that if the king (or chinook) salmon, which is also the most valuable species, wouldn't cooperate, well, they would grow silver salmon instead.

His listeners undoubtedly breathed a deep sigh of relief and applauded Mr. Hemphill vigorously.

The strain on Richard of running the ranch and saving Round Valley in his spare time was severe. Coached by Curt and assisted by Lewis, he became virtually a professional lobbyist for the duration, working the ranch during the day, driving to Sacramento at night, or flying in and out of Covelo's dinky airport on the west side of the valley. Elmer held the meeting in Covelo that Richard had asked for, and it went off well. A poll was taken, and five hundred people signed their names, saying they were opposed to the dam. Only seventy-one refused to sign. Richard kept up the pressure, but what he was waiting for, the big gun with which he hoped to blast the corps, was Gardner Brown's analysis.

He could not resist calling Gardner from time to time, and at last his persistence was rewarded. Gardner called to say he thought his study of Dos Rios would bring the benefit/cost ratio down from 1.6 to a completely unworkable 0.7.

Richard at first was incredulous. Could Gardner really substantiate such an enormous discrepancy? Or, to put it another way, could the corps really have been so incompetent or unscrupulous?

Gardner reassured him. There were many ways in which the corps could be challenged, he said. A small example: They were putting value on the numbers of recreationists who would visit the lake but ignoring the fact that the available access roads would seize solid under the traffic.

Richard almost danced a jig.

"When can we get it confirmed?" he asked. "Can we announce it now?"

"Oh, gosh. I don't know. I mean this is entirely provisional. You'd better not put my name to it yet, until I've run through it more thoroughly."

"But it's going to be something of that order?"

"Yes, you can say that."

"How long before we get the finished report?"

"Give me a month."

"No. That's too long. The corps is going to send its report to Washington in a month. We've got to have this on record before then."

"I'll do my best. I'll try."

Curt put out a press release immediately to announce Gardner's conclusions without naming him. Curt said you had to use every opportunity you got to hit the media.

"It's a funny thing," he quipped. "They're supposed to be interested in what's new. But they often don't think it's important unless they've heard it before. This can become what they heard before."

Only one major newspaper picked up on Curt's press release, and that was *The Sacramento Bee.* In a five-paragraph down-page story, Richard was quoted saying: "If we're not careful Northern California may die of Southern California's thirst." And yet the silence of the Bay Area papers was strange. Neither the *San Francisco Chronicle* nor the *Examiner* mentioned the story, yet the *Chronicle* had always been particularly chauvinistic where water was concerned. It had fought the State Water Plan with thunderous editorials, and might have been expected to pounce on this new angle.

Someone who did notice it, however, was the *Chronicle*'s promotion manager, Phelps Dewey. This slender, astute, and engaging man was a key figure in the battles the *Chronicle* had been waging against its rivals. He worked all hours at high pressure, and like many others he revitalized himself by wandering off into the wild river canyons of the north. He was already familiar with Round Valley, and he had begun to think of buying a piece of land there, perhaps even one far-off day retiring there. The dam seriously threatened what had become an important part of his life, and he mentioned it to a venerable editorial writer, Templeton Peck, who brought the matter up at an editorial board meeting.

The editorial board was a longtime institution at the *Chronicle.* It consisted of the men, like Templeton, who enshrined the newspaper's policy in prose. They in turn invited staff members or outside advisers who they thought might help them with information. It met every day, and still does. In the sixties it happened in a room adjacent to the editor's office, and the editor himself presided.

In 1967 the editor was Scott Newhall, a fearless buccaneer admired by his staff and backed up with the full confidence of his proprietor, Charlie Thieriot. The *Chronicle* was supposed to be a Republican paper (Hearst, of course, being Democrat), but it took strong, idiosyncratic stands on a multitude of issues across party lines. More important than party politics was its allegiance to Northern California as opposed to the south, and particularly on water issues.

Templeton Peck already knew Lewis and Curt, and before long they were both invited to board meetings to advise the paper on the campaign against Dos Rios, making certain that their case would at least be reported.

Gardner Brown's report arrived from Washington in March, all thirty pages of it. Gardner was merciless in his criticism, and his thin chuckle seemed to permeate the pages. The project, he said, would cost at least another $50 million. The water it produced, far from being worth $27 an acre-foot, would be worth no more than $8. The flood control benefits had been exaggerated by 17 percent, the recreation by 10 percent, and the hydroelectric power by 20 percent. Then, with barely disguised gusto, he went on to explain.

First he hit them with a study that showed federal flood control projects in the past had regularly finished up costing twice what they were estimated at. "No private construction company could have remained in business with such a performance record," he noted. For one thing, he pointed out, it would be thirteen years before the project was completed, and in the previous thirteen years costs had increased 30 percent. Why shouldn't they increase by that much again? Yet the corps had allowed only a 20 percent contingency figure for the whole project.

Then Round Valley, according to the state, was worth about $13 million more than the corps wanted to pay for it. And the tunnel, the famous Grindstone Tunnel through the mountains was, even according to Gianelli's men, a "technically difficult undertaking," through a "complex geological stratum" and as much as five thousand feet deep. The state would have allowed 30 percent to cover unexpected difficulties. The corps allowed only 15 percent. There's another $11 million right there.

The fish hatchery, he said, was much too small, and he brought expert opinion to bear on that. Then there was the question of the rock fill. The corps had still not shown satisfactorily that the borrow for the dam was really where they said it was, and that alone could lead to the most tremendous cost overruns. Even the state had reservations and considered putting in a concrete arch dam instead, at an extra cost of $100 million or so.

As for the benefits, there were many more detailed criticisms. However, none of them affected the issue nearly so much as his critique of the values assigned to the water supply, which accounted for almost 90 percent of the dam's value. And here it was mainly a matter of whose projections you believed. Both Gardner and the corps agreed that taking the salt out of sea water was a coming thing, but they put quite different values on it. The corps gave no figures at all in its report. Gardner produced seven pages of figures, graphs, and tables to show that water from the sea would become so cheap that by the time the Dos Rios water got to Southern California it would only be worth $8 an acre-foot. The difference amounted to almost $19 million a year—the difference between a golden goose and a white elephant.

Richard was delighted with the results. Gardner warned him that the corps, with the resources they had available, would try to drown his criticism in a sea of counterargument, but what Richard wanted more than anything was grounds for a serious controversy. He had the report duplicated and sent copies to Colonel Boerger, to General Dillard, to the corps in Washington, to Clausen in Congress, and to Senator Collier. But the copy he paid particular attention to, the one he thought would do the most good, was the one he delivered personally to Ike Livermore.

20

Leading Ike to the Water

WHEN REAGAN came to office as governor in 1967, the main topic of the conservationists in California was survival of the redwood forests. Reagan had already offended them deeply by a careless "seen one, seen 'em all" remark about those phenomenal trees. Nobody expected the environment to benefit much from his time in office, and so it came as a considerable surprise to find two respected, nature-friendly men appointed to strategic positions. William Penn Mott, who had fought an honorable battle in defense of parkland in the Bay Area, became director of Parks and Recreation. The other, Ike Livermore, a walking oxymoron who was both a "big lumber" man and a Sierra Club member, was appointed administrator of the Resources Agency, which made him overall boss of the Parks, Fish and Game, Water, Forestry, Conservation, and Agriculture departments.

In reality, Reagan had little or nothing to do with these appointments. They were made by his shrewd, young appointments secretary, Tom Reed, one of the millionaires in Reagan's entourage, in the knowledge that his leader's image needed adjusting. Reagan was a novice in these areas of government, but he did know that trees promised to be a whole lot of trouble. Water policy was generally undisputed, and Gianelli was appointed first as the best man to get on with the water job. Livermore was chosen to oversee the agency and mediate the looming crises in the forests, where water, it was naively assumed, would play no part.

Ike's acquaintanceship with Richard, even without the Thacher connection, was not unnatural. Their families moved in similar circles, and had similar origins. It was quite possible that their forebears had crossed paths more than a hundred years earlier. When Angus Grant was logging up by the Donner Pass, Horatio Gates Livermore came through from the East looking for opportunities to do the same. Though his efforts to create a lumber enterprise were unsuccessful, one of his sons was luckier with a quicksilver mine farther west at Knoxville, in Napa County, and the family was secure and very comfortable from then on.

Ensconced in the upper strata of society, inevitably Republican, the Livermores went on to play an important part in the commercial and political life of California. Ike's father was a civil engineer who had surveyed the entire catchment area on the American River basin for Sacramento's water supply. He was lucky enough to have a brood of five sons, all of great stature, considerable competence, and good health. One of them, Putnam Livermore, became chairman of the state Republican party during Reagan's governorship.

Not far from the mine at Knoxville, the Livermores turned eight acres of mountain land into a family retreat on an exposed hilltop in the forest. It could be reached easily from both Sacramento and San Francisco, and as the family spread between those cities, it was frequently used as a gathering place. They called it Montesol, and gradually added to it through the years. At the time he was appointed to government, Ike Livermore was the treasurer and a major shareholder of Pacific Lumber, one of the world's largest lumber manufacturers with sawmills and company towns on the lower Eel River. Even so, he was not quite the orthodox timber man that his position suggested. In 1990, at the age of eighty-something, still a healthy, strapping man, he looked back with as much pleasure on the trees he saved as on the ones he cut down.

"My feelings are due very largely to this place," he said, sitting out on the broad earth terrace of his ranch house at Montesol, in cool fall sunlight, with lightly wooded slopes dipping away on all sides. "I spent all my boyhood summers here, and two winters during the influenza epidemic in World War I. It gave me a potent appreciation of the outdoors—nature and open space."

His love for woods, mountains, and horses led him, as a young man in the early thirties, to combine a conventional business education with packing in the Sierras. Packing was a popular recreation industry in those times. People paid to be led on mules into the mountains for prolonged camping and fishing trips.

He chose to write his junior business school thesis on the packing business, and circled the whole High Sierra on a motorcycle to do it. That led him to form the High Sierra Packers Association—"probably the world's smallest trade group"—which still exists. The Sierra Club asked him to solve some contractual problems they were having with their packers, and he thrived on the challenge. His self-confidence combined with a good political instinct to make him a born mediator. The Sierra Club came to depend on him more and more.

"In those days, packing was the political heart of the Sierra Club. I was made a director, and served from 1940 for ten years, excluding the war. All I'm saying really is, my environmental feeling is very closely tied up with the wilderness."

He was, by upbringing, position, and temperament, perfectly suited to straddle hotly debated issues. His self-deprecatory manner deflated belligerence and pride. His genial warmth readily convinced people with opposing views that he understood and respected their positions. Frequently they failed to observe how tenaciously he held to his own. What they thought was a compromise usually came very close to the solution he had privately determined in advance. David Brower, the doyen of the western environmental movement, has since written in a tribute to Ike that "the sun never sets on a Livermore argument."

Ike's conviction that it must be possible to simultaneously conserve and exploit nature and the wilderness has never seemed to him, as it has to others, contradictory. In the thirties the issue hardly arose. Since then, population pressure on parks and wilderness has increased enormously while forested areas have greatly diminished. Ike resigned his Sierra Club directorship—"I was always a rebel director anyway"—in 1950 partly because packing had become less acceptable politically to the club.

In the sixties, when Reagan appointed him to handle the bitter fight over the redwoods, he had to make his mind up about one of the great debates of our time: Does protecting the environment mean leaving it alone, or can we use it and save it at the same time?

There was no question where he stood emotionally. People had to be able to interact with nature. To lock it away in a museum could not be right. Economically, too, it would be ruinous to stop cutting trees, mining minerals, and, where necessary, adapting nature to our needs. All his experience told him that compromises could be arrived at, people could be persuaded, things could be managed, the damage could be contained and made acceptable without stifling growth.

The Sierra Club and others were claiming that all but 5 percent of the redwoods had gone, and that what was left should be preserved. In particular, environmentalists abominated the clear-cut, a harvesting method that razed large sections of forest to the ground, exposing the soil. Ike, who was still on the Sierra Club Advisory Board, thought his club members were being hysterical and inaccurate, and hasn't changed his view to this day.

"Take that famous percentage figure—you hear it all the time—only five percent of the redwoods are remaining. I take strong exception to that. They have never defined what kind of redwoods they're talking about. There's an enormous difference between the grove type—the huge, primeval trees—and the sidehill stuff, which in many cases is half fir.

"I still say, the primary problem is erosion. Obviously if you clear-cut in areas with very friable soil, that's very, very bad. But it's well known in the Pacific Northwest that a lot of the best logging is clear-cut logging, and in good areas the forest rises again, just like a cornfield."

Conservationists, though, were not inclined to put their faith in reasonable behavior by lumber companies. There was great pressure from the Sierra Club and others to create a national park of redwoods. Ike recalls those trying times with great enjoyment, clearly convinced that he did his best in difficult circumstances.

"I remember some of the press accounts when I was appointed, saying 'This man is a walking contradiction. How can he be a lumber man and also a director of the Sierra Club? Maybe he cries every time he cuts down a tree.' Anyway, *National Geographic* got out a tome about the tallest tree in the world. The Sierra Club leadership persuaded them to do it. Big headlines. It was in Redwood Creek, near a town called Orick."

Orick is in the far northern part of the state, between Eureka and Crescent City. Around Redwood Creek was a big block of privately owned redwood forest.

"The publicity immediately started to increase to get a grand Redwood National Park. It built and built and built, and I was right in the middle of it. The first six months I was in Sacramento, that's about all I did."

The expectation had been that Ike would somehow deflect this campaign, but Ike was determined to make his boss understand that environmental problems were real ones, and that their values had substance. Reagan became visibly impatient with him.

"I almost got fired that time," he remembers, "when I mentioned to Reagan and the cabinet that these were very potent forces, that we couldn't just ignore them. It was obvious some kind of compromise was needed."

Ike juggled, pressured, threatened, and cajoled the federal government and the lumber industry. He found a sixteen-thousand-acre block of timber belonging to the Forest Service, called the Redwood Purchase Unit, and eventually a trade was done, a compromise arrived at. Redwood Park was created, and it did, fortunately, include the "world's largest tree."

Although Ike's attitudes were the despair of many militant ecologists who thought no compromise was any longer possible, they were also well to the left of California's business establishment. The lumber companies believed that even the slightest supervision of their activities would be an outrageous interference. Ike, on the other hand, was beginning to realize that the industry, sooner or later, would have to accept some control. He had always argued for the so-called multiple-purpose approach, as in the national forests. These are supposed to be managed on behalf of the people as a resource as well as for recreation. Now he began to hear more and more evidence that the system was being abused and manipulated in favor of industry and private development.

In 1967, he started to call for rules governing forest practices. The *Ukiah Daily Journal*, among other papers, was reporting that story at the same time as the news broke about the Dos Rios Dam. The lumber barons rejected, with confident scorn, the very idea that they should share their plans with a public agency.

Ike Livermore takes pride in the forest practice rules he did eventually set up. "As far as I know," he says, "they're among the stiffest, if not *the* stiffest, in the country." But that was much later. When Richard Wilson came to talk to him about Round Valley in 1967, he was in the throes of his struggle with Reagan and big lumber over the redwood issue. The last thing he expected or wanted was to have to fight a battle on a quite different front. Only friendship and hospitality persuaded him to listen at all. He said "Amazing!" at suitable intervals, and hoped the matter would go away.

Back in Sacramento he felt obliged to make some kind of inquiry. He sent a letter to Gianelli, two floors below him, saying in effect, What's this I hear about a high dam that will flood a town and move three thousand people, including a thousand Indians? Why haven't you mentioned the serious political problems that would necessarily follow?

In reply, he got a long account assuring him that the question of whether to flood Round Valley had been "vexing" the state for years. But now, as it turned out, investigations showed that they had no option. It was the only economical choice. Fortunately, Gianelli went on, his staff and the corps had been pleasantly surprised to find only very minor opposition in the valley. It was true that the supervisors had "expressed some concern" about losing tax revenue, but they were coming around to the idea that recreation could make up for it.

"General Dillard told me informally a few days ago," wrote Gianelli, "that he had discussed the situation with the local leaders and is convinced there will be no difficulty with the inundation of Round Valley. At this point in time the political problems associated with inundation of Round Valley appear to be more imaginary than real."

Inundation is a good word to use when you're trying to avoid "flood" or "drown." Ike might have guessed that there was some wishful thinking between the lines, but there were many other pressing matters on his desk. He tried to put Dos Rios aside for another time but found he couldn't. His director of Fish and Game, Walter Shannon, came to him with much concern. His department was in the middle of an investigation into the likely effect on fish and wildlife of a dam at Dos Rios. He was sure the damage would be severe, and a major effort would need to be made to compensate for it. But his investigation could not be completed until 1971. Pressure was building to cut his program. The water contractors thought he was wasting their money, the money they would have to pay for the Eel water when it arrived at their faucets. If the Corps of Engineers was now to take over the project, it would become a federal matter. The Feds wouldn't be able to get going for a year. They'd be under pressure. The research wouldn't be done properly, and they'd end up with the same mess as they had on the Trinity River. What mess? asked Ike. Well, Shannon told him, before that dam went in with all its hatcheries they had a steelhead run of six thousand. Now they were counting only two hundred.

And Richard would not leave him alone either, pursuing him with information, turning up at his home in San Rafael and at Montesol, but particularly at his office in Sacramento. Richard remembers the effort he had to make to get to Ike.

"He had this huge desk, with all these different projects scattered over it, marked with red tags saying 'EXPEDITE! EXPEDITE! EXPEDITE!' Getting him to focus on the dam was an enormous job. The thing had been so downplayed. It was totally blocked out of the press. It was big news in Willits and Ukiah, but, hell, nobody knew anything in L.A. or Sacramento. Or if they did, they didn't care. It was just a wart on the elephant's butt.

"I said to him, 'This is the biggest water project in the West. You have to be engaged in it. You're in charge of resources.' But he had the Water Resources department, with Gianelli, under him, and he thought they were taking care of things. So he was constantly thinking of reasons not to make a decision. He asked questions, wanted more information. Then he'd go into cabinet meetings and come back with arguments from the corps and from Gianelli, saying 'How do you account for this, or for that?' It was like doing a tutorial."

But Richard knew it was worth it. Of all the people to whom he had an entry, none had a fraction of the influence Ike could wield. He sent press cuttings, copies of speeches, results of the poll, and reports from the supervisors, most of which contradicted what Gianelli and the corps were telling him. Then, in April, he took Gardner Brown's "Critical Review of the Dos Rios Project" to Ike's office and told him that he would be glad to bring the author down from Seattle to make a presentation in person if that would help.

Mr. Brown went to Sacramento, and he was mightily impressed to be ushered through the corridors of power. He says: "It was marvelous to have access. Marvelous that this man could take my work to a person that counts, and force that person, despite all the other pressures, to listen to my arguments. Of course it *should* be done in an open way, with equal access on both sides, but if it's going to be done by influence, thank God for once the influence was on the right side."

Forced or not, Ike listened. Together with all the other pieces of information Richard had brought him, it eventually made him realize that he could not just let this project slip by him. He sent a copy of Gardner's report to Coloner Boerger and asked for his comments. The colonel, frigidly polite, wrote back that his people were studying it. Since the corps Interim Report was a draft sent only to federal, state, and county agencies for review, he said, "We did not anticipate analyses by private consultants who have neither the basic data nor background to participate."

He certainly did not let it interfere with his plans. Privately he let Gianelli know that Brown's criticisms were all but groundless and wouldn't affect the outcome.

This was the critical time that Richard had been aiming for. The corps had completed its report, and announced to the press that it had been sent off to Washington with the blessing of General Dillard, and notice was given to the world at large that it had until May 3 to say why this dam should not be built, or forever hold its peace.

The *Ukiah Journal* received the press release and swallowed it whole, splashing the news across its front page: CORPS OKEHS DOS RIOS DAM. ROUND VALLEY DOOMED.

Richard and Lewis didn't know whether to laugh or cry. "It's ridiculous," they said to each other, "but what do we do?" They sent ten dollars to Boerger's office for two copies of the report, and Curt sent out a press release from Lewis protesting that the corps was rushing this project through. Nothing happened. Nobody cared. Even sympathetic editors like Newhall were still reluctant to believe that there was any solid case against the dam. They didn't want to find themselves exposed as supporting some rich man's private interests.

The corps had a fully functioning public relations department in San Francisco. The Met had a very experienced lobbyist in Sacramento, in the imposing shape of Bill Fairbank. They were all seasoned veterans with much credibility. Also they were well placed strategically, for while the *Chronicle* despised the Met, it had no beef with the corps, and the *Bee* was better disposed toward southern water interests. Curt's main task from the start was to convince somebody, anybody, that there was even the seed of an argument. Lewis remembers how he went about it:

"Curt would work on planting one word in their minds. The key word was 'controversial.' Every time he referred to Dos Rios in front of them, or in press releases, he always called it the controversial Dos Rios Dam. We laughed about it years later. It was as if the name of the town were Controversial Dos Rios. But at that point, early on, there was no controversy at all."

Curt continued to bombard the media, trying to create a presence. He scheduled a press conference for April 17 to announce the new Save the Eel River Association, and Gardner Brown's report. Richard lectured the press about the folly and extravagance of Dos Rios. It was still the age of telegrams, and Curt had Richard send a long Western Union cable to the corps in Washington protesting: ACCELERATION OF SCHEDULE BY CORPS OF ENGINEERS FOR DOS RIOS PROJECT AND LACK OF ADEQUATE HEARINGS AND INFORMATION HAVE DENIED PUBLIC RIGHT TO REVIEW AND COMMENT ON THIS $400 MILLION PROPOSAL FOR LARGEST DAM AND RESERVOIR PROJECT IN CALIFORNIA.

He felt strong enough now to make the demand he had prepared for months before, and in his telegram insisted on a ninety-day extension of the corps deadline. Then they sent copies to Reagan, to the two California senators, Kuchel and Murphy, to Clausen, to the secretaries of the army and the Interior, to Collier, to Belotti, and to Ike.

"I don't know what it is about telegrams, but they work," said Curt. "I guess people always think words are worth more when they cost more."

Whatever it was that did it, Curt's press campaign finally paid off. The *Chronicle* and the *Examiner* both gave sizable space to the story, and they broke through the news blackout.

"A huge dam the Army Corps of Engineers wants to build on the Eel River at Dos Rios would be matched in size only by its wastefulness, it was charged yesterday," said the *Chronicle* on the morning after the press conference.

"Richard A. Wilson, a rugged six-foot-two, 195-pound Mendocino County rancher-cattleman, brought his war against the U.S. Corps of Engineers to San Francisco today," began the *Examiner*'s story that evening, under a two-column picture of Richard standing before a map of the reservoir, dressed in a plaid shirt.

Both stories were long and fairly comprehensive, while *The Sacramento Bee* did a three-paragraph squib. None of the papers wanted to go into benefit/cost ratios for their fickle readers, and a good part of the evidence was never mentioned, but for the first time Richard felt that at least some of the case against the dam was being presented to the public. Then to their supreme delight, Curt's "controversial" buzzword found its hive. *The Sacramento Bee* adopted it, and put out a long column of editorial, cautiously describing the controversy and saying that Dos Rios needed much more public debate.

"Opponents of the project, led by the newly formed Save the Eel River Association, contend the dam is not needed because other, smaller projects would do less damage and produce sufficient amounts of water. They have argued only one official public hearing has been held. They have called for full public disclosure of all arguments. Their request should be granted by federal and state water engineers, state legislators, and congressmen."

This coming from the most conservative of the major papers, and the one closest to the hearts of senators and assemblymen was a triumph. In a later interview[1] Curt said: "The corps was hopping mad about that, but the more they screamed and hollered that it wasn't controversial, the more the papers believed that it was, and that's where we got started."

Meanwhile the corps was stung into making a foolish mistake. It put out a press release claiming that the project had gone to Washington with "the concurrence of the state of California," suggesting that the state had approved it. The wording eventually found its way to Ike, and he felt he could not stay out of the ring any longer. He wrote Boerger a three-page letter of criticism and reproach, telling him the state had given only "preliminary approval" to proceed with planning, and that he would need many more assurances before he could recommend it to the governor.

"Press releases that seem to be emanating from the Corps of Engineers appear to indicate complete and unqualified approval of this project by the state of California. If these statements originated from your office, I do not feel this wording is proper . . . ," he said, and sent copies to all his staff as a way of making sure that it would get into the papers. It did, and Scott Newhall finally had all he needed to jump on the bandwagon with a major editorial titled: DAM QUESTIONS.

It repeated Ike's criticism of Boerger and, putting its own adjectives and adverbs at Richard's disposal, reiterated his charges that the dam "would drown out unique Round Valley, the historic town of Covelo . . . would usurp rich agricultural lands, ruthlessly displace an Indian community, and produce human and economic havoc.

"Involved here is the largest single water project in the state's history. It concerns matters that have duly agitated the people of its area and also involves another gigantic raid upon water supplies that Northern California will surely need. It demands and should receive most careful investigation and thorough public review."[2]

21

Spring in Round Valley

SPRING IN ROUND VALLEY was a hard season to define. Often, toward the end of January, the weather might turn quite summery for a week or two, misleading both plants and people. Then as the Pacific airstreams swung around, the valley would be plunged back into mists and hard frosts or long weeks of drenching rain.

But since summer in Covelo meant the scorching hundred-degree heat that boiled the sap out of plants and set the landscape shimmering, residents were grateful for those months from April to June, even if the long succession of cloudless T-shirt days was broken by an occasional sudden dip into frost, or the inevitable heavy shower when the hay lay cut in the fields.

The wild plum trees were the first to flower, brandishing thick sprays of luscious white blossoms against a skyline of snow-capped mountain peaks. The apple trees, which were plentiful in Round Valley, soon followed. The oaks were slow to show new growth, but the squirrels brought them to life with outbursts of scampering and rowdy chatter. The creeks settled down in their beds, baby barn owls were launched into staggering flight at dusk, and on the airfield west of town, where the children raced to collect colored eggs at Easter, the field was a dazzle of blue, gold, yellow, and crimson wildflowers.

It was a busy time for ranchers, and despite his increasingly heavy schedule of meetings, hearings, and speeches, Richard was still a working rancher.

"I worked daily on the ranch. Often I drove to San Francisco or Sacramento at night. Or I flew. I worked weekends, and used the telephone a lot."

The Covelo road was unusually busy that spring. As well as the usual traffic of Ray Polsley's trucks, the daily bread deliveries and the regular mail and parcel services, there were engineers, officials, legislators, and bureaucrats coming and going constantly. The airport, too, was busy with light planes. All the agencies and associations with an interest in the dam came to check out the "doomed valley" to see what the fuss was about, and to try their hands at easing the project through.

The businessmen in town who supported the dam were irritated by Elmer Bauer's success in rallying opposition. It undermined their ability to negotiate with the corps as they tried to get the best deal they could for the new Covelo by the lake. Jan Stewart was still the leader and mouthpiece of the group, which called itself the Covelo Action Committee. With him were Jim Fisher, Walt Winters, and the Graviers. Other supporters were Danny Thomson, who owned Dan's Market at the entrance to town, and the attorney, Judge Weber. They and others often met in Jan's cavernous hardware store across from the post office, discussing how to make their plans for the relocated town more acceptable. Often they had with them one of the visiting engineers—maybe Charles Elmore or Colonel Boerger—or the planning commissioner, Barney Rowland, who was an interested advocate of the project. Visiting supervisors met with them, and Jerald Butchert of the Eel River Association came through.

The corps was glad to quote them, and for a while helped Jan Stewart to speak publicly outside the valley. His stand did nothing to improve his business prospects. People in the valley began to boycott his store. He was one of the first to be hurt by the growing hostility between the two sides, and he claimed to have been physically threatened. Nobody was surprised to find that a taste for violence had not been entirely lost in Round Valley.

Hostilities also festered between those who opposed the dam. Not all of them supported Richard. Some deeply resented his assumption of leadership, and preferred to do their protesting independently. Lois Hurt was one of those, but she had an important network of contacts in the state Farm Bureau, and worked hard to convince her colleagues in the south of the state that the dam would never fill up, and that the water of the Eel was so loaded with silt as to be unusable.

A young Covelo cowboy, Dusty O'Ferrall, wrote a song about saving Round Valley and a group of his friends put it out as a 45 record, to be played at Farm Bureau functions. Although they resolutely ignored Richard's part in the campaign, and even now deny him any role, their efforts certainly helped to spread awareness.

Elmer Bauer was back to building his new house when Jerald Butchert came to visit him, hoping to strike a compromise, but Elmer was in no mood for that. Butchert made some remark about Jan Stewart, which set Elmer off.

"I laughed at him. 'If you only knew it,' I said, 'takin' Jan around to make those speeches, you're just unifyin' the people against you, see. You're helping us, and I thank you for it.' "

It was a ploy, but Elmer says Butchert fell for it.

"You know," he says, "they never took him out after that. And I accomplished what I wanted to do. But they pulled a fast one on me, too. I had a cousin up here then—he's dead now—John Bauer. And he was for the dam, and so they kept quoting him: 'Bauer said this, and Bauer said that,' and people thought it was me. I had to put a piece in the paper that it wasn't. I remember Jim McCombs's brother telling Richard, 'I'm going to punch that John Bauer.' "

By the beginning of May the grass in the hayfields was reaching maturity and the seedheads were beginning to form. It stood tall, but never as tall as the native grasses that had once covered the open areas a hundred years before. Then the grass was as high as a man, and the Yuki (for want of a better name) knew the place as "Meshakai," or "the valley of the tall grass."

Those Indians who survived the first hundred years of white occupation had settled into a way of life that more or less suited them. Ida Soares says there were few left who even knew their ancestry anymore, whether Concow or Wylackie or Nomelackie or any of a half dozen tribes, let alone the white strains mixed in.

"I have every race in the world in my family," she said. "We're all intermarried. I worked on the enrollment, and I know. We're at the place now where there's just a drop of Indian blood in a child."

The way of life that developed among them was, with some exceptions, subsistence farming. There was some poverty, a good deal of junk and litter, an element of crime, and some notable success stories like that of Norman Whipple. Outwardly it was untidy, and Norman recalls that on weekends, when as a child he walked in and out of town, there were many old men drinking and sleeping in the ditches. As a community it did not seem very attractive to white people. Although there was always a core of devoted Indians like Ida Soares and Vivian Frasier working to maintain the identity and conscience of the tribes, white onlookers saw mainly evidence of disagreement and failure. However, it was no business of theirs (beyond sporadic conflicts) until the prospect of the dam suddenly made Indian attitudes significant.

To visiting engineers, like Baumli, Elmore, and Boerger, and to the businessmen in town who, like Jan Stewart, were mostly from other states or places, the desire of the Indians to keep their way of life was incomprehensible. Charles Elmore expressed the feeling of all of them when he told an interviewer: "We thought the Indians were in pretty poor shape. We figured all along we'd be doing them a favor by creating a whole new economy."

Clearly from their point of view it was just a case of explaining and making their offer attractive enough. Their first meeting with Warren Lincoln confirmed this belief. When they were confronted, in early 1968, by Lincoln's dismissal and a new, intransigent attitude, they could only explain it to themselves as the result of intrigue. Somebody else, they felt, had gotten to the Indians. Of course, in a sense they were right. Richard and Elmer had done their best to encourage the Indians to stand firm, but what Elmore and his faction seemed unable or unwilling to grasp was the element, beyond economics, that created the unlikely alliance between Richard the wealthy landowner, and the indigent Indians of the reservation. They shared an appreciation of what has come to be called "spirit of place."

Despite their past miseries and deprivations, despite the mixing of blood and races that had so diluted their tribal identities, the Indians retained a strong sense that the valley was theirs. And this did not apply only to old families there. Other Indians came from as far away as Oklahoma, Arkansas, and Louisiana. Ida knew them.

"They worked in the mills here, they bought a piece of land, they built homes, and they were going to stay."

Unlike white Americans, who can think of the entire country as theirs, the Indians of Round Valley were accustomed to viewing the hills that ringed them as the boundaries of their territory. In the valley they were safe; on the hills they were exposed.

"I don't even like to go to the hills," said Ida. "I never visit the hills. Never. It's not that I don't like them. I liked sittin' on my porch and lookin' at them. That was the reason I didn't want the dam. I hated to see the Indian people uprooted again, which was not mountain people to begin with. We don't know what to do up there."

Lou Cannon, in his *Cry California* article[1] quoted an anthropologist from San Francisco, A. E. Treganza, who had knowledge of the Yuki in Round Valley. To relocate the Indians in the hills, he protested, amounted to "racial extermination." And he went on to say "the adjacent hills are not suitable for any type of habitation, white or Indian. If the area were suitable, it would have been inhabited 2,000 years ago and used by whites in the last 150 years."

But these opinions were not shared by most of the people Ida and Norman encountered, and they were constantly called upon to explain their opposition. The pressure on them was growing palpably, and wherever Norman Whipple or Ida Soares went, they were likely to be asked, "Have you made up your minds yet?"

Charles Elmore did his best to bring them around. Norman remembered him as a nice guy, and felt rather sorry for him, for walking into such a tense situation.

"It was already getting to the point where you had Indians on one side of the room and whites on the other. When the colored guy came in, I can remember hearing, 'No damn colored people goin' to tell us what to do!' I tell you, that poor man. And he was tryin' to make a name for himself.

"And Colonel Boerger was, too. One time he said to me, 'This will go down in history, and my name will be up there: Colonel Boerger, director of construction.' That was a big mistake."

But for all the talking, neither Boerger nor Elmore had offered the Indians anything more than two acres of scrubland in the hills in exchange for every acre they held in the valley, and it seemed they had no authority to do a better deal. There were private citizens, however, who could.

Judge Weber was one of those who seemed most eager to bring the Indians behind the dam. He was an attorney who had moved in recently from Southern California and been elected judge. He owned a good many acres of hillside in the southeast corner, and Ida was convinced that he had been sent up there "to work the dam." As she put it: "One day he said, 'Ida, I just got to talk to you,' and I said, 'Judge, if you want to talk about the dam you can go to damn, 'cause I'm not gonna talk to you today. I got other things to do.' And he said, 'When can I talk to you?' And I said, 'I'll let you know.' "

As a church leader Ida spent much of her time in the room at the back of the Methodist church, the same modest church where the "Whipping Minister" had invoked God's word in 1879. It stood less than half a mile from her home north of town, and Weber came to see her there.

"So he brought the map out," Ida recalled, "and he pointed up there by the Mina road and said, 'This is where you people are going to be.' And I said, 'You can't really tell me on a map where I'm going to be.'

" 'Well, it's going to be here someplace,' he said. Then he pointed down by the Covelo road. 'We're gonna build a shopping center down here. Safeway is all ready to come in, and there's other stores, and they got a motel, and lodges, and things.'

"And I said, 'Well, why do you want it down there?' 'Well, Ida,' he said, 'to tell the truth, the water will stand there at the same level all the time.'

"And I said, 'Well, what's going to happen at this end, where you're putting us?' 'Well,' he said, 'water will probably not stand that long, and you people will probably have to walk about three or four miles before you even get your foot muddy.'

"I just let him go on. 'It'll be good for you,' he said. 'You fellows can come down any time for recreation.'

"I said, 'Judge Weber, I don't like to tell you this, but you just wastin' my valuable time.' "

Norman's obduracy and Ida's recalcitrance baffled the dam boosters who, being preoccupied themselves with mercenary considerations, were led, all too easily, to wonder whether these two might be holding out for some kind of favor. The sweet smell of corruption began to taint the atmosphere.

"We had a guy come in with the planning commission," said Norman, "who was going to do wonders for us. Take us out and bribe us, you know. He used to wander about town all the time. I remember once he approached me. 'Well, Norman,' he says. 'Did you make your decision? Why don't you just vote this way—I'll take you to dinner with your family. We'll go to San Francisco.'

"And the corps. They were in here every day, doin' their homework. They had spies."

Ida leapt in. "Yeah. They had sneakers out. But when we saw them, the Indians would go to their houses and keep quiet. They knew they had something big to protect. I told them, 'Watch your mouth. Be there at the meetings to support your tribe. If you've got something to say, get up there and say it the way you feel about it.' "

Eventually, recalls Ida, Boerger came to her and said, "Well, Ida, what do you really want?" Driven by anger and frustration, and by the fear that despite all her efforts the white men would once again dislodge the Indians from their homes, Ida responded with belligerence, and in the only language her persecutors seemed to understand.

"I said, 'I want to go where you gonna put the rest of the people. All the business is going to be built down that way, where the water will stand year-round, and we gonna be stuck up here. To me that's not justice.'

"He said, 'Well, what do you want?' And I said, 'I want a motel, I want a casino, I want a new home, I want to be down there where everybody else is, Colonel. What's wrong with us, you can't put us down there?'

"He said, 'Well, it's just that all the business—' "

" 'I don't care whether it's business or not. If it goes, I'm going down there. I'll be the first one, and don't you forget it.' "

Visibly impressed by this outburst, Boerger replied, "Ida, I believe you will."

There was some bitter satisfaction in having wrung such a tribute from her adversary, but it was all bravado. She did not want any of those things—not for herself or for her tribe. She wanted only to be left in peace on her porch to gaze at the mountains, and believed sincerely that her community would not survive the dislocation of the dam. Between them, Norman and Ida were agreed on that.

Norman used every device available to procrastinate. He recalled long negotiations over the cemeteries.

"Indians really protect their cemeteries," he says. "First the corps said, 'We'll leave them where they are and cement over them.' But some Indians wanted them relocated. That drug on a long time, but it was a stalling game. We knew what we were doing. We were stalling them, until we'd decided."

The stalling couldn't go on forever, though. By the middle of May they could hold off no longer. There had been enough meetings. People were changing their minds from day to day, and it was time to vote.

22

Scuttling Belotti

WHILE TEMPERS and opinions heated up in Round Valley through April and May, the temperature in Sacramento remained frigid. Lewis and Curt, together with lobbyist John Zierold and their new allies in the conservation movement, were attempting to light a fire over the issue of the dam, but it wouldn't catch. Even despite the recent newspaper editorials, politicians remained coldly indifferent.

Richard felt impelled to spend more time at the state's capital. It was a killing commute—in time, in money, and not least in wear and tear on himself and his family, but he could no longer count the cost. Outraged as he was by the glacial disregard of the politicians for this vital issue, he was also not a little impatient with the efforts of his colleagues. He thought they were being too damn polite.

Richard's approach to lobbying was different from that of many of his new associates. It was a good deal less gentlemanly. Many of them, he knew, had no real hope of saving Round Valley, but regarded the campaign as a means to an end. Richard, by contrast, was determined that the valley would be saved, and was willing to take risks in that cause. His intention was to break the hold that the water lobby had on the Dos Rios project, and expose it to public criticism. The Department of Water Resources was equally determined to protect it from the political arena. They warned legislators of the danger of making this second phase of the water plan a political football, reminding them of how drawn out and damaging the water battles had been in the fifties. Dos Rios, they insisted, was a fait accompli, provided for in the 1960 legislation, properly authorized by the state, and ready to go. Leave it alone.

The message was duly noted. Richard roared up to the senators and assemblymen on the water committees much as he drove his pickup on the ranch, but was everywhere turned away or ignored. To John Zierold and the other old hands he was like a bull in a china shop, and they were fearful that he would damage their connections with his impetuous behavior.

One day, in desperation, he turned to Bob Lagomarsino, who was chairman of the Senate Natural Resources Committee. Lagomarsino had once been mayor of Ojai, where the Thacher School was located. He had had dealings with Richard before and could not just turn him down. He passed Richard on to his committee consultant, Bill Kier, to talk about the issue.

Kier was a marine biologist with a fascination for politics and a strong leaning toward conservation. As with all committee consultants, his job was to write bills and advise on issues. Kier had established working friendships with consultants on other related committees, and in particular with Ronald Robie who worked for Carly Porter's Assembly Water Committee and with Louis B. "Mickey" Allen, who did the same job for the Senate Committee. He brought them both together at an informal meeting, and let Richard make his pitch.

Kier remembers now that Mickey Allen made a spirited defense of the dam. This was not surprising. His uncle was Senator Harold "Bizz" Johnson, a powerful supporter of federal water projects, and he had been brought up in the ethos of engineering miracles. Not so Ron Robie, who had a legal background.

"Robie was a real open-minded kind of guy," says Kier. "He sympathized with Richard's story of being rebuffed everywhere he turned. His line was, 'The guy deserves his day in court.' "

Richard seized the opportunity with enthusiasm and gratitude, and Robie, like many others after him, found Richard to be a compelling witness. It was the mixture of urban sophistication and simple rural morality that won him over. As Robie admitted many years later, it was not so much what he said as what he represented. "He brought a certain city respectability to what appeared to be a 'hometown save-our-territory' thing. As I recall, his argument was: 'This is a lovely place. There are Indians here. We shouldn't flood it.' He didn't point the finger at Los Angeles and say, 'You're stealing our water.' It was more focused on why you shouldn't build the dam. So it was less threatening. The water industry was terribly threatened, for the simple reason that for years they had projected Dos Rios as the next step."

Though nobody could tell at that time where the conversation would lead, Richard felt that he had at last broken through the skin of indifference and found warm blood beneath. Richard continued his lobbying efforts unabated, and together with Curt and Lewis stirred up as much controversy as he could. A lot of their energy went into trying to throttle Assemblyman Frank Belotti's bill to finance recreation at Lake Covelo. It was a battle that had to be fought on two fronts—with the politicians in Sacramento and with the supervisors in Ukiah.

Belotti's bill was making its way through the committees in Sacramento. The supervisors supported it, the Eel River Association commended it, and nobody on Richard's side had been able to stop it. In March, Ike Livermore actually helped it along by suggesting an improvement in the wording. He was attracted by the money-saving element, dangled like a sale item before the state. For a mere $2 million down, the state got a $25 million present from Uncle Sam. But, Hurry! This offer expires when Dos Rios goes to Congress.

With Jim McCombs and Elmer, Richard was offended by any public statement that conceded even the possibility of the dam being installed. Most of the supervisors could not understand this position. To them it was simply insurance. They might be on record as opposing the dam, but surely they had to protect the county against all eventualities? Be reasonable, they said. If the dam goes in, we'll need the state's money.

Only Joe Scaramella stood out, and objected to Belotti's bill at every opportunity. Jim and Nita McCombs made sure that Joe was kept in touch with their campaign in Sacramento and San Francisco. In mid-April, when the San Francisco papers first admitted the existence of an opposition, Joe decided to push harder. He suggested an open meeting—effectively a "town hall" meeting—when all those opposed to the dam could combine forces and coordinate their strategies. Mayfield found the idea most distasteful. He tried to put a damper on it, pretending that he couldn't really see the point, but his usual allies deserted him. Harvey Sawyers was by now listening to his constituents in Round Valley, and found that nearly all of them opposed the project. Joe's plan swept through, and the following Tuesday a jam-packed crowd overflowed the chamber.

It was a scene of triumph for Richard and his group. It happened to coincide with the news of their first significant victory. A telegram was read out to the jubilant masses from the Board of Engineers for Rivers and Harbors in Washington, granting an extra thirty days in which to submit evidence for or against the dam. The deadline was changed to June 3, and it meant that Richard was close to his first objective. It was becoming increasingly unlikely that the project could be authorized that summer. A precious delay was within reach.

Joe attacked Belotti's bill again, and wanted the board to oppose it. He said it was tantamount to condoning the project, and there was a heated verbal scrap, but he lost that round. The supervisors still wanted to play it both ways, and John Mayfield was deputed to go to Sacramento and give the county's qualified support.

Richard and Lewis were thoroughly alarmed. They saw that the bill would knock away one of the main props of the opposition, and give the supervisors a reason to vacillate on the issue. They tried to persuade Belotti to drop the bill, but he wouldn't listen.

As it happened, the next hearing they had to attend to dispute Belotti's bill was before Robert Lagomarsino's Natural Resources Committee, and there, on behalf of Mendocino County, stood John Mayfield. They watched him carefully as he made his case. They knew Mayfield's brief was to make it clear to the committee that though the county felt bound to support Belotti's bill, it was adamantly opposed to the dam.

What Lewis thought he heard Mayfield say was that the county was in favor of the dam, and he rose in his seat to contradict him vehemently, and to insist that the county was on record against it. Mayfield's displeasure was undisguised, and he came looking for Lewis afterward to express it.

Most of the daily business of the legislature is done not under the capitol's great gilded dome, but in a modern, brightly lit annex where the governor and most of the legislators have their offices. It is in that building's broad marbled hall that the journalists and lobbyists hang out waiting for news or favors. That was where Richard and Lewis went after the hearing, and Lewis recalls seeing a large and dour Mayfield advancing menacingly upon him.

"He started yelling at me and picking a fight, and I was really losing my temper. Richard had to grab me, and no damage was done, but it's the only time in my career as a lawyer that anything like that ever happened. Mayfield went stamping off, and Richard said, 'For God's sake, stay cool. I'm the one who's supposed to cause trouble. You're the lawyer who's supposed to take care of it. And now you're getting into a fight.' He was delighted. By that time we were pretty hetted up.

"And just about then, a TV guy came up to us and said, 'Are you the guys who are fighting the dam?' "

The 'TV guy' was Bob Simmons from KNXT, the CBS affiliate in Los Angeles. Lewis had assumed that he was attracted by the brawl, but in fact Simmons had been looking for them. His pal, Lou Cannon, had tipped him off that there was a good news segment waiting to be made, and before long Simmons and his crew were in Round Valley, filming. Lewis was ecstatic.

"A fifteen-minute program, in Los Angeles, on Channel 2. We couldn't believe our luck."

KNXT was an unusual TV station. It had begun to air environmental issues before anyone else. Bob Simmons thinks it was the best TV newsroom in the country at that time, doing a lot of land use and conservation stories. Dos Rios was a "natural" for him, and after talking with Lewis and Richard he arranged to go up to Round Valley to look around. Like Lou Cannon and Gardner Brown, Bob Simmons was suspicious of wealth. He had only seen Richard in his Brooks Brothers suit, so obviously at ease among the affluent legislators and lobbyists in Sacramento. He drove into the valley very unsure of what to expect.

"I knew from Lou that he had a lot going for him. I found his driveway, after some trouble, and drove in thinking I'd see this rich rancher. When I got out and looked around I heard somebody swearing. He was lying on the ground under a Jeep, pounding on the brake drum with a ballpeen hammer and swearing like a trooper.

"I called, and he came wriggling out from under, muddy from head to toe. I took a liking to him immediately. And he had a marvelous perception of the real issues up there, beyond his own selfish interests. He understood what was at stake, socially, ethically, and politically in the valley. I thought he was just outstanding, and a wonderful television interview."

As with Gardner and Lou, the Wilsons took it for granted that he would stay with them, and he was touched by Susan's grace and hospitality. They also had a common interest in gardening. She had established an organic vegetable garden that, being a rarity at that time, surprised him. He remembered it because it became a significant factor later in their story.

"She was just a darling person. Rather quiet—not much to say—but a steady, mellowing influence. He had quite a temper at that time. He was inclined to fly off the handle. She calmed him down. And she was very interesting because she had become so well acquainted with the Indian community, and was able to tell me a great deal about their background and history."

Susan's unassuming role in the fight is not an easy one to define, but it was of prime importance. Although she was uncomfortable with large groups of people, she conveyed a sweet sensitivity in close conversation. Among the state employees who wandered through the valley working for various agencies were some who fell under her spell. Richard's ability to employ the state's own facilities to frustrate the state's intentions, was often due to Susan's influence and hospitality. There was one young soil engineer who became so devoted to her cause that he even serenaded her after dark at her bedroom window, not with love songs but with secrets from the state files that he thought might help her campaign.

In other ways, by pushing for improvements in the valley, she helped to promote an image of a thriving community. Scandalously, the Covelo High School was the only public school in California to lack accreditation. She took advantage of Richard's visits to Sacramento to pester Assemblyman Belotti relentlessly about it, so that he sometimes found himself under attack from both Wilsons on separate issues, which did nothing for his composure.

During Bob Simmons's visit Richard had no difficulty persuading Byron, the state's helicopter pilot, to fly Simmons and his cameraman around just as he had flown Gardner Brown. It was a hair-raising flight, Simmons said. The cameraman insisted on repeating the same maneuver again and again. They would fly low in the canyon over the waters of the Eel and then shoot sharply up a thousand-foot bluff when the entire valley was suddenly revealed before them. Byron remarked, with unconvincing humor, that he hoped the thing would keep flying because "a helicopter's got as much glide as a greased crowbar." Only when they were on the ground did the pilot tell them that he'd been sick as a dog all night, and worried that he might faint at the controls.

Bob Simmons recalls: "That was the year I covered the Democratic National Convention in Chicago, and all the violence of San Francisco State. It was such a relief to get away from those stories and sneak up to Round Valley to deal with things I understood and felt at home with."

As with all like-minded people who came close to Richard's campaign, Bob Simmons became intoxicated by it and stayed with it to the end.

"I couldn't come on as a visible partisan—working for KNXT—but I did what I could. When we put the film on the air, a woman who lived in Los Angeles but had grown up in Covelo—Virginia Brody—wrote me a letter and told me how interested she was in it. She was unbelievably helpful. Through her they got the use of copying machines, mailing lists, postage meters. It enabled Rich and Curt to flood the state with material and give the impression of being much bigger than we really were.

"I don't think there was ever more than half a dozen of us."

The half dozen, at that time, included Richard, Elmer, Lewis, Jim and Nita, Curt, Bob, and, almost immediately, Virginia Brody. Two or three more central figures joined the band before long, but it was never more than a handful. Of course there were many more who played vital roles in the crusade. They were generally allied to organizations like the Sierra Club, Trout Unlimited, or California Tomorrow, but they had broader objectives, and the valley's survival was not all-important to them. It was that small group gathered around Richard that forced the pace. Though they did not all share Richard's conviction that the thing could be done, they were fired up by it, and all of them—or at least those that survive—look back on those days as having been among the most thrilling and purposeful of their lives.

Belotti's bill continued to make its way through a seemingly endless sequence of committee hearings, and at each one the Round Valley partisans showed up, making it almost a weekly commute. Finally it arrived before the Senate Water Committee. Looking around desperately for ammunition, Richard thought, Who better to kill the bill than their very own state senator, Randolph Collier?

In spite of Richard's early attempts to influence him, Collier was still publicly supporting the dam. In April he went to the inauguration of the huge underground powerhouse of the newly constructed Oroville Dam, the latest awesome achievement of the Corps of Engineers. He gave a speech and to the dismay of the "dambusters" he called for a speedy construction of the Dos Rios Dam. Better to vote another billion dollars in bonds, he said, so that Dos Rios and all the other north coast dams could be built to save his constituents from flooding.

Yet, a month later, testifying before the Senate Water Committee, Collier was whistling a different tune. He called Belotti's bill "ill-timed," because, he said, the State Department of Water Resources was using it to get the legislature in favor of Dos Rios Dam. Furthermore, he said that as a member of the Finance Committee he would oppose Belotti's bill when it came before him in May.

How and why did Collier swing around? Richard insists, unconvincingly, that Collier was persuaded to "do the right thing," but the right thing for Collier may have had more to do with his power base than his conscience. Richard's cousin in Los Angeles, Richard Grant, was president of the California Portland Cement Company, and a member of the six-man National Affairs Committee of the Portland Cement Association, a powerful lobbying group at both state and federal levels. In April, Grant wrote to Richard offering assistance. Freeways can't be built without cement, and Collier, of course, depended heavily on the freeway construction industry for his support. The rest of the story must be left to speculation.

Belotti's bill went on to the next stage despite Collier's testimony, but there was another consequence to that day's work of tremendous importance to Richard. It signaled, in fact, another significant victory. The chairman of the Water Committee, an austere, scholarly lawyer by the name of Gordon Cologne, used the occasion to announce a decision. He was widely respected for his knowledge of water issues, and represented, at its best, the orthodox view of water development. He was quite clear in his mind that the Dos Rios Dam, and others to follow, were absolutely essential to the state's well-being. Up to that time he had assumed that this view could be taken for granted, and that the project would proceed fairly easily to Congress under the existing authorization.

But Carly Porter, influenced by Ronald Robie, had pressed him hard with the need to have some kind of public discussion, and he announced at the end of the day that his committee would seek permission to hold interim hearings on the Dos Rios project. Richard's pleas before Robie, Allen, and Kier had finally borne fruit. Cologne saw that the corps had been forced to extend the review period, that the timetable had been disrupted. He saw that something might have to be done to push the project through. Richard could not have hoped for better. In his view, the water lobby was being forced, finally, to open the can of worms.

In Washington, thoughts rather similar to Cologne's must have been occurring to Col. A. D. Wilder. He was the resident member of the Board of Engineers for Rivers and Harbors, which had the responsibility of reviewing all the army's projects before they were sent to Congress. As the only colonel among a roomful of generals, it was his job presumably to spare them from embarrassment. The telegrams of protest from Richard hardly ruffled his composure, but now he was getting some rather pointed inquiries from congressmen and senators on the Hill. This was too close for comfort. Like Cologne he, too, now realized that this project might not slip through unnoticed, and he decided that a trip to the West Coast might be both pleasant and informative.

Wilder was a tall, suave engineer, balding and courtly, with a distinguished record and medals to show for it. With other staff members from Washington and San Francisco he flew into Ukiah and fed the public relations machine with a tour of Lake Mendocino, the project Hank Pape had helped to build. Then he had lunch with the supervisors. A three-column photograph appeared in the *Ukiah Journal* of Wilder and four others lined up at the old Palace Hotel. On his right is a civilian staff member from Washington. On his left stands a younger lieutenant colonel, deputizing for Boerger; then Charles Elmore, and then, facing the other four, John Mayfield.

There is an odd quality about the picture that intensifies as one examines it. All the men, including Mayfield, stand almost at attention, with their thumbs in the regulation position along their trouser seams. The four engineers are looking fixedly at Mayfield, and fairly beaming with admiration and gratitude, although Elmore has had to twist his neck unnaturally to do so. This is particularly strange because Mayfield, a big man, looks like anything but an object of affection. It may be that he is trying to smile, but beneath his beetling brows is something much more like a scowl, and the picture makes him look overbearing and dangerous.

No doubt the instructions of an inept photographer are partly to blame, but the picture leaves an unavoidable impression that these engineers will do anything for this guy to get their project through, and Mayfield looks like a man who knows it.

The following day after a tour of the valley, Wilder was invited to meet with Covelo residents at Gravier's store. The event turned into one of the more farcical episodes in the story of the dam. It seems that Jan Stewart thought it would be better to get the supporters of the dam off to his hardware store to talk to the colonel uninterrupted. He probably had a point. It is unlikely that Elmer's crowd would have listened very patiently to their speeches. Stewart enlisted his mother to guard the door against the opposition, while the engineers and supporters were ushered in at the back. But the plan failed, as Ida Soares remembers well. She went there with a number of others, including Bud and Trilby Niesen, who were white. They found the door locked, and pounded on it until it opened.

"We wanted to get in, and his mother was standing there and—these are white people now—Mrs. Niesen said, 'I want to get in there.' And she said, 'Are you for the dam or against?' And Mrs. Niesen said, 'I'm against it,' and she said, 'You don't get in here,' and she said, 'Oh, yes I do,' and she forced her way in, and the rest of us burst in after her."

Recriminations, it seems, had already begun to fly and the meeting was getting noisy.

"That big officer that came, Colonel Wilder, he said, 'Let's just stop a minute and ask a civil question here. How many of you want the dam?' And I demonstrated and said, 'We don't want no dam. You go to hell.' "

Opponents of the dam later told the *Journal* that they didn't think they had been heard, though Ida certainly was. They thought the colonel had spent most of his time with Stewart's boosters, and Richard said it was like a comic opera.

Recollections of the meeting itself are scattered, but one remark Wilder made seems to have stuck in several memories. Asked why not build a smaller dam that wouldn't flood the valley, he replied: "Oh, you know us. We're just like a bunch of beavers. We love to build dams. The bigger they are the better we like it."

Nobody, it appears, bothered to inform Colonel Wilder that on that very same day, with exquisite timing, the Indian Tribal Council announced the results of its referendum on the dam. The Indians had finally made up their minds, and voted to oppose it.

Even now, with so many against the dam, the supervisors could not bring themselves to harden their position. Mayfield continued to insist that there was no need to add to the 1964 resolution, although he knew full well that it was inviting confusion, as recent events had shown. Richard's group continued to view him with the utmost suspicion, and on the day of the photograph, one of them thought to ask Charles Elmore whether he knew that the board of supervisors was formally opposed to the dam. Elmore said he didn't and that there was nothing on record in his office about it.

This seemed outrageous. They put the same question to Colonel Wilder in Covelo. Did Colonel Boerger's report to Washington include the fact that Mendocino County was on record against the Dos Rios project? Wilder said it did not. Richard, Elmer, Lewis, and Jim were all furious, and determined to bring the matter to a head. They persuaded a sympathizer, Burt Banzhaf, who was running as a supervisorial candidate, to ask the supervisors on the following Tuesday to pass a resolution against the dam. Before he could speak, Mayfield produced what he said was a transcript of a telegram from Wilder, now back in Washington, saying that he and all other agencies were now fully aware of Mendocino's 1964 resolution. Clearly, he smirked, no further action was necessary.

Banzhaf backed off, but so suspicious were they now of Mayfield that Richard checked with Western Union to see whether such a telegram had actually arrived. Western Union said no. Banzhaf rushed back to the board to confront Mayfield with this iniquity, but Mayfield silenced him with a blow of the gavel, and ended the morning's session before he could open his mouth.

Through the lunch hour the rebels entertained each other with accounts of what they would do to Mayfield that afternoon, but again he forestalled them. An assistant clerk brought in the original telegram. Western Union in Ukiah knew nothing about it because it had been relayed from San Francisco by the corps. Far from retiring red-faced, Richard persisted with his demand for a new motion. The 1964 resolution, he said, did not mention the Dos Rios Dam, only flooding. The board's position was obscure, and he wanted it clarified. Now Avila came to Mayfield's defense. He said they were more concerned with pinning down the state on recreation, if and when the dam was built. Ernie Banker added that he didn't believe harassing the corps would achieve anything. The skirmish ended inconclusively, and was put off to another day.

Meanwhile, Belotti's bill was still alive and due to come before the Finance Committee on May 28. Richard arranged for Elmer, Ida, and others to come to Sacramento to testify before the committee and to have lunch with Ike Livermore. The lunch was a success, but the hearing was postponed to June 11. Elmer came down again with Jim McCombs, only to have the hearing postponed two more weeks. Tired of these cat-and-mouse games, Elmer managed to get into Belotti's office early on the morning when it was next due to be heard. All the opposition Belotti was generating must have finally gotten to him. Possibly he already knew that Collier's influence on the Finance Committee would be too great. What followed became one of Elmer's favorite anecdotes.

"Belotti looked up and said, 'What can I do for you?' And I said, 'You can pull that bill. It isn't going to do anyone a bit of good.' Well, he looked at me a minute and said, 'Let me announce it.' And he did. Just went out and withdrew it. After all that fighting. Lew said, 'You did it so easy.' "

All the arguing and maneuvering, the plotting and counterplotting in Ukiah and Round Valley, had focused attention on the local issues, and at first the water lobby had been well pleased, thinking the problem could be contained and dealt with there so that no larger issues would come up. But now enough heat and noise had been generated to interrupt the dam-building schedule. The water interests became aware that unless they took a hand, the true importance of the Dos Rios project to the state, as they saw it, risked being overshadowed.

Senator Cologne quickly came to agreement with his counterparts in the Assembly to hold joint public hearings. They were certainly not expected to reveal any fundamental flaws in the project. On the contrary, they were intended to set the public's mind at rest. By all means let those local people show their distress and detail the damage. Let them demonstrate how hurtful it is to be displaced by a reservoir. Then show the world how much care would be taken to compensate them, to repair the damage and mitigate the losses. And then show how and why their problems could not begin to outweigh the importance of the dam to the general good of Californians.

As Boerger persistently put it in his speeches around the state, this dam was the key to prosperity. Growth in Southern California translated directly into more jobs, more taxes, more services, more political punch to extract more funds from Washington. Millions of people were affected. More water for the Central Valley meant more produce, more land under cultivation. Who could object? Who could doubt the benefit?

What these rosy prospectuses really implied, however, and what no politician was foolish enough to spell out, was that if the water supply failed to keep up with population growth, the sins of the past might eventually catch up with us. There would be no new miracles to make up for the unearned increments already extracted. The pyramid scheme had to keep building, and woe betide those who try to break the pattern. They would be faced with reality. They would have to make up what their forefathers had stolen from the future. They might actually have to be the first generation to pay for their resources what their resources were worth.

The closest they could get to saying this was when Met chairman Jensen, for example, exclaimed that for Los Angeles to be deprived of the water from Dos Rios would be disastrous. All his cohorts in Southern California immediately echoed his warnings. Gianelli agreed. "Disastrous," he said. And if the public at large could not quite take seriously a disaster that was thirty years down the road, the legislators at least could be relied upon to see it clearly. In any event, it was time for the water establishment to bring on the big players and put Richard's little mutiny in perspective.

The first hearing of the Joint Water Committee was scheduled to be held in Ukiah on August 17 at the Veterans Memorial Hall. Following that there would be another in Sacramento at a later date. The game plan now was to let the protestors vent their anger in Ukiah and then, having shot their bolt, with no more ammunition to bring to the second hearing, the major agencies could dispose of the objections in a peaceful and orderly manner, and the next phase of the Water Plan could get under way again.

Richard knew it was time to broaden his campaign, and he was ready. There were people in Southern California waiting to be contacted, and he planned to start with Virginia Brody.

23

The Brody Bunch

IN THE EARLY YEARS of the century Christian Science became a fashionable religion in Berkeley and gained many converts. As a result, a teacher by the name of Barton decided he had better get his family out before it was too late. It was not the theological contagion that frightened him, but a much more serious medical threat.

The newly enlightened disciples of Mary Baker Eddy had lost all faith in hygiene and modern medicine, and were putting the health of their families in the lap of God. They sent their children to school with whatever diseases God had given them, and the young Barton children were coming home with an endless succession of coughs and fevers contracted from all the little Christian Scientists. It would only be a matter of time, he thought, before they caught something lethal.

When he heard that Covelo was looking for a school principal, he took the job, thinking the farther away the better, and so his daughter Virginia spent her early childhood in Round Valley. That was up until 1920, when her father identified an even greater danger. He became afraid that his daughters might marry some worthless local lad, and moved them all out again. It has been a family joke ever since that the "worthless lad" might have been good-looking young Joe Long, the boy next door, who was a friend of theirs. Joe, as it happened, went on to build the Long's drugstore empire and make multiple millions.

Instead, Virginia became active in the trade union movement in the forties, and went on to marry a labor organizer named Marvin Brody. Even though her marriage took her far away, she never forgot Round Valley. She cherished the memory of her days there, and the unusual people she knew. Her brother Max was taught to hunt by the same Otto Kaser who showed Richard Wilson, as she says, "how to carry his twenty-two through a barbed-wire fence without shooting his toe off." She kept up friendships with members of the old families, and maintains them still.

These days the Brodys have their home in Ukiah, across the street from her friends, the McCombs, but in the sixties they lived in Los Angeles.

"It was in San Gabriel," she says, "and we always went to the L.A. County Fair, and to the Mendocino County booth, because I was supportive of it. So I'd read whatever papers they put out and when I read about the dam, I couldn't believe it. How could they dream of it—drown that beautiful valley? What an awful thing to do!

"My husband said, 'I told you, when everybody voted for the water plan in 1960 that they'd take your valley.' He's a political man. He works in Sacramento.

"I wrote to people I still knew. I wrote to Otto, but though he loved the valley, he wasn't political. Then I wrote to Vera Hurt in the valley—she'd been my sister's best friend—saying, 'What's going on? What can we do?' So she turned the letter over to Richard Wilson. One day when he came to Los Angeles, he dropped by, in his laconic fashion, and talked about what was happening. And of course I quickly signed up as a volunteer."

Throughout his campaign Richard displayed one of the major attributes of a successful politician: He was phenomenally fortunate in his choice of supporters. Virginia Brody, an attractive blonde with a powerful personality, was a dynamo just waiting to be set in motion—"an organizer at heart"—as she puts it. They sat under an alder tree in her backyard, with vodka and a Jack Daniels and talked about who was for the dam and who was against.

"My first question was, 'What do we put together down here?' and he liked that because he hadn't gotten anything going in Southern California."

It quickly became obvious that Virginia's job would be to spearhead a letter-writing campaign, to spread the word in any way she could, and solicit letters of protest to the governor, and to southern legislators.

"You know," she said, "you should get Marvin in on this when you're in Sacramento. He knows the scene so well, and he could bring the auto workers in behind you."

Richard looked bemused.

"Well, how do we make that connection?" he asked.

"Look, in Marv's local alone you've got eighty-five thousand guys working their butts off on the assembly line, and come vacation time, what do they do? They stuff their guns, fishing poles, and families—in that order—into their RVs and I bet every one of them heads north for the great outdoors and the wild rivers. It should not be difficult to persuade them that the rivers need saving.

"They may not know Round Valley, but it's dollars to doughnuts they know the Eel. That's where you'll get them.

"Anyway, talk to Marv. His local's got a good progressive liberal for president. He could help."

As he got up to leave, Richard said, "You should probably meet Jerry Barnum. He's a lawyer in town. If you need anything, give him a call."

Superficially Jerald Barnum was everything Virginia Brody was not. She described him later as a "straitlaced, uptight Republican lawyer," and with years of courtroom appearances behind him, his formality at first was formidable. His correspondence dripped with Dickensian turns of phrase like "your good selves," and he eschewed anything so vulgar as the first person pronoun, preferring always to describe himself as "the writer."

The select firm of Cosgrove, Cramer, Rindge, and Barnum was not quite the museum for stuffed shirts that Virginia might have imagined, as Jerry Barnum is quick to point out. For one thing, the firm had worked a long time for Harry Chandler, who had come to Cosgrove in the twenties in unusually desperate circumstances.

"Chandler was indicted for running arms to some republic in South America. He used to be represented by a different firm, but they gave up. There was no way to deny the charge. They didn't know what to do, and frankly I don't think we did, either. But Harry Chandler came over to our office, and three days before it went to trial, the group to whom he had run arms became the government that indicted him, so of course the case was immediately dropped."

In celebration of such good fortune, the firm was hired to defend the *Los Angeles Times* against its many detractors. Jerry Barnum, who was a libel lawyer, had plenty to keep him occupied because the *Times* never settled a case. However, Cosgrove, the senior partner, had another specialty: water law.

"As long as Cosgrove was living he stood at the apex of water lawyers. The thing about water law is that you can't understand it unless you've been at it for ten or twenty years. I never had water law at law school."

Jerry picked it up on the job, working for private water companies, including the five Dominguez sisters who had become fabulously wealthy through a lucky oil strike. In his water dealings Jerry found himself constantly in dispute with the Metropolitan Water District, particularly over boundaries.

"We fought the Met over three water districts and took them to the U.S. Supreme Court on each occasion. We fought pitched battles. They never forgave me, and I never forgave them. Nobody had ever opposed them before, nor to my knowledge since. You don't. You simply fall in line.

"It's cheaper to think they're God. If you do what they want, it's free, and your fees to your client will be pure gravy."

Jerry was in an unusually privileged position because Cosgrove's policy was to keep the firm strictly away from politics, including personal politics. None of them were even allowed to join service clubs, like Rotary or Round Table. It seriously limited their chances for social advancement, but it left them marvelously free to express their opinions.

On the other hand Cosgrove did make a point of belonging to the Los Angeles Chamber of Commerce—one of the ways in which one sealed one's bond with the city—and Jerry Barnum sat on the chamber's Water and Power Committee, in part he says because the Dominguez sisters wanted him to go and listen. Known to everyone as "Patch" because of a distinguishing splash of white in his hair, he became a famous dissident on the committee, the only one to argue with the chairman.

"The others would have liked to, but didn't dare. If you took a position antagonistic to either the Department of Water and Power, or the Metropolitan Water District, you'd suddenly find you didn't have any water business. Things are done that way down here all the time. But nobody could touch Cosgrove."

Barnum's outfit remained small and personal, and relied on a few important clients. Chandler was one. The Citizen's Bank another. A third was Mike Connell, who left a fortune in endowments and needed lawyers to keep his charities in order. Connell devised his charities so that they would also help his various nieces and nephews, including Richard's stepmother, Marjorie, who were appointed to administer the largesse, and were assured of a good income by doing so. After Marjorie's death Richard succeeded to some of her various directorships. Naturally when Richard began looking for ways to make a dent in the Southern California water establishment, he went to Cosgrove, and Cosgrove introduced him to Barnum.

"I don't think he knew quite what he wanted at that time, but it revolved about the idea that we'd clean house up there in Sacramento. That's Richard for you. I made some suggestions. I'm sure I pointed out how difficult it would be. I didn't think he'd get as far as he did."

The Water and Power Committee was chaired by another lawyer, Henry Lippitt, Jr., who worked out of an office in the same building on Spring Street that Barnum occupied. As it happened they had been at the same boarding school together, back east in Massachussetts, and considered themselves to be good friends.

"I always admired Henry, and I think he had a high regard for me," recalls Barnum. "He was a gentleman. I'm not. I tell the truth, but that's all."

There was another important difference between them. Henry Lippitt drew much of his income from representing utilities, and he was devoted, heart, soul, and wallet to the Metropolitan Water District, the State Water Project, and, of course, the Dos Rios Dam. Once a month, through the late sixties, they both walked to the committee meeting at Bixley Street and there these two friends attacked each other mercilessly.

"That's the way lawyers are," Barnum reflected happily. "Then they walk out of the courtroom arm in arm."

The Los Angeles Chamber of Commerce could be regarded as the ultimate stronghold Richard Wilson would have to take by storm if he were to save his valley. There is no better way to appreciate the power of the interests concentrated there than to read through a list of the members, which Jerry Barnum readily provided. Here were the men who paid the pipers in Sacramento, and who often called the legislative tunes. These men, for the most part chairmen, presidents, or chief executives, represented a dazzling array of American industrial heavyweights. Among them were American Airlines, Bank of America, Lockheed, General Dynamics, Standard Oil, American Cement, Pacific Telephone, Prudential Insurance, the *L.A. Times,* Litton Industries, Union Pacific, and on and on.

Yet, in reality, they were largely indifferent to water matters. They depended entirely on the Met and the Los Angeles Department of Water and Power, both of which were ruled by Joseph Jensen. His supremacy baffled many. For as long as Barnum could remember, Jensen had been on top of that pile, and Barnum had never been able to understand why he remained unchallenged. By 1968 he was an old man, decrepit and, according to some who watched him shuffle out of meetings, apparently incontinent. The Met has a portrait of him taken that year, and with all its resources it could do no better than show a smart, mean old man trying to smile.

Jerry saw him often and remembered him quite well.

"He was stooped, bald, and saggy-baggy if you know what I mean. I always thought he was a bit dotty, but I may be wrong. We used to go home on the same red trolley on Saturdays at noon. He'd eat his luncheon before the trolley left, over at the cafeteria in the Pacific Electric building. It was a strange thing to watch. He wouldn't spend more than a quarter on anything he'd eat. Nobody ate with him. If you went by him and said 'Hi, Mr. Jensen,' he wouldn't acknowledge your existence. A little old shriveled-up guy, eating a twenty-five-cent lunch all alone.

"Contrast that with the dragon who ruled over the world's biggest water empire. I don't think anybody there ever stood up to him. If you took a line on your own, he'd see to it that you didn't bother him again."

Richard went on about his business, moving through the familiar city landscape, meeting and talking and looking for opportunities to advance his case. It is hard to count the ways in which power and influence are exerted. Much of it derives simply from familiarity. Spring Street, at the heart of old Los Angeles, was where Isaac Van Nuys once built an opulent mansion in the 1880s, and it was where his real mother's uncle, Daniel Grant, went to work as a director of Grant Brothers in 1906. A few blocks away, on 7th Street, was the site where Daniel's wife, Nannie, was raised, and on that same site Alexander Pantage built a theater that one of Nannie's nephews operated through the depression.

John Cree Wilson's reputation in the city was maintained and amplified by his oldest son, John Wilson, Jr., who had now almost equaled his father's eminence. He had become chief of staff of the Samaritan Hospital, and had married a member of the O'Melveny family, one of the oldest and most revered legal names in Southern California. Other members of the Grant family were embedded in the city's business heirarchy.

Richard had access everywhere and was listened to, but money runs by its own rules, and having it doesn't mean you can talk others into giving it up. The great majority of the business community in Los Angeles stood behind the Henry Lippitts of that world, taking it for granted that it would be economic folly to stem the flow of water to the south. Afraid that their Colorado water would soon be confiscated by Arizona, they were convinced that Dos Rios would be their salvation.

Jerry Barnum on the other hand was skeptical of the Dos Rios project. To him it looked like just another replay of Mulholland's aqueduct, with Los Angeles, as usual, destined to carry a major part of the burden. The people of the city had no idea how much they were paying for their water. As well as charging them directly through water rates, the Met was also empowered to levy taxes to cover its costs. A good half of the construction costs of the state project would be covered by the Met, which typically hit Los Angeles the hardest. Yet—and this was an extraordinary situation to arise in a great city—the Met was a power unto itself, free of public scrutiny and able to elect its own directors who kept their interests secret.

The chamber of commerce, which he thought should be taking a more sober and balanced view, was dominated by water lobbyists like Henry Lippitt. In Jerry Barnum's eyes, Lippitt was acting out of turn. As chairman of the chamber's committee Lippitt should be impartial, and yet a more partisan voice for water projects was never heard. As soon as the outlines of the Dos Rios project were published, he had created a subcommittee consisting only of himself and one other like-minded water official to examine the proposal. Not surprisingly, they had reported that it was absolutely essential to the future well-being of Los Angeles.

Jerry Barnum, a lone voice in this particular wilderness, observed the charade with some cynicism. He raised his objections on principle, but, like Lewis Butler, he assumed it was in vain. With conventional wisdom solidly behind the corps's plans there seemed little hope of any real debate being permitted. The only other voice of dissent was that of Councilman Bernardi, asking why Los Angeles should pay through the nose while the Met nourished newly minted subdivisions and communities all the way to San Diego with cheap water.

When Richard came to announce his uprising in the north, Jerry welcomed him with avuncular affection, glad to know that he would have good company when the waters of the Eel finally closed over both their heads.

As for Richard, in his wanderings around the city, he heard only what he already knew: that he would never find support unless he could prove that Dos Rios was uneconomical and that there was another, better source of water. Nevertheless, he worked the ground as best he could, encouraging whatever little shoots of discontent he could find, and looking for allies.

Soon after Virginia Brody saw the film on KNXT, she heard from her husband, Marvin, that the UAW had voted to support the Save the Eel River Association and had made their Los Angeles offices available to her. As Bob Simmons had rightly recalled, this was a priceless gesture. It gave them access to the mailing lists, the printing machinery, and the franking machines. Pretty soon after that, two thousand reprints from *Cry California* arrived at her door. They contained Lou Cannon's evocative ten-page article and a weighty critique of California's water policy by a former public health official. Virginia started mailing them off.

"A lot of it was hit or miss. I just used my ingenuity, going through the phone looking for organizations that might be supportive. Anthropologists. Indian specialists. People at UCLA. There was an anthropology professor at Modesto, and his wife, Kay. They put out so much material against Dos Rios among their circle.

"I said to Richard later, 'I've no idea whether anything I'm doing is effective or not.' He said, 'Well, the letters are coming into Sacramento. That's what counts.' "

Eventually Virginia Brody, the "110 percent" Democrat and labor agitator met with the rock-ribbed Republican lawyer, and found that for all his reserved manner, Jerry Barnum had a lively appetite for controversy and was a fount of information that had come his way through his years of practice. After a few sticky moments, they got on very well. The water business has always made strange bedfellows, and Virginia had to face the fact that it was the Democrats who had planned this outrage on her valley, and it was a few buttoned-down Republicans who offered the only hope of saving it. She found more and more to like in him.

"I got him to go on a public radio station from USC—they'd run anything you wanted to talk about, and they had an elite listener group. This man Barnum and I got on the air, and he found it really rather hard to do. But I talked aesthetics, and righteousness and justice, and he talked facts. And in the end it was fun. He was a splendid man."

24

And the Maps Came Tumbling Down

On June 10, seven days after its deadline, the corps's Board of Engineers for Rivers and Harbors in Washington, D.C., issued its findings. The generals saw no reason to interrupt the progress of the project. The storms of protest that Richard and Curt had whipped up on the West Coast made scarcely a ripple in Washington, and whatever Colonel Wilder had learned in Round Valley seemed to have had no effect on the issue.

Communications received from residents of the area, they said, were evenly divided. They gave as much weight to Stewart's Action Committee as they gave the opposition. They noted that Mendocino County was opposed, but that all the other counties were in favor. Although the Indians, too, were opposed, there was plenty of time, they said, to take care of them and deal with their problems.

"The urgent need for flood control and water supply is of sufficient national interest and importance to support construction of the Dos Rios Dam and reservoir as a federal project." That was the conclusion, and in ordinary times, that should have been that. Onward and upward to authorization.

It was fortuitous that Don Clausen, the Republican congressman for the north coast, was on the Public Works Committee and on the subcommittees that dealt with flood control and with rivers and harbors. Richard had been writing to Don regularly. His first long letter in January, enumerating his serious doubts about the dam, concluded by offering his "100 percent support" for Clausen's reelection in November of that year.

The Met has a lobbyist in Washington, named Bob Will, who recalls Clausen saying that he was always bothered by Dos Rios. On June 12, Richard took his older son, Alex, on a trip to Washington. By courtesy of Senator George Murphy they were given a VIP tour of the White House, which pleased Alex tremendously. Richard also spent some time with Don Clausen. In a press release three days later, Clausen said he had "notified the state of California, the Eel River Association, and counties involved that the proposed Dos Rios project will not be considered by the Congress during the present session."

Clausen had done his bit. In 1969, after his reelection, he was glad to be able to acknowledge Richard's "generous contribution" to his campaign, which would no doubt have been made anyway.

Although there was cause for celebration in June, Richard was under no illusion that he had achieved anything more than a stay of execution. The statement issued by the engineers in Washington still represented exactly the attitude and beliefs of all the official agencies in California. The corps and the Department of Water Resources, as well as the Southern California agencies, continued their activities without pause.

Norman Whipple says that in June, sometime after Wilder's visit, Colonel Boerger asked if they could have a private discussion, and he replied (perhaps on Richard's advice) that he would want to have the Tribal Council's attorney present. He says the approach was never made again.

Richard also had refused, on an earlier occasion, to meet in private with Boerger, and when the suggestion was repeated he said they should not meet alone but on a platform in a public discussion. Soon after that exchange, he received an invitation from Henry Lippitt to debate with Colonel Boerger and others at a meeting of the Water and Power Committee at the Los Angeles Chamber of Commerce building.

To Richard it seemed a shrewd enough plan on their part. The meeting would take place on the water lobby's home ground, just one week before the first hearing in Ukiah. The Met, the state, and the corps all had speakers scheduled. With the exception of Jerry Barnum, the audience would be composed entirely of their own men. Between them all, he supposed, they thought they could squelch this interloper and put his little guerrilla band to flight. For good measure they had added to the platform the very engineer who had ruffled Richard's feathers at the Lake County fairground by suggesting he would never be able to master such complicated issues. No doubt they also hoped to get a preview of anything new that Richard might be planning to offer as evidence at the hearing.

In fact Richard planned to bring some new ammunition with him. He and Curt had been on a trip north to Trinity County, and they had come back with a fine selection of dirty pictures. The dirty ingredient consisted of a hundred yards or so of muddy rocks that separated some boat ramps from the water at Trinity Lake. He owed the inspiration for these provocative images to a pipe-smoking lawyer in Weaverville, a phlegmatic man of acute wit and intelligence and a sardonic smile, named Al Wilkins.

Weaverville is the county seat of Trinity County, which stretches north from Mendocino and inland from Humboldt. At its northern end it includes the Trinity Alps, an attractive range of mountains heavily forested (and logged) where gold was once mined. Weaverville has inherited a number of picturesque buildings from that time, and it attracted Al and his wife, Marne, when they came up from Los Angeles in the early sixties. They badly wanted to raise their family somewhere else, and Trinity looked like the place. They found a piece of land outside town and made plans to build their home.

"It was all pristine and beautiful," he says. "There weren't any lawyers here, so they named me assistant DA."

Almost immediately he became involved in a controversy over a big subdivision. It was called the Travis Ranch, and it belonged to Occidental Petroleum. It lay just inside the county line, a few miles north of Henthorne. Some developers had decided the time was ripe to buy it, subdivide it, and sell it off.

"They were going to blade in some roads, hack it up into eight thousand parcels, and sell them off to people in the cities as 'conversation pieces.' That's what they told me. Leaving us with all the problems of schools, roads, all the other services. It was a perfectly horrible use of that land."

Richard Wilson was watching it, too, because it was uncomfortably close to Henthorne. That was how Al and Richard met.

Eventually Al garnered enough support to be able to send the developers elsewhere. Meanwhile, he had discovered an even greater threat to the county. Someone tipped him off to what the water engineers had in mind for the Trinity River. He got hold of the state's bulletin 136, and was horrified at what he saw. Dams everywhere.

"The county was a member of the Eel River Association, so my wife, Marne, attended the meetings, and the more we saw of that the more we realized that it was being subverted by the Metropolitan Water District. We tried to get Collier to take a position, but he wouldn't. All this time, the Dos Rios thing was starting down there, so finally we got together with Dick and Curt." As a lifelong Democrat dedicated, he says, to unstuffing Republicans, Al calls Richard "Dick."

From Al, Richard heard about broken promises on the Trinity River. First, he learned that the river was dying. It was already silting up after only five years because the engineers—in this case they were with the Bureau of Reclamation—were not letting enough water run past the dam. Just like the corps, they had promised to care for the river. They built hatcheries and swore there would always be enough water. But when it came to competing with the demands of the State Water Project, the river always came second. From Trinity Lake they siphoned the water away to the Sacramento Valley. Below the dam, creeks brought sediment into the river, and the flow was not sufficient to flush it out to sea. The spawning beds were ruined. So Richard discovered what Ike Livermore had already been told. The salmon and steelhead runs were deteriorating fast.

The second thing he learned was that Trinity Lake (also known as Clair Engle Lake) was turning into a disaster for recreation because of the very problems he had been predicting for Lake Covelo. Namely, that as the water was withdrawn into the Sacramento River system in the summer, the level dropped and left the recreation facilities stranded in a very unscenic mess. These were the pictures he took with him to Los Angeles in August.

Jerry Barnum, together with some sixty or seventy businessmen, was present to hear Richard speak. They were gathered at four long tables to enjoy a frugal lunch. Jerry had some caustic remarks to make about the chamber's cheap silverware and its generally stingy fare. The speakers sat at a separate table on a raised dais. The turnout was good, possibly because the redoubtable Joseph Jensen himself had decided to come, and Richard noticed that he was sitting close to the speakers beneath the dais.

Promptly at one-thirty, after the meal was over, Lippitt introduced the speakers, saying he was sure they would all learn a great deal from the occasion. Afterward, he added pointedly, they would vote on a resolution to recommend speedy construction of the Dos Rios project. Then Colonel Boerger spoke at length. He was not at his best. Perhaps he had said his piece too often already. He was fidgety and distracted, but of course his case was what all those present, except Richard and Jerry, wanted to hear.

The two civilian engineers followed and Richard spoke last. He recorded on his notepad that the audience seemed listless, and he did his best to wake them up. His stump speech had improved out of all recognition and it carried considerable punch. It was nice to be there, at Bixel Street, he said, because only a few blocks away, on Virgil, was the house where he had been born. Now he lived in the north of the state, but he had been asked to come and tell them as taxpayers why the Dos Rios Dam was a poor venture. The truth behind these apparently conventional projects, he said, was sometimes so startling it might be hard to believe.

Take, for example, the flood control this dam was supposed to offer. "If you were standing at Fernbridge during the infamous flood of 1964, and the great Dos Rios Dam was built, you would not have been covered by thirty-five feet of water—only by thirty-three and a half."

Take the recreation, he said. The project contradicts itself. Water storage and recreation are incompatible. How can you enjoy a lake when the water level is going up and down like a yo-yo? He told them about the stump-riddled brown banks and mud flats he had seen, and the resort owners left high and dry in a financial crisis, trying to make a living in a ghost town.

He told them that Dos Rios was at the heart of the most unstable geological area in the state. Any miscalculation about the nature of the rocks in the vicinity could add hundreds of millions to the cost. He told them about Gardner's analysis, and some of the inconsistencies he had uncovered.

"Have there been any hearings in the Los Angeles area," he asked, "relating to the largest proposed water project in the state of California? The answer is *no,* because the project cannot stand public scrutiny. This project has been planned and pushed through by a few people in Sacramento and Washington."

He finished with a ringing appeal for caution and wisdom while handing out his pictorial evidence of dirty work at Trinity Lake. Unfortunately the pictures were not in great demand. Most of the audience had long since left. Jensen was one of the few to stick it out to the end, but when Richard looked down he saw why. Jensen had fallen asleep.

"It really annoyed them when I handed out the pictures," Richard says. Jensen started to snore, but nobody had the courage to prod him. Lippitt made a halfhearted attempt to have the resolution passed in favor of the dam, but Jerry Barnum put a stop to that by saying there weren't enough members present to vote on such a controversial issue. Richard noted that Boerger looked sicker than ever. So Richard's first public foray into the stronghold of the water lords ended not with a bang but a snore.

The Los Angeles farce was on a Monday. The committee hearing was due to open in Ukiah the following Friday, but the legislative circus came to town the night before. Two dozen senators and assemblymen, with their consultants and secretaries, drove up from Sacramento after a thrilling day of high jinks in the air, put on by the Metropolitan Water District.

In his waking moments, Joe Jensen was as determined as ever to bring the Eel to Los Angeles, and he chartered a plane big enough to fly both the Senate and Assembly Water Committees, as well as various officials and engineers, over the entire state water system. Boerger, Clausen, and Gianelli were on the passenger list as well, and various directors of the Met came to join in the fun. They flew from the Colorado to Dos Rios, while the complexities of the system, its marvels and its shortcomings, were explained to them. There was no reason to doubt the commitment of these legislators to the State Water Plan, but it did no harm for the Met to assert its presence. Bill Fairbank was there, too, of course, knowledgeable, affable, and persuasive as ever, doing the lobbyist's job at its best.

The Third House, as the lobbying community in Sacramento was dubbed, has enjoyed a colorful history of openly lewd and scandalous episodes, in which the late Art Samich set the high-liquor mark, but by the sixties business was generally conducted with decorum. This is not to say that booze, girls, and pay-offs no longer played any part in California politics, but that the majority of lobbyists accomplished their ends by honorable and legal means, and these were certainly the ways Bill Fairbank chose. For one thing he knew the water business. His advice to legislators was solid and valuable. He had come to Sacramento fully qualified, and was lucky enough to have a dramatic career in the Pacific war to tell about as well. He would certainly not deny offering entertainment and hospitality, sometimes lavish, but the principal inducement for following his advice was that it usually brought applause and gratitude from one's constituents. The Met operated a very sophisticated public relations campaign, and was generally able to convince voters that their water projects benefited everyone.

Frank Fats's bar and restaurant, a short walk from the capitol, is still a favorite rendezvous for lobbyists and politicians. Today it has been remodeled, and behind the blank exterior and heavy solid wooden door, it glitters in an ultrasophisticated display of veined black marble, mirrors, and dragon motifs on heavy brocade. The presence of lobbyists is easily discerned. Any presentable stranger walking in past the bar and looking around is greeted by slight nods of acknowledgment from carefully groomed men, all concerned lest this be someone they ought to know but can't remember.

In the sixties the restaurant was less pretentious, but no less well patronized. The negotiations that brought the State Water Project into existence were often carried out in an upstairs room at Fats's, and Bill Fairbank remembers being present at many of them with Bill Warne, Ralph Brody, and the other major players. Later he followed the Eel River Association around, dropped in on the other action groups, and flew legislators from one end of the state to the other. A handy overnight stop when inspecting water facilities was Las Vegas, and the Mendocino supervisors were among many who stayed there as part of the great "Metropolitan Mystery Tour" of California.

Inevitably, Bill Fairbank was on personal terms with all the legislators significant to his work. It was his business to know, as well as they knew themselves, where they stood on these intricate issues, and his political dowsing rod had begun to twitch in the neighborhood of a few of the senators.

Senator H. L. Richardson was one. Bill Richardson, a Republican from Southern California, demonstrated how Dos Rios cut across conventional political lines. Richardson, the huntin', fishin', guntotin' Birch Society conservative, felt sympathy for those embattled ranchers living the western dream in their cowboy valley. More surprising still, he was worried about the Indians and the fish, in that order. As a result, the corps and its allies were not brushing off the Indian problem quite so nonchalantly anymore.

Then there was Senator Al Rodda, a very different kind of man, a teacher from Sacramento and a man of tremendous conscience and conscientiousness. He was as concerned with education as he was with irrigation, and worried that water was siphoning money away from schools. He had taken the trouble to drive up to Round Valley on his own account to see it for himself, and was more ready than most to listen to what Richard had to say.

The third waverer was Senator Jim Mills, a Democrat representing San Diego. He should, by all that's reasonable, have been a staunch supporter of the Dos Rios project. San Diego was top of the list of cities whose water supply was threatened, but he had already expressed serious doubts about the project. Of the nine senators, they were the only ones to cause Bill Fairbank any concern, and among the fifteen assemblypersons (which included one woman, Pauline Davis) there was no apparent break in the ranks.

Lewis Butler drove up to Ukiah that Friday morning in a green Plymouth station wagon he had just bought. He thought it would help to ferry the supporters around. It was his personal response to Metropolitan airpower.

"The Metropolitan had flown up in their airplane and had a big dinner for the politicians. We had this rinky-dink little bunch of people with no political power at all. I don't know why I bought a green car," he says. "Richard saw it and said, 'My God, you even look like you're with the corps.' "

Virginia Brody was there. She had been visiting Round Valley, and came down to Ukiah with a contingent of people opposed to the dam. She remembers being in the company of Grace Long, "a lovely old lady whose family was deeply divided. Her oldest son supported the dam. The rest of the family didn't. There were lots of feuds like that. All the Coveloites met at a restaurant there, called Fjord's. Curt Roberts was there, too—little, white-haired, thin, energetic, humorous, mad. Then we all went down to the Veterans Hall."

It was a packed agenda, with a surprise right at the start. Jan Stewart sent a telegram to say he would not testify because of "threats of violence." Chairman Carly Porter read it out loud; the committee had no idea what to make of it, looked blank, and moved on quickly to the speakers who were there.

There were thirty-four of them, and twenty-seven of those were opposed to the project. An inspiring day for the dambusters. Colonel Boerger led off in his assured, didactic manner. He was back on form, Richard noticed, spelling it out for the committee, in full command of the detail. He regaled them with the benefits, the water, the power, the recreation, and of course the flood control. He had a new, neat twist to dramatize the flood control, and it stuck in Jim McCombs's memory for many years. At peak flood, he said, the dam would hold back enough water in just a few seconds to supply the whole county of San Francisco—not just the city mind, but the entire county—for a day. Very impressive, thought Jim, but why is he talking about supplying water to San Francisco?

Then Richard began the attack on the dam.

"Coolly, methodically," said the *Ukiah Daily Journal* that evening, "Wilson chopped away at many of the points made by the corps." With the benefit of months of study, practice, and effort, and lending to his words the weight of his conviction, he led the charge effectively, scattering the corps figures right and left as he went. Lewis followed with a fiery assault on the corps itself, threatening a congressional investigation of its methods, in particular the money he accused it of spending on public relations efforts to sell its project.

A long list of opponents followed. One of the most moving was Joe Paul of Trout Unlimited, a burly, vigorous man with an eloquent tongue. It was left to him to introduce the case that Richard had never felt he could depend on. The dam, said Paul, would "destroy more long-term basic values than it will create.

"The Middle Fork of the Eel River is a precious, free-flowing, unspoiled waterway that qualifies for wild or scenic status and should be preserved as such for future generations. It is a unique resource of that rare and dwindling species of summer steelhead, and a critically important winter range of coastal black-tailed deer.

"There are alternative sources of water," he insisted, "infinitely less destructive to the ecology of California. These alternatives cry out for exploration. . . . We don't deny the need of our exploding population for water," he said, "but I don't think we can afford the luxury of applying nineteenth-century solutions to twentieth-century problems. We have a responsibility to the citizens of the twenty-first century who will be confronted with the enormous costs and tragic losses in natural resources."

A surprise witness appeared during the course of the afternoon. Senator Collier made an impromptu speech, in which he also called for more investigation, and slapped the corps for "taking on ninety-five percent of somebody else's business." Nobody can quite remember when he spoke, but most people do remember that as he was standing there chastising the army, there was a crash and all the corps maps fell off the wall to the ground. Cheers rang out through the hall, and the "rinky-dink" band of rebels felt that a blow had been struck by providence.

As at Willits, the protestors met afterward to congratulate each other on a good showing. They were well covered by all three of the main newspapers. Joe Paul, in particular, got a lot of space in the *Chronicle* and *Examiner,* but as the days passed a colder reality dawned on them. All their fine words would be slowly stripped of emotion, as the practical committee consultants carefully extracted the information from their heated testimony, and laid it before the agencies. The corps and Gianelli's department would have two months to contest the charges brought against them, and modify their plans to defuse the opposition. Then in the cool formality of a Sacramento committee room, the Department of Water Resources, the Corps of Engineers, and the Metropolitan Water District would reassert their authority. There would be no more opposition. Only new evidence would be allowed, and there was none. With reams of paper and exhaustive testimony the water lords would remind the legislators of what California could never afford to forget. Before anything else, there has to be water. Better take it while you can.

25

"Let Me Tell You About Those Fish Guys."

THE CAPITOL BUILDING in Sacramento is as splendid as any in the country. It stands, glistening, at one end of a forty-acre park landscaped and planted with trees, shrubs, and flowers from around the world to advertise the wonderful versatility of California's climate. Under its 120-foot-high gilded dome, the government, the Senate, and the Assembly do their daily business.

It was built in the 1860s when high-minded people believed that men who did their work in grand and noble buildings would act with greater honesty, selflessness, and idealism. Not all commentators have found the theory to hold up in California. If the standards of our lawmakers were truly elevated by this inspiring structure, some would say, then one can only shudder at the thought of what they could accomplish in a barn.

Viewing them from the thirteenth floor of the Resources Building, a few blocks away, Ike Livermore was reported to have said, early in his government career, "Why, those gosh-darned legislators, they just authorize anything they want."

Bill Gianelli, on the eleventh floor, had a more seasoned view of government business. He had spent years testifying before water committees during Brown's first term as governor. He knew all the principal figures and what to expect from them.

This was just one of the many differences between the two men. Gianelli was a short, combative man with a hot temper and good white teeth that flashed often from his round, close-cropped head. He was a flamboyant figure in Reagan's administration, and his style contrasted strongly with the subdued decorum of the old-money Republicans like Livermore. There was a persistent rumor that he used to drive between projects in a chauffeured limousine, equipped and provided by agribusiness pals. He has always denied this, and takes great pride in saying that he and his department spent $1.5 billion without a hint of scandal or corruption. In truth, those who opposed Gianelli never seriously considered him tainted in any way. Just excessively zealous in the wrong cause, which he of course considered right and pursued to the utmost of his ability. Together with his high-profile activism and colorful slanging of opponents went an incisiveness and a loyalty that endeared him to most of his staff. There was no question where you stood with Bill Gianelli. If you were for him, he'd stand by you. If you were against him, watch out.

At the beginning of 1968, Dos Rios scarcely crossed Gianelli's mind. It was a given, a federal gift that could not conceivably be rejected, and it was in the very competent hands of the army. If Gianelli needed things to worry about, he had them in plenty without that. He had taken on the job of finishing the State Water Project that Pat Brown and Bill Warne had started eight years earlier, only to find himself $600 million short. Though it was unthinkable that the job would not be finished somehow, it taxed all his department's ingenuity just to keep the work going ahead.

Gianelli opened the year in style with a boisterous mud-slinging match. He made a speech attacking what he called "special interests"—a favorite target of his—for sabotaging the state's plans. State Senator George Miller, the chairman of the Finance Committee, replied in public that Gianelli should be fired for referring to him and others as "political extremists." Jerome Waldie, the congressman from Contra Costa County was equally incensed. Their disagreement was just one more episode in the unending argument about what to do, or not to do, with the delta, a serious source of contention just a few miles down the Sacramento River, and the nexus and perplexus of the whole grand water design.

The delta is a broad spread of islands formed where the Sacramento and San Joaquin rivers meet, about sixty miles inland from the Pacific coast. Formerly their combined waters washed unrestrained over an area of almost a million acres before escaping through a narrow channel to the big saltwater bay of San Francisco. In the early part of this century, much of this wetland was reclaimed, and more than seven hundred miles of waterways have been fixed in place by aging levees protecting and irrigating some of the richest land in the state.

This is the natural outlet for two fifths of the water that falls on California. Whatever is done to water in the great Central Valley will be felt in the delta. And whatever battles are fought over water, the condition of the delta becomes a central issue.

Although the Dos Rios Dam was always justified by the need to supply water to Los Angeles, it was impossible to keep the delta out of the picture. That water would first have to pass through the delta, and it would play its part, together with the other blocks of water from Oroville and Shasta dams, in keeping the delta fresh and supporting fish, factories, and homes from Sacramento to Stockton to Suisun Bay.

The delta is an area unlike any other in California. The islands vary from a few acres to thousands of acres in extent. They are composed of the silt swept down by the rivers through eons of time, and the material is so rich in organic matter that, when dry, it is combustible like peat. It was the custom for decades to burn off the grain stubble in the fall, and those who lived in and around the delta will always remember the sweet but pungent haze of smoke that drifted through the fall air, from the smoldering rice fields.

There are boat docks everywhere, and the delta is a paradise for those who like to fish for striped bass, for duck hunters who build their blinds in the remaining marshes, and for people who like to float idly along canals between saloons and inns. It also grows $300 million in rice and other commodities every year. It supplies water to, and receives effluent from, a belt of oil refineries, power plants, steel and plastics factories, and other heavy industries clustered along its southern shores from Antioch to Pinole. It acts as a reservoir for much of Southern California's drinking water. And finally it serves as a barrier against the salt water from the bay that would otherwise (and sometimes does) intrude and threaten agriculture and fisheries.

Every one of these interests would like to command priority over the fresh water in the delta, and it would be hard to compile a list of more conflicting roles. The delta is a permanent, raging argument, where every water interest is opposed to every other. It has become, fittingly for such a convoluted ball of waterways, the Gordian knot of California water politics. Among those who would have dearly loved to play the role of Emperor Alexander the Great and slice right through it was William Gianelli.

Gianelli's favorite solution to the problem was a simple one. It was to construct a canal around the delta, and ship all that expensively acquired fresh water directly into the southern aqueducts. The scheme—loved by some, heartily loathed by others—was known as the Peripheral Canal, and it was much closer to the forefront of Gianelli's mind than Dos Rios. Both the dam and the canal were authorized parts of the State Water Project, but Gianelli considered Dos Rios to be a shoo-in. Getting the canal was the true challenge.

The delta has always been a factor in Gianelli's life because he was born on the edge of it, in Stockton. What the city of Sacramento is to its river, Stockton is to the San Joaquin. A smaller city because it does not lie on a transcontinental route, it was nevertheless an important link between the southern valley and the bay, dealing mainly in produce and beef. Gianelli's father came from a small village north of Genoa, and crossed over on a cattle boat with four brothers at the turn of the century. All five of them made their way to Stockton, where a cousin had a grocery business.

Bill Gianelli grew up tough and outspoken in the Italian manner. His father was a laborer, his mother took in sewing. He worked hard to become the only member of his family to go to college, and had to break his education once to earn money. It should not be surprising that a man with his background was more likely to identify with the farmers, the producers, the ones who made California grow, and less with the duck-hunting gentlemen of means, the conservationists, and the anglers whom he refers to scornfully as "those fish guys."

His circumstances today are very different from those he grew up in. There is still water on his doorstep, but now it's the Pacific Ocean. He lives on Pebble Beach, a rich, guarded development on Monterey peninsula south of San Francisco. Although his neighbors are likely to be millionaires, his house and those around him are relatively modest. Location is what sends the value through the roof. Pebble Beach has one of the world's most exclusive golf courses, and Gianelli plays a lot of golf. Though he's spreading a little at the waist, he keeps in shape. Still vigorous and temperamentally hot, he also has a sweetness about him that's often seen in men who appear to have banished doubt from their lives. He can survive three hours of conversation on disputed topics without once conceding that there might be two sides to a question.[1] In Gianelli's universe, what Gianelli knows, goes. If you agree with him, there's no gainsaying it—he's smart enough to be right most of the time. If you disagree, no man could be more wrong. Take the State Water Project, for example, and those misguided enough to oppose it. As he talks about it he gets increasingly frustrated. Toward the end he's almost shouting.

"The water projects have provided a degree of control that was never provided by the state of nature, and the people who benefited by it don't want to give it up. They just bitch. The fish guys always bitch about water projects. They're never for 'em. And that's one of my pet peeves. Let me tell you about those fish guys—they've been one of my big— They'll say: 'The striped bass—look what's happening to them!' The goddamn striped bass! The water projects always get blamed, but they never get any credit. Look at the recreation that's provided in Southern California around those reservoirs. San Luis, the reservoir there. The recreation. Projects are always put in the part of the bad guy. And that's wrong."

Gianelli was sometimes referred to in the press as a "master of gamesmanship," but it is hard to imagine this choleric enthusiast engaging in diplomacy as he continues to rally his troops from Pebble Beach.

"When you get the no-growthers and the anti-dammers and the pure environmentalists and the fish guys all opposing water projects, they won't happen in the future. We're in trouble. People will put up with a certain amount of shortages for a period of time, but after a while they'll say enough is enough, and then they pay through the nose to correct their former errors.

"In Southern California, if they can't flush their johns, or fill their swimming pools, they're going to say, 'Well, to hell with those anti-dammers and environmentalists. We want a water supply that's adequate to our needs.' But the trouble with that is, when they make that decision it's twenty years too late. You don't build these projects overnight. I betcha, if things go on the way they are for fifty years, they'll kick every environmentalist out of the legislature, and it'll flip over the other way."

Like many of those he later worked with he completed his education at Berkeley just in time to be swept into the world war. He went in as a second lieutenant and returned as a major and a hero, to compete with many other heroes on the job market. A job offered by the state reminded him of his fascination with the uses of water, which survived from a childhood on the delta.

"I was a Sea Scout. In Stockton the Sea Scouts do a lot of things on the delta. The deep-water port was constructed in 1932, and a big training base, so we had a sailboat. So I was oriented kinda water-wise, and I was also oriented agriculture-wise. During the semester I stayed out of school, I worked for the Department of Agriculture, going around on crop surveys."

Gianelli took the government job, to become an assistant hydraulic engineer, measuring snowfall in winter and distributing irrigation water in the summer. It was a grassroots introduction to water politics.

"It got to be a very emotional subject; in fact, one time one of the farmers took a shot at me—from a long way away—because he felt I'd turned off his water when I shouldn't have."

He soon discovered that the practical work in the field did not intrigue him nearly so much as the almost byzantine legal complexities of water rights. Besides, spending six months of the year in the mountains did not fit too well with raising a family. He got himself transferred to the water rights section of the department, embedded himself in Sacramento, and eventually became the man in charge.

In California—in the West in general—water rights are a matter of life and death. From the days when Haggin fought Miller over the San Joaquin River to the present, the most expensive and convoluted court cases were those fought over water, and it was the issue of water that has several times threatened to break the state in half. After ten years of acquiring expertise in the subject, Gianelli was persuaded by the state engineer, Harvey Banks, to move over with him into a reorganized department devoted principally to getting the State Water Project started.

He recognized later that it was the most critical move of his life.

"Immediately after I got involved, about the beginning of 1957, the legislators started to fight. For two years, the legislature was deadlocked on the water issue. The people in Northern California said, 'Look, we may have surplus water but we don't want to let it go and not be able to get it back when we need it,' and the people in Southern California said, 'We have a tax base, but we don't want to finance this project and then find we don't have the water from it.' So there was this north-south conflict."

The governor, Goodwin Knight, appointed fourteen lawyers to devise a constitutional amendment to solve the problem. Gianelli was their engineering consultant. They worked seven days a week for months, all to no avail. The legislature refused to accept their solutions. Meanwhile the pressure from the southland for more water was intensifying, particularly when the federal courts decided that much of the Colorado water would be cut off and given to Arizona.

"Los Angeles had been pretty much taken care of [by expanding the Owens Valley supply], but San Diego didn't have a damn thing other than the Colorado River. So the pressure came from the San Diego area, and Riverside, and the big agricultural interests in Kern County who were not able to get water from the federal projects because of the acreage limitations."

The northern senators fought hard against the plan to take their water south, but what tipped the balance, in Gianelli's view, was the flood of 1955. It was his first direct experience of how a catastrophe at one end and an appetite at the other can combine, like the stick and the carrot, to move the donkey of public opinion. It was pointed out, and driven home again and again, that a big dam on the Feather River would have saved the cities of Yuba and Marysville. Finally, when a new governor, Pat Brown, took a new approach to solve the disputes in the legislature, the pressure for flood control in the north had grown enough to swing the balance.

"There was a groundswell for a major project that involved flood control in Northern California and water supply in the San Joaquin Valley and Southern California," Gianelli states in his characteristically dogmatic manner. There is no question that he believed the project to be in the state's best interests, but talk of a groundswell is disingenuous to say the least. It was an organized campaign with heavy support and financing from the south that put the message across.

Playing a significant part in this campaign of persuasion was the Corps of Engineers, which eventually built the dam. The corps is always required to assure Congress of "cooperation by local interests," and this gives it a mandate to inform and interact with those interests. In practice this was usually taken much further, and translated into a full-blown propaganda campaign on behalf of the project. A proven and effective technique was to stimulate the creation of a body of citizens in favor of the project—a sort of Fans of the Dam Club—into which other interests could funnel money and other kinds of assistance. These associations often assumed a quasi-official status, and to uninformed newspaper readers easily passed as branches of government.

The Feather River Project Association fulfilled this role from 1956 and it lobbied enthusiastically for the dam, collaborating closely with southern water interests to push out news stories and to counter criticism. At last the years of effort paid off. Enough of the public bought the flood control story to push the project through.

At this moment of political triumph, Gianelli found himself in a sticky situation. There was friction within the department, and Gianelli added to the irritation. Perhaps he had made himself too visible for comfort. He was offered a refuge in Los Angeles, but he chose private practice instead. For six years Gianelli used his experience with water rights and water law to help farmers overcome difficulties with acreage limitations. He negotiated contracts for all the major water users along the Sacramento River, and for others on the delta.

Then came the election that Brown lost and Reagan won. There was no question of Warne remaining. He and Reagan had slugged it out verbally in public. So there was an urgent need to find someone who would get on with building the water project, and obviously what was needed now was not a politician like Warne, but a can-do administrator. Gianelli's credentials were impeccable. He was soon at the top of the list. Reagan phoned him in the middle of December, before he took office, and said: "You've been highly recommended to me. Will you come and be my director of Water Resources?"

Gianelli says he knew nothing about Reagan, and asked to talk a few minutes.

"I was concerned about whether he had any philosophies I'd have to follow, and whether he was going to support the project, because I didn't want to be thrown to the wolves. He said, in effect, he didn't know a damn thing about water, but he knew the project was good for the state, and wanted to finish it. So I said, okay, I'll do it. Just like that."

The beauty of the Dos Rios project, from the water lobby's point of view, was that you could explain the need in so many different ways, according to whom you were addressing.

To agribusiness, you could say it was really meant to expand agriculture. In another variation on the San Fernando gambit, most of the water would be surplus most of the time. Not only do you get what you contracted for, which was almost half of the total amount, but you get the surplus, too, at knockdown prices.

To the general public you said the water was absolutely essential to supply the growing population in Southern California, and guarantee them the living standard that every Californian had the right to expect.

And to those with a growing concern for the environment you said the water was essential to keep the delta healthy, salt-free, and full of fish.

True or false? That depends on how you look at it. The conflict between these points of view was the crux of the problems that continue to harass California twenty-five years later. Do you strive, at great risk to the environment, to maintain a constant supply of the resources people think they need? Or do you learn, painfully, to live with what the environment can safely provide? Richard Wilson at Dos Rios wanted the state to confront the issue early and open Pandora's box. Livermore became, reluctantly at first, his champion.

Gianelli, the honest soldier, was on the front line defending the conventional wisdom that had served California and his generation so well. The source of his strength is his uncompromising position on the uses of water. It's simple. It's direct. In twenty-five years it hasn't changed, and he is not shy about expressing it.

"Let me give you my basic philosophy, because it permeates these projects. California is an arid state. It gets a hell of a lot of rain for three or four months of the year, and then it doesn't have any. On the other hand, it has climate, it has soils, it has a lot of things it can do with adequate water. But given Nature's way of handling the supply, these things couldn't happen unless you build big projects to hold water over from winter so you can use it in summer.

"So I come from the standpoint that water projects are good for the people of the state of California, whether they be big farmers or little farmers or duck shooters or whatever. I just feel that if California is going to be the number one state of the Union, it's gotta have its water supplies developed.

"Now that runs me counter to the no-growthers, it runs me counter to some of the environmentalists. A lot of the opposition comes from special-interest groups who are no-growthers or against corporate farms.

"The no-growthers will tell you that the way to control growth is to control water. Well then, why not go up and do away with the hospital on the hill here? Or do away with electricity? To use water to control growth is a misapplication. You ought to control growth by zoning, proper planning. But politicians don't have enough guts, at the city or county level, to zone properly. The department didn't authorize this water project. The people of California did. We're still ruled by majority vote in this country. My answer is very simple. Don't come and bitch to me. Go to the politicians who decided this thing. I'm carrying out the mandate of the people.

"Then there were people advocating that if you dried up Imperial Valley, you could have enough water for California. But the politicians adopted the policy that agriculture was important to California. I took the view that my job was to take care of the water needs of California. It was not to try to control growth, not to do away with irrigated agriculture or corporate farms. It was to supply the needs of California however they occurred.

"I don't think the state can afford to have forty percent of its water supply go to waste in the ocean, when there are needs for it in other parts of the state. The big demand for water developed south of Sacramento. They are real needs. I don't think it was my job to say 'If you develop this water project you'll have too many people in Southern California.'

"I used to say, in my talks, that Tijuana, in Mexico, was the fastest-growing metropolitan area in the West after World War II. Half the houses had plumbing but no water, but it still grew. People are going to come to California whether you have water or not. All you're going to do if you don't have it is make their lives a whole lot more miserable.

"That's not so absurd. Look, we've got a water shortage here right now [in 1991]. I don't like it, because I can't flush my toilet every time I take a pee. That's not my standard of living. I can get by on a gallon of water a day—I did that in the army when I was overseas—but I don't like it. So if you're going to have a standard of living you're accustomed to—and we like to think we have a higher one than any other country—then I want a toilet I can flush every time."

And to all of this, the no-growthers, the special interests, the environmentalists, and those fish guys can only reply with questions.

How many rivers can you empty before there are no more fish? How many more acres can you irrigate before the earth turns to salt? How many millions more toilets can you flush before you wonder where it's all going? Is it really okay to turn the whole of Southern California into Tijuana because we lack politicians with guts? Who wants to be number one and king of the castle, if the castle is a dung heap? And finally, aren't there better ways to grow than by consuming more water?

Gianelli has no patience with those questions now, any more than he did in the sixties. He and the others working around him were the can-do leaders of the GI generation, now reaching middle age and at the height of their executive vigor. They had no reason to doubt the philosophy that had sustained them all the way through from the war. They were men who had made it the hard way. It was not lost on them that the argument seemed to be between those who had had to work for a living, and those, like Wilson, Livermore, and Butler, who had the luxury to choose a living to work for.

In Gianelli's experience it had been proven that man's ingenuity would always be equal to any practical problems that might arise. Technology, unhampered by sentimentality, could provide an ever rising standard of living for an increasing population. They were the stewards of the American dream, confronting the stewards of the earth, and they regarded those who raised obstacles to progress as being either dreadfully misguided or venal.

The huge Oroville Dam on the Feather River was the keystone to the project, and at the beginning of 1968 it was just about finished. The broad concrete canals that would carry the water south were creeping steadily across the landscape. Already they were servicing Napa County and the general area of the bay with smallish deliveries, but the project's destiny would be fully realized in the next two years when the water would first flood over many hundreds of thousands of thirsty acres in the San Joaquin Valley and then, finally, be sucked into the biggest pumps ever built and rammed two thousand feet up and over the mountains to Los Angeles.

In a project this size, the water is counted by the million acre-feet and fractions thereof. One million acre-feet is a truly colossal amount of water. As a column of water covering the area of a football field, it would rise nearly two hundred miles high. There would be enough water to fill the World Trade Center—all of it—two thousand times; enough to give every man, woman, and child on the face of the planet three luxurious, American-style showers.

The State Water Project was committed to moving more than four times this amount of water up the San Joaquin Valley every year, and half of it over the mountains to Los Angeles. And all of it would pass through the delta on its way to the southern aqueducts. To get these enormous facilities financed and built despite the lack of funds, Gianelli was ruthlessly cutting out the trimmings, and cleverly rescheduling the construction program. He was also frantically peddling contracts for the full capacity of the project, drumming up commitments that would ensure its financial integrity.

It was designed to deliver 4.2 million acre-feet, and if contracts were signed for the full amount, then payments for the water would eventually meet the cost of building and maintaining the whole facility. In any ordinary year, even without Dos Rios, the project could deliver the full amount, because there would be a surplus in the delta pool flowing naturally from the rivers. But in dry years, when the project depended on water that had been saved, there would be a 900,000 acre-foot shortfall. The state hydrologists calculated that sometime during its hundred-year life there would be another seven-year drought as bad as the record drought of the late twenties. The function of the Dos Rios Dam was to safeguard the state against defaulting on its contracts during such a cycle of drought.

In a practical sense, the argument came down to the contracts, and the water rights that stood behind them. For Gianelli, so long as he was in charge, his personal reputation was on the line. The thought that the state could default on its contracts was unthinkable, and until the beginning of 1968 he didn't think it. Then he began getting memos from Livermore asking him to explain this or that aspect of the Dos Rios project.

Gianelli had been appointed nine days before Ike Livermore. It did not cross his mind, or Ike's—or, one can safely assume, Reagan's—that there would be anything more than a formal relationship between Livermore and Gianelli. Gianelli had simply assumed that his department would operate independently, dedicated to an engineering project about which there could be no disagreement. Ike Livermore would be nothing more than a "communications link," as he put it later.

As Ike grew more and more doubtful about Dos Rios, he realized that he would have to assert his authority over Gianelli. The struggle became fierce. For a while there were many who believed that only one of them could survive, and they gave Gianelli the odds.

26

Famous Amos and the Doody Report

FOLLOWING the Ukiah hearing, Richard and his allies were under intense pressure to find ways to influence the legislators at their next meeting in October. None of them felt that their testimony at Ukiah would carry much weight against the arguments of the water lobby. Since when, they had to ask themselves, had emotional pleas for restraint had much effect on affairs of state? The only argument they had made that could disqualify the dam came from Gardner Brown, who said the water could never compete with desalted water from the ocean. The corps had responded promptly by *raising* its benefit/cost ratio another three points from 1.6 to 1.9. When Ike Livermore asked, politely, for an explanation, Colonel Boerger replied that they had *underestimated* the value of the water. Desalinization, he said, was much too expensive and could not be relied on to get any cheaper. Gianelli's department had figures to show that the water from Dos Rios was worth at least $29 an acre-foot coming out of Grindstone, rather than the $26 they had calculated earlier.

Serendipity, indeed. The discovery came just in time to save the project from rising federal interest rates. It was obvious that with the Department of Water Resources being the source of all data, proving the engineers wrong would be next to impossible. And Gardner Brown's assertion that the water was only worth $8 was made to look like fantasy.

The media were not so quick to dismiss it, though. Having embraced the existence of a "controversial Dos Rios," they were delighted with the idea of this "Lone Ranger" from the north holding the mighty corps up to ridicule, and they kept repeating his figures. Richard, Lewis, and Curt strengthened their resolve and hoped for a lucky break. Sooner or later, they felt sure, the combined efforts of various groups would generate an irresistible wave of environmental awareness. It was growing in every quarter, on every issue—highways, air pollution, forests, fish, toxic chemicals, groundwater. In all likelihood, these concerns would resonate with each other to create an effect greater than the sum of the parts. It was in the air, and they could all sense it. Rachel Carson's *Silent Spring* had introduced the first nightmarish notion of an invisible but deadly chemical menace back in 1963. Ralph Nader was seriously undermining confidence in the ethics of the manufacturing industry. Los Angeles was battling smog. The Sierra Club and the Wilderness Society were beginning to expose abuse of the land. As a result of the Vietnam War and the free speech movement, young people were learning to question authority.

So far, so good, but it was not far enough. It might take a decade to gather the necessary force to reverse the trend. Meanwhile governments and companies were still free to propose the most monstrous projects in the name of progress and profit, without opposition. In a mainstream backlash against student demonstrators, voters clung blindly to the old values. Reagan had again shown his political mastery by recognizing this fact, and had solidified his hold on his conservative constituency by allowing himself to be demonized on the campuses of California.

It would be a brave man who bet his shirt on turning public opinion around in a year. That was just the kind of bet Richard took without blinking. After all, if he was going to "clean house in Sacramento," as Jerry Barnum deduced, then why not clean up the rest of the mess while he was about it? Richard had become the reincarnation of a phenomenon from the past, a Republican revolutionary, and he began by looking up and down the state, county by county, to see where he could foment rebellion.

In Trinity County, Democrat Al Wilkins was a willing accomplice. Al was already comparing his own activities to those of the American rebels of the 1760s. Together with Supervisor Hazel Wilburn he called for "united public action" to stop more dams on the Trinity River. With a keen sense of the humor of it, he said they would join with other groups and function like the "committees of correspondence" formed by American patriots before the Revolutionary War. Their immediate purpose was to take Trinity County out of the Eel River Association.

"I don't think there will be a future for Trinity County if they put in more dams," he said, and proposed a meeting at the Civil Defense Hall in Weaverville. "After the dams go in," he added, "they'll probably declare the whole county a recreation area." For recreation, read disaster!

From Al came a flood of information about the effect of Lewiston Dam and Clair Engle Lake on the river and its wildlife population. Even more damaging to the dam builders was his claim that he had unearthed information to show that all these consequences had been foreseen and inexcusably ignored.

In Humboldt County, where the pro-dam forces were most numerous and economic arguments for the dam were at their strongest, a resistance movement was beginning to brave public opinion. Richard had spoken in Eureka, rallying fishermen to his cause. Although the single daily paper, the *Times-Standard*, was firmly committed to Dos Rios and flood control, it had an outdoor sports columnist, Ray Peart, who disagreed, and said so in print. Like Richard, he found that his views impelled him to take action. Others emerged to support his view that a more sensible response to flood danger was to move out of the way of it. He went into local politics to promote flood zoning among other things, eventually was elected supervisor, ran his own television program, and became a beacon of environmentalism.

In Mendocino County, the militia was already mobilized, and the battle continued to swirl around the supervisors. Mayfield had engineered a new job for himself in Sacramento, but his replacement, Charlie Barra, was even more outspoken for the dam. The McCombs were kept on their toes. One night, late in the game, they were called out in an emergency by a friendly clerk of the board of supervisors. Barra had turned up unexpectedly at a meeting of the board's water committee, and was trying to force through a pro-dam resolution while nobody was looking, but Jim McCombs managed to talk it down.

Lake County was hostile territory but had its own reasons to be disgruntled with the corps over the routing question. Napa and Sonoma were no help. In Marin, however, Richard not only had the tacit support of the Brahmins but also another bit of luck came his way. The tragedy of Dos Rios was being echoed in Marin as a farce, and Boerger found himself in the part of the helpless buffoon.

It happened that Colonel Boerger and his wife had settled into the small Marin community of San Anselmo. They found a house they liked, and, already in 1967, Frank Boerger was contemplating keeping this as their ultimate home. Ironically Boerger, who had been able to maintain such cool detachment from the problems of the embattled residents of Round Valley, now found himself having to take the heat personally.

San Anselmo was one of a cluster of prosperous communities, which included Kentfield, nestling between the northern arm of San Francisco Bay and the ridge of low mountains along the coast. Small creeks carry the winter rains off the eastern slopes down to the bay. Tamalpais Creek runs into Corte Madera Creek, and both of them were inclined to flood after heavy rains. Because of the value of the real estate, Congress authorized a small flood control project. About eleven miles of the creeks were to be contained in concrete by the Corps of Engineers at a cost of some $5 million.

Some of the inhabitants of the choice property around Tamalpais Creek got a look at what the engineers had planned for their little stretch of sylvan paradise, and recoiled in horror. They saw, winding among their trees, what looked like an endless cement trough for hogs. Arguments broke out between those in Larkspur who would benefit and those upstream, including the eminent Kent family, whose environment was to be violated. It was Dos Rios in miniature. To add to the irony, because of the celebrity of the persons involved, it probably received more publicity and generated more heat than did the Dos Rios saga. The Boerger family found itself swept back and forth by the tide of remonstrations, which did nothing for the colonel's morale. Dignified residents, pillars of the community, lay down in front of bulldozers and were carted off to jail. Roger Kent, the patriarchal Democrat, was happy to appear on Richard's SERA letterhead, and his support was more than nominal.

Over on the delta Richard was also finding unlikely allies, united in their common determination to rub Gianelli's nose in the dirt. Senator Miller's stinging rebuke of Gianelli had been delivered at that same meeting of the Eel River Association where the counties voted 7–2 for the Dos Rios Dam. At that time, both Miller and

Congressman Waldie—the men Gianelli had styled "political extremists"—had favored the dam. Tactically, it meant more fresh water for the delta. But what they both now had to realize was that they needed to make common cause with conservationists everywhere, to fight what they saw as the ungovernable thirst of the Southern California water lobby. In other words, if they wanted support from the San Francisco–based environmentalists, like Butler and Heller, in their fight against the Peripheral Canal, they would have to change their tune on Dos Rios.

In Los Angeles, Jerry Barnum did his best to keep the colors flying at the chamber of commerce. Henry Lippitt, at the next meeting of the Water and Power Committee, again put the resolution to support the dam. This time, Jerry wrote to Richard, the meeting was packed with water officials, thirty-five more than expected.

"Yours truly laid his thin neck on the block and it was chopped off after several faces were red and stammers uttered in response to the writer's question why consideration of a $450 million project was committed for study and recommendation to a [sub-] committee with only two members. When the chairman asked for a show of dissenters' hands, the writer alone raised his."

Richard did all he could to fan the flames of discontent in the south, supporting a major effort by Virginia to bring the matter to the notice of Southern Californians. Her husband, Marvin, had also testified at Ukiah on behalf of the auto workers. He made sure that his members were told all about it in their newspaper, and were asked to spread the word.

Clearly the most important thing was to bring all this activity into focus in Sacramento. Curt was doing what he could with the media and behind the scenes. Bob Simmons continued to cover the story in Los Angeles. KRON did it in San Francisco. There were televised debates, at one of which Norman Whipple walked off in disgust. Richard and Lewis were lobbying intensely in Sacramento, overshadowing the efforts of the Planning and Conservation League lobbyist, John Zierold, who was beginning to feel a chill.

Then, in early September, Richard first got wind of something big, something that could swing the whole issue of Dos Rios in their favor. It could be the stroke of luck that they had longed for but never expected. A dissident source in Gianelli's department tipped him off that an explosive document had just made its appearance at the

Sacramento headquarters. It had been completed by Southern California engineers and it showed that there was no need to build the Dos Rios Dam for another ten years, if at all. This information was so disconcerting, he was told, so potentially disrupting of the department's plans that the report was being kept secret. In fact it was even being kept secret from Gianelli because, his mole told him, "Gianelli has a habit of shooting messengers." Reportedly, Gianelli's deputy, John Teerink, had told his underlings "not to bother Bill with it."

Richard's joy was matched only by his frustration. Unfortunately it would be physically impossible for his contact to obtain a copy of the report. He could only identify it as a ninety-three-page memorandum from James Doody, the district engineer in Southern California, to Teerink. The subject was "Present and Future Water Supply and Demand in the South Coastal Area." Only six complete copies existed, and it was to be kept confidential.

From that moment Richard could think of nothing but how to get a copy of the "Doody Report." None of his other contacts were even close to it. Without the document itself they could do nothing. Somewhere in the files of the Department of Water Resources in Los Angeles sat ninety-odd pieces of paper that could blow the Dos Rios Dam sky high, but they might as well have been on the moon. He had no way to get them, no way even of knowing in which of a thousand file cabinets they were.

About a week later, out of nowhere, Richard got a phone call. The caller identified himself as Amos Roos. He said he worked for the Department of Water Resources in Los Angeles. He had heard Richard speak. He had been following the progress of Richard's campaign. He was sympathetic, and believed that the department's policies were outdated and hidebound by obsolete thinking. Was there something he could do to help?

Was there! Richard told him exactly what he could do. He could find the Doody Report and bring it out. Even on the phone, Richard could hear Roos blanch.

"I'll see what I can do and call you back," he said, and hurriedly hung up. Richard could not remember a time when it was harder for him to keep on with his work, as he waited and waited. Several days later Roos called again. He had found a part of the report. It was in sections, distributed among the workers who had contributed to it. He had made a note of some salient paragraphs. Here was one, from page 89.

> Contrary to general opinion that there would be a supplemental water demand by 1990, present and future supply is adequate to 2000. This 10-year difference has important consequences, since it means that investment in new importation facilities can be postponed 10 years longer than was anticipated.

Richard's heart leapt. What else could it mean but that the whole argument for the dam was false! That Jensen and Gianelli and Boerger, in unison, screaming "disaster" and "only the dam can save us" were either deceived or lying through their teeth. But where had this information come from, and when? Roos explained that this report combined the results of painstaking studies in population growth, in groundwater resources, in economic projections for industry and agriculture, and in the prospects for reclaiming wastewater. The bureaucratic process was grinding on, doing its work, amassing data, monitoring change, sifting and analyzing regardless of policy on high. Richard for once had good reason to be grateful to the bureaucracy.

Roos offered to bring as much of the information as he could to Richard, but he could not smuggle out the report itself. He'd be risking his job.

"A copy will do," Richard said. "Can't you copy it?"

"How can I?" Roos replied. "I don't know where the rest is. And I don't have any business looking for it."

"Well, can you copy the part you've seen?"

"That would be really hard for me to do."

"Well, Amos," Richard said, in his most presidential manner, "I can only say that this is the name of the game. You wanted to help. With this document I believe we can stop the dam and change the course of water policy in California. I don't believe the department has the right to sit on this information. I don't think you believe that either. I understand the risk you're taking, so I am just going to give you the name of a man in Los Angeles who is utterly reliable. If you decide to do this, call him." And he gave Roos Jerry Barnum's phone number.

Jerry received a call almost immediately to tell him that a package would be delivered at his office. It was left there by hand by an anonymous messenger. It contained a copy of a section of the report. Jerry examined it. It was fascinating, tantalizing, but it was not enough. They had to have it all. They were now scarcely two weeks from the hearing. Roos spoke to Jerry, then to Richard. Having gone so far seemed to have emboldened him. Richard explained that for the evidence to carry weight at the hearing, Jerry Barnum would have to say that he had a "true copy" of the document. Roos bit the bullet. One night he let himself back into the empty office. He told Richard later that he spent some of the most harrowing hours of his life tracking down the rest of the report, but he finally got it all together and took it out.

At home he studied it, made two sheets of notes, and sent the whole package over to Jerry's office in Spring Street. The following day, after work, he appeared at Cosgrove, Cramer, Rindge, and Barnum in person. Jerry was glad to be able to say afterward that he liked the man.

"I always had a question," he said. "When you're employed by the state, aren't you supposed to support the state, rather than talk to Jerry Barnum on the side about what's wrong?

"But Roos was quite positive in what he believed. His reasoning on what was wrong with the Department of Water Resources was very acute. He didn't like the way they tried to lord it over the little guy. I thought personally he had a much better way of doing things than they did. He was rather chunky—stout, a great talker. Yes, I liked him very much. A brave man."

The report was a gold mine. If anything, it was too rich. There were the seductive phrases like "the supplemental water demand is somewhat less than has been thought" and "investment in new importation facilities can be postponed ten years longer than was anticipated," which were almost enough in themselves. But embedded in ninety-three packed pages were carefully researched details about sources of water that the dambusters had never dreamed of finding.[1]

All along they had wanted to show that there were better and cheaper alternatives to Dos Rios. This had been a dilemma for Richard. He had hardly wanted to be regarded as the prince of NIMBY, buying influence to build dams in other people's backyards. There were other, smaller projects in the Central Valley that could be built with less ecological damage, and he had at times asked, Why not those? But he knew why not. They weren't big enough, they were expensive, they were already accounted for, and, most important, the whole concept was wrong. In reality, what he believed in was conservation, not expansion, of the system.

He knew the water should come from subsidized cotton crops, from water wasted in unlined canals, from water lost in evaporation through wasteful irrigation methods, from water sent to the ocean in pipes and drains loaded with toxics. Unfortunately, people weren't ready to hear his story. Now suddenly, like a gift from God, came this astonishing revelation. The water didn't have to come from anywhere. Los Angeles was already sitting on top of it.

Page 74 said it all. "It was found that there is much more groundwater in storage than was previously believed. Moreover, the cost of using it is far less than importing water or drawing on other sources."

How much of it was there? "The safe yield of the south coastal area is expected to be about 900,000 acre-feet per year." More than Dos Rios could provide, and at only one fifth the cost. And safe yield meant the absolute minimum. No fuss. No legal battles over water rights. With even a fraction of the effort that had gone into planning Dos Rios, there would be much more.

It was ridiculous. No wonder Gianelli would have to be protected from this lethal knowledge. How otherwise could he justify his huge, expensive, destructive dam to take water at five times the price to a place that already had it? Nor was that all. There were other ways in which Dos Rios was made to look like an expensive folly. Reclaiming wastewater in Southern California, said the report, would cost only a quarter the price of water from Dos Rios. And another way of winning was to take the surplus water in wet years and bank it underground to be drawn up in dry years. A typically bureaucratic footnote here pointed out that this might not fully deal with the problem because there was already such an excess of water down here that there might not be room for all the surplus.

Richard hurried down to Los Angeles to meet with Roos and shake his hand. Among themselves they were already calling him "famous Amos," though his celebrity was very restricted. They made many copies of the report, but kept their treasure and its provenance secret. Lewis Butler was in raptures of delight, and Amos Roos, now reconciled to his role as the Daniel Ellsberg of conservation, was feeding them with more and more. He got a copy of a memo put out by Doody confirming that Teerink was keeping the report under wraps.

A week later, Gianelli gave a pep talk to his senior staff before the all-important hearing in Sacramento. Characteristically full of confidence he said they had the legislature solidly behind them, they had the money to build the tunnel, and Dos Rios was as good as done. The people on the north coast who felt their water was being snatched away, he said, would have to be educated to realize that their best interests were being looked after.

"Bill Gianelli just hasn't gotten the message," Amos remarked.

According to Amos, the consensus in the office was that Gianelli was in a great hurry to build Dos Rios, and that was why the corps had been brought in. Not so much to save money after all, but because the state engineers were too busy finishing off phase one in the south. It all made perfect sense from their point of view. Gianelli had other dams to build after Dos Rios—the dams on the Trinity that Al Wilkins was so worried about. Hearing the news live, like this, out of the mouths of real people, gave it a tremendous urgency. The battleship of state was coming right at them. It would drown them all if it wasn't stopped. Well, now they had a torpedo.

Richard, Jerry, Lewis, and Curt went into a huddle, trying to figure out how best to use their secret weapon. They decided that it would have maximum effect if it were released halfway through the session, after the stuffed shirts had rambled through all their tedious justifications. Give them rope to hang themselves, and then get in the one-two punch in time to hit the evening papers. Jerald D. Barnum, the water lawyer from Los Angeles and the soul of rectitude and respectability was the obvious person to present it.

The tactical problem was, what to hit them with first. Was it that simple quote telling them they had ten more years to think about it? Or was it the information about the other sources of water? After some agonizing, they decided to go for the ten more years.

But there was yet another potentially serious problem, and that was how to get themselves on the agenda without giving the game away. Save the Eel River Association made a formal application to speak to the committee. The committee replied that since they had already made their presentation in Ukiah, unless they had something new and relevant to offer they would not be allowed to speak. The association said it did. What is it? asked the committee. We're not telling, said the association. Well, you'll have to take your chances then, said the committee.

It was a Thursday, a lovely fall day in Sacramento. The committee was sitting in room 4202 on the fourth floor of the north wing. It was a large room with a gallery, rather ugly and entirely suitable for such a bloodless occasion. In the audience were many from Covelo. Ida was there, and Jim McCombs. And of course Richard, Curt, Jerry, and Lewis. Since that day, Lewis has been involved in many controversial matters, in and out of government, but nothing he can recall compared with that event.

"I was never much of a lawyer, in my own view," he says, "but the high point of my legal career, my political career, anything else, was the day we had this thing and Gianelli didn't even know it existed." The joy of recollection led him into a cloudburst of mixed metaphors. "We just sat there like we were sitting with a bomb. We let them hang each other because we had the smoking gun that was going to blow them out of the water, and they didn't know we had it."

To make absolutely sure that nobody missed the explosion, they had photocopied fifty copies of the report and planned to distribute it to the press as soon as Jerry made his appearance on the stand. He was on the agenda to speak, but rather far down the list. They sat together and savored the approach of the climax.

Gianelli opened the proceedings with a lengthy statement. Dos Rios was necessary, he said, because the state had made contracts to deliver a certain amount of water. It was beyond a question of need now. In fact it no longer really mattered whether the water was needed. A contract had been made, and Round Valley had to go. Actually the water might never even be used to fulfill the contract. Unless a dry cycle like 1928 to 1934 came around again, it was quite possible that the dam could be built and the valley flooded and the water not needed for decades to come. It was being flooded in case. Because of the contracts.

But of course, there was always the flood control. And the recreation. Listening to Gianelli's self-confident phrases, with that bomb ticking away, it was so easy to read between the lines. The ghosts of Mulholland and Chandler flitted across the ceiling among the beams of sunlight, blessing the proceedings. Water and growth, they whispered. Never mind what reasons you have to give. First get the water. It will be used for sure. The smart will get rich. The rich will get richer. The poor will get jobs. Then they'll want more water. One dam leads to another.

For the Covelo contingent, knowing what they knew, it was like being with Alice in Wonderland. The project and the contracts were now the only things that mattered. When Gianelli said, "We have brought our information on all developments up to date," it was hard not to burst out laughing, knowing what had been kept from him. But he drove on in sublime innocence, talking about the dams that would certainly follow after Dos Rios. They would have the St. Helena Dam, and the Burnt Ranch Dam, and the Eltapom Dam, and the Butler Dam.

An unusual word kept cropping up in Gianelli's texts and speeches. He was said to employ a speechwriter named Candy Johnson, and it may have been her word, but he obviously liked it. The word was *vex*. It was as close as he ever got to dealing with the real problem. "Vex" was to "agony" as "inundate" was to "drown." The department, he would say, was vexed by the problem of inundating Round Valley. It was a stylish nod. It acknowledged the existence of a problem that could not be solved on a slide rule. Too bad. That's life. Now let's get on with the business of mitigation.

There was no vexation about Round Valley in today's speech though. What had it ever gotten him? Rudeness and rebellion! Today Gianelli played hardball.

"With regard to the possibility of developing water supplies on north coastal streams other than the Eel, the department's studies indicate that it is not a case of the Eel or the Trinity rivers but rather a matter of timing of construction or development. Both streams will be needed to meet long-range projections of future statewide water demands. In fact, projects on the Klamath River as well as Trinity will eventually be needed."

The only life-forms for which he spared a little vexation that day were the fish in the Trinity, which, he said, would be "more vexing than the Eel."

Gianelli's presentation took almost an hour to read. He ticked off objections raised to the dam, one by one, dismissing them all as groundless or irrelevant. By the time he had finished and dealt with some desultory questioning, it was almost lunchtime. He excused himself, and left his deputy John Teerink to watch over the hearing.

Boerger followed with much the same format, devoting himself to reasoned rebuttals of criticisms by Gardner Brown and others. None got more than polite acknowledgment. When he came to describe the damsite itself, he could not disguise his satisfaction. The symmetry and steepness of the canyon walls were ideal, he said, and, quoting a renowned geologist, he added, "The Dos Rios damsite is the most favorable site for a high dam that I have seen anywhere in the Franciscan terrain of the coast ranges."

To deprive a dam builder of such an opportunity would be too cruel. For all the sterile language, the impassive stance, and the claims of objectivity, there were genuine (and unquantifiable) emotions stirring in the breasts of those engineers. The pretense that they were mere stolid workhorses content to do, or not to do, as the public commanded was more dangerous in its way than having public affairs openly influenced by the wishes and dreams of poets and philosophers. These hidden passions, regarded as illicit, unable to find their expression in the usual, natural terms, were channeled instead into bureaucratic aggrandizement, and a mean-spirited disparagement of emotion in others. Those were the rules of their game. "If we're not allowed to have feelings, then neither are you."

The labored recitals of "facts" continued to clog the atmosphere of room 4202 through that Thursday afternoon. Bill Fairbank, tall, presentable, authoritative, with a resonant actor's voice, staked his claim for the Met by pointing out that they were paying for half the project. He wanted to make the dam even bigger, and he argued for less water for the fish. He wanted to buy the approval of Mendocino County by compensating them for the tax revenue they would lose, and helping with schools and services while the dam was being constructed.

"District representatives worked with local water leaders in the north coast area through the Eel River Association and other groups, in order to keep in touch with local problems, attitudes, and desires. This contact has served as a constant reminder that flood control is that area's primary and immediate need."

Richard might have asked who was reminding whom, and for what purpose. The perpetual harping on flood disaster was always intended to distract attention from other interests. He and Lewis listened as the water lobby declared its interests more frankly than usual, knowing themselves to be before a sympathetic jury. Henry Lippitt came to boost the dam along, knowing only that his friend and adversary was there, but not what he had up his sleeve. Various other water contractors joined in the clamor for the dam, but not everything went their way.

William Penn Mott for the Park Service voiced his dislike of losing the valley, and the Indian history and archeology that would be drowned with it. Even the Bureau of Reclamation, committed to support the dam, had to deplore the loss of the valley. After all the bureau had been created by Theodore Roosevelt for the job of irrigating just such a place. The strongest criticism came from Walter Shannon of Fish and Game, who insisted that the fish runs would be irreparably damaged.

The growing dissension within Ike Livermore's Resources agency was pleasing to the opposition, but as the testimony dragged on into the afternoon, they were beginning to worry that they might miss the television and evening papers with their sensational disclosure. At the three o'clock recess, Lewis approached the chairman, Gordon Cologne, saying they had vital evidence the committee should hear soon, evidence that would affect the whole proceedings. Cologne was not impressed. He told them they would have to wait their turn. It was beginning to look serious, and Richard slipped away from the committee room. Soon after, Senator Collier came in.

Jim McCombs remembers this moment most clearly.

"He came in all easy like. He was chewing on something—sunflower seeds, I think—and he kinda went over to the side of where the committee was sitting, and he crooked his finger at Senator Cologne. I can see him now, white hair flying, chewing, and beckoning. He was a very powerful man. Cologne went over there and they whispered a minute, and Cologne went back to his seat and said we could have three minutes."

Nobody could have looked less like a torpedo primed to explode than Jerry Barnum in his lawyerly three-piece as he stood up to testify. He had his script in one hand, and the Doody Report in the other, and in classic Dickensian style he began: "Ladies and gentlemen, I am a lawyer from Southern California representing the Save the Eel River Association.

"Today I hold in my hand a true copy of a memorandum dated August 21, 1968. It was prepared by the Department of Water Resources—the same Department of Water Resources which has been working arm in arm with the Corps of Engineers on the Dos Rios project. Like the corps, the department is here today urging you to expedite approval of the Dos Rios Dam in order, as they characterize it, to meet a critical need for water in Southern California by 1990."

Jerry waved the Doody Report at the committee.

"Its subject is titled 'Present and Future Water Supply and Demand in the South Coastal Area.' It gives this definition on page ten, and here I quote: 'Supplemental water demand is the difference between water supply and demand.' Unquote. Then it indicates that 'the supplemental water demand is projected to begin around 2000. This differs significantly from the value derived from earlier studies, in part because of the use in this study of recent data not available in previous studies. Ten additional years of data provide a clearer picture of development trends.'

"It further states, in plain, positive terms on page eighty-nine that 'It is of particular significance that the supplemental water demand is somewhat less than has been thought. Contrary to general opinion that there would be a supplemental water demand by 1990, present and future supply is adequate to 2000. This ten-year difference . . . means that investment in new importation facilities can be postponed ten years longer than was anticipated.'

"Ladies and gentlemen," said Jerry with a triumphant flourish, "according to this report you have called this meeting at least ten years too early!"

Richard was just in time to catch, out of the corner of his eye, a pale John Teerink slip out of the room as Jerry went on to list the other ways in which the report said the water could be provided. Rubbing in the message, he said: "It all adds up to this. The people of California—not the Met, not the corps, not the department—the people of California, the taxpayers, have a minimum of ten more years to plan for the most economical and efficient use of our most precious resource. Water.

"We say that development of water resources is not an end in itself, and should not be used simply as a means whereby enlargement of public agencies or extension of their authority results.

"The Save the Eel River Association has never opposed meeting the water needs of Southern California. We have steadfastly said, however, that Dos Rios is not the answer. We have said Dos Rios is not feasible economically by congressional standards. We have said there was no justification for moving the people of Covelo and the Covelo Indians off rich agricultural lands in order to build it. We and geological experts have said there is serious question whether the highly unstable ground in the Eel River Canyon would support a 730-foot-high dam. We have said that by the time the Eel River water reaches Southern California in the 1990s few, perhaps no one, will be able to afford it.

"We have asked many questions concerning many things about Dos Rios. They have never been answered. This report, a true copy of which I now file with this committee, tells us why.

"Thank you."

Recollections of what happened then, a quarter of a century ago, differ dramatically. Jerry Barnum, ever the cynic, says his rhetoric got the same reaction from the committee that Lewis got from the Indians in Covelo: phlegmatic indifference. On the other hand, Lewis the idealist remembers all hell breaking loose. He was so caught up in the drama of the event that at first he actually recalled having made the speech himself. What is certainly corroborated is Gianelli's hasty return to the committee room.

He burst in, red-faced, having apparently run all the way from the Resources Building to say something like, "I won't be called a liar," to which Cologne calmly responded that nobody had called him anything, but had simply read from a report. To which Gianelli replied: "What he said isn't true. We could stand here all day and argue about it. It doesn't mean what he said it means." But nothing he could do or say would dilute Lewis's pleasure at seeing a water lord finally caught with his pants down. "At the end of that hearing," he said, "we really thought we might win."

If the dambusters had hoped for an epiphany on the dais, they were disappointed. The committee members neither burst into song nor exchanged high fives with the opposing team. They simply dragged the hearing on to its conclusion and went home, but Curt got the report out all over California, and although they missed the evening papers they got very good coverage the next day.

For once, public ignorance worked in their favor. In fact they were wrong about a salient part of their case. The "supplemental water demand," which Jerry had so gleefully announced to be ten years further down the line, was actually calculated on the assumption that Dos Rios, or something like it, would already have been built. But once Jerry's slogan of "Ten More Years" had been uttered, the engineers were never quite able to get rid of it. Slowly but surely it ate away at their position. In any case, the rest of the evidence from the Doody Report was very revealing and bound to cause them endless trouble.

As Mickey Allen and Ron Robie, the committee consultants, got down to drafting their respective reports, the senators and assemblymen had much to ponder. Gianelli was right to suppose that the great majority wanted to support him, but they could not help being disturbed. The opposition would not lie down. It kept popping up with some new embarrassment. Cologne was unalterably in favor of taking water from the north coast, but he felt obliged to appear impartial. He announced that his committee had engaged yet another engineering consultant, Clair Hill of Redding, to investigate the Dos Rios project and report back, but even this maneuver backfired.

Nobody supposed the report would be unfavorable. Clair Hill shared all the orthodox values of the water establishment. His was one of the companies likely to bid for some of the work on Dos Rios, and Clair Hill himself was a member of the government-appointed California Water Commission. He unwisely used his position on that body to accuse Jerry Barnum of libel for suggesting that Gianelli had suppressed the Doody Report, which of course prompted laughter in the wings. Suing a libel lawyer for libel was funny enough. The idea of Gianelli suppressing a document he didn't know existed made it hilarious. It was all too much, even for the staid *Sacramento Bee.* In a stern editorial it said Hill's appointment would "raise the question of propriety . . . if not . . . possible conflict of interest."

Then the November elections were upon them. They needed to get back to their constituencies, to defend their seats or campaign for others. Things suddenly were not going so well for the water boosters, but they had bought themselves some rather expensive time.

27

Ike Hits the Roof

NOT ALL THOSE who advocated the dam felt the need to express remorse over the fate of the valley. Some Covelo merchants, such as Jan Stewart, saw nothing but good in it, while remote bureaucrats such as Bill Warne appeared to feel no compunction at all. However, most of them had the decency to shed a few crocodile tears. The army's public relations man, Eugene Huggins, for example, said:

"The thought of inundating Round Valley is most distressing. It is a gorgeous spot. Few valleys could match its beauty. . . . They say we are a vast, impersonal organization not concerned with human values. . . . [but] . . . we are thinking of human values all through the Sacramento and San Joaquin Valleys and the Los Angeles area."

The slogan of the "greatest good for the greatest number" served the engineers well and it was certainly one that Gianelli lived by, but as a catchall philosophy Ike Livermore found it hardly appropriate. One might as well let everyone take home a square inch of the *Mona Lisa,* or a brick from the Taj Mahal. From the first moment that Richard told him of the threat to Round Valley, Ike felt an involuntary twinge of sympathy. It was not due to the social and political ties between them. Those simply helped to lend credibility to Richard's accounts of causes and remedies. It was just that Ike did not believe in flooding valleys, and in this respect, as in others, he was fairly unique in the upper echelons of government. It was a feeling born in his youth, through his admiration of the Sierra and of John Muir, who saved Yosemite and founded the Sierra Club. Since he belonged to a politically potent family with money, he was able to think of matching his feelings with deeds.

It was Ike's lifelong ambition to do something toward the ultimate restoration of the Hetch Hetchy Valley, which was stolen from Yosemite by San Francisco for its water supply. His father, the Sacramento engineer, had seen it before it was flooded, and told Ike it was by far the most beautiful part of all Yosemite Park. The Shaughnessy Dam—the same dam that John Cree Wilson had driven mule teams to build, the dam that Hank Pape had modeled with such pride and enthusiasm in his youth—was the means of Muir's worst defeat, a catastrophe that was said to have broken his heart. Ike Livermore retained a photographic image of that entrancing valley before its devastation, and the ache caused by its loss never really left him. He believed that San Francisco now could find other ways to slake its thirst, and he made a number of attempts to have studies done on the project of reclaiming the valley. The almost derisive lack of understanding he encountered left him sensitive to the blind areas of engineers and bureaucrats, and he approached the problem of Round Valley with a well-developed skepticism about their claims and promises.*

This was only part of Richard's great good fortune. He was also lucky that the "water guys" were so deeply entrenched in their certainties about the excellence of their project. They could not imagine anyone in a responsible position among them taking a different view. For many months Ike was too busy to do more than record what was fed him from both sides of the issue. It was probably in September of 1968 that his instinctive dislike of the project developed into a full-blown rejection. By then he had heard a great deal, and after a meeting with Butchert and two supervisors from Marin and Humboldt, he drew up an exhaustive list of questions, problems, and criticisms. There were 117 items, and they ranged from broad economic matters through political calculation to personal—and in some cases scathing—observations. From that time on he regarded the dam as a solution that was worse than the problem.

*Ike's last vain effort to reclaim Hetch Hetchy was made in the eighties in connection with a proposal by Donald Hodel, President Reagan's second secretary of the interior.

Ike's decision to oppose Dos Rios led him to a rather shocking revelation. He discovered that he had virtually no control over the most important department of his agency. While he was nominally in charge of all the departments, his acknowledged ignorance of water matters had led him to be satisfied with this charade.

Ike's bluff and hearty manner, his imposing physique, his outdoor history in the mountains tended to distract from another aspect of his character. His real work since leaving school had been as an accountant. He was a stickler for form and liked things to be done by the book. He liked order and systems. The scribbled notes he made of his daily business, all meticulously stamped with his initials and the date, are descriptive of a mind that flourished within a structure. Penciled observations and key phrases lie strewn about the page like dream fragments of a Chagall, and then they are drawn together and interpreted with circles and long swooping arrows, and separated off again by wavering dotted lines. There is a charming lightness of touch about these pages, a suggestion of an imagination trying to get free of chronology and purpose, hemmed in by that web of relationships.

In the free use of question marks, underscorings, blue brackets, and other marks of emphasis, the play of emotions can be seen flickering across the page. Here's Reagan confiding his feelings about beauty. Is it real? How can I rely on this? Why is he referring to Clausen? Reagan's reiterations are circled across the page like a daisy chain, attended by little blocks of doubt or deduction floating in blue brackets. So different to Richard's relentless lists, driven into the paper with heavy lead.

Ike's tendency, one senses, is not to dominate by sheer force but rather to shape events on the jujitsu principle of guiding rather than frustrating the momentum of his opponent. Dealing with his other directors on issues he understood had been constructive and congenial work and demanding enough to justify his leaving water alone. Now that Richard had forced him to confront the latter, he had to call on other less amiable resources, and his reluctance to do so is not surprising. Beating Gianelli into submission was a difficult cause to justify, but he saw that he would have to establish his authority over the water department if he was to influence policy.

How could this be done, given his ignorance of such a highly technical and complex matter? Only by stressing that there were other considerations even more important to the state than water. Such a notion was, as yet, unheard of in California. All the emphasis to date was on mitigation. His other departments were all subject to water needs. They were there to do the best they could in the circumstances. The primacy of water was a fact of life. Indeed it was quite usual for Gianelli to say, when others proposed actions that inhibited water development, that "a few of us are governed by the facts of life."

Now Ike was about to embrace the heretical proposition that protection of the environment could rival the importance of water: that it might even take precedence. Both he and Richard knew that for Ike to make such a declaration would call forth howls of rage from the most powerful economic interests in the state. Once Ike was convinced that Dos Rios had to be stopped, a tacit compact was arrived at. Richard would be the "bad guy" out there, ranting and railing, digging up the evidence, lobbying and networking. Ike would proceed with patience, tact, and some cunning, appearing only to respond to the unavoidable pressure of public opinion and gradually insisting that he, and not Gianelli, had responsibility for a resources policy that put water in its proper context.

He was helped fortuitously by a decision pioneered by Caspar Weinberger and his close aide, Earl Coke, to adopt a cabinet system for Reagan's administration. Ike had been hired as administrator of Resources, a title that conveyed a rather fussy association with budgets and rules. Now he became secretary for Resources, which had a much more resonant and inclusive sound to it, and helped in his campaign to make the title real. For some months he carefully avoided any public expression of opinion on Dos Rios. Instead he besieged Gianelli and Boerger with questions, confronting them with information that was flowing into his office from Richard and Curt. During that same period he began to challenge every move that Gianelli made that seemed to undercut his authority. Since Gianelli had been led to believe by Reagan, and by Warne's example, that he had a special dispensation to act independently, the clashes came fast and furious.

When it finally dawned on them—and we are talking here of Gianelli's senior staff, the Corps of Engineers, the Metropolitan Water District as a whole, Henry Lippitt and his ilk, and the great landowners of the San Joaquin—when it dawned on this mighty establishment that Livermore was probably a traitor in their midst, the significance of it horrified them. The governor's decision to ratify the dam was all they needed. The hearings had all been intended to validate that decision. They had been confident that when push came to shove, they would have all the political muscle they needed to persuade Reagan to go for it. Right next to Reagan, acting as his secretary for Cabinet Affairs and controlling access to the governor, was their committed ally Earl Coke, who later became secretary for Agriculture and understood, if anyone did, their desire for more water. But now it appeared that there was an Iago at court, whispering slanders in the monarch's ear. They determined to get Ike out.

The first attempt surfaced in *The Sacramento Bee* almost immediately after the hearings. The paper published a "persistent rumor" that Ike and two of his directors were going to get the sack immediately after the November election. The rumor, it said, was circulating in "various state and federal offices and in sportsmen's circles."

The influence of sportsmen should not be underrated. Spectacular hunting opportunities are always within reach in California, and many legislators and government employees took their weapons to the hills and marshes any chance they got. This phenomenon could lead gun-toting conservatives to find themselves in bizarre alliance with posy-picking conservationists. Now they were getting anxious about the fate of Walter Shannon, the director of Ike's Fish and Game department. Shannon was a popular figure among fish enthusiasts, but his health was failing, and he had already told some that he would have to leave before his term was up. All the same he was holding on as long as possible, and he was severely critical of Dos Rios—not just for its likely consequences but also for the dismissive way in which his department's work had been treated by the engineers. He had been making his feelings known for months. The water faction had been gunning for him, and was making his job untenable. He told his friends he was going to quit, and why. The word got out fast, and those who were glad to see him go added to the story their own wishful thinking that Ike Livermore would go, too. They threw Stearns, the conservation director, in for good measure and hoped that the wish, having fathered the thought, would lead to the act.

On the evening of the day Ike read about his impending dismissal, his brother Putnam, the chairman of the state Republican party, phoned and read him his political obituary from an editorial already set in type at *The Sacramento Bee,* but not printed. It described the internecine struggle and said of Gianelli: "Apparently he packs the most muscle of the four within Ronald Reagan's inner circle."

Ike took it seriously enough to call Reagan's office. Bill Clark, who was Reagan's executive secretary at the time, assured him that he had heard nothing to support the story. The editorial never appeared. The rumor faded but never died, and talk of Ike's resignation recurred again and again.

As Ike maneuvered to make his authority over Gianelli weighty and palpable instead of being the paper tiger that Gianelli took him for, he braced himself for a bumpy ride. He had absolutely no reason to believe that Reagan, whose environmental record was poor, would share Ike's point of view. Ike knew very well that the redwood park had been achieved only because Reagan had seen it as politically advisable, with Ike's job on the line if it turned out badly. He foresaw the same scenario this time, but with far more powerful adversaries.

Then an extraordinary thing happened. On the tenth of December, with the election over and the Republicans having won the Senate, Reagan called on the phone.

"Ike," he said, "I hate to see a beautiful valley destroyed. Just between us, I feel we should pause in destroying a beautiful valley."

He explained that he had thought it was all a federal project. He hadn't realized that the state had a part in it, and that he would have to approve it.

"Ike," he said, "you know, I'm really not so bad on conservation. I really hate to see beauty destroyed." He repeated several times more that he didn't want to destroy the valley. He said they should "hang loose" and he particularly wanted to know what Don Clausen would have to say.*

All the sources of Reagan's newfound interest in the valley will never be known, but some of it was due to a lucky combination of Richard's foresight and Lou Cannon's friendship with Bill Clark. Lou had sent his *Cry California* article to Clark. It included three pages of photographs, the same pictures Lew Butler had packed into his "big red books." There was an aerial shot of George White's mansion (taken, of course, from Byron's state-owned helicopter), a nice picture of Ida's Methodist church, and some intriguing close-ups of old-timers Cliff Foster and Edith Murphey. But the winning entry was a full-page shot of some young Hereford cows, dappled by spring sunshine, ambling beneath a blossom-laden bough.

According to Cannon, Bill Clark took advantage of an electioneering trip with Reagan to thrust the magazine upon him, and he was

*These phrases were noted down by Livermore at the time, in his own handwriting.

moved by the pictures and the clear sincerity of Lou's prose. It aroused in him the feelings he held for his own ranch, colored by the cowboy mythology he had absorbed in Hollywood and a surprising concern for the plight of Indians, which seems to have been common among moneyed Republicans of that era.

Seven days later Don Clausen, safely reelected to Congress, came to talk with Reagan and then made an appointment with Ike, asking particularly that they meet in private. Ike regarded Clausen as his protégé. He had guided Clausen's selection as a candidate for the First District, and had secured the financing of his campaigns, but he knew that Clausen was "understandably in the pocket of the timber industry," and would be no help with the dam. The conversation was revealing. He was astonished to hear Clausen say, "You know, I'm pretty darn lukewarm about Dos Rios."

It didn't do enough for his district, he said. Only 5 percent of it was flood control, and there were no other benefits. He said that for one thing he was worried about the poor measures being taken to protect the fisheries in California.

"I'd just as soon find another solution, but going up against the Department of Water Resources, and the Metropolitan and the construction industry would be worse than the redwoods.

"Ron knows it would make him politically vulnerable. We need to spend more time with him after hours, with a glass of Napa Valley wine. Bring Bill Gianelli into it if you want to."

Apparently Reagan had felt that it might be a good idea to let the crisis build up for a while. Perhaps they could find an alternative to Dos Rios. Another river, maybe. The Klamath? The Van Duzen? The Mad? But we must improve the fisheries, not just mitigate.

They talked about Ike's hopes for what he called "reverse migration," meaning that it would be better to think of ways to bring the people to the water, instead of destroying valleys to take the water south. They discussed changing highway financing to promote rapid transit systems that could open up the north, and talked about moving the railroad out of the Eel Canyon altogether and bringing it in from the east instead. Ike considered Clausen a very decent fellow. He had had to turn against him over the redwoods affair, and he had taken it hard. Now he was relieved to hear Clausen's reservations about Dos Rios and to hear him say that Reagan's thinking was "close to yours and mine."

On the other hand, it was clear that Reagan did not want to be publicly identified with that attitude. He had already learned a lot about the uses of Teflon. He seemed to be encouraging one policy while reserving the ability to defend another. Ike had to assume that if he could find a way during the coming weeks to make the governor's veto an acceptable choice, then he would make that choice because it was where his heart lay. But when it came to the point, would Reagan even want to stand up to the pressures that were sure to be brought on him to bring that water south?

Ike's task was clear. He would have to assume responsibility for water policy. If it couldn't be done, he would have to resign. If it could be done and his policy was rejected, then again he would have to go. His chances of survival did not look good, but his mind was made up. He would make his stand on Dos Rios.

Gianelli, likewise, was determined to retain the authority he had assumed from the start. He, too, seemed to feel that he had Reagan's personal confidence, and he believed that to let Livermore meddle in these matters would be disastrous. For months he had been complaining about special interests interfering with the noble works of state. Now these interests were coagulating into an "ism," which he had to view as a serious threat. Conservationism was gathering strength all around him, and he could not but be aware that its insidious propaganda was eating into the very heart of the Resources agency.

He clung to the belief that his department was in no way comparable to the others. Bill Warne had made it an independent force, and Gianelli strove to maintain that de facto autonomy. In spirit he felt himself to be Ike's equal rather than a subordinate. He spoke out in public on water policy in a way that none of the other directors did. Belligerent and self-assured, he gathered around him his armies of water officials from Southern California, his irrigation district contractors from the Central Valley, and addressed them like a commander-in-chief.

They loved it. He and his speechwriter knew their audience would delight in epithets like "posy-pickers" and "Chicken-Little emotionalists." After Lewis Butler's group had fought a successful battle to limit development around Lake Tahoe, Gianelli uttered his famous definition of a conservationist as "a judge who bought his place at Lake Tahoe last year."

He had every reason to feel confident. He had Reagan's personal promise that the State Water Project would be completed and its contracts honored. Therefore Round Valley had to be filled with water, whatever the inconvenience to those who lived there. All the alternatives that had been put up by the opposition spelled nothing but trouble to him. He foresaw immense legal complications in gaining access to groundwater reserves. He saw great public resistance to feeding recycled wastewater into the household supplies of Southern California. He thought attempts to take water from agriculture were wrong, and wouldn't work anyway. It was Dos Rios or nothing. He flew his colors proudly, and they were black and white. If he needed evidence that he was at war, the unleashing of the Doody Report must have been his Pearl Harbor.

On January 16, Jerry Barnum told Curt Roberts, on the phone, that a Metropolitan official he spoke to was certain Ike was on his way out, and Curt passed it on to Ike. Vague threats to unseat him were coming from all directions. A public works official in Humboldt, named Guy Kulstad, phoned him after he had been up there to speak in Eureka. There was a plan afoot, said this informant, "to cut his throat" with vague allegations that he was misusing his office to provide secretarial help to Richard Wilson. At the same time, Kulstad told Ike that Gianelli had installed a private line to his office so that his conversations would not be overheard.

It was evident that both sides felt they were being conspired against, and were justified in doing whatever was necessary to win the day. Having what amounted to two secret agents planted in the Department of Water Resources helped Richard tremendously. If he had any qualms, they were stilled by his belief that information was being wrongly withheld from Ike, and he made sure that Ike heard it all. Amos provided a running commentary on Teerink's efforts to save the department from the embarrassment of the Doody affair. Jerry had copies of letters before they had even been sent. There was one in particular, drafted for Gianelli to sign, that was supposed to account for the contradictions exposed at the hearing. It was so inept that Jerry and Curt were salivating over the damage they could inflict if Gianelli approved it (which he apparently did not).

It had been made obvious to Richard, and it was now being drummed into Ike, that water engineers considered their craft to be impenetrable by ordinary men. Like priests defending a cult, they belittled all efforts to understand them and resisted the intrusion of any ideology that conflicted with their dogma. It seemed that the scent of north coast water had driven them into a frenzy, and that all efforts to dissuade them were automatically dismissed as impossible, irrelevant, or inadequate.

Now that Ike had been identified as an unbeliever, too, he felt himself to have been targeted by members of the water establishment, and fought back with zest. He took every opportunity to diminish their influence and ridicule them. The complicated mathematics of statewide water control and the delta pool concept gave him plenty of chances. He would ask Gianelli, for example, why the Dos Rios project was being credited with 900,000 acre-feet, when other figures showed it would only be delivering 600,000, and the labored explanations were easily made to look suspect.

Ike had a lot of fun with some balance sheets he got the corps to draw up, showing how costs would change when the interest rate was raised. This would have serious long-term effects on the cost of the project, but it could not, of course, change the first costs of construction. The corps (which must not tell a lie) sent back two columns of figures, one for 3¼ percent and one for 4⅝ percent. Some individual items changed because the split between state and federal shares was affected by long-term costs of things like recreation and water supply, but the columns added up to exactly the same total.

Ike says he showed the figures to Reagan as a blatant example of how the corps was "cooking the books." He still claims they were phony, but in fact they were theoretically correct, and as an accountant he probably knew it.

In water circles in Sacramento it was well known long before the committee reports came out who was for and who was against the project. Bill Fairbank knew that only two of the seventeen members of the Assembly committee were opposed. On the Senate committee things were shakier.

The three who had been doubtful had since confirmed their opposition. Bill Richardson, the tough little man from Arcadia, liked to fly around the state looking for happy hunting grounds. One day he flew into Round Valley. He was impressed with what he saw and took a moral stand against destroying a fragment of the Old West. He was unlikely to make a politically embarrassing issue of it, but his thinking was too close to Reagan's for Bill Fairbank's comfort.

The other two were equally worrying. Al Rodda, who had never disguised his dislike of the project, had actually circulated his written objections among his colleagues. Senator James Mills had also become a convinced opponent. He enjoyed considerable seniority and respect in the Senate, and for him to come out against Dos Rios was troublesome.

Fairbank felt it essential to forestall the pressure that these three might bring to bear on the governor. Ike was asked in January to receive a delegation of eight of the heaviest guns from Los Angeles that Fairbank could muster, including Jensen and the Met's general manager, Henry Mills. He agreed to see them on the twenty-third, and on the day before got a letter from Fairbank thanking him for offering to "spend an hour or so" with them. What Fairbank did not say was that after leaving Ike, they would all be lunching with Reagan and Gianelli at the Sutter Club, a lunch apparently arranged by Gianelli to which Ike had not been invited.

Ike heard about it accidentally, and in the privacy of his office hit the roof, an exceptional feat for such an easygoing fellow. When he came down he first made sure that he *would* be at the lunch. Then, on the back of an agenda he wrote a heading—"Gianelli—Intransigence"—and below it he compiled a long list of transgressions—occasions when Gianelli had cut him out of the loop or performed end runs around him or simply failed to cooperate. It was clear to Ike that it was time to make an open stand.

Although he was outraged by the Sutter Club incident, he chose a different, less personal issue to fight on, and one for which he could expect to win outside support. The day before the lunch, Gianelli had released news that he was appointing three fishery experts to advise his department. All three were from Washington State, and were known to have little respect for California's own Fish and Game department. Ike, of course, had not been consulted, and was being treated in this matter, as in others, as having no useful part to play. Gianelli's purpose in hiring these experts was well known in the agency. The idea had been put up formally by the Association of Water Contractors, the private companies who would eventually buy the water, and the same people Gianelli had worked for in private practice. They thought all this effort to protect fish was a waste of their money, especially on the Eel. Their auditors claimed the dangers to fish runs were "grossly overstated," and wanted these experts to cut out the frills and the foolishness.

By appointing them unilaterally in this high-handed manner, Gianelli had not only breached a directive issued by Ike a year earlier but he also seemed to be expressing open contempt for Fish and Game, and for Livermore's authority. Ike got hold of Gianelli on January 24 and took him to task, but he was unrepentant on the main issue. On the same day Ike talked briefly to Reagan and then sent him a letter saying "an irreconcilable conflict of wills" had arisen. Gianelli, he wrote, insisted on this authority to hire any and all consultants as and when he chose, and would not retract.

"He has also in a number of other instances displayed a regrettable lack of awareness for the overall objectives of the Resources agency, in the broad context in which I view them." Ike said he could not run the agency effectively in these circumstances and added: "If in your good judgment you do not feel able to back me up on this, then I see no other course but to offer my resignation," and said he would want to be out in thirty days.

If they had only known it, the moment that the water officials in Los Angeles had been praying for had arrived, but Reagan did not seize it. Instead, during the following two weeks, flurries of conversation and negotiation took place in private. First Bill Clark took a hand. Then Ed Meese, who was succeeding Clark as Reagan's executive secretary, came in to broker an understanding. They flattered, cajoled, and argued that both men were badly needed.

To be sure, it would have been difficult to replace Gianelli at that point—he had such a firm grasp on the financial intricacies of the State Water Project in its last stages. Reagan might well have found Ike more expendable, but clearly he was beginning to see some political merit in Ike's point of view. Ike insisted at first that Gianelli drop his experts. Meese suggested it would be better not to expose Gianelli openly in that way, but to come to some internal agreement. Ike grasped at the opportunity to present an agenda for changing the way things were done. It required Gianelli to apologize, to acknowledge his failures to comply, to allow other departments a more vigorous role in his project planning, and to give up his practice of bypassing Ike and going directly to the governor via his ally Earl Coke. It seems that Gianelli choked over this final condition. He said it was like giving Livermore a veto over his administration, and he, too, offered to resign. Meese again smoothed things over.

Gianelli promised to be good, Ike offered forbearance, pride was accommodated and face saved. Both men swore that they respected each other, and indeed despite their violent disagreement throughout that year, Ike says they were never openly abusive. There were occasions when Gianelli stopped signing his memos "Bill," and that was about as personal as it got. However, Ike did emerge from this melee with a degree more authority than he had wielded before.

There was another series of points that he set out about specific projects, and it is unclear now what became of them, but visible through them was Ike's determination to shift the emphasis away from water for its own sake to an approach that gave more balanced importance to all the resources. It was the first tentative step toward seeing the environment not as an obstacle in the way of resource exploitation, but as a resource in itself. In other words, what Richard Wilson began by refusing to have his ranch flooded out had finally brought about a serious attempt to create an environmental policy for the state of California.

Until the Dos Rios question was finally resolved, Livermore and Gianelli remained at loggerheads, and the dispute was aired in the press as other organizations joined in on both sides.

To Gianelli's claim that one of his experts, Milo Bell, had a gilt-edged record of success with saving steelhead and salmon in the Columbia River, the National Wildlife Federation said those same famously abundant fisheries were in crisis, with some runs down by 50 percent because of the dams. Joe Paul wondered out loud whether Gianelli had "hired the embalmer of salmon and steelhead on the Columbia to preside at the final rites for the same species on the Eel, Trinity, and Klamath."

Trout Unlimited sent a long telegram of protest to Senator Richardson, who since the election had become chairman of the Senate Committee for Fish and Game. He in turn wrote to both Ike and Gianelli, asking what the beef was between them, knowing full well what it was, of course. His intervention also strengthened Ike's hand, so Ike and the fish guys got good mileage out of that affair. Then, just as the story was cooling, another bigger one broke.

Ronald Robie's report for the Assembly committee was presented, and brought forth its expected endorsement of the dam. (Although Robie himself said later he opposed it personally, his job was to present the committee's views). None of the arguments made by Richard, Lewis, or Jerry cut any ice with them at all, but they wept tears over the Indians and the fish and asked for more consideration for both. This was soon followed by Mickey Allen's Senate report, which was even more enthusiastically pro-dam. It took up the idea suggested by the consultant of building it even bigger and higher. Six senators signed the report.

Ike prepared himself for the possibility that Reagan would feel obliged to decide quickly. This was the optimum moment for the water lobby to push for approval. Ike had heard no further word from Reagan about his feelings on the matter. Usually he followed the advice of his cabinet, but the other members, apart from Coke, were undecided. The water guys seemed confident of getting their way, and it was evident that Reagan was telling everyone what he wanted to hear. Ike began work drafting procedures to decide the issue and announce a decision, and he was preparing for the real possibility of his own departure.

Then Senators Al Rodda and Jim Mills put out their minority report, condemning the Dos Rios Dam. Their arguments were almost identical to those that Richard had been championing, but with them came the astonishing news that two more senators had changed their minds.

Mervyn Dymally, a black senator originally from the West Indies, said he had signed the report by mistake, thinking it was just a year-end wrap-up, and that he was unalterably opposed to displacing the Indians, while another senator, Jim Wedworth, said he, too, had been misled.

Senator Richardson, who was already opposed, told the press, "I do not believe my constituents sent me up here to 'power' people out of their rights and resources." So that made five senators against and only four in favor. The unthinkable had happened. The Senate committee had reversed itself, and Gordon Cologne was left twisting in the wind.

Even John Harmer, a Mormon who did sign with Cologne, made a bitter protest, which he insisted on having printed in the report. He said: "In my opinion, someone should be most severely criticized and chastened for allowing the state to be committed to the delivery of a certain volume of water with only the vaguest notion of where that water would come from and what would be necessary in terms of the dislocation of people and the destruction of natural resources. . . . It seems to me to be the ultimate in contempt for the public good to have committed us to such a project." Richard could not have put the case more angrily himself.

Speaking to *The Sacramento Bee,* Ike could hardly disguise his pleasure. "This thing is really startling," he said. "With this new report I don't see how we can decide anything for at least sixty days. This whole thing puts me and the governor in a pretty tight spot."

Ike's next smart move was to put the governor in an even tighter spot by writing a long letter to the *San Francisco Chronicle* countering criticisms of Reagan's environmental record, which he knew were entirely justified. After citing the few examples he could muster of Reagan as the environmental knight, whose "record rings loud and clear," he finished by insisting, "I cannot recall a single instance where a decision was made by the governor that was inimical to the philosophy of concern for the quality of our natural environment."

The reality of a major split in the state government over water policy was now common knowledge, and Ike thought it as well to declare the matter openly in terms of Gianelli's differences with the Fish and Game people. Gianelli, being rooted in the instrumentalist tradition that all natural resources existed for the benefit of man, was one of the first to employ the term "wise use," which has since become the slogan for commercial interests opposing the environmental lobby. He liked to taunt conservationists by calling them "preservationists," accusing them of wanting to protect nature from any and all interference by man.

Ike cutely appropriated Gianelli's label and pinned it back on Gianelli. He convened a conference within the agency to resolve differences, and, implying that the water guys were entrenched in the status quo, he publicly characterized the dispute as "the environmental people against the preservation people," while presenting himself as a neutral arbiter.

The point was lost on Gianelli, however, who insisted that more dams still might be needed, just for flood control alone. Two weeks later he sent out copies of an incendiary speech prepared for the Commonwealth Club in San Francisco, where many of the frankest utterances on water matters were made.

California, he said, could not afford to let "narrow self-interest" interfere with water developments that benefited everyone.

"We've had a lot of yik-yak from people who have sectional problems. I don't care whether it's a group that is way far out or a sectional group with its own self-interest"—a broad enough charge to include everyone from the delta to Round Valley.

On the same day, Rodda issued another critical statement to the press and Randy Collier called Dos Rios a white elephant, while the Mendocino Board of Supervisors, unanimous at last, wrote to Ike asking to be received by the governor so that they could present their case against the dam.

By now it was clear that an opportunity existed for conservationists to take the initiative. Much had changed since the election. Nixon was in the White House. Cranston was the new senator for California, and was expressing doubts about Dos Rios. In the last year of his administration, LBJ had signed authorizations for $5 billion worth of water projects, none of which had yet been funded. The interest rate was finally up to 4⅝ percent, which had a profound effect on their viability. A fifth of them were for California, and money was tight because of the war.

Another consequence was that Lewis Butler went to Washington as an assistant secretary for Health, Education, and Welfare. Someone would have to take over the Planning and Conservation League. It was plain to Richard that this was the most useful instrument available for pursuing his aims, and so he assumed his third presidency in twelve months.

28

Ike and Gianelli Fight It Out

THE REMARKABLE turnabout in the California Senate did not simply happen. Richard and Curt had been in almost constant touch with the major players in Sacramento, and it is impossible to convey how much effort this campaign had demanded of them. In his testimony to the committees, Colonel Boerger pointed out that he and his staff had engaged in at least fifty meetings in Round Valley and Ukiah, to ensure, as he put it, that the public was kept informed of the corps's activities. Richard certainly matched and maybe even doubled that score. At times he and Boerger were following each other around the Rotary, Kiwanis, Lions, and Round Table club luncheons like acts booked on a vaudeville circuit.

On top of this came the exhausting series of Senate and Assembly committee hearings, frequently postponed at the last minute, which had him commuting between Covelo and Sacramento weekly. Added to this were several trips to Washington, an unending series of phone calls, a constant flow of correspondence from Covelo and his San Francisco office, and a good deal of time spent in serious study of subjects ranging from the evapotranspiration rates of alfalfa to the energy output of geothermal fields in the Imperial Valley. And all this on his own time and nickel.

If he had not enjoyed the privileges of wealth and connections, the effort would have been doomed from the start. In reality the task required him to operate in most respects as a privately funded agency running parallel to the corps and the water department. He, Curt, and Lewis had to keep in touch with dozens of senators and assemblymen and their staffs, feeding them information, countering arguments from the other side, writing press releases, papers, speeches. By the time Lewis left for Washington, Richard was completely immersed in conservation politics. Taking over the Planning and Conservation League made the best kind of sense.

In March the PCL put out a clarion call to conservationists everywhere to inundate Governor Reagan with letters and telegrams opposing Dos Rios. On the same day, Trout Unlimited distributed almost exactly the same appeal. A few days later the *Ukiah Journal* printed a bulletin from Elmer Bauer, who was now president of the Round Valley Conservation League, asking everyone to write a "short letter today" to Governor Reagan. Save the Eel River Association did so, too, and the letters began to flow.

In the middle of this new concerted effort to frustrate the dam builders, a snippet in the *Examiner* reported the impending departure of Col. Frank Boerger from the district office, and his probable retirement from the army. Fortunately for him, he was remembered for other things than Dos Rios. The deepening of a ship canal, the enlargement of a harbor—those things at least had made his stay worthwhile, but he would never see that bronze plaque on the high dam at Dos Rios. If it was to be built at all it would be built without him.

It was a wet year in the valleys, and a flood interfered with the great cotton growers in the Tulare basin. Jim Boswell, who ran one of the San Joaquin's greatest enterprises called Ike to discuss water. Connected to the Chandler family by marriage, he personified both the world's wealthiest agribusiness conglomerates and the Los Angeles business establishment, and he made it clear to Ike that they wanted the north coast water. The flood was a nuisance, but it was more water they needed, not less, even if "a small town has to go under." Ike noted the phrases down. "Our whole economy is based on it," Boswell asserted. "We'll pay whatever it costs. Do it *now*!"

Jerry Barnum wrote to Richard that Henry Lippitt was getting nervous. At a chamber of commerce meeting, Lippitt castigated the *San Francisco Chronicle* for distorting the facts, and insisted on calling Rodda's report the "minority report," even though it was already a majority report.

"He's braying," said Jerry, and most people could see it. Lippitt had reason to be nervous. Jerry was behind him at every turn. Whenever he made a statement in public Jerry contradicted it. When he wrote to the *L.A. Times,* so did Jerry. When he pontificated in the chamber's newsletter, Jerry circulated his own response, as well as explaining to everyone that "Dear Henry" was in the pocket of the utilities and it was time to get an impartial chairman on the job. Jerry Barnum had not enjoyed himself so much in years.

From the end of the hearing through April of 1969, he was busy with Amos, rooting around in the substrata of Southern California, looking for better sources of water. Amos would dig up pertinent information and discuss it with Jerry on the phone. The conversations were recorded and transcribed for Richard to read. Amos came across a study made by a department engineer, with a figure for groundwater capacity that took their breath away. In the underground basins of Chino, San Gabriel, Bunker Hill, Los Angeles, Raymond, and in Orange County there was room for almost 7.5 million acre-feet, and reading his account was like taking a stroll beneath the earth's crust. The idea was simply that in wet years you would store the surplus there, and in dry years pump it out. Cheap, simple—and no need for dams. On the phone Amos rehearsed a fantasy conversation with Gianelli:

"How much water do you anticipate, Mr. Gianelli, will be 'wasted' out to sea before the time when Oroville Dam is no longer adequate?

"What is the total available underground capacity south of the Tehachapi?

"What steps are being taken to allow the use of the underground capacity to store the 'wasted' water? Who is working on the hydrologic, geologic, and legal problems?"

The answer to the last question, of course, would be, Nobody! Jerry knew what a pain a water rights lawsuit could be. It was the only area where he was in sympathy with Gianelli. In Southern California people would spend millions to defend them. He tells the story of a case in point.

"Our Mr. Cosgrove tried the O'Neill case in Orange County. Every morning twenty experts would depart the premises carrying little bags and picks and shovels to gather rocks to show what kind of banks there were on an underground river in Orange County. Well, it would break the average fellow, but today that O'Neill family must have three or four billion as a result."

Yet surely the same principle of eminent domain that operated in Northern California, where nobody had the money to defend their rights should operate here, too. The state would have to grasp this nettle eventually. Building obsolete dams was just a way of avoiding the real issue.

Then Richard turned up another source of water.

"Let me try this on you," he wrote to Jerry. "Oroville Dam was supposed to produce all the water needed for the State Water Project. But the northern contractors filed for more than was expected and, being in the county of origin, had priority. So it looked like the project would be short. This is the argument for Dos Rios.

"But those northern contractors, it turns out, can't sell all that water. They want to sell it back to the state. But the state won't buy it, because *it would undermine their argument for Dos Rios.*"

Jerry thought it would be too confusing for legislators or the public to understand, but Amos said it was an essential argument, and added, "Tell Richard if he were a carpenter as good at hitting the nail on the head as he is here, I'd have him build my house."

Yet another source of water was discovered, and was connected with the changing practices of agriculture. Agriculture used 90 percent of all the water delivered in California. The smallest saving there would be more than enough to keep Round Valley dry. Now sprinkler irrigation was being developed, requiring only a fraction of the water used by old-fashioned flood irrigation methods. But what if farmers did save water in the Central Valley? How could that water become available where it was needed? The complexities of transferring water provided by a federal agency, at bargain prices, to another utility served by the state were all but insuperable under the existing rules. How much easier to flood a valley than to change the rules.

The more they went into it, the more it became apparent that it was not water that was lacking, it was the political will to rationalize California's resources. Given that, Gianelli could hardly be blamed for harping on "the facts of life." He took his case to a convention of the Irrigation District Association, at Sacramento's El Dorado Hotel, where he could be sure of unqualified support.

"Those who cry that engineering works have ruined our natural environment and destroyed our natural resources do not know, and do not have the responsibility for quenching the thirst of agriculture, industry, and employment and providing water-oriented recreation."

And Henry Lippitt was there the next day to warn that Dos Rios was in danger. Half the letters opposing the dam, he said, were coming from south of the Tehachapi . . . a treasonable state of affairs that gave Virginia Brody cause for pride. On the same day, Jerry Butchert in Eureka told the Eel River Association that if they didn't get the Dos Rios Dam, the Eel would slip out of their grasp forever. It was their last chance to get that water, and he, too, was agitating for a meeting with the governor so that they could state their case.

The Dos Rios story had become an epic, with a cast of thousands, and all of them it seemed wanted to see the governor. Scarcely any of them did, but a good many got as far as Ike, and as the day of decision loomed nearer for the governor to make a decision, Ike's offices thronged with partisan groups. The most hopeful sign for him was that while a number of important figures had veered away from blind adherence to water above all else, none had gone the other way.

Among the most dependable supporters of the dam, of course, was Carly Porter, sponsor of the State Water Project, chairman of the Assembly Water Committee, and a close collaborator with Bill Gianelli. Ronald Robie, his committee consultant, remembers calling on Reagan with Porter and Gianelli a little earlier in the year when Porter was lobbying strongly for Dos Rios. To Robie's amazement, Reagan now seemed to view Dos Rios with some distaste, and he talked about the pleasure he took in the streams running over his own ranch in Malibu. They were alone in the governor's office, and according to Robie, Reagan turned on Gianelli and said, "You'd pave over Yosemite if I gave you a chance."

Reagan's sympathies for free-running streams may have had something to do with Porter's own surprising change of mind. Ike went to see the old man in his office, and noted how frail he seemed—"obviously failing, slow in speech, but mind still sharp." It was there that Ike first ran into a rumor that must have been started by the water guys to discredit the opposition.

Porter said he was extremely suspicious of the motives of those who wanted to save the valley. He had visited it back in August—incognito, he said—in the company of General Glasgow, who commanded the Corps of Engineers Pacific Division. It had looked to him like a dying community. Someone it seemed had been putting out the rumor that Lewis Butler was planning to buy up the valley as a speculation, an idea that Ike found utterly absurd.

However, the most unexpected thing Ike learned that day was Porter's own change of heart about the project itself. He told Ike flat out: "If I had a billion dollars to spend for the State Water Project now, I would not be ready to approve Dos Rios based on present facts."

On March 17, 1969, the *Los Angeles Times* published an article about this new water war between the north and south. The big difference this time, it said, was the growing strength of "an aroused group of individuals and organizations striking back on every point, from environmental dangers to cost/benefit figures." It gave a lot of play to Richard's arguments and involvement, and then quoted Lippitt, Jensen, and the usual water lobbyists as saying the case against the dam was highly exaggerated and false.

It concluded that Ike had not yet made up his mind, and quoted him as saying: "But when I do, that will be the state's decision. And if the governor overturns my decision, then I do not believe I would be of much more use to him."

It was a bold statement to make, and Ike said afterward it had not been put quite so intransigently, but he stood by it with Reagan, and it clearly had an effect. Two days later, the *Times* published an editorial berating Gianelli for his attempt to pin the opposition on "narrow interests."

"We suggest that the opposition is not 'narrow.' As for the issue itself, while undoubtedly holding emotional overtones in the area involved, it is primarily an economic one as far as the rest of the state is concerned." And it warned the Reagan administration to be careful "lest water users of Southern California wind up buying a white elephant." With that one editorial, Richard considered that his strategy of attacking the dam on economic grounds was vindicated.

Richard kicked off the month of April with a rally for the North Coast Rivers Association in Eureka. He said it was time for the north coast to set a precedent by demanding written agreements to protect their interests before any more projects were authorized. Elmer Bauer said three hundred letters opposing the dam were hitting Reagan's desk every day, and Norman Whipple spoke movingly to defend the valley.

Then Rodda was in the press again, this time appealing directly to Ike to shelve Dos Rios rather than expand California's indebtedness. *The Sacramento Bee*'s water reporter, Wilson Lythgoe, confirmed that hundreds of letters were pouring in, mostly opposing the dam, and that Bing Crosby was one of the writers. On the other hand, Ike was having to deal with heavy pressure from Jensen, from the California Water Commission, and from the Central Valley. The intensity of the fight increased at every level. Ike kept copious notes of visits, phone calls, and correspondence and they indicated that both sides were fighting for their lives.

There were many signs during this period that the water interests were losing their automatic preeminence. The Senate's reversal had certainly punctured their invincibility. Some were talking about the water lobby being in decline and saying that the battle was practically over, but a little thought quickly disclosed the folly of that conclusion.

It was true that the so-called water lobby had been able to inflate its significance to awesome proportions, and that the conservationist campaign had stuck a pin in the balloon. A lot of hot air had escaped, but there was much more than air inside that skin. There was a $10 billion agricultural industry, there was an equally potent industrial complex, and California's prosperity still depended entirely on these sources of income. To imagine that they had lost their power because of a change in political perceptions would be dangerously naive.

Ike knew that on any night Ronald Reagan might dine with any of a hundred powerful men who could persuade him that to deprive California of the north coast water would be to cripple the state he loved. There were many highly qualified civil servants around him who sincerely believed that same truth. They could tell him that the whole subject had been grossly distorted for obscure motives, that the future of what was virtually a nation was being held hostage to the inconvenience of a couple of thousand people who didn't want to be moved, even though elaborate plans were being made to take care of them.

On April 16, Ike heard that the Eel River Association, led by Jerry Butchert, was seeing the governor. Ominously, Ike's attendance was "not required." On April 24, he countered by bringing the Covelo deputation into the governor's office. It was a small group, consisting of Richard, Curt, Jerry Barnum, Norman Whipple, and Joe Russ, another Indian from the valley. Richard made his case on the economics of the dam, using charts and pictures. Jerry Barnum talked about the alternate sources of water that he and Amos Roos had been pursuing over and underground. Jerry's recollection of the experience of presenting a case to Reagan was idiosyncratic and less than flattering.

"He had a perpetual smile on his face. He looked at me as though I were the most interesting person he had ever listened to, and I knew he was bored stiff. But he was a character, that fellow. He could sway anybody. I don't think Reagan ever knew a darned thing. I got the feeling he was looking at me because, as a movie actor, he was supposed to. A peculiar duck."

Then Norman Whipple began to speak about what the valley meant to his people. It is a strange thing that Norman, who had never really meant or wanted to live in the valley, was by far the most eloquent about it. In his simple, homespun language he evoked the injustices Indians had suffered in the past. He described how the army had driven his ancestors into the valley at gunpoint a hundred years earlier and was now threatening to drive *their* descendants out. The valley was theirs by treaty, he said. So many treaties had been broken. Would there never be an end to it?

There was no question now of the effect on Reagan. He was visibly moved, almost to tears, and according to Richard's later account, Reagan said there and then, "Agreements are made to be kept, and we should live with them." All those present at that meeting were in no doubt that if any one moment had to be singled out as crucial in saving the valley, then that was it.

A date had been set for the critical cabinet meeting. It was to take place on Monday, May 12, and as if by divine plan many of the conservationists' best efforts came to fruition during those last tense days. On the very day of the Covelo group's visit with the governor, the public embarrassment of the corps at Tamalpais Creek reached its climax. Forty-three conservationists were arrested, giving the *Chronicle* a fine opportunity to jeer at these "slide rule Noahs" and the "destructive outrage" they were committing in the name of flood control.

An article Bob Simmons had written months before under a pseudonym also appeared with perfect timing. Naturally it was very critical of the corps and the dam. Originally intended for *Reader's Digest,* it found a home instead in a magazine called *Human Events.*

"It was the journal of the John Birch Society," Simmons, the liberal Democrat, recounted afterward with relish. "It had a great many right-wing readers in Orange County. I played up the Indian story and the implication of this rancher being trod on by the big federal government. What began to happen was that Republicans all over the county, many of whom Reagan knew and many of whom had helped finance his campaign for governor, began to send him copies of this article." And the proof of Simmons's success lies in Ike's files today—a reprint of his three-page article, stamped "Compliments of Senator H. L. Richardson."

On Monday the fifth of May, the supervisors from Mendocino County arrived in Ike's office. Ike knew from Richard how much confusion and conflict they had gone through over Dos Rios, and he was most impressed to find them, on this occasion, unanimously fed up with the dam. All of them were finally convinced that, whatever benefits might one day come to the county, they would never be worth the long years of uncertainty and delay that this project entailed.

Joe Scaramella and Augie Avila were both against it on all counts. The others thought it better to kill it now rather than have it hang over their heads for another fifteen years. Ike felt true sympathy for their predicament, and it remains one of his strongest recollections of that time. It supported his belief that he was taking the right stand. All in all, as the last week before the decisive cabinet meeting began, he felt he had about as good a case as he would ever have. A considerable number of influential people had either come out against the dam or had expressed reservations about it. The only important legislator who remained solidly behind it was Cologne.

In the Assembly, a new Republican chairman of the Natural Resources Committee, George Milias, had become its most outspoken critic, and Bill Kier took some credit for that. Milias had a congenial committee consultant named Rod Tuttle. Kier says, "I took him out to cheap lunches and pumped him with my concern for Dos Rios."

It was Tuttle who eventually led Milias into a meeting with Rus Walton. Walton, another character in this large cast, was an enigmatic figure at Reagan's side, with the title secretary for Program Development. He had come out of the advertising industry, and played the ultraconservative version of a very sixties role, as Reagan's combination guru, Jiminy Cricket, and Minister for Enlightenment. According to Kier, "Walton saw himself as a very bright person in a desert of intellect. He belonged to Mensa [the club for people with high IQs] and contributed to their publication. He saw his job as trying to provide for his boss some fresh insights on things."

Walton was already inclined toward conservation. He had sent

Meese and Ike a remarkable memo a month earlier passionately praising Bill Mott when he made a stand against the corps's story that Lake Covelo would make a wonderful state park.

"Let me say strongly that I think William Penn Mott's statement before the cabinet this morning (the long-range implications of Dos Rios and the future development of this state) was a *most important and profound statement.*

"It is essential that he and Ike Livermore be given some time to expound on this in the near future, not simply in reference to Dos Rios but attending to the entire subject of where will this state be twenty-five years from now (environment, social conditions, metropolitan development, and the 'new California' idea, et al.).

"Such commitments as water projects (and freeway systems and other public works) *do in fact determine living patterns for years to come.* And it makes no sense at all to establish or expand projects which can only lead to additional implosion in areas which are already congested, already polluted, already infested and already almost politically, economically, and sociologically enervated.

"The essence of leadership—and courage as well as vision—is involved in this one. *We can invent the future!*"

Whatever influence Walton had over Reagan would clearly be an asset. As for Milias, he had already told Ike that he thought building Dos Rios would be "a grave political error." Among those close to Reagan now, only Earl Coke was resolutely in favor of the dam. Clark was against it and Meese veered that way. Weinberger, who had taken over the state's finances, said his "instincts were against it," and the others were neutral. Provided Reagan stuck to his usual policy of following the cabinet's lead, Ike felt he had a good chance of having his decision ratified, but with so much at stake he knew there was every possibility that outside influence could still tilt the table.

Ike had one more outstanding problem to deal with. How could Reagan cut off Dos Rios and still continue to say, as he had done consistently, that the state would honor its commitments to the water contractors when the state's own water department insisted there was no other way to do so? His solution was to lift himself off the horns of that dilemma and impale Gianelli on them instead. He wrote Gianelli a memo:

"Please describe in not more than two pages of typewritten text what, in your opinion, would probably be the reaction of your department toward selecting alternate courses of action should the decision be:

> a. Not to flood Round Valley
> b. Not to recommend authorization of any dams in the Middle Fork Eel River until further studies are made."

Gianelli's verbal reaction to this request can only be imagined. His written reply came back up from the eleventh floor on Wednesday. The bureaucratic terminology could not disguise the surly undertone. Reading between the lines and summarizing freely, it said in effect:

> First we'd tell you again that Dos Rios is the only good plan.
> Then we'd try to comprehend why on earth you'd want to kill it, and what other projects you might be dumb enough to stop.
> Then we'd wonder how to account for all the money we've already spent on it.
> Then we'd look around, with little hope of finding another project that could possibly do the job.
> Then we'd try to figure out how to fund such a project, given that there's no money.

Knowing that his comments would be read by Reagan, Gianelli gave the governor an obvious loophole. He said he could see no reason to withhold authorization because they could then use federal dollars to go on planning the dam and the state could still stop it any time thereafter simply by refusing to give the corps a contract.

Ike added this sheet to a number of others that he had gathered as background material for the governor to read. They included numbered lists of factors in favor and factors against, alternate sources of water offered by all the parties to the dispute, a long letter from Jensen justifying the dam with Ike's itemized response, various cuttings and quotes from relevant letters, a short history of the betrayal of the Indians in Round Valley, and a tally of letters received so far.

He sent one copy of this bundle to Gianelli for comment, and it came back with remarks jotted in the margin that showed him to be plainly disgusted. Under the summary of correspondence—62 in favor, 2,440 against—he scribbled sarcastically: "Perhaps project sponsors and opponents should hire PR firms to promote letters to responsible officials, who could make decisions by tallying 'for' and 'against.' "

On another page Ike had listed what he called "issues stemming from the Dos Rios decision," and they all consisted of more or less radical attempts to bring environmental consideration into the discussion of water projects. Below the last item, which was Ike's call to have all these matters delegated to him, Gianelli added.

> 14. Whether this administration intends to encourage or discourage water resource development
> 15. Whether past efforts of State Water Project sponsors should be repudiated
> 16. The importance of maintaining financial integrity of SWP

These were not the comments of a man who would take defeat lying down. Obviously Gianelli felt that the state's interests and his own dedication were being trivialized. Since he was excluded from the cabinet meeting, surely he would be bound to take some action to make his feelings known before Monday. Certainly the fight was not over yet.

During that week in May, everybody in the office was drawn into the drama. Ike was universally liked as a person, and his secretaries doted on him. Most of the career people and politicians around him thought he was far too nice a person to be tangling with a power structure like the water lobby. They were all fearful that it would be his undoing, and that the Metropolitan, if not Gianelli, would find some way to strike him down. The atmosphere between his office on the thirteenth floor, and the water department two floors down crackled with tension, and the press was dancing in attendance, looking for clues to the eventual decision.

Ike kept his counsel, and the press was left grasping for straws. On Monday morning they were still none the wiser. Jackson Doyle in the *Chronicle* started a long piece saying, "A major and possibly decisive phase of the cat-and-mouse game that has long been played over . . . the highly controversial Dos Rios project will climax in Sacramento today. State Resources Secretary Norman B. Livermore, Jr.—perhaps the coolest and most widely respected of Governor Reagan's top aides—promises to make his formal and final recommendations to the governor and his cabinet this morning.

"This does not mean, however, that Livermore's report will be made public—now or at all—nor that Reagan will announce his own decision immediately, although he could.

"Livermore noted that department heads do not sit on the cabinet—and the disputing factions have not been invited this morning. . . ."

In fact the cabinet meeting was delayed until the afternoon, and Ike spent the morning in his office making sure he had his brief and his props well prepared. Both Richard and Curt called to wish him luck. Only after lunch, when he was getting ready to walk the two blocks between the Resources building and the cabinet offices, did he hear that Reagan had been closeted in his office throughout the lunch hour with an extremely high-powered delegation from Southern California and, presumably, with Gianelli. The news was chilling and he could not brush it aside. It was only with great difficulty that he recovered his composure.

He reviewed his brief once more before leaving the office. A sealed envelope had been thrust into his folder of papers, and he noticed it then for the first time. It was addressed to him and marked: "PERSONAL—TO BE OPENED JUST BEFORE THE CABINET MEETING."

He slit the top of the envelope and pulled out a memorandum sheet with a simple message typed on it.

"This is just to let you know that you have *our* support on your stand on the Dos Rios project, and that we are proud of you and respect you for it, whatever the outcome!"

It was signed by Marty, Zoe, Patty, and Joanne, his four secretaries.

He had almost reached the capitol building before the lump in his throat went away.

29

Reagan Decides . . . or Does He?

REAGAN GOVERNED CALIFORNIA from a suite of rooms and offices on the ground floor of the annex to the capitol. The public was excluded by a door leading off the main hall, and in an anteroom beyond this door the press had gathered that day, hoping to pick up some inkling of a decision on "controversial Dos Rios." Ike passed among them, outwardly jovial and confident as he fended off their questions, and then entered the cabinet room adjoining the governor's office.

The room is large and high ceilinged, with a soothing view of the park through tall windows. Nancy Reagan attended carefully to the ceremonial aspects of her husband's position, and she had decorated one of the walls with plaques, memorabilia, and photographs from Reagan's unusual career as actor and politician, so that there was no mistaking who was the governor. Ike took a seat at the large table in the center of the room and prepared his exhibits as the others assembled. He had several charts blown up to illustrate some of the anomalies he had detected in the corps's calculations, and there was a short film of Round Valley spliced together by Bob Simmons and his crew that he hoped to show.

Reagan's cabinet consisted of only a handful of people—his immediate aides and the secretaries of the four agencies. Gordon Luce, who had Business and Transportation, and Spencer Williams, who ran Human Relations, had not taken a position on Dos Rios. Agriculture, which was originally one of Ike's departments, had been taken away and inflated into a full-blown agency of its own at the insistence of agribusiness. Earl Coke was doubling as secretary for Cabinet Affairs and for Agriculture. Ed Meese, Reagan's executive secretary, was the only other member of the cabinet.

These five all had jelly bean privileges. Jelly beans were a passion of Reagan's, and a jar of them was passed around the table at the start of every meeting, in a quasi-religious ritual. It was considered proper, says Ike, to take only two or three. Seated on chairs along the walls were Mike Deaver, Tom Reed, Paul Beck, who was Reagan's press secretary, and a dozen or so other advisers. They constituted the second echelon, which got no jelly beans and took no part in the discussion unless asked.

That afternoon along with the jelly beans came something even more to Ike's taste. Earl Coke handed out copies of a three-page memo from Rus Walton to Reagan. It was a surprising document. Recalling the abuse of the Indians in Round Valley since 1850, Walton claimed that they had a moral claim to their land, even though all treaties had been broken. He finished:

"Surely this—of all administrations—should take a stand for morality and the protection of individual rights. Even if there were no alternatives for developing the necessary water resources—*and there do seem to be*—certainly this administration cannot accept the despotic dodge that the greatest good for the greatest number is a defense for violating the individual and his rights.

"We should not be a party to the duplicity, the treachery, the thievery, the broken promises, and the violation of individual rights that have been perpetrated on these Indians by previous administrations and generations."

And there, laid out for him if he wanted to put it on, was as good a suit of Teflon as Reagan might ever hope to wear. Surely Walton would not have bothered if he hadn't thought it would appeal.

The governor entered from his office and sat down, urbane, relaxed, and smiling as always, and after a little chatting Ike began his presentation. He had timed his talk precisely and spoke for less than half an hour. Most of the details he needed to refer to had already been distributed in the form of information issues during the previous week. Among them were two lists—points for and against the project.

The "points for" had been supplied by Gianelli. They were longer and there were more of them, but Ike included them all rather than be accused of misrepresenting the department, and there was nothing that had not been heard a hundred times before.

The "points against" were succinct and deliberately ordered with the more emotional issues last. He pointed out that the national economic climate was against expensive water projects and that this one seemed to have come out of left field without proper preparation or integration into some north coast plan. Mendocino County was against it, and now even Humboldt County was worried about the effect on its fishing industry.

In his easy, rumbling voice Ike suggested that there were many factors that the engineers had simply not taken into account, and that to rush into this project without examining them would be wrong. Agriculture might not need so much water after all, and population projections were apparently being revised downward. He played on the enormous discrepancies between the corps figures and those of Gardner Brown, and pointed out that many significant legislators had serious doubts about them. Ike reminded his listeners of the multitude of other sources of water that had surfaced during recent months, and suggested that they should be seriously analyzed.

Even while he was talking, he wondered what would happen when he stopped. Would Reagan, as usual, acquiesce and follow the majority at the table? Or had the people from Southern California finally gotten to him? Would he suddenly, shockingly reveal his own unilateral decision to endorse the dam and put an end to Ike's government career?

Ike had a stark appreciation of just how unpredictable Reagan could be, and he understood the perplexity of the water interests. Where was Reagan's power base? How could you get to him? He didn't seem to be in anybody's pocket. Just a bunch of assorted millionaires with a conservative ideology. There was no knowing which way he might jump.

Toward the end of his talk, Ike pointed out that environmental awareness had grown at an astonishing rate during the previous year, and that it was now a factor of considerable political importance. Then he declared his personal conviction that the valley should not be flooded and that a public statement should be made to that effect, to relieve the inhabitants—particularly the Indians—of the economic and psychological stress of having this project hanging over their heads. He sat down and waited.

Ike recalls that there was little discussion. Earl Coke reiterated that he felt the dam was needed to fulfill the state's commitments. Reagan looked brightly around the table. Nobody else had much to add. Reagan said that of course the state must meet its commitments, but he wanted to keep faith with the Indians. Gianelli's department should be instructed to find some alternative. There must be other places to build dams that didn't destroy beautiful valleys. He turned to Ike.

"You and Earl can work out a press release tomorrow with Paul Beck. I'm going to New York on Wednesday. It would be best to keep this to ourselves until I'm on the plane."

That was that. The kicker Ike had been waiting for didn't come. It was done, but it seemed too good to be true. What had Reagan actually said? When he and Coke fought over the wording of the press release the next day, the vagueness of it became apparent. Clearly what Reagan hoped to produce by putting Ike and Earl Coke together was a statement that would offer hope to everyone, from Joe Jensen to Norman Whipple. In other words, a masterpiece of confusion. Ike had drafted his own release in anticipation of a good result, and it stated unequivocally that Round Valley would not be flooded. Coke refused to go along with anything so categorical, and produced a draft of his own. He tried hard to introduce wording—"weasel words," Ike called them—to imply that the dam was simply being postponed while the engineers looked around for "alternatives." He tried to limit those alternatives to the Upper Eel watershed. It was obvious from Gianelli's statements that no alternative would ever be found by his department or by the corps with the same economic value as Dos Rios. They would come back six months later saying, "Look, we tried, but nothing else will do," hoping that by then the political atmosphere would be more conducive to their plans. Ike fought for a couple of words that would broaden the scope of the revision and give it at least the appearance of a serious intent to look elsewhere as well as on the Eel River.

As they went through the drafts, starting with Coke's version and ending with a hybrid, Ike's assistant rated each one. The final version was scored as a 72 percent victory. The remarks attributed to the governor in the press release had a pious ring to them.

"I am very concerned about the Dos Rios project with its resultant flooding of Round Valley," Reagan was quoted as saying, "and I want to know about other alternatives that may be feasible."

And later he was supposed to have said: "There are very serious questions in my own mind about protecting Round Valley. It is a place of great natural beauty. Another concern I have is for the community of Covelo and for the future of the Round Valley Indians, who have inhabited the valley for centuries.

"With these factors in mind, as well as our commitments to deliver water to the south under terms of the State Water Project, I have determined that all alternatives must be completely analyzed."

All the same, despite the mealymouthed phrases, conservationists were determined to make it a victory by treating it as such. Milias, next day, called it "one of the most significant and far-reaching decisions to preserve the quality of California's environment made in the past decade. . . . The governor has virtually assured us that the unique scenic and recreational values of the north coast and its precarious ecology will not be disturbed."

When Richard read the statement, he saw of course that it meant no such thing. He joined ostentatiously in the general jubilation, but he knew it was a stall, and no more. At best, what it did was to level the playing field. It acknowledged that there were good reasons on both sides of the issue. The fight would go on, but it was no longer David and Goliath. From being an unknown rancher in a forgotten cow county, Richard had become the president of an important conservation association and a lobbyist to be reckoned with. The environmental movement had achieved a degree of influence and cooperation on major issues that it had not known before, and public opinion was swelling in its favor.

Now, in the effort to turn Reagan's well-meaning phrases into a decision, maybe the real issues would get a public airing. Glad as he was that the Indians had given Reagan a moral peg to hang his hat on, the arguments were so much broader and more crucial. During the past months, Richard had been trying to conduct a dialogue with Ike on his "watershed" proposal. The concept of a self-contained watershed economy was a natural vehicle for the ideas that seemed most important to him. He wanted to reinvigorate rural communities, put a true value on natural resources, preserve the environment, revive the dignity of agriculture as a way of life, expose the false glamor of city cultures, and bring brains and ingenuity back to the land.

He intensified his efforts to convey these notions to Ike, as an antidote to the water interests who claimed that California's water should always be free, and go where it could do the greatest good for the greatest number. Ike was a willing listener. He, too, saw the necessity of switching the emphasis, from dollars per acre-foot to an assessment of the true value of California's environment. When the water guys began their counterattack, they gave him a platform for these ideas.

After the initial shock of betrayal, the water establishment comforted itself by saying that Reagan's remarks were just a political ploy to disarm the opposition, and that they would get their dam in the end. The chambers of commerce, the Eel River Association, and the other "merry dowsers," as the *San Francisco Chronicle* called them, rose up and declared, "Dos Rios is not dead." A vigorous proponent was General William Glasgow, the corps commander on the Pacific. He wrote and spoke widely, condemning "hardy, single-purpose preservationists" for maligning engineers and distorting the truth. He and Gianelli seemed to speak with one voice, and undoubtedly made plans together to rescue what they could from the debacle.

Their first move was to contain the damage and keep the funds flowing. Gianelli drafted a letter to General Cassidy, commander of the corps in Washington, for Reagan's signature. It seemed again to limit the scope of the search for alternative projects to the Eel River basin. They knew they must not let the Eel River slip from their grasp. It was the key to the whole north coast. Earl Coke got Reagan to sign the letter. Ike was never consulted, nor even sent a copy.

The letter went out on May 22. The news got back to Ike soon enough, and on June 2 he confronted Ed Meese with "this unconscionable breach of protocol." Then he went through all the issues raised by it. This was just what he needed to get his own agenda back on the table. It included a fundamental review of the State Water Project and of the chain of command within Ike's agency, a new emphasis on environmental planning, and Reagan's commitment to saving Round Valley.

The talks went on intermittently for a month. Ike's notes indicate that he pursued Meese relentlessly to bring these matters to a conclusion, while Meese was presumably having to counter Coke's influence with Reagan. Finally Meese told Ike that Coke had been reprimanded, and that Reagan would *not* go back on his promise to Round

Valley. He simply could not say it in public until some other way had been found to satisfy the state's contracts. However, Ike had Reagan's verbal permission to tell conservationists that "this administration will never permit the flooding of Round Valley." And, finally, they agreed that Ike should write letters to Glasgow and others that would be widely publicized, putting Ike's case on the basic issues.

The result of this effort came to be known as "those three letters" and it caused the biggest uproar in water circles that anyone could remember.

To Glasgow, couched in the usual courtesies and pleasantries, he wrote that the old mathematics did not add up anymore. It was no longer good enough to value a valley only by the dollars that its inhabitants could hope to extract from it by their labors. There was, by implication, an intrinsic value that had to be considered.

Nor could it be right to flood out one set of people in order to protect another set from flooding, especially when they had put themselves deliberately in a floodplain knowing what the consequences might be.

Nor was it good enough anymore to design a water project and expect authorization *before* figuring out how to protect natural resources like fish and wildlife.

The corps, he said, was out of touch with public opinion if it thought these were just the ravings of extremists. The feeling was widespread, and all four major metropolitan newspapers in San Francisco and Los Angeles opposed the dam.

To Henry Lippitt, he put the heretical notion that counties of origin might want more in the way of benefits for their water.

"As our society gets more complex and competitive, water at its source is indeed becoming more and more a saleable commodity rather than being free for the taking. . . . Why should not the north coast counties be paid for the export of their water, just as they are now being paid for other exported materials, such as agriculture and forest products, for instance?"

To Ira Chrisman, whose California Water Commission had its office three floors below him, he wrote that in his opinion water projects should be made to go through environmental committees in the legislature as well as through water committees. New criteria should be established to assess water demands. Population projections were declining. People were seeing other uses for rivers, like rafting for example. It was time to reexamine the plans as well as some of the figures put out by water departments that seemed designed to confuse and baffle the public.

Water officials and boosters could barely contain their fury. For the first time, the principles they had suspected Livermore of harboring were actually stated openly. Jensen wrote to Reagan asking him to denounce his secretary for Resources. All the water interests unleashed a flood of abuse against environmentalists for going to extremes, for sacrificing future generations, and plotting the downfall of the state with a "zero-growth" mentality. Gianelli was at the front line of the assault. He seemed to spend all his spare time issuing press releases and ranting at water-oriented functions about the iniquity of the conservationists. The correspondence between him and Ike became more and more strained, to the point where Gianelli was telling Ike, in so many words, that he didn't know what he was talking about. Reagan, meanwhile, was making reassuring noises to the water establishment, saying that Ike was merely putting ideas on the table to stimulate debate.

In October, Henry Lippitt dared Ike to repeat his inflammatory remarks to the Los Angeles Chamber of Commerce in person, as Richard had done a year earlier, and he obliged them. Once again howls of indignation echoed all the way to Sacramento, accusing Livermore of undermining the State Water Project and implying that he was incompetent to exercise any authority over it. Somehow, though, the old Southern California magic didn't seem to work anymore. The water officials all got up and shook their sticks in unison, a spectacle Jerry Barnum observed with cynical amusement, and yet the conservation bandwagon rolled right on past them into 1970.

In Mendocino County, strangely enough, it was dèjá vu. Colonel Boerger's replacement, Colonel Roberts, turned up in Round Valley in the company of Charlie Elmore and asked the Indians, including Norman Whipple, what it would take to get their agreement to the dam. Richard protested loudly that the corps was ignoring the governor's directive to pursue other alternatives. The difference was that now, as opposed to 1967, he was heard and reported.

Then the Met and Henry Lippitt flew the Mendocino supervisors down to Los Angeles and put together a plan to compensate Mendocino County for the revenue losses it anticipated. The supervisors once again fell into disarray as glittering prizes were dangled before them, and they went through another series of tortured meetings and disagreements.

This was the year when Reagan would run for reelection, and the big power brokers in the south assumed that he would have to come to his senses, but Reagan had begun to realize that there was as much of a constituency in conservation as in big business. He worked both sides of the aisle with consummate skill. A typical example of his expertise occurred on October 7, when one minute he was standing on a platform with Gianelli wearing a hard hat and celebrating the starting of the mammoth pumps that would take the water over the Tehachapi, and next minute he was whirling away by helicopter to the inauguration of "Environmentalists for Reagan," in Sacramento.

For another year Gianelli and Livermore went on slugging it out with speeches, letters, and memos symbolizing the struggle between an emerging green movement and the overconfident utilitarians who were used to having it all their own way. As the battle progressed, the weakness of the water interests became more and more apparent. The patches of dogma that had covered the cracks were peeling away, and the agencies began to leak like sieves. Within these bureaucracies were young professionals with their own doubts and criticisms who now found an outlet for their dissatisfaction with the old guard. Amos Roos was getting his groundwater information from an engineer who believed that Teerink and Gianelli were locked into attitudes twenty years out of date.

Al Wilkins in Weaverville had a similar experience. As his North Coast Rivers Association made more and more noise, biologists with both state and federal agencies came to him surreptitiously to support his views and tip him off about this or that report. Al was determined to expose the damage that had been done to the Trinity River, which he felt was being deliberately concealed by the new director of Fish and Game to protect Gianelli's interests. He was told that the studies begun by Shannon showed just how bad things were on the Trinity, and he asked for a copy of the report.

It was refused. He insisted, and was told that it was incomplete and subject to review. Unimpressed, he went to court and sued the department. Finally, with an injunction, he forced the agency to send him the incriminating document. One success led to another, until finally he and Hazel Wilburn were able to get Trinity County out of the Eel River Association altogether.

"It all took a lot of time and expense," Al said later, with that understated manner and laconic smile so characteristic of him, "but we didn't feel it. We felt it was really mysterious that we *could do this.* The Bible says: 'They that wait upon the Lord shall renew their strength.' We were active and involved with a thing of such consequence, and getting away with it, and being sustained in the effort. And so you had to conclude that you *weren't* really doing it. I don't know where it was coming from. So often you wish you could find that same sort of direction and feeling of rightness."

However, the water guys were still in full cry, and the corps and the DWR were still busy in the Eel watershed. Then, early in 1971, a startling headline hit the *Chronicle*'s front page: BIG ERROR ADMITTED ON STATE WATER PLAN.

And Jackson Doyle wrote:

> State water officials are finally conceding that they have long planned to transport too much Northern California water to the Southland too soon. . . . New findings, which could well spare one of the nation's most celebrated wild-river systems—the Eel, the Trinity, and the Klamath—from "development," will be submitted . . . to the California Water Commission tomorrow.

Gradually the details emerged. Population projections had sunk by six million for 1990, and by nine million for 2020. Gianelli's department had not been able to keep the lid on the news any longer. He made a statement to the press, and reading it is almost painful. With language contorted to minimize the effect, there was no hiding the facts. Jerry Barnum had been right after all. They had called their meeting ten years too soon . . . and possibly they might never have to call it at all.

Yet the water interests would not abandon their interest in the north coast. It had become clear to Richard, Al, Ray Peart, and others that their rivers would never be safe as long as the south could consider them to be available. Populations would still increase, the pressure for more water would grow. Another governor, or even the same governor in a different situation, could give way. The only answer would be to lock them away for good, by law. For a long time there had been talk of trying to get the rivers federally protected. A Federal Wild and Scenic Rivers Act existed already, which could prevent development.

At this opportune moment a new and very significant figure joined the cast. A Marin County supervisor named Peter Behr was running for the Fourth District senatorial seat, which covered Marin, Napa, and Solano counties. He was an avowed conservationist with a long record of successful battles in defense of the bay and the coastline around Point Reyes. He was very much admired in densely populated Marin, and at the end of 1970 he won the seat handily.

Behr was seen as an unusual figure in Sacramento. He was a Yale law graduate and a World War II naval veteran, but beyond that he was obviously a man of superior culture and sophistication, and these mandarin qualities seem to have impressed and even awed his contemporaries.

Ronald Robie, himself a short, fast-talking, bustling ball of energy, remembers Behr as being "tall and sort of patrician, charming, rather British-sounding, a very honorable man, and a fine legislator whom everybody liked and everybody disagreed with, because he was a liberal Republican."

Behr took his seat in January and within three days shocked the entire establishment by immediately launching a major piece of legislation. The shock was caused in part by the importance of the bill, but mainly by the fact that it had nothing to do with his own district. It was a bill to create California's own wild and scenic rivers act, and to lock up the Eel, the Trinity, and the Klamath forever. All those rivers were in the district of Randolph Collier, dean of the Senate.

Collier was openly offended and privately furious. He was also now chairman of the Senate Finance Committee, through which all such bills must pass. Even though a sufficient majority of his committee was actually in favor of the bill, he ensured its defeat by juggling the membership at different hearings and by his manipulation of the voice vote. This voice vote rule was a cherished privilege of committee chairmen. It allowed them to announce how many votes they heard, and sometimes Collier heard voices nobody else could hear. Still, even though the bill crashed, it picked up a lot of goodwill on the way, and it was obvious that it would be tried again.

Peter Behr began undeterred in 1972 with a modified version of his "Wild Rivers" bill that was calculated to pick up even more votes. Naturally he received the wholehearted support of Richard's PCL and all the other conservationist groups. This time Collier responded by running with a bill of his own, a "Protected Waterways" bill to do the same kind of job but much less so. The water interests supported him as the lesser of two evils. Behr saw that he would never get his bill through Collier's finance committee with the rules as they were. He had no option but to try to change the rules. Committee votes would have to be recorded by roll call, and he introduced legislation to that effect.

For a rookie senator, this was heroic presumption, and yet amazingly enough he succeeded. Behr's victory was electrifying, but Collier still wielded immense influence. He kept his bill on track, and modified it as it went through so that it approached Behr's. Both bills advanced through the Assembly in tandem. Even those who voted for Behr also voted for Collier's bill rather than displease him. Behr's bill had compromised slightly. There was now a twelve-year moratorium on any major construction on the Eel, and total exclusion on the other rivers. Collier's bill at first gave no protection to the Eel, but as Behr's bill flourished, Collier's was amended to come closer and closer, and most people recognized it as a "spoiling" bill.

Finally, in November both bills were passed by the legislature and sent to Governor Reagan. He did not hesitate for long. He signed Behr's bill. The Eel River and Round Valley were safe for at least twelve years, and in all probability, forever.

30

The Aftermath

IT WOULD BE PLEASING to be able to say that Round Valley went on to become a happy, prosperous rural community, but reality writes a messy scenario. In early 1971, just when it seemed that all Richard's efforts were about to be rewarded, something in the valley went terribly wrong. Wrong, that is, from Richard's point of view.

A man with a very different kind of vision put his faith in the valley's future. He had made several million dollars selling lots in the back hills of the Sierra, and he bought a 28,000-acre ranch on the southern edge of Round Valley to promote his own subdivision. His plan was to sell 8,000 half-acre lots, on a development called My Ranch. Despite opposition from every relevant county department, the supervisors authorized it on a 3–2 vote. To Richard and many others it promised to be as big a catastrophe as the Dos Rios Dam.

Everything to do with Round Valley was big news now. The *San Francisco Examiner* called it "the biggest lot-sales subdivision ever approved in California." Fully developed, it would bring 30,000 people to a valley with a population of less than 2,000. Instead of being flooded by water, the valley would be overrun by salesmen, speculators, and retirees in recreational vehicles. Such an enormous influx of people would surely obliterate the character of the valley.

That this problem should land on Richard's doorstep with the force of an asteroid was irony on a grand scale. One reason Peter Behr had been doing so well with his bill was that legislators were getting the message clearly now from their voters that conservation in all its forms was popular. Environmental concern was spreading rapidly, just as Richard and others had predicted. People were getting excited about problems they had not even known to exist a year or two earlier. They were discovering untested preservatives in food, toxic emissions in the atmosphere, radiation hazards, groundwater pollution, and oil spills like the one at Santa Barbara that was still tarring the beaches.

As editors woke up to the fact that these subjects sold newspapers, the level of public debate rose dramatically and spread to every area. In Sacramento, in late 1969 for example, three councilmen were whipped out of office because they were too cozy with a commercial developer who ignored environmental considerations. *The Sacramento Bee* said, "The losers . . . were probably among the best financed candidates in the field. In another era, they could not have been beaten."

This, and similar events, led to a public examination of how planning commissions were appointed, and the shocking (though predictable) discovery was made that they were all controlled by developers.

A problem that PCL and California Tomorrow had particularly helped to expose was the damage caused by a long-running boom in rural land speculation. It reached a climax in the late sixties. Big ranches in remote places, like the Travis ranch that had brought Richard and Al Wilkins together, were being sold off in lots to city dwellers, often on the basis of exaggerated hopes and false promises. Widespread frauds had been exposed, and people were getting angry about the hundreds of thousands of acres being taken out of agriculture, only to be abused and left derelict.

Earth scraped clear of vegetation for house sites and roads was washed into rivers and streams by the rains, followed often enough by effluent from houses. Fish and Game wardens reported hundreds of miles of trout streams ruined by siltation, unlikely to recover for decades. And now, one of the biggest such schemes in the history of California had dropped right in Richard's lap. There was no alternative but to fight this off, too.

Jeff Dennis, the developer, was a brash, glad-handing ex-fighter pilot, who wore his business suits cowboy style, with hat, buckle, and boots to match. He flew his own plane and jet helicopter, drove around in a custom-built Cadillac station wagon, and described himself as being "in the happy business." He was a gutsy opponent who believed absolutely in his right to do what he wanted with his own land. He refused to scale his development down to something that Richard and others thought reasonable and many in the valley supported him, believing that he would at least bring in money and economic opportunity.

Some thought Richard was more offended by Dennis's personal style than by his project. People with old scores to settle cast Richard as the arrogant elitist trying to block the ambitions of a self-made man doing it the American way. For his part, Richard suspected corruption in local government. Even though the planning commission was against the plan, he had stumbled upon a clandestine meeting between Dennis and one of the officials in a nearby town.

The divisions in the valley followed more or less the same lines as before. The family feuding and mutual recriminations were if anything even more bitter. Richard has kept a page from the *San Francisco Chronicle* that was sent to Susan by someone in the valley. Scrawled over a description of the My Ranch project are the words, "We, too, fought to save the valley, but not for this."

That message encapsulated Richard's own dilemma. If the valley was indeed saved, what was it for? And if it remained as depressed and underpopulated as it was, wouldn't the water guys be sure to return another time, with more success? Was he going to spend the rest of his days guarding the valley with a "No Entry" sign? He was getting tired of advocating what he called "the politics of *no.*" His position on just about every issue was "Stop it" or "No more" or "Keep out."

Curt Roberts was keener than ever to run Richard for high office, even for governor. Jerry Barnum was equally convinced that Richard should get into politics. Certainly his performance over Dos Rios had been brilliant and, for a beginner, astounding. Yet he could not bring himself to enter the arena, holding the views that he did. Who would risk money to finance a campaign for a politican who could only say no?

There was another, more visceral reason for rejecting the lure of political power. Ronald Robie put his finger on it when he called Richard "a rural person." He had been particularly effective, Robie said, because despite his style and sophistication he had made it clear to everyone that he was genuinely committed to the country. He did not want to leave it.

Instead he began to throw his energy into the valley. If he was going to beat out My Ranch—which eventually *was* done with a referendum—then it was up to him to leave something better in its place. That was the beginning of a new and vital phase in Richard's life. His mind was already bursting with ideas about revitalizing rural communities, and his first thought was to find some way to bring a more social atmosphere to Round Valley.

Jan Stewart's business had gone bankrupt, largely because of the strife over the dam. It seemed fitting to Richard to make of that big store building, where the corps had plotted its "new Covelo," something that would bring people of the old Covelo together. He bought it at auction, had it rebuilt as a fine restaurant with a bar and public rooms, and named it the Round Valley Inn. At the other end of the same block was Rohrbough's magnificent old flour mill, defunct for many decades, but with its original, elaborate milling machinery still in working condition. Thinking that as a historic monument it could be a tourist attraction and an outlet for local crafts, he bought that, too, as well as a few small buildings in between. Inevitably he saw this development as the nucleus of something that would be more like a town. Across the street from the mill was another long wooden structure that had originally served as a theater, and this also he acquired, hoping to restore it to use.

To Richard, bringing people together, cutting across the cultural rifts, was the most urgent need. The valley lacked a newspaper and he saw that as an essential ingredient, so he assisted in founding the *Round Valley News,* and supported it with charitable donations. In an uncanny way, he was repeating in Round Valley what his great-uncle had done in Albuquerque, but from different motives, and with a different end in view. Angus Grant had simply gone with the grain of progress in America. Richard might have been trying to repair the damage that Angus's headlong pursuit of progress symbolized.

It was an interesting period for rural California. It was the beginning of the drift back to the land. Young people, disillusioned with the war and corporate America, were trickling into the back country to try out their own social experiments with communes and homesteading. The hill land that Ida Soares had scorned as only fit for rattlesnakes, they found ideal for their purposes, and they could buy it for only a few dollars an acre. Others, less radical, came to the small towns to try the clean air, the good water, and the quiet life. They came to Round Valley as schoolteachers, as carpenters, mechanics, or jacksof-all-trades. Some came in to build Richard's restaurant, and stayed. One well-known Bay Area typographer, Jim Robertson, moved his entire publishing business to Round Valley. Richard and his family, alienated from a good part of the old community by the fighting over the dam and My Ranch, found he had more in common with these new people. They brought life and fresh ideas, but the big problems still remained. How to bring jobs and money to the valley.

Wondering how he could stimulate new economic vitality, he reached out to people of all kinds. Rod Shippey, the county's agricultural adviser, an avuncular fellow with a merry sense of humor, was one of them. Ray Peart, by then involved with the Planning and Conservation League, was working on ideas for what he called "Appropriate Rural Technology." Al Wilkins had some interesting ideas for funding these experiments, and together they created the Institute for Man and Nature. With Ray, Al, "Uncle Rod," and others, Richard compiled lists of crops and products that might flourish in Round Valley and tried hard to develop and finance them. Self-sufficiency was one of the slogans of the seventies. Richard brought in people with ideas on the subject from all over the world. John Seymour, whose books on the small farm were famous, came to visit the garden; and so did the economist, E. M. Schumacher, who was celebrated for his book *Small Is Beautiful.* New connections suggested themselves all the time.

The most ambitious idea emerged through Susan's passion for gardening, and it was to make Round Valley a new mecca for organic gardeners. In Santa Cruz they came across one of the most extraordinary men ever to set foot in the valley. Alan Chadwick was teaching horticulture at the university at the time. He was an Englishman originally, though he came to California from South Africa, and the story of his background is as confusing as it is intriguing. He had been an actor in the Shakespearean mold and allowed it to be known that he was the offspring of an ancient English aristocratic family. Certainly his manner was as haughty and extravagant as might be expected from a noble thespian. What was not in doubt was his supreme ability as a horticulturalist and the magnetic influence that he exerted over his students.

In Santa Cruz his talent and his electric personality had won him a following of young people who treated him as their guru. Chadwick was a fanatic for the classics and for classical method. He drew inspiration from as far back as Virgil and the Georgics. He had nothing but scorn for contemporary culture, and celebrated the primeval life-force in everything around him. To hear him lecture on, say, "the lascivious rhubarb, voluptuous in its giving" was an experience to be had nowhere else. It was Richard's idea to seduce him away from Santa Cruz, which has a wonderful growing climate, to the challenging frosts and temperature swings of Round Valley. After all, he told him, it's no trick doing it in Santa Cruz, but do it up here and everyone will know you're a genius.

Chadwick, who knew that he probably *was* a genius, jumped at the chance to prove it, and early in 1973 he began work on a garden in Covelo. He was the self-proclaimed inventor of the "biodynamic French-intensive" method of gardening, and nobody could deny the exuberant abundance of delicious fruits and vegetables he was able to coax out of his beds. All forms of machinery were despised; only hand tools were allowed, and the labor was extremely arduous. The young people he gathered around him from the cities had never had such efforts demanded of them before. They responded with total devotion and, of course, discovered strengths and physical qualities in themselves they had not suspected, which only increased their admiration. He made a start on a piece of land donated by Richard just outside town, and his acolytes quickly followed him up from the south, content at first to live off their own savings for the privilege.

The inhabitants of Round Valley had never seen anything like it. What they took to be real live hippies had invaded their territory. These strange beings, men and women, wandered around almost naked—for in Round Valley only certain prescribed areas of skin, above the neck and between the knees and the ankles, were normally considered decent—and yet it was clear that they worked all the hours that God gave. In fact they slaved for Chadwick and put up with frequent abuse and tantrums to receive his wisdom.

A wet winter turned Chadwick's garden into a marsh, and Richard invested in a larger and better piece of land. The Covelo Village Garden Project was transplanted but it grew and flourished even faster. Nothing but perfection would do for Chadwick. He laid out on his thirteen acres a garden designed for eternity, with fruit trees of all kinds, places for ducks, geese, and hens, and features such as a *claire voyer,* a *bosquette,* a dove cote, and a lily garden, borrowed from classic French and English traditions. His students brought down from the mountains the stones he needed to build his ponds and borders, all carried by hand, for there could be no compromising with the internal combustion engine. To Chadwick horticulture was magic and could never be achieved by compromise.

In the microcosm that was Round Valley, Richard had found a workshop of just the right size to put his ideas on trial, and they seemed to be prospering. Among the many people drawn there by the excitement was a young postgraduate, Steven Bundy, the son of President Johnson's hard-line national security adviser on Vietnam, McGeorge Bundy. Desperately in need of a break in both his academic career and personal circumstances, he came in 1973 as Richard's unpaid assistant and general gofer. Today, as a law professor in Berkeley, he recalls his astonishment and exhilaration.

"It took me months to get used to his vision of the world. He seemed almost prophetic in his insights into the limitations of American society. And of course events really made him seem like a Cassandra, in that that was the year of the Yom Kippur war, the Arab oil embargo, and the collapse of the stock market.

"Suddenly his resource-based, low-technology, environmentally sensitive, localized vision of the world came to seem extraordinarily powerful."

With all these influences at work, it truly seemed in those heady years as though some real transformation might be accomplished in the valley but Richard deserved recognition for much more than saving a valley, grand as that achievement was. Largely as a result of his energy and determination it was never again possible for a major water project to be planned in California without the environmental and social cost being evaluated first. In consequence, no high dams—widely known now as "killer dams" for their effect on fish—have been seriously contemplated in twenty-six years. Nor has the Corps of Engineers won authorization for a single big project since Dos Rios.

Soon after Behr's wild rivers bill was signed, an optimistic article appeared in the Santa Rosa *Press Democrat* authored by Rus Walton. It was devoted almost entirely to the opinions of Richard Wilson:

> "Our problem is not so much population growth, as it is population compaction," comments Wilson. "The Behr bill will turn off that neon arrow that has been sending people to live in Southern California.

"I think we are heading into a period of more natural, sensible growth. A time of greater responsibility in land development and environmental protection."

Wilson is especially scornful of business interests that built on the floodplains at the mouth of the Eel River. Those interests joined the water lobby in an effort to kill the Behr bill.

"Those fellows knew about the floods when they built there. But they went ahead anyway. They should not be able to have the taxpayer come running in every so often to save them from their own stupidity.

"People have to learn to take the consequences of their own actions. These guys want free enterprise without the risk. They want the government to cover their risks, but leave their profits alone. That is not free enterprise."

Wilson feels that politicians are beginning to find the courage to say "no" to powerful interest groups to which they once kowtowed. The enactment of the Behr bill may also mark the end of another era: the power of state Senator Randolph Collier (D-Yreka). Collier, who has been in the Senate since 1939, also authored a wild rivers bill. It was a ploy, an attempt to kill or weaken the Behr bill. The plot failed. The governor vetoed Collier's bill. Not many years ago the Collier measure would have sailed through the legislature and been signed by the governor—any governor. But those days are gone forever.

Given Walton's position in the administration, it must be significant that he says nothing about Reagan's role in saving the rivers or the valley. Walton was right to point out, by inference, that the governor, any governor, would have found it expedient to sign Behr's bill that year, because of the pro-environment context that Richard had done a good deal to stimulate.

Reagan's environmental effort peaked in the first two years of his governorship. Even Ike, who has always remained loyal, agrees that after 1970 Reagan lost interest. Ike's agenda for reform, which seemed so promising in 1969, did not fare well, and he stoically took blame that should not have belonged to him. By 1972 Reagan had moved far away from conservation to other political pastures that promised to nourish his presidential aspirations better, and his presidency, of course, is generally considered to have been an environmental disaster. Nevertheless, Reagan liked to assume the mantle of

"Savior of Round Valley" when it suited him, and Richard never begrudged him that title.

One day in August Richard came to the garden to tell Chadwick that Governor Reagan would be visiting to inspect, for the first time, the valley he had saved. To Chadwick, who was a supreme snob, this represented just the kind of challenge and opportunity he adored. His work and his vision would be on display before the highest authority in the state. He set about preparing for the event as though the queen herself were coming.

A special vegetable bed was created, on which one of his apprentices would demonstrate the laborious double-digging technique at the base of Chadwick's method. Another apprentice would be sowing flats, and another transplanting. Chadwick planned a twenty-minute tour of the garden to move the governor, with military precision, from one work station to another, culminating in a stroll down the *claire voyer* to the raspberry beds, where the two great men would commune in private.

The day dawned, much as all August days dawn in Round Valley, under a blue sky with the sun stealing over Dingman Ridge, striking the upper foliage of the oaks and then for a blessed hour or so bathing the valley in its first cool rays. Leaves and petals, still fresh and moist, bounced the light back with an intensity that gradually faded as the sun rose higher. By ten in the morning all the moisture was gone, and the sun struck hard through the surface into the hearts of things. The hills were burnished gold, the sun a pool of molten silver. The temperature was climbing to one hundred degrees and a heat haze rose from the tarmac when Reagan's twin-jet Cessna Citation landed.

Peter Behr had driven up from his home on the coast and was waiting, "cap in hand" as he says, by the runway with Richard and Ike Livermore. A school bus was at hand to transport journalists and members of Reagan's entourage. To Elmer Bauer's everlasting pride, his new car had been chosen to take Reagan around the valley. Behr thought the plane seemed too big for the short runway. He was afraid it would tip over on its nose trying to stop short of the hillside, but Reagan emerged unperturbed as always, in coat and tie, unprepared but also seemingly unaffected by the heat, which was becoming intense.

On the plane with Reagan were a number of his security men, who quickly went off to check out the various venues that had been planned for Reagan's tour. The itinerary included a lunch put on by Susan at the Wilson residence, and a meeting with all the town's notables at the Round Valley Inn. But the first and most elaborate event was the garden tour.

Steven Decater, one of Chadwick's original apprentices, remembers the blue-suited agents arriving and how incongruous they seemed to him in that context. The greatest threat to the governor's security was one that Alan Chadwick had discovered at the last moment. A hornet's nest was attached to a lintel above a place where Reagan would pass, and imagining all kinds of horrors he insisted on having it removed. Since insecticides were naturally forbidden, this was a delicate task to perform in daylight, and the bodyguards watched nervously from a distance.

Chadwick had prepared himself for the encounter with great care. He wore an immaculate blue, doubled-breasted suit jacket over a pair of pure white Bermuda shorts, blue socks, and shoes. It was, in effect, a tropical version of full-dress, appropriate for official ceremonies. Steven Decater was stationed in the garden workshop, where hand tools were maintained and equipment built, and when Reagan came through, followed by Peter Behr, Richard, and Ike, Steven's job was to demonstrate the equipment they used. Then Chadwick lectured them on his principles and philosophy, Steve shook Reagan's hand, and the party moved on.

He watched as Reagan and Chadwick separated themselves from the rest of the group, and the two men walked down the path toward the soft fruit beds. They were equally tall and distinguished in their different ways, two professional spellbinders at work. Chadwick was bristling with his sense of the importance of the occasion while Reagan, the accomplished performer, relaxed as he presented himself for the cameras. They stopped among the raspberries, as planned. From the shadowy interior of the workshop, Steve watched them through the shimmering heat, across the newly made beds. He could hear nothing of what they said. He just saw their movements and expressions, and he *knew* something then, something that became even clearer the more he thought about it later.

He captured a moment and froze it in his memory. Reagan with his hand to his chin, looking judicious. Chadwick with an arm flung wide in a grand gesture and a visionary gleam in his eye. It was a tableau: The Governor meets The Genius. But what Steve also saw and remembered was the sight of two old actors putting on a show, projecting their fantasies. "It was neat to see them together like that," he says, but it came as something of a shock to recall that these were the men who ruled his world.

Steven was not the only one to have difficulty distinguishing Reagan the actor from Reagan the politician and Reagan the statesman. The confusion was felt eventually across the world. Some suspected that having been an actor Reagan must be working to a script provided by others. Those who came close to him knew this was nonsense.

It is true, as Ike Livermore himself recalls, that Reagan scarcely ever put forward policy initiatives, preferring to leave that job to his chosen cabinet. However, his judgments were his own. They were based on certain strong beliefs, and his acting experience had taught him to present them with soap-opera simplicity.

He knew better than anyone the value of identifying the *feeling* that lay behind any message he had to deliver, and it was that feeling, be it optimism, defiance, resolution, concern, admiration, or heartfelt sympathy, that he was at pains to project. He knew that Americans vote not with their minds but their hearts, and he was proved right throughout his career. Only in retrospect did the minds become engaged.

Undoubtedly he employed the same talent in personal dealings with his subordinates. No governor or president ever inspired more loyalty in his staff and followers, and not a few were left stranded by his administrations to wonder how they had been persuaded to suspend their judgment in favor of the great communicator. It may be a necessary quality in any successful politician to inspire others to take the brunt of difficult and controversial policies while seeming to be detached from them. Reagan raised the art to a new level.

Already, in his management of the Dos Rios issue in 1969, Reagan was showing exceptional mastery of the technique. Both Ike and Bill Gianelli had the best of reasons for the stands they took, and any governor might have given both of them credit for a well-considered case. Reagan (with Ed Meese's assistance) went beyond that. He managed to give each the impression that his heart was with them. Even after the decision, Reagan left Gianelli believing that his hand had been forced. If Dos Rios was not exactly a blueprint for Iran-Contra, it was at least a sketchy outline of what was to come.

Victory has many fathers. Former Senators James Mills of San Diego and Al Rodda of Sacramento each felt that they had played the primary role in blocking the Dos Rios Dam. Probably the fish guys, Joe Paul and David Lennihan, could claim it as their triumph, too, if they were still alive, but most of those involved in the political processes of the time give Richard the lion's share of the credit. Richard himself, however, believes that the critical engagements of his battle were fought and won for him by a shadowy group of Republican éminences grises, and that the job was done far from the public eye in back rooms and across the polished veneer of elegant dining tables.

"There was a group of people, like Jack Hume, Grover Turnbow, the Mailliards, Palmer Fuller, Dean Witter, and others. They were older conservatives who *knew* California, and they could appreciate what was going to be lost if you went ahead with these projects. They were people you could talk to about this, and they made Reagan understand. I don't know how many dinners and receptions it took, but somewhere along the way he got the message."

The penalty for this victory of influence was a crucial delay in public awareness of the underlying issues. Richard wanted to confront the public with the concept that all natural resources must be given a value *before* they are extracted, and that this price must be paid to balance our account with the environment. He wanted at least to open a debate on whether the best measure of health in a society is how much it consumes. But Reagan used the "Indian question" to shelve Dos Rios, and water developers have clung to that explanation for decades. Being the politician he was, Reagan neither would nor could face up to the real issues in public. Ike's attempt to open up the subject dwindled for lack of support. The press, which failed so miserably to explore the issue at the outset also lost interest too soon.

The Indians of Round Valley had a good case, and Reagan's sympathy was certainly genuine. However, as an example of caring government it was lost among other policies Reagan espoused, such as the budget cuts that threw so many handicapped people on the streets. As a plank in an environmental platform it obviously carried no weight at all.

The wave of public opinion, stimulated by Richard and his associates, swept Reagan a good deal farther down the environmental stream than he had meant to go, and secured the protection of the rivers. Being the consummate politician that he was, he extracted what benefit he could from it, but "Environmentalists for Reagan" notwithstanding, conservation was not his thing. Conserving resources put too much of a crimp into the rosy scenario of boundless opportunity he liked to project.

By the time Ike and Reagan came to Covelo to celebrate its reprieve, all hopes of a brave new environmental policy had evaporated. Although Ike retains a fondness for Reagan the man, he was disillusioned by his policies. He did later agree to help the president-elect in his transition to the White House, but declined to take office under him again and was spared any association with Reagan's subsequent record.

Most of the prominent figures on the side of water development remained convinced that sooner or later the engineers would return to the north coast of California. Col. Frank Boerger, who retired from the army to a private consultancy in Marin County, was one. Virginia Brody recalls that she and her victorious allies used to describe their campaign as "The Battle of Boerger's Butt," and the Colonel was heard to concede that "they really thrashed us," but as a parting shot he promised that in thirty years' time the water guys would be back (however, he and Charlie Elmore would not be there to see it, and Curt Roberts would not be there to contest it; all three died prematurely in the eighties).

Bill Fairbank, also retired but still magisterial, says: "In my humble opinion, in the next twenty or thirty years you're going to have to do something on the north coast. Unless of course California changes track. That's the big question. What is going to happen to agriculture, to the subsidy program, to big farmers? What is going to happen to California's gift of food supplies, not just to the nation but to the world?"

Legislators, lobbyists, and corporate farmers echoed these warnings, and with such powerful interests still active, even California's Wild and Scenic Rivers Act didn't seem such a safe haven after all, but there was a federal equivalent, and a successful effort was made to have the Eel River federally protected. A significant figure in this campaign was Ronald Robie, who had been appointed to Bill Gianelli's old job as director of water resources by Reagan's successor, the much more environmentally friendly Governor Jerry Brown.

Robie has an interesting comment on the Dos Rios project that strips away some of the bureaucracy's camouflage.

"I talked to people at the department about it," he says. "I had a lot of close relationships with engineers who worked there, and they, to a person, agreed that the Dos Rios Dam was a real turkey. The department was pushed into a corner of defending dams because they were the agency that was *supposed* to defend dams. They thought if they ever let anybody kill a dam then they could never build any more.

"I became director at the time the moratorium on the Eel was running out. I consider the most important accomplishment of my term was getting the wild rivers into the federal system."

The pity of it, in Richard's view, is that it took so long for California to acknowledge its true circumstances. Only now, in the nineties, is California emerging from denial, to confront the fact that water cannot be developed regardless of other considerations but, like all resources, has to be valued and conserved. After a severe seven-year drought, the state has had to revise its attitude. Surplus water in wet years will now be banked, in groundwater basins and reservoirs. Federal legislation has been passed to permit farmers to sell their water rather than use it to grow unneeded or subsidized crops. The value of irrigated agriculture no longer goes unquestioned.

It must also be said that Richard, who was fully aware of the need for these changes a long time ago, sees the intervening twenty-five years as a period of wasted opportunity. So much wealth was squandered in unproductive ways. The great financial crisis that California struggles with today, trying to care for its citizens and resolve their conflicts, should have been foreseen. Those unearned increments that are gone forever could have restored the state's impoverished schools, plugged many a hole in the crumbling infrastructure, and above all, helped to resolve the racial conflict that has plagued her cities.

Much of California's early wealth and many of her problems derive from the refusal to treat immigrant labor and other minorities with dignity and consideration. They are now present in large numbers and are making their resentment felt in dramatic ways.

Jerry Barnum, establishment lawyer though he is, has always been appalled by the niggardly prejudice of white Californians against blacks and Latinos. Soon after the riots in Los Angeles, while Richard Riordan was still campaigning to be mayor, I met Barnum at the California Club, and we walked from Flower Street across Hope, Grand Avenue, Olive, Hill, and Broadway to Spring Street. Barnum's hair is all white now. His back is bent as the result of an old skiing accident (it was Dr. John Cree Wilson who operated on him), and we could move only at a slow shuffle.

When we arrived at the corner of Spring and Sixth, he waved his arm at the street and said: "Look at this." It was then that I realized what a change had occurred in those few blocks.

It was a strange and portentous sight. The buildings that had once housed all those brisk white lawyers were desolate, empty, and blind to the world. The Rowan Building, from which Barnum and Lippitt used to walk to the chamber of commerce meetings, was barred with chains and padlocks. The glass doors were partially shattered and boarded in, enlivened by graffiti over the grime. All along those blocks of Spring Street, where the movers and shakers of Los Angeles once operated within strolling distance of each other, only the sidewalks were busy. An incongruous immigrant life had embedded itself in the buildings at street level, carving up the once-elegant shop spaces into kiosk-size apertures, advertising brightly colored objects for small sums ending in ninety-nine. It was as though a new life-form had found refuge in the decaying carcass of an extinct species.

"I don't see how we'll ever be able to recover from this," he said, and there will not, of course, ever be recovery in the sense of things returning to the way they were. The frontier closed many decades ago, and the state has been living off its inventory. Now it must learn to survive on its wits, its labor, and, one hopes, on a more humane and social concept of statehood.

In 1909 Lord Bryce, the British ambassador to the United States, came to Berkeley, California to speak. He was a man of wide-ranging experience, who admired America and wrote extensively on it. About California, and echoing de Tocqueville, he had noted that "the most active minds are too much absorbed in great business enterprises to attend to politics."[1]

His own country, smaller and more heavily populated than California and already stripped of most of its resources, was then still the dominant world power. Against this background, he asked his audience: "What will happen when California is filled with fifty millions of people, and its valuation is five times what it is now, and the wealth will be so great that you will find it difficult to know what to do with it? [Then] the real question will be not about making more wealth or having more people, but whether the people will then be happier or better."

Much wealth has come and gone in the interim. More people and more wealth will undoubtedly come in the future. The real question, Bryce's question, remains to be answered. Britain, no longer Great in the old sense, became too dependent on the wealth of its empire, and has struggled painfully for decades to find a new source of greatness in its people. California, with the frontier closed, and its resources severely diminished, faces a similar dilemma. Wilson would say that California must learn to value its people and its environment above wealth; only then can they hope to be happier and better than they were.

31

Epilogue

I CAME TO ROUND VALLEY in 1980 looking for land, and met Peter Herman. One of his jobs was to operate the town dump, which in those days was still a pretty free and easy affair, the garbage crisis not yet having come to bury us. Another job he took quite seriously was that of "alternative" real estate agent. He knew who owned the land I was interested in. He knew who would sell and who would not, and he was savvy about avoiding problems with the county. He knew what day of the week *not* to be seen building because that was the day the inspector came by, what kinds of septic system to build that the county would never approve, and other such useful information.

At the time I had my eye on two pieces of land. One was a nice quarter section in the valley, and Pete told me who owned it. The other was a parcel in the hills above Covelo belonging to a woman named Betsy Belotti. She lived in San Francisco and I called to ask if she would come down on her price, but she said she had decided against selling because her land would become lakeside property when they flooded the valley. That was my first introduction to the Dos Rios Dam, and for a while it had me worried. I asked Pete about it and he said the person to talk to was Richard Wilson. So, that evening I found myself driving up to the same ranch house that Lou Cannon, Bob Simmons, and Gardner Brown had visited years before.

Richard told me that he thought the dam was no longer a possibility. The so-called moratorium on the Eel River was due to expire in 1984, but the Department of Water Resources had lost interest in Round Valley. In any event, there were moves to put the river under federal protection. Richard and I met frequently after that, and began a firm friendship. My baby son played with their youngest daughter, Sarah, a latecomer born only three years earlier. The Wilsons' hospitality, well recorded by so many, was undiminished. It was lavished on me and my family, and I learned quickly to love and respect them all.

Even if there could be such a thing as an objective account of a man and his work, this book would not be it. On the other hand, I have tried to remain open and aware of all aspects of Richard's character, as a true friend should, believing that a person's achievements are all the greater for being won in spite of those quirks of temperament and attitude that we all inherit.

During my first years in Round Valley it became obvious that the community was once again in decline. The energy crunch had bitten into the economy, inflation was at an all-time high, and more and more of those who were attracted to the valley in the flowering seventies were being forced out by financial necessity. The Garden Project, sadly, was no more. For five years Chadwick had driven his devotees to create something genuinely marvelous, but he personally became more autocratic, histrionic, and unpredictable with every passing year. Like many of his kind he was unable to foster leadership in those around him, and when he fell ill and had to leave, none of his apprentices could find the moral authority to take his place.

In the hills the communes shriveled and died, and only marijuana growers did well in their weird, paranoid subculture. The lighthearted enterprises, more characteristic of the Berkeley campus than of a cow and timber town, closed down one by one. The Wild River Cafe was no longer wild. The door of Tom Lawrence's Epicycle repair business was always locked. The alternative school at the "hippie" land trust had to close. The bright lights that had been lit in those optimistic years to project an image of a different kind of rural community were gradually extinguished. As the dream faded, Round Valley was revealed with all its old prejudice and belligerence intact.

But not everything was the same. Robertson's Yolla Bolly Press persisted, survived lean times, flourished in others, with a fine body of work that drew on the natural beauty of its setting. Yet another press was established, an environmental publishing house called Island Press. Although it was the offshoot of an even more adventurous plan that eventually failed, the press continued to profit and expand. And though the old mill still stands empty and forlorn, a permanent site has been built alongside it for an annual blackberry festival that the valley's residents have embraced. Today a circle of redwood stands surrounds a small roofed stage where bands play and fiddlers contest for prizes every August.

With the dying of the Garden Project, Richard largely withdrew from the prominent position he had played in the valley. Instead he made his efforts where they seemed to bring a more lasting result. He was on the Coastal Commission for seven years, one of only two commissioners who could be depended upon to oppose developers. His miserable experience with the Louisiana-Pacific Corporation made him a sworn enemy of its chairman, Harry Merlo whom he accuses of a "cut-and-run" lumber policy that has stripped Mendocino County of a major sustainable resource. He was able to prevent the construction of logging roads that might have ruined large areas of national forest, and spent several more years as a member of the Forestry Commission.

Nevertheless, radical environmentalists now disparage his record and claim that he is not doing nearly enough; that the gentlemanly approach of men like Richard and Ike is too feeble and compromised to meet the challenge. Indeed, the influence that Richard wielded at the time of Dos Rios is not available today. The old conservative establishment that worked its magic on Reagan has dispersed and died, and today's government responds to the harsher demands of the aerospace, agriculture, and timber industries all in decline.

Despite all Richard's efforts, the Eel River has suffered. Salmon and steelhead runs have dropped to a small fraction of what they were even ten years ago. Overfishing in the Pacific is blamed for some of the losses, but few doubt that indiscriminate logging on the Eel watershed is a major factor. The devastation that Dan De Quille portrayed in the Sierras 130 years ago has its counterpart today on the Mendocino Coast Range, with similar consequences for the rivers. That resource-hungry machine Angus Grant helped to drive west still has momentum.

Richard never gave up his belief in a watershed-based economy, and for a while his ideas were hotly discussed in the county, but that, too, faded as economic adversity focused people's attention more on personal survival. Always this social fragmentation, this failure of people to see themselves as part of a social organism, the very thing Richard's ideas were planned to promote, was what brought those ideas down.

Perhaps there has never been a time when people would willingly embrace the kind of society Richard has in mind. It is essentially a society rooted in frugal virtues. "Use it up, wear it out, make it do, or do without," are his watchwords. People, it is well known, thrive on adversity but rarely choose it. When viewing the rural past through rose-colored spectacles, we may forget that life on the land has always been a battle with adversity. Rewarding, certainly. Character building, undoubtedly. Easy, never. Given no choice but self-sufficiency, many might rise to the occasion and fulfill themselves marvelously. Given the choices that America's consumer-oriented culture offers every moment of the day, through one medium or another, very few have the vision and tenacity to see it through.

To some in Round Valley Richard has always been and always will be a hero. To others, who were either offended by his initiatives or disillusioned by their collapse, he remains a troublemaker, a dilettante, an "inheritance prince" with delusions of grandeur. There was a time in the early eighties when he thought seriously of moving his entire cattle operation to some other state, where ranching was easier and where he and his family would not have to carry such a burden of notoriety. The thick vein of resentment that has run through Round Valley society since the days of George White is still an important feature of the community, and it was heaped on the Wilsons in plenty.

It took a tragedy to soften its effect. In April of 1984, people gathered at the blackberry festival site for a different kind of event, a memorial service for Richard's elder son, Alex. He was killed at age twenty-three, riding a bull at a rodeo, a sport at which he exceled, and the entire valley put its passions and prejudices aside to sympathize.

Alex was buried on consecrated ground at Buck Mountain, and all thoughts of moving away stopped there. Seven years later, after trying to ignore an aching back, Susan was diagnosed with a swift and terrible cancer and within months she had joined her son in the mountain graveyard. With Susan gone and nobody to care for her house and garden, Richard lost his attachment to the valley. Her absence opened a great chasm in his life, and in an attempt to fill it he took a step he had previously resisted and became part of the state's political life, by assisting Governor Pete Wilson in the transition of his Resources agency from the Deukmejian administration.

In the valley itself other saviors with different ideas come and go, their efforts usually dissipated by those same old divisive tendencies. A Belgian baron had his brief period of fame and glory before retreating in defeat. A retired realtor has bought a large chunk of property to breed pedigree bulls, but has yet to show signs of incipient evangelism. Another exotic arrival with more public ambition is Roland Hoehne, a Bavarian industrialist. He fell under the spell of the valley a few years ago, when he first bought a vacation home on the hillside. Before long he had staked a large amount of his own money on the future of Round Valley. His contribution, an elaborate workshop and office complex, rears up on the edge of Covelo, among the cows and hayfields. In early 1994 his own highly specialized engineering business was still the only occupant, but on the "build it and they will come" principle, he puffed serenely on his pipe and waited, as so many of us have waited for so long.

In Sacramento it seemed, at first, that Richard might follow in Ike's footsteps as California's resources secretary under Governor Wilson (who is no relation). Instead he became director of the California Department of Forestry, and as much an object of suspicion and abuse as he ever was in Round Valley. Once again he has put himself at the heart of an almost insoluble problem and, given California's dire budget crisis, has little money to spend on it.

Environmentalists and timber companies alike are angered by his apparent inaction, but as always he refuses to defend himself or his reputation. Only once, in all the years I have known him, has he ever deliberately asserted a personal achievement. During the years of Reagan's presidency he watched with increasing dismay as society tore itself and its values apart in the much romanticized feeding frenzy of the eighties. To Richard junk bonds and leveraged buyouts were the theft of the unearned increment taken to extremes; and the deficit, which stood then at $3 trillion, was the visible measure of the nation's ability to deceive itself. The problem hit close to home when the financier Charles Hurwitz took over and stripped the assets off Pacific Lumber, one of the last major lumber companies on the West Coast with a reasonable attitude toward timber harvesting.

One dark winter evening Richard roared up to my front door with a steak and a bottle of wine, as was his custom, leaving deep tire marks in a newly seeded lawn. Disgusted with what was going on in the forests of the West Coast, I reproached my forestry commissioner friend for letting it happen.

"Jesus, Ted," he cried. "I stopped them from taking all our rivers. What more do you want?"

He has, of course, given more, and continues to do so. Frustrating and underappreciated as his efforts in Sacramento have been, he believes that the consequences of his quiet reorganization there will eventually surprise his radical critics. Now near the end of his first term as CDF director, and uncertain whether Pete Wilson's administration will survive the election, his thoughts return more frequently to the Eel watershed. Using all the clout he can command, he is mounting an effort to restore the watershed after decades of abuse, to give the salmon a chance to recover, and to give Round Valley some hope of a viable, agricultural economy in the future. The timber has gone. Ranching can never support more than a few families. For Richard the real problem of Round Valley has always been the body count, the critical number of people you must have to make a remote community flourish. What will bring these urban refugees to Covelo is still anyone's guess. Will it be Hoehne's dream of small, high-tech businesses, computer connected to the outside world; or Richard's hopes for watershed-based, resource-related activities?

They must come soon to vindicate the faith and vision that Richard Wilson, above all others, mustered to save this glorious valley for posterity. The water guys are waiting.

Elmer Bauer: "I'll tell you something about Richard. If he's your friend he'll stand by you. I think that of him."

Ida Soares: "We thank God for Richard. He was our door. He opened the door. This is what the Indian respect of him. He led the way. The writing in *The Sacramento Bee* on the first trip we made said: 'Richard Wilson and his Indians made their appearance in the state capitol today.' "

Lou Cannon: "Covelo farmer Richard Wilson spent a few thousand dollars and enlisted the aid of a handful of Indians, conservationists, journalists and farmers. . . .

"On paper the outcome was pre-determined. The unwillingness

of Richard Wilson to concede this, and the integrity and concern of Ike Livermore, a resource administrator whose own resources are largely inner ones, brought about a different result than anyone had anticipated.

"The voice of the people can still be heard when people take the trouble to speak out" (*San Jose Mercury-News,* May 13, 1969).

Ike Livermore: "They'd say: 'Stick to the facts.' I'd say: 'Look, emotion is a fact. The solitude of the wilderness, the beauty of a flower—those are facts.' "

Does the Water Story Ever End? An Afterword

Robert Gottlieb and Ruth Langridge

MORE THAN thirty years have passed since that fateful cabinet meeting in 1969 when Ronald Reagan made a decision that interrupted the plans to build the Dos Rios dam at Round Valley. The water industry, that once powerful coalition of private interests and public agencies, suffered a devastating defeat at Round Valley, all the more surprising given the industry's significant clout during that period.

But has water politics really changed since the defeat of Dos Rios? Can the water industry still flex its muscles as effectively as it did between 1940 and 1970 when it successfully promoted massive water projects? Is there even a coherent coalition of water interests today advocating the construction of more large dams? And what new groups have formed to challenge this once powerful lobby and its vision that if you build it, they will come, and if they come, you just build again?

In the ten years that followed the Dos Rios battle, the nature and direction of water policy remained uncertain. The water industry in the Central Valley and Southern California still coveted the north coast rivers. However, during the 1970s, a more expansive environmental movement succeeded in promoting federal laws and regulations that provided new tools to safeguard rivers and estuaries throughout the west. For the first time, environmental protection was defined as a legitimate goal of water policy. But despite these constraints, the water industry continued to seek out and lobby for additional imported water supplies.

The next big battle to erupt was over the fate of the Sacramento Bay Delta. Once a vast tidal marshland largely covered by tules, a series of changes to the land had degraded the Delta's ecosystem and transformed it into a water development way station. Beginning in the 1940s, first the Central Valley Project and subsequently the State Water Project began to channel huge quantities of water from the Sacramento River southward through the Delta, leaving even less water remaining to support fish and wildlife. By the 1970s, the Delta had become the key to a transportation bottleneck hindering water development. The question was whether it would be unblocked to permit more northern water to flow south, or whether there would be a paradigm shift in water policy, as suggested by the Dos Rios episode.

The fate of the North Coast rivers, including the Eel, thus became intertwined with the battles over the Delta, most notably in relation to the water industry's campaign for a Peripheral Canal. This facility, already proposed at the time of the Dos Rios battle, had become the water industry's solution to transporting water around the degraded Delta to the large irrigating farms on the west side of the Central Valley and the urban regions of southern California. The Peripheral Canal, proclaimed Earle Blais, Metropolitan Water District's chairman at the time, was nothing less than "the final solution." Indeed, it appeared that the water industry's objectives had remained the same as during the Round Valley struggle: promote water development to stimulate new growth to insure new water development. The only difference was that now a few environmental measures had to be thrown in. However, despite being dressed up with fish ladders and screens and assurances that North Coast rivers were not the target of such a facility, the Peripheral Canal went down to defeat in a 1982 referendum. The opposition was led by an alliance of northern California communities, Delta-based agricultural interests, statewide environmental groups, and a budding movement focused on growth issues in southern California. The forces arrayed against the Peripheral Canal had become more complex and varied in their goals than in the Round Valley situation, and despite significant lobbying the water industry received a stunning defeat. The failure to pass the Peripheral Canal provided a second crucial turning point in California water politics.

Throughout the next ten years, the Delta remained center stage, becoming the focus of a drawn out process by the State Water Resources Control Board to establish a balance between water quality and the effects of diversions and water transport. This culminated in yet another jarring event for the water industry, the 1986 Racanelli decision, where the courts established a more extensive public stake in water decisions and required the Board to consider "all competing demands for water." This decision, coming on the heels of another critical court decision, *National Audubon Society v. Superior Court of California,* seemed to serve notice that a *status quo ante* in water policy was no longer possible. In Audubon, the court held that the long-standing diversion of water from the tributaries of Mono Lake to supply the City of Los Angeles needed to be reevaluated, taking the public trust into account. And the public trust provided a powerful new impulse in water law, challenging the cycle of water development and growth and essentially providing a more formal role for the environment in water decisions.

In apparent recognition that new players now had a seat at the table, in the early 1990s a Three-Way negotiation process was initiated to resolve California's ongoing water wars. Included were the agriculture interests (primarily the large irrigation districts), urban interests (primarily the development-oriented water agencies), and environmental interests (primarily Northern California-based and focused on Sacramento Bay Delta issues). By granting environmentalists a seat at the table, water industry players finally seemed to acknowledge that the rules of the game and the parameters for negotiation had changed. Protecting the fish and the environment of the Bay and the Delta were reluctantly acknowledged. But how much protection? And was anyone missing from the table?

The Three-Way process never got very far. After Pete Wilson was elected Governor in 1990 some of the agricultural interests pulled out, fearful of the changing climate concerning water development and hoping they could maneuver better with the new Governor. But Wilson couldn't budge the process either, and a stalemate set in. Other voices emerged as well, contributing to the deadlock. Agriculture, for one, was not a monolith. Small irrigation districts and family farm advocates challenged the notion that the big irrigation districts (like the Westlands Water District, now represented by that one-time Round Valley nemesis, Jerald Butchert) should speak on behalf of all farmers. Nor were the big urban water districts, like MWD, without their own critics, including a new generation of "smart growth" advocates and more environmentally-oriented elected water officials who established their own association (Public Officials for Water and Environmental Reform or POWER). Even the environmental movement had become complex, as a new form of advocacy, environmental justice, identified and worked for solutions to the environmental needs of inner city communities.

These developments set the stage for another round of negotiating initiatives in the early 1990s. The catalysts were two pieces of federal legislation. In 1992, the Central Valley Improvement Act required the Bureau of Reclamation to release 800,000 acre-feet of Central Valley Project water each year to protect the valley's rivers and the Delta's fisheries. When several species of fish in the Delta were listed as threatened under the Endangered Species Act, the US Fish and Wildlife Service proposed the entire Delta as critical habitat, and a "Club Fed" of various federal agencies threatened to impose a water quality plan on the whole region unless agreement could be reached on how to protect the fish. This galvanized urban and agricultural water suppliers dependent on Delta exports. Fading quickly were the dreams of building big new water projects; now it was a matter of maintaining an existing supply of northern water. The listings spurred new negotiations that eventually included the environmental community, and in 1994 a Bay-Delta Accord was signed by state and federal government agencies. The Statement of Principles represented the first time that the three big interest groups had come together on an agreement that included the goals of balancing environmental protection with assurances for reliable supply. A year later, a new negotiating or collaborative process, called CALFED, was formed. Composed of 14 federal and state agencies, and many, though not all, of the interest groups, CALFED's mission was to solve the new dual objective of protecting the environment and improving water supply reliability. Could two such potentially conflicting goals result in an enduring coalition, or would the water industry attempt, and be able once again, to flex its muscles?

By 2000, after five years of negotiations, the CALFED participants reached an agreement that included both new storage and greater environmental protection. The agreement also specified that an "isolated conveyance facility," the scaled-down version of the original Peripheral Canal, would not be built, but instead suggested that a "through-Delta" solution needed to be explored. While some of the interest groups voiced cautious optimism, the consensus was still fragile, and the California Farm Bureau and the Regional Council of Rural Counties eventually decided to sue to stop the agreement. However the times had changed; it was clear that the water industry was no longer a monolith, that new forms of more participatory decision-making were being explored, and that the environmentalists had established a significant voice in the political process. But had a true paradigm shift in water policy occurred?

As the new century begins, it is obvious that the story hasn't ended and, given the extent to which water politics is embedded in deeper issues of land use and development, it is unlikely to be resolved in the near term. While some of the debates never seem to change, like how to fix the Delta, others do. Take MWD, the water industry behemoth to the South. In 1999, a new Latino leadership assumed power at the MET through the selection of a new general manager. This decision by a still largely conservative board of directors was partly in recognition of the changing political and demographic landscape of Southern California and the role of some elected Latino officials in challenging MWD's traditional methods of operation. For the first time one could hear talk at MWD headquarters of such unlikely ideas as environmental justice and watershed management rather than simply the pursuit of the traditional agenda of development. Yet MWD was still in the water and growth business, given its desire at least to construct additional and expensive infrastructure to bring the water to the high growth/limited water supply areas at the urban edge.

Even more compelling is the development of an emerging coalition in southern California of groups and advocates championing the cause of the Los Angeles River as a community and ecological asset. This advocacy contrasts with the L.A. River's historical transformation into a concrete flood control "freeway," an anti-environment cutting through the heart of the urban region. "Re-envisioning the

Los Angeles River" is becoming as strong a place-based ethic in the heart of urban southern California as any of the other water struggles of the last three decades.

Within agriculture new voices, such as the California Alliance with Family Farmers, are identifying the importance of a connection to the land and the idea of stewardship and sustainability, rather than the conventional focus on profitability, as the measure of farming. Water use and availability are figuring prominently in this new equation. Farmers are beginning to approach the question of what to grow, how they view their land, and ultimately their commitment to continue farming itself, as a sustaining activity rather than simply as a commodity-driven business.

And within the environmental movement, the commitment to issues of justice is being broadened to consider issues of place. It is not only environments that need to be valued, but communities and cultures. This concern about what Charles Wilkinson has called an "ethic of place," could be seen in the original battle to save Round Valley, described so eloquently by Ted Simon. The efforts by Richard Wilson, the Round Valley Tribes and others in the community to stop a dam that would destroy their homes identified this commitment to place and the values attached to it. The fear of displacement that led to saving Round Valley affirmed the meaning and importance of a community's cultural roots and history.

The struggle over Dos Rios also became a turning point for the Eel River. In the early 1970s, the lower Eel was given significant protection against further development through the state and federal Wild and Scenic Rivers Acts. But yet another battle, this time for protection of the upper Eel River, was just beginning. In the early part of the twentieth century two dams were constructed on the upper Eel River. Water stored behind those dams was diverted through a tunnel into a powerhouse in the farming community of Potter Valley, and then into the Russian River. Known as the Potter Valley Hydropower Project, the facility created an interbasin diversion that contributed to the gradual degradation of the main stem of the Eel and its once renowned fisheries. When the power project came up for relicensing by the Federal Energy Regulatory Commission in 1972, new environmental legislation required consideration of the declining fishery. Following the defeat of Dos Rios, communities on the Eel River, the Round Valley Tribes, environmental organizations and government agency staff increased their efforts to restore the upper Eel River and its fisheries. Russian River water interests who had promoted the continuation of the diversion to support local growth, faced a new challenge. And for the first time, decommissioning the two dams became a possibility. This battle, even more protracted than the Dos Rios story, has continued for nearly three decades. And while this water story has not ended, changes have taken place. It now appears likely that less water will be diverted from the Eel River in the future, that the goal of restoring the fisheries in both the Eel and Russian rivers will remain high on any future agenda, and that a regional dialogue on water policy will be seen as necessary.

And the water story still goes on. A few years ago one of us received, unsolicited, a poster from Walter Hickel, former Secretary of Interior and Governor of Alaska. The poster was promoting yet another Alaska-to-California water scheme; this one called the "Alaska-California Sub-Oceanic Fresh Water Transport System." Similar to such proposals as shipping an iceberg from Alaska to the port at San Pedro, this one sought to demonstrate, through a series of drawings, how a 2000-mile aqueduct could transport "pure Alaskan water from the abundant rivers of Southeastern Alaska to the arid Southwestern United States." Under the drawings was the following text: "Big projects define a civilization. So why war—why not big projects?"

For much of the twentieth century, the water industry has tried to think big thoughts and enact big projects. Those that were built became far more controversial and problematic than their masterbuilders and water industry advocates had anticipated. With the defeat at Round Valley, and the subsequent history of water policy in California and the West, the dreams about mega-water projects fueling an unending cycle of growth and development have faded. That is the big change. But the water story hasn't ended. Communities throughout California are still tackling the relationship between water and growth. While we have come to recognize that people who live on river systems like the Eel, and even the Los Angeles River, are intimately tied to them in their culture and everyday life, the future of these watersheds remains open-ended. But by protecting and nurturing these watersheds, we can strengthen our capacity to reconnect with our places and identify with what Helen Ingram has called the "community" value of the water in nearby and distant parts. The lesson of Round Valley is that, perhaps in the decades to come, an ending of the water story will still be found.

Robert Gottlieb
Los Angeles
Ruth Langridge
Berkeley
October 2000

Source Notes

1. In the Wake of the Flood

[1]The army engineers recorded a flow of 4.5 million acre-feet: See Corps Interim Report on Dos Rios, p. 29. Cotton irrigation figures are for 1972, and come from *The California Water Atlas,* p. 84. For a good general account of the distribution and uses of water in California, this excellent and entertaining work, published by the state under the aegis of Governor Jerry Brown, is unbeatable.

3. "Oh Shame, Shame! Where Is Thy Blush . . . ?"

[1]*History of Mendocino County, California,* by Lyman Palmer, San Francisco, 1880. Reprinted in Fort Bragg by the Mendocino Historical Society in 1967, and quoted in *Genocide and Vendetta.*

[2]*Genocide and Vendetta,* by Estle Beard and Lynwood Carranco (Norman: University of Oklahoma, 1981). Much of the information in this chapter is drawn from this valuable source, now hard to find. See acknowledgments. The rest comes from conversation with inhabitants and from oral histories such as *Mendocino County Remembered,* a two-volume work edited by Bruce Levene and published in Fort Bragg by the Mendocino Historical Society in 1976.

[3]*Genocide and Vendetta,* p. 221.

4. "As Far as I'm Concerned, They Can Have It."

[1]Interviewed by the author in 1992. See also Oral History Program, Bancroft Library, University of California, Berkeley.

[2]See Eel River Investigations carried out by the Bechtel Corporation in 1959 for the Metropolitan Water district of Southern California, which details five combinations of eleven different dams.

6. Timber, Gold, and the Railroad

[1]*Virginia & Truckee,* by Lucius Beebe and Charles Clegg, Berkeley, 1963.

[2]Ibid.

[3]Pseudonym for William Wright. See *The Big Bonanza,* reprinted 1947 (New York: Alfred A. Knopf).

[4]*Virgin Lands,* by Henry Nash Smith (Boston: Harvard University Press, 1950), p. 187.

[5]*The Spectacular San Franciscans,* by Julia Altrocchi (New York: Dutton, 1949).

[6]William Smythe. See *Rivers of Empire,* by Donald Worster (New York: Pantheon, 1985), p. 104.

[7]*Our Land and Land Policy, National and State,* by Henry George, San Francisco, 1871.

[8]*Rivers of Empire,* pp. 171–172.

7. "They Have Stolen the Unearned Increment."

[1]*California: Land of New Beginnings,* by David Lavender (New York: Harper & Row, 1972), pp. 13 ff.

[2]The story was retold by James R. Page in a memorial to Van Nuys, published privately in Los Angeles in 1944 and printed by the Ward Ritchie Press.

[3]*Water & Power,* by William Kahrl (Berkeley: University of California Press, 1982).

[4]Ibid., p. 443.

8. Strange Fruit

[1]This paeon of praise is quoted in a biography of Sartori by George M. Wallace, published by Security–First National Bank of Los Angeles, 1982.

[2]*Water Atlas,* p. 46.

[3]*Factories in the Fields,* by Carey McWilliams, Santa Barbara, 1971.

[4]As told in a letter from Allan Balch to Preston Hotchkis, and published privately in 1958 to commemorate fifty years of the camp. "In the campaign [for the presidency, 1911] between Hughes and Wilson, Hughes made a

speaking tour around the country, coming into California from the north and speaking in San Francisco and Los Angeles. Will Crocker was the chairman of the Republican State Committee. Hughes wired Will Crocker to know how he should treat [Governor Hiram] Johnson. Crocker asked Nicholas Murray Butler and Fred Henshaw to discuss the matter with him and prepare a telegram to Hughes. Fred Henshaw hated Johnson, and those of you who knew him there remember that he had a strong character. He influenced Crocker, with Butler's approval, to send a telegram to Hughes to ignore Johnson. . . . Naturally, Johnson was furious and turned all the votes he could against Hughes. The result in California was that the majority for Wilson was about one thousand. California was the pivotal state and as a result of this telegram and its influence on Hughes, Hughes was defeated and Wilson elected President, with all that followed."

9. Another Country

[1]*New York Times,* November 20, 1966.

14. How the Corps Lost Its Innocence

[1]For a more complete account see *Cadillac Desert,* by Marc Reisner (New York: Viking, 1986).

[2]Speaking to Eel River Association in Willits, July 1972.

[3]Speaking at "Timber Trading '85" in London, March 5, 1985.

20. Leading Ike to the Water

[1]With John N. Sutthoff in 1976—"The Dos Rios Project," a research paper.

[2]*San Francisco Chronicle,* May 19, 1968.

21. Spring in Round Valley

[1]*High Dam in the Valley of the Tall Grass,* summer 1968.

25. "Let Me Tell You About Those Fish Guys"

[1]Interviewed in December 1990.

26. Famous Amos and the Doody Report

[1]Most of the material surrounding the discovery of the Doody Report is based on correspondence, transcripts of telephone conversations, and copies of reports retained by Richard Wilson in the files of SERA.

30. The Aftermath

[1]Lord Bryce, *American Commonwealth* (New York: Macmillan, 1913).

Bibliography

Adams, David Wallace. "The Deep Meaning of Native American Schooling." *Harvard Educational Review,* vol. 58, no. 1 (February 1988).

Andrews, Ralph W. *Glory Days of Logging.* Seattle: Bonanza Books, 1956.

Bain, J.; R. Craven; and J. Margolis. *Northern California's Water Industry.* Baltimore: The Johns Hopkins Press, 1966.

Bald, F. Clever. *Michigan in Four Centuries.* New York: Harper & Row, 1954.

Beard, Estle, and Lynwood Carranco. *Genocide and Vendetta.* Norman, Okla.: University of Oklahoma Press, 1981.

Bowers, Claude. *Jefferson and Hamilton.* Boston: Houghton Mifflin, 1925.

Boyle, Robert H., John Graves, and T. H. Watkins. *The Water Hustlers.* San Francisco: Sierra Club, 1971.

Cleland, Robert Glass. *The Cattle on a Thousand Hills.* San Marino, Calif.: Huntington Library, 1951.

Clover, S. T. *Constructive Californians.* Los Angeles: Saturday Night Publishing Company, 1926.

Coleberd, Frances. *Hidden Country Villages of California.* San Francisco: Chronicle Books, 1977.

Cooper, E. *Aqueduct Empire.* Glendale, California: The Arthur H. Clark Co., 1968.

De Voto, Bernard. *The Course of Empire.* New York: Houghton Mifflin, 1852.

DiLeo, Michael, and Eleanor Smith. *Two Californias.* Covelo, Calif.: Island Press, 1983.

Downey, Sheridan. *They Would Rule the Valley.* San Francisco, 1947.

Dumbrille, Dorothy. *Up and Down the Glens: The Story of Glengarry.* Toronto: Ryerson Press, 1954.

Earle, Alice Morse. *Home Life in Colonial Days.* New York: Jonathan David, 1975.

Fradkin, Philip L. *A River No More.* Updated edition, Berkeley: University of California Press, 1996.

Goldsmith, Edward, and Nicholas Hildyard. *The Social and Environmental Effects of Large Dams.* San Francisco: Sierra Club, 1984.

Gottlieb, Robert, and Irene Wolt. *Thinking Big: The Story of the* Los Angeles Times, *Its Publishers, and Their Influence on Southern California.* New York: G.P. Putnam's Sons, 1977.

Hawke, David. *The Colonial Experience.* Indianapolis: Bobbs-Merrill, 1966.

Hill, Gladwin. *Dancing Bear.* Cleveland: World Publishing Co., 1968.

Holiday, J. S. *The World Rushed In.* New York: Simon & Schuster, 1981.

Hotchkis, Preston. *The Lost Angels.* Los Angeles: Ward Ritchie, 1958.

Hundley, Norris. *The Great Thirst.* Berkeley: University of California Press, 1992.

Johnson, Paul. *Birth of the Modern.* New York: HarperCollins, 1991.

Kahrl, William, ed. *The California Water Atlas.* Sacramento: State of California, 1972.

———. *Water & Power.* Berkeley: University of California Press, 1982.

Lavender, David. *California: Land of New Beginnings.* New York: Harper & Row, 1972.

———. *The Great Persuader.* New York: Doubleday, 1969.

Levene, Bruce. *Mendocino County Remembered: An Oral History.* Ukiah, Calif.: Mendocino County Historical Society, 1980.

Mantoux, Paul. *The Industrial Revolution in the 18th Century.* New York: Harper & Row, 1965.

Marx, Leo. *The Machine in the Garden.* New York: Oxford University Press, 1964.

McWilliams, Carey. *Factories in the Field.* Boston: Little Brown, 1939.

Nadeau, Remi A. *The Water Seekers.* Bishop, Calif.: Chalfant Press, 1950.

Page, James R. *I. N. Van Nuys.* Los Angeles: Ward Ritchie, 1944.

Phillips, Herbert L. *Big Wayward Girl.* New York: Doubleday, 1968.

Reisner, Marc. *Cadillac Desert.* New York: Viking, 1986.

Samish, Arthur, and Bob Thomas. *The Life and High Times of Arthur Samish.* New York: Crown, 1971.

Smith, Henry Nash. *Virgin Lands.* Boston: Harvard University Press, 1950.

Strauss, William, and Neil Howe. *Generations.* New York: Morrow, 1991.

Steinbeck, John. *The Grapes of Wrath.* New York: Viking, 1939.

———. *In Dubious Battle.* New York: Penguin Books, 1979.

Stone, Norman ed. *The Times Atlas of World History.* London: Times Books, 1989.

Tocqueville, Alexis de. *Democracy in America.* New York: Alfred A. Knopf, 1980.

Treadwell, Edward. *The Cattle King.* Santa Cruz, Calif.: Western Tanager Press, 1981.

Turner, E. S. *Roads to Ruin.* London: Michael Joseph, 1950.

Van Dyke, John C. *The Desert.* Tucson: University of Arizona Press, 1980.
Wallace, George M. *Joseph Francis Sartori.* Los Angeles: First National Bank of Los Angeles, 1982.
Worster, Donald. *Rivers of Empire.* New York: Pantheon, 1985.
Weinberg, Albert K. *Manifest Destiny.* Baltimore: The Johns Hopkins Press, 1935.
Wright, Esmond. *Fabric of Freedom.* New York: Hill and Wang, 1961.

Documents

California Legislature

Joint Legislative Committee on Water Resources, Acreage Limitation Hearings, Bradford S. Crittenden, Chairman, 1947
Senate Fact-Finding Committee on Water: Sacramento Hearing, Joseph Jensen's testimony, October 8–9, 1959
California Senate Committee on Water Resources, The Dos Rios Project, Sacramento: California Senate, Gordon Cologne, Chairman, 1969
California Assembly Committee on Water Resources, the Dos Rios Project: California Assembly, Carly Porter, Chairman, 1969

Department of Public Works

Division of Engineering and Irrigation, Bulletin #9, Supplementary Report on Water Resources of California, by Paul Bailey, 1925

U.S. Army Corps of Engineers

Hagwood Jr., Joseph Jeremiah, *Engineers at the Golden Gate,* (San Francisco: U.S. Army, 1981)
Water Resources Development, 1963
Transmittal Letter, Eel River, to House of Representatives, 1965
Supplementary Data on Dos Rios Dam Project, October 1968
Interim Report on Water Resources Development for Middle Fork Eel River, 1967
Flood Plain Information, South Fork Eel River, 1968 and 1969

Department of Water Resources

Bulletin No. 3, The California Water Plan, 1957
The 132 series of bulletins on the California Water Project
Bulletin No. 136, North Coastal Area Investigation, 1964
The 160 series of bulletins on Implementation of the California Water Plan
Bulletin No. 171 Upper Eel River Development, 1967
Bulletin No. 173, South Fork Eel River Study, 1968
Office Report, Alternative Plans for Development of the Lower Trinity and Klamath Rivers, 1967
"Memorandum Report: Present and Future Water Supply and Demand in the South Coastal Area," mimeographed, Southern District [The "Doody Report"]

Bechtel Corporation
Final Report on Eel River Investigations, 1959

Bureau of Reclamation
English Ridge Unit, 1969
Round Valley Unit, 1964
Eel River Division, North Coast Project, 1964
Northwestern California Plan, preview, 1965

Acknowledgments

My story of the events surrounding the controversial Dos Rios Dam, while based in part on reports in the press and on official documents, depends most heavily on interviews with surviving protagonists. To these patient people, many of whom I have pestered mercilessly, I offer my sincere gratitude. Richard Wilson himself, who must many times have wished the book had never been conceived, has been unfailingly helpful even when he could not know whether my efforts would reflect credit on him or not. Ike Livermore, likewise, has been most kind, courteous, and forthcoming, and access to his files was an invaluable resource. To William Gianelli I am deeply indebted for his spirited presentation of his own point of view, and my thanks go also to the fifty or more engineers, legislators, conservationists, and others who have helped to point me in what I hope was the right direction.

For historical background I have had to rely heavily on the previously published work of reporters and scholars. Most immediately fruitful were Donald Worsters's *Rivers of Empire,* Marc Reisner's *Cadillac Desert,* William Kahrl's *Water and Power,* Leo Marx's *The Machine in the Garden* and Carey McWilliams's classic *Factories in the Field*—all wonderful books to read and to learn from. For background on Angus Grant's origins I must thank my friend Heather Chisholm Chait, whose family happens to spring from the same corner of Ontario and who shared with me a journal of a pioneer ancestor. For the wild history of Mendocino County I turned most often to the pages of *Genocide and Vendetta.*

Writing this book has been as much a labor of duty as of love, and it will, I hope, go some way to repaying the debt of gratitude I feel to this hospitable country. There are many individuals I should thank for the help they gave and the tolerance they have shown over the years, and I can only mention a few. Chief among them are Virginia Sharkey, for shedding some brilliant light on the story at a dark period, and my son, William, who has lived half his life in the shadow of this "work in progress." I am grateful also to Norma Schlesinger and Eric Hansen for their help and encouragement, and to Professor Gardner Brown, of the University of Washington, for looking through the manuscript.

In my experience it is never possible to anticipate how people will receive words published about them. I can only say that I have no feelings of animosity toward any person named in this book, and for those I have been privileged to meet, regardless of their points of view, I have only goodwill and respect. Undoubtedly there were some whose part in these important events I have failed to record. To them I offer my apologies.

One last note: Generally these days it is usual to employ the term *Native American* as a mark of respect to the indigenous peoples of this continent. However, those described and quoted in these pages, including Native Americans themselves, invariably refer to *Indians,* and it would ring false for me to do otherwise. I hope it is clear that no prejudice is felt or intended.

Index

ABOUT THE AUTHOR

TED SIMON has a background in science and engineering, daily paper journalism, music, the restoration of ancient monuments, restless travel, agricultural innovation, and a lifelong devotion to food and wine. His urge to wander culminated in a four-year journey around the world on a motorcycle that led to the international bestseller *Jupiter's Travels* and its sequel *Riding Home.* He has lived in England, France, and California and is at work on another travel book exploring his connections with Eastern Europe. He has one son.

ABOUT THE TYPE

This book was set in Plantin, a classic roman typeface named after the famous sixteenth-century printer. Plantin was designed in 1913 by Robert Granjon for the Monotype system. Its even strokes and lack of contrast make it a highly legible face. It was, later, the typeface on which Times New Roman was modeled.